UNDER THE ORIOLES NEST

by
Charles J. Palmer

Edited by
Michael Huth

Whisper Ridge
Press

Published by Whisper Ridge Press
an imprint of MetroWest Inc.
822 North Spring Ave.
LaGrange Park, IL 60526

Library of Congress Control Number 2001098505

For all Contacts:
Telephone or Fax: (708) 354-2125
E-mail: teamhuth@sbcglobal.net

Second Printing - 2003
Printed in USA

*Nature speaks to us
only insofar as we have
ears to hear and souls
to understand.*
*Charles J. Palmer
1933*

*I believe Charlie would have dedicated his story to his family,
and to all those who in life's toiling, find the beauty around them,
be it in nature or in human interchange.*

*I dedicate this book to my Grandparents and my own parents,
Lois and Ken, all of whom taught me the value of honest labor,
and exposed me to the beauty in the world around me.*

ACKNOWLEDGEMENTS

My thanks to Robin Swenson for his preservation and sharing of the manuscript with the extended family.

Thanks also to Jonathan Huth for his preservation and selection of the family photos used to illustrate the book.

Special thanks to Caroline Huth who designed the entire layout and cover of the book

And thanks to my wife, Pat, for her assist and encouragement.

CHARLES J. PALMER

EDITOR'S FORWARD

This true story is, in many ways, a simple one. Its simplicity of life is much of its charm, but I think you will find two things quite remarkable about this adventure story, which begins in 1933.

First, in today's complex weave of interdependent services and high technology, it is almost unbelievable that such a pioneering adventure actually took place only two generations ago. Just before my birth and for my first decade or so, my grandparents and their children forged a living in the most basic way amidst a true frontier. Perhaps Charlie's questioning whether he was an artist or a technician is the answer to their success. His balanced capabilities in both areas, along with the focus, dedication and talents of the entire family, unfold in a story of challenge, progress and reward. But more than anything else, it is story about people, and a broad spectrum at that.

Secondly, buried within the story you will find the fact that this saga was written by a man with only an eighth grade education. Certainly this is not obvious from the level of prose. His style is both effective and charming – I always knew him as a story teller. To be sure, the original manuscript needed some tuning to read smoothly, some restructuring, but I can assure you that you are reading Charlie's story, not mine. The style, vocabulary and enchantment are his.

Charlie died in 1962, the manuscript unfinished. Charlie's grandson, Robin Swenson, received a typed copy from Charlie's son, Bruce, in 1981. He made many copies for the extended family, but the text lay otherwise untouched for another 19 years. The advent of scanners in home computing opened the door for easy entry of the text into a computer, and in late 2000, I began the project of taking the text to a new level.

Margin notes were collected from Charlie's son Harris' copy. A search through old family papers uncovered some early proof copies of the manuscript, and along with them several key documents. There was one untyped chapter in Charlie's hand, and two drafts of an introduction to the book, one by Charlie and one by his wife, Flora. Rather than use them as the introduction, I have included their contents in the text since it tells how the book came to be, at Flora's near insistence. And most helpful was an index, listing the proposed contents of the three final chapters, not done due to Charlie's death. This was a signpost for my completion efforts. Thus, the final chapters were crafted by me to bring Charlie and Flora's story to a conclusion. Finally, I consulted with Lois, Charlie's youngest daughter and my mother, the last living link to that generation, to clarify and expand on the multitude of stories and events contained herein. For those who must have the entire story, I have included an epilogue - the story of the resort, the land and the family beyond Charlie's death.

A glossary is included at the back of this book for several reasons. Since this story was written about 50 years ago, there is some vintage language; words I chose not to replace in order to retain his style. Then there are some 'Palmer-ized' words, unknown outside the family.

Far from a simple family history, Charlie draws the reader in and carries him to the many venues that the Palmer family was fortunate to experience, some in unfortunate times. That this verbal storyteller did indeed set this story down in writing for us is our great fortune.

Enjoy the adventure!

Mike Huth
2001

Chapter 1

EMBARKMENT

A small group of people had gathered to see us off, their casual, intimate conversation suggesting long-standing friendships. They had arisen early to wish us godspeed and wave farewell to our small caravan of but two vehicles. Although we had given much time and thought to our itinerary, we could not answer their many questions except in generalities. Nor could we put a finger on the map and say definitely, this is where we are going. Like many emigrants, we would see the country first, then choose some likely spot on which to settle. Many times these very people had seen our car, loaded with camping equipment, headed for some obscure place from which we were sure to return, but now a large platform truck, towering high with our belongings, told them quite a different story.

Here in the fertile soil of church, school and social life our family had taken root, each filling his or her small communal niche in a matter-of-fact way. Now this fledgling family tree was to be torn from its urban rooting and planted in some remote spot as yet undiscovered.

The reasons for our embarking on this venturesome enterprise were twofold. First, the hand of a cruel depression lay heavy upon us, and industry had turned thumbs down upon men of my age. At fifty, I belonged to an army of industrial casualties too old for employment. As father of a family, I could not accept the empty idleness thrust upon me, nor the philosophy which held that youth was the measure of a man's worth. Thus came our determination to find a new life in the wooded country far to the north.

The memories of our early camping days influenced our thinking, and our revolutionary plan to build a summer resort was a welcome challenge to our pent-up energy. Still vivid in our minds was a small, log cabin nestled beneath tall pines beside a spring fed lake, and it was toward this bit of remoteness we were about to set forth. Here a crude roof and walls would give us shelter of a kind until we could explore the countryside for a permanent stopping place.

Then, too, there was the second reason for our going, less important, perhaps, but not without its own significance. The Burlington railroad switchyard, like a monstrous dragon, was slowly closing upon us, blowing its fiery breath upon our house and its environs. Already, it had consumed many of our neighbors' homes, until only the lethargy of the depression held it in check. Though we had long since become accustomed to the cacophony of bumping cars, screeching wheels, escaping steam, clanging bells and shrill whistle blasts, it had not always been so, for when our old home had been built, it stood in the quiet seclusion of a suburban prairie.

These were the obvious reasons for our going, the ones given to our friends and neighbors. They were the sum total of our rationalization. Yet somewhere within my own subconscious mind was quite another more subtle reason, perhaps, but quite as compelling in its persistency. Was this not the call of Nature to which we were responding, an inherent urge to identify ourselves more closely with the great out-of-doors? For half a century, I had watched the gradual merger of flowering prairies into blocks of industry. Where once I had heard the wild sweet song of the meadowlark now came the harsh cry of a newsboy. Slowly but surely the imperceptible hands of time were forging a city from the green fields of my boyhood days. I wanted to get away from it all, to escape time with its exacting demands. I longed for a place where the sun was wanted for its warmth and splendor, not for the split seconds man had attributed to it.

But what is time? Scientists cannot assert its real existence, nor whether it flows or is eternally static. To my credulous mind the answer lies in the moving hands of the clock, for they have ever set the tempo for my feet. When man first devised the sundial, he thought he had captured time, but when he added a spring and a wheel and clasped it to his wrist, he found, alas, that time had captured him.

2

Our family had lived in the very shadow of big business and high finance, though we understood little of them. Trusts, corporations, monopolies - in a sense these were responsible for our plight, for had we not become hopelessly enmeshed in their broken-down gears? Now a ray of hope had come, a plan of escape from the insecurity of a collapsed economy. Each day, the load on our truck reached a little higher, and a varied array of things strained at the taut canvas about

them. There was just enough room for essentials, so much of our furnishings were to remain behind in the big, seven-room house.

Varied, too, were the personalities, the temperaments and potentials of the individuals who awaited, anxious for this day of

Palmer House in Cicero, IL

departure. How would our children react to such a new and strange environment, and what measure of courage and fortitude did their mother possess for so venturesome an enterprise? Only time would tell.

My own contribution lay more in know-how, born of experience, together with a talent for creativeness. The recollection of my schooling, confined as it had been to the grades, still haunts me as an era of bondage made tolerant only by an occasional day at hooky. I shall never forget the joy and freedom of vacation time, those delightful days of leisure when I explored the woods and prairies about Chicagoland. All too soon came the responsibilities attendant to maturity, though with them came no diminishing of my love for the great outdoors. Young manhood had found me in a quandary—whether to follow a natural bent for mechanics or submit to an insatiable craving for art. The hard and fixed demands of the former were ever in conflict with the abstract callings of the latter, and I moved periodically from one absorbing realm to the other. Fashioning things with my hands, whatever the circumstances, had always been the source of my greatest satisfaction. Few were the tools of trade that were unfamiliar in my grasp. But a quick temper, a measure of intolerance and egotism, and a definite lack of business acumen were liabilities that had to be considered. Now, upon distant

3

horizons, we would seek a common denominator that would absorb both my dual talents and my unwanted years.

Flora, one of four sisters whose early graying hair was a family characteristic, was my wife and mother of our four children. She had been a grade school teacher, though her forte really lay in mathematics. Beyond her academic training lay an insatiable yearning for knowledge. No circumstances would stay her hand from the big dictionary should a word arise to challenge her. Not only had she a motivating spirit, but from her font of wisdom came the cement that alone could bind our unlike natures into a singleness of purpose. Many a camping trip had proven her worth, and her love of nature knew no bounds. Possessed of a strong mind, she could be stubborn and unyielding. She much preferred the freedom of outdoor life to the restrictions of good housekeeping. All things considered, she was well qualified to cope with adversity and the uncertainties that lay ahead of us.

At twenty, Harris, the older of our two sons, had finished Morton Junior College. His interests lay in the realm of nature, and his love of woodcraft surrounded him with many wholesome friends. An ardent archer, he enjoyed the making of his equipment equally to its use. Often in our loft I have seen bolts of Osage orange or lemonwood, or yew staves from Oregon. From these he fashioned his bows, and from Port Orford cedar or northern pine, his arrows.

Greater than his knowledge of woodcraft was his interest in geology. I keenly watched his bent in this direction, and from my own meager knowledge of this subject, encouraged him as best I knew how. As a keen-nosed hound follows a trail, so he followed the meandering of streams and the contour of hills to better understand their relationship. He was ever interested in the great forces that had tilted mountains and leveled plains. Such a background, then, I considered fitting for the business ahead.

Bruce had been our problem child. At eighteen, he was an individualist, strong-minded and showing signs of genius. On occasion, I despaired for his future, but not his mother. Her confidence in him was steadfast. She had many times confessed to a lack of wisdom in his upbringing, but a nature as unconventional as his, I had told her, was the product of both heredity and environment. Unlike Harris, with his host of friends, Bruce confined his friendships to a few, indeed choosing those who few would or could challenge his ideas with understanding. Our walls echoed with controversial problems,

4

the solutions of which lay only in the minds of an Edison, Ford or Einstein.

In tenacity of purpose, Bruce had no equal, unless it was his own mother. Her oft-used quotation, "Stick to your aims - the mongrel's hold will slip, but only crowbars loose the bulldog's grip" held for his youthful mind the challenge of the crowbar alone. At a tender age, he had learned the power of leverage, and a porch railing without spindles and a picketless fence had once testified to his trials with his first lever. His mind and hands were ever busy with cams, gears, levers, wheels and figures.

Of the quartet of children, there remained two girls - Ruth, our first-born, and Lois, our last-born. In temperament, they were as dissimilar as were the boys, and in looks, unlike matching peas in a pod. I bow in ignorance to the law of genetics that cast these four children from the same mold. Ruth was obliged to remain behind, for she had already chosen her future in marriage. She was the quiet, efficient and happy wife of a young chemical engineer, Ed Swenson, and in his hands we left her, a bit reluctantly but with no misgivings.

Thus is set down a brief appraisal of those whose hopes lay within the little caravan that stood, anxiously waiting to start.

Conspicuous on this eventful day of our departure were my in-laws, the Walkers, who lived but a block away. Manora, Grace and Blanche, together with their elderly mother, had been interested in our undertaking and spared nothing toward our happiness and comfort. As we stood grouped about the towering truck awaiting the moment of departure, I felt the warmth of a small hand upon my own and turned to look into the moist eyes of my mother-in-law. For a moment, we stood in silence, as I waited to hear in words the message I read upon her time-wrinkled face.

"Well, good-bye, Charlie," she said, "I'm sure that you and Flora are going to be successful, for you both have the cajene to make a go of it."

Little did I realize then how many occasions I should recall that bit of optimism so timely spoken. With reassuring pressure on her thin hands I replied, "Yes, Grandma, we'll make a go of it somehow."

A blast from the roundhouse whistle shrieked a warning note as commuters hastened by. This, too, was the time for our departure. Now small gifts, tokens of friendships, were hurriedly tendered us. A

5

napkin covered basket was not the least of these, and the last, a bobtailed cat, was pushed gently through our sedan window. The two boys high on the seat of the truck waited with dwindling patience as the early June sun grew dim in the acrid atmosphere over the great switchyard. A flock of pigeons dipped a farewell salute in their flight toward pellets of grain among the box cars, and I took one last look at the old home. The big house somehow now stood out of focus, its familiar lines a myopic blur.

I waved a signal to the boys and we were off, the grind of starters, varied pitch of gears, vacuum hum of tires, all sound effects in a bit of life's real drama. Lois was the last to get aboard, having slipped away to her grandmother's refrigerator for a bottle of milk, mindful of the bobtailed cat she had adopted. At sixteen, she had an avid appetite for life which was reflected with naive enthusiasm in her affection for all creatures, large or small. She lived entirely in the present, and looked only with reluctance upon the prospect of ever growing up. With her new friend, she was parked comfortably in the back seat.

Many misty miles rolled by before I could appreciate the passing landscape, for I was deep in retrospect. Flora finally broke the silence.

"Daughter," she said, "are you sure you put that black box in the car, the one with the mortgage and insurance papers in it?" The reply was a stifled sound that might well have come from the cat. I knew then that our youngest was still under the spell of her good-byes. Polishing her glasses, Flora continued, "I wish you would open the box and hand me Grandfather Adams' autobiography."

This proved the open sesame, for no sooner had she obeyed than she exclaimed, "Gee, Mom, are we pioneers too?" Turning back the faded cover of the old document, Flora scanned its yellowed pages, then affixed a finger and read aloud:

"'I shouldered my whip and drove six yoke of oxen hitched to a sixty-hundred wagon, very cheerfully if not gracefully.' Lois," her mother said, inclining her head toward her daughter, "do you know what oxen are?"

"Sure I do. They're cows, aren't they, Mom?"

"Well, not exactly. They're steers. And about that wagon, you had better explain that, Charlie. You understand those things, and moreover it was your grandfather and not mine."

"Well, Lois, a sixty-hundred wagon was one big enough to carry three tons. That would mean a half a ton for each yoke of oxen. Also known as a Conestoga wagon, it could hold a whole family, with their belongings. A large canvas shelter was stretched over wooden hoops, and now of course you'd recognize it as a covered wagon."

"He was my great-grandfather, wasn't he, Pop? And how could he whip the farthest oxen?"

"Well, let's answer your questions one at a time. He was my mother's father. That would indeed make him your great-grandfather. And now about that whip. Made from plaited rawhide, it was known as a bullwhip, and it took lots of skill to crack its great length over the ears of the oxen, especially the near ones. Did you know," I continued, "that grandfather used no lines?"

"Then how could he steer the steer?" she laughed.

"The animals were trained to respond to the call of gee and haw," I answered, "so that they turned either to the right or left as he wanted them to."

"Was that when he was a forty-niner, Pop?"

"No, this was later than that. I think he left Independence, Missouri in 1862 for New Mexico over the Santa Fe Trail, but that story will keep very well for another day." I asked my wife why she had chosen that particular sentence for her text.

"Well," she said, "when I saw Bruce and Harris climb to the seat of the big truck this morning, I recalled your grandfather's experiences and wanted to refresh my mind. Yes, perhaps we are pioneers, Lois, modern pioneers on rubber," was her mother's belated reply.

With Flora at the wheel, I took over the faded papers and turned to the account of his earlier days, when as a forty-niner he had crossed the Great American Desert.

I said farewell to the dearest on earth and started with a large wagon train of eager pursuers of wealth.

What had we in common with this old pioneer? I thought of those heavy iron-bound wheels and their wooden hubs that thumped from side to side, then of our own air cushioned tires that turned swiftly and truly as planets in their orbits. Settling deeper into the upholstery I closed my eyes. There, hunched over a wooden seat, booted feet braced against the incessant lurching, I saw an old bewiskered man, squint-eyed, weather-beaten and worn. On and on he went, not for a day, not for a week, but for what seemed forever.

*How can I tell of those long, long years that followed? Whose pen
can write intelligently of those trials, privations, solicitudes,
hardships, disappointments, fears, hopes, anticipations, successes
and failures? I shall not attempt it. Even now my heart recalls its
anguish and I almost faint as I write.*

Not much in common, I mused, returning the old papers to the
safekeeping of the tin box. Perhaps in spirit at least we might travel
with this pioneer, for weren't his aims our aims, his dreams our
dreams? He had sought security in the yellow gold of California. We
would seek ours among the lakes and streams, beneath the blue skies
of northern Wisconsin. Suddenly I was awakened from my reverie.

"What about your Grandfather Palmer, Pop? Was he a pioneer,
too?" Lois asked.

"Well, he was a wainwright, if you know what that is."

"No, tell me."

"A wainwright is a man who builds wagons, and as there weren't
many factories then, he had to make everything himself, even the
wheels with their heavy iron tires."

"Iron tires? Then he couldn't get a puncture, could he? Why don't
we have iron tires on our Studie?"

"Now, Lois, act your age. You know very well why. My grandfather," I continued, "came with his family by wagon from Albany, New
York, to Fort Wayne, Indiana back in the 1840's. I think that would
make him a pioneer, don't you?"

For a moment, there was no reply, then she asked, "What about
your grandfathers, Mom?"

"Well, the Walker side of the family goes pretty well back in our
history, to Pilgrim days, I'm sure. According to records, my
Grandfather Walker graduated from Yale Law School, then struck out
west to Michigan where he founded the village of Capac. That's where
I was born, you know. He was a lawyer, a judge and a state senator,
I've been told."

"Oh, boy, what a man!"

"And Charlie, did you know that Grandfather Walker was once a
regent of the University of Michigan," Flora said turning to me, "and
helped frame the constitution of the state? I wish I had known him
better. I was just a girl when he died."

"Now for my mother's father, Grandfather Warren; he, too, was an early settler in Michigan."

"Then I must be full of pioneer blood!" Lois exclaimed, tossing up her bobtailed cat.

So the passing hours devoured endless miles of concrete. We were rapidly leaving the prairie state behind, and no longer could see the pall of smoke that marked Chicago on the horizon. We came upon the boys where they had stopped before a low viaduct. Bruce was standing on the abutment. He signaled a six inch clearance and was watching while Harris slowly piloted the truck through. They took the lead again, and our little caravan settled down for a long run that would end only with the setting sun.

The blur of passing landscape soon had my head rolling with drowsiness. Flora was at the wheel, and I was too far gone to note her mischievous smile as she winked at Lois. Our truck was about to pass from Illinois into Wisconsin at the small town of Big Foot. As our own wheels touched the dividing line, my ear drums burst with a deafening "BLOTTO!" fairly exploding from the lungs of Lois and her mother. When I had pried the cat from my shoulders, I realized I'd been a victim of our old traveling game. My mask of indifference hiding my chagrin hadn't robbed the perpetrators of their triumph, and shouts of laughter filled the car.

North and west we traveled over the gentle hills of southern Wisconsin, when once again we came upon the boys and the truck, parked well off the highway. A rear tire had blown. Flora spread an old blanket for Bruce to lie on while he adjusted the jack position. Harris was spinning the tire wrench, while Lois, holding her cat, stood nearby, watching in interest.

As the clicking jack slowly raised the truck, she casually asked, "Got a puncture?"

"No," came Bruce's sardonic reply, "but the air is beginning to show through."

"Now, Son," his mother said, "that wasn't nice."

"Well, she shouldn't ask foolish questions," he retorted, as he lifted the heavy wheel from its spindle. We spelled each other with the tire pump, each contributing a hundred strokes.

As Bruce wiped his hands on an old shirt he said with some contempt, "It's about time someone made a puncture-proof tire."

"Someone has," Lois replied.

"Who?" Bruce snapped.

"My great grandfather, and if you don't believe me you can ask Pop."

When our heavy load again rested upon all four rear tires and the tools had been gathered, we loitered in the warm sunshine to stretch our cramped legs and relax from the tenseness of the journey. Clumps of cowslips dotted a green meadow beside the highway, a spring brook heavy with watercress sung its way through a culvert at my feet, and a yellow butterfly clung lazily to the pavement. For just one brief moment I was barefoot again. Had I heard the fluid notes of a bobolink, I might well have been playing hooky on a day in June, long, long ago.

The sight of the wicker basket soon corralled my thoughts and brought our children together for the tidbits beneath its napkin cover. Having the boys with us was comforting as we sat upon the soft green shoulder of the highway. While we rested, they recounted their own experiences. They hadn't forgotten the family game either, as they blottoed each other simultaneously at the state line. Despite the blowout, it had been a worthwhile stop, this hour of idleness, for it sent us on our way again with little or no thought that we were hardly more than a band of roving gypsies.

Harris took a place in the sedan with his mother, and Lois and I eagerly mounted the truck beside Bruce. As I piloted the lumbering vehicle, the noise was so great that there was little hope for conversation between us. For many uneventful miles, through Janesville, Madison and the Dells, we set the pace for the sedan, then gradually our speed was checked by a long and heavy drag to the summit of a hill, where a beautiful valley lay spread out before our eyes. With a fresh grip on the wheel, I sat back with satisfaction to coast down to the velvety floor below. Before realizing our predicament, we were speeding beyond the limits of safety, and I quickly, but foolishly, jammed on the brakes.

"Ease 'em up!" Bruce shouted as we swerved dangerously to one side, "or they'll freeze and throw us. Now give 'em a little at a time!" he directed as he applied the emergency brake himself. "If we can make that bend ahead, we'll be all right." Careening perilously we followed the arc of the curve, and at last we straightened out for a long and safe run. We stopped to cool our smoking brakes and wipe our perspiring palms. As I cut the motor, Bruce's face broadened into a smile as he heaved a sigh of relief. "Pa, that was a close one!" And so it had been.

After checking over the load and finding that it had not shifted, we took once more to the highway, but I now found myself parked safely beside Flora who had once again taken the wheel of the sedan.

We were entering unfamiliar country now, and with my newly found freedom I drank in the endless panorama opening before our eyes. From the flat expanse of valley floor on either side sheer rock walls rose, capped by dark bands of forest, vivid against a cloudless sky. This was country in which a cowboy might feel at home, for here were great weathered buttes, bathed in the depths of their own purple shadows. Here, too, were cactus, jackrabbits and coyotes to put him in his element. What a perfect setting for Grandfather Adams' covered wagon train, and if Indians were needed, they, too, were here to add reality to the picture.

Geologists call this the driftless area, for its vast and rock-ribbed surface remains unscarred by the ice movement that had scoured the rest of the state. Ancient continental glaciers in their southward trend divided above and joined their forces below this interesting country. Scientists came from foreign lands to study its phenomena and peck at the roots of its long vanished mountains with their hammers. Mile upon mile we rolled through this interesting and unglaciated country.

Flora reminded me of the time when, in our indecision to pitch our tent, we had passed up many a desirable spot, lured always by the charm that lay beyond the next hill. Finally, in desperation we had made camp in darkness, and the following morning, the Idaho sun found us tucked in among overturned car bodies, tin cans, windswept papers and rubbish in the midst of a town dump.

The ever-lengthening shadows would soon merge into darkness, and we kept watch for a convenient camping place. When at last we saw our truck pull from the highway and park beneath the turning blades of a windmill, we knew the boys, too, were tiring of this long day's journey. We drew alongside, and found our big milk can already filled with water.

A farmer, pointing a horny finger toward the western horizon, was saying, "Better make your campfire over against that big rock, don't forget to close the gates and be sure to put out your fire."

When all was ready, I called for Lois, who was nowhere to be seen.

"Now where can that girl be?" I shouted.

"If I know my daughter," her mother said, "she's exploring that big red barn." And so she had, for at the honk of our horn, she came running, remembering, no doubt, the time she had been inadvertently left behind.

The setting sun kindled the tousled head of the rocky escarpment, and as we drew within its welcome shadow we cut our noisy motors and crawled wearily to the ground. We pitched our tent and built our fire in the prevailing silence, then watched distant hills fade into darkness. As we partook of a hastily prepared meal, fingers of light reached bits of weathered wood, lichen covered rocks and soft mullein leaves about a woodchuck's hole.

"Daughter," Flora said, poking idly at a burning ember, "tell me, what did you see in that big red barn?"

In reply, Lois crooked a finger atop her head. "I saw a cow with a crumpled horn," she mumbled hoarsely.

The sedan seats had been made into a bed and Flora and I were comfortably settled, but we could not sleep, for the old home still tugged at our heartstrings. As the moon looked down upon us, we talked quietly of other camps, of the Big Horn range, Crater Lake and Lake Tahoe in the high Sierras. When mention was made of the Guadalupe Mountains in New Mexico, Flora rose and made her way to the children's tent. She would see to the door flap, that it was securely buttoned, and the canvas floor, that it was tight against any intrusion, for she had not forgotten the rattlesnake, centipedes and scorpions we had killed on that occasion.

The tantalizing aroma of coffee and frying bacon in the crisp morning air sent our appetites soaring. With breakfast over, we reluctantly turned our backs upon the big rock. A herd of freshly milked cows ambled toward us as we neared the creaking windmill where we stopped long enough to shout our appreciation to our wayside host, then we were on our way. As we advanced further into the driftless area, we came upon great rock formations rising from the valley floor. Some took on the semblance of turreted castles, others, Mayan temples friezed about in bas relief. Another rode the blue distance like a battleship on the high seas. For centuries these huge monoliths have withstood the elements and still stand as monuments to an enigma that sent the great ice sheets around and not over them. Through this interesting but lakeless country thousands of fishermen annually rush toward their favorite waters beyond, with seeing eyes perhaps, but with little understanding.

Mid-afternoon found us in a region devoid of habitation, where our path lay through a wilderness of aspen and popple, beyond an open swamp, buttoned about with muskrat houses. From brown waters on either side rose a never-ending chorus of frogs, and red-winged blackbirds joined the serenade from their precarious perches on slender reed rushes. Eventually we saw the distant hills that would lift us to a higher, more auspicious land.

Thus far on our journey we had seen little to remind us of the devastating depression that held the country in its throes. Surely it was not evidenced in the herds of cattle that grazed serenely in green pastures, not in the creatures of the forest and swamplands through which we passed. Nature had a way of caring for her own, even to the crows that rose from crushed rodent morsels on the highway before us. Perhaps the wilderness with its bountiful lakes and streams and its mellow soils would do as much for a wayfaring family. Who could say?

At a small city by a river, from the long bridge that attended it, we looked down upon granite boulders strewn topsy-turvy in the amber water beneath. Soon the church spires of Black River Falls vanished from our rearview mirror. Once more we were in glaciated country, and over its newer hills and younger valleys our vehicles played fox and hound until first Eau Claire, then Chippewa Falls were behind us. When at last forests of conifer darkened the horizon we knew we were approaching our destination. Our thoughts reached out now to the little log cabin that would mark the end of our journey, and I wondered if we should find it empty as when we had last seen it.

"I'm afraid it will be a tight squeeze for a family of five," I said, a little pessimistically.

"Well, maybe so," replied Flora, "but the landscape won't be forever rushing by, and we'll have room enough to stretch our legs." As an afterthought, she added, "You know we'll be in it for only a few days at the most."

So we counted the hours until we would cross its threshold, 'til we could wash our travel stained bodies in the cool waters that mirrored its image. Long since, concrete highways had given over to gravel, and seldom could we glimpse our truck except on some turn where it crawled slowly from its own billowing dust. Someone has said that great armies travel on their stomachs. So, too, do small caravans, and when we came upon the truck parked beside the road, we could guess the reason. Bruce wanted to continue on to our destination before eating, but not so Harris. He was all for a hot meal in the adjacent town. There had been words between them, and their mother lost no time in suggesting a compromise.

"Don't you think we had better send for some wieners? We can have them hot in no time," she said. "We are just too dirty to go into a restaurant, Harris. How about it?"

After some bickering, her plan was accepted, but not without a provision by Bruce. He insisted on having poppy seed rolls with hotdogs. "And get a jar of peanut butter!" he shouted to his brother, whose appetite had already started him on the way. Across the river lay Spooner, the northernmost point in our long and tedious journey. Here in its strategic setting lay the metropolis, if one could call it so, of a vast recreational area of blue skies, woodland lakes and meandering streams. Little did we realize then the part it was to play in our own venture.

When Harris finally emerged from a canopy of age-old willows, his arms filled with groceries, water was boiling merrily over our fire. Soon enough the magic of Bruce's poppy seed rolls restored camp morale, and hastily spoken words were quickly forgotten.

At last we were on the last leg of our journey. Lois had demanded a seat beside her brothers, for with her bobtailed cat, she meant to be first to set foot over the threshold of our new living quarters. The sun was low on the horizon as we made our way through the leafy bower and turned westward on the highway. Although we closed our windows against clouds of dust, we were obliged to stop until the truck had put distance between us.

"Two days on the road," I said as we pulled off by the entrance to a cemetery. "The speedometer reads close to five hundred miles – not so bad considering roads and all."

"How far do you think your grandfather had gone by the end of his second day?" Flora asked.

"Oh, about forty miles or so, maybe, depending upon the circumstances, the weather, the wagons, the nature of the country and such things." Soon we were on our way again, the old pioneer still with us in mind and on our tongues.

"Did he know just where he was going, I mean like some town or mining camp?" Flora asked as she lowered the sun visor into position.

"He was not alone, of course; he was one of perhaps twenty or thirty wagons, as he says there were nearly a hundred souls on the march. He said, too, that he'd never forget those four months of hardship and suffering while crossing the Great American Desert. Think of it, Flora, four long months on the road compared to our two short days, and here we are complaining about a little dust. Why, Granddad lived in a world of dust, powdered alkali that stung his eyes and parched his throat; dust from turning wheels and cloven hooves that clung to his clothing and settled in his food. Dust, wind, rain and sleet - he took them full in the face, not on a glass windshield like ours. But back to your question, he says he stopped at a little California town called Rough and Ready, while the rest of the party continued on. Rough and Ready, I like that name, don't you? It sounds so romantic and fairly rolls off your tongue."

"What a trek that must have been, and how can we even think of ourselves as pioneers," Flora mused.

We had just gotten grandfather to his destination when far ahead we saw the children had arrived at last. Was the little cabin still there among the pines to greet them, or was our last mile to be one of disappointment? How slowly the Studie went. There it was, as we had once seen it, deep in the splendor of the spent day, our very own little Rough and Ready.

Chapter 2

THE SEARCH

The morning sun found its way into our new quarters to coax the household awake. The freshness of springtime quickened our pulses, and we were burning to be outdoors in search of the acres that would assure us hope and security. Nature's extravagance was bewildering, but we knew that nothing was ours by divine right, that only through achievement might we hope for success.

Although the old familiar lines of concrete and steel had given way to soft undulations of pine boughs, we still looked about with stereotypical eyes and evaluated what we saw with city trained minds. For a time, we could lay no hand to the plans we had so meticulously worked out. Virgin timber had long since disappeared and a new forest had risen in its place, and this, too, was being threatened by the woodsman's axe, for pulp cutters were busy satisfying the hungry maws of distant paper mills. Cut-over land had little place in our scheme of things. On the contrary, much of our success would depend upon preservation of the woods, its lakes, streams and wildlife.

We were in the land of the Chippewa, and here remnants of this once proud people still eked out a living as had their forefathers before them. Fish, game, wild rice and other growing things were theirs for the taking. The more industrious worked on farms, about sawmills, as cutters in the woods and occasionally as guides. From the dark hands of their squaws came fine specimens of bead work and basketry for the souvenir market. Many had forsaken their racial strain, woodsmen having taken Indian wives to bear their children. Yet there were many who could still boast of pure Ojibwa blood.

Though we came upon a few prosperous looking farms, this was mostly marginal land with light soils and a short growing season. Hardly a day passed in our wanderings that we did not come upon some old abandoned farm, defeat written all over its dilapidated buildings and weed grown fields. To make ends meet, farmers became woodsmen as well, and woodsmen, farmers. Corn, beans, potatoes, pulp logs and rough lumber; these were their seasonal commodities. We had given little thought to agriculture, nor had we any thought of squatting like the Indians and living off the land, for our ideals were higher and our ambitions on quite another plane.

Woodsmen, Indians, jackpine farmers were the obvious things we saw, the pigment that gave color to a truly frontier picture. There were other things, spires of spruce against a golden sunset, the flash of a buck's tail, a leaping fish, the drumming of a partridge – matter-of-fact things to the natives, but full of meaning for us in our scheme of things to come. Few days passed that we did not come upon something of unusual interest; a bird, a tree, an animal or perhaps a small reptile. Our biggest discovery, however, came in the realm of intangibles with the realization that this northern latitude gave us one whole extra hour of daylight to do with as we pleased. Though it was a real contribution, we knew we were simply robbing Peter to pay Paul, for we would find our winter days correspondingly shorter.

Though we were on the go most of the time, the weatherman was not always cooperative. When a two day storm finally subsided and the sun peeked into our windows, we took once more to the outdoors. Things needed doing before we could again start to explore the wilderness that lay about us in all directions. The wind had loosened the canvas covering over our truck and rain wetted some of its contents. Water found its way through holes in the cabin roof. Flora had her first washing to do, and provisions must be had. In all, it was indeed a long, busy day, but when we went to bed that night, it was with the assurance that the morrow would find us on the move.

We had hardly retired, it seemed, before it was time to rise. Breakfast over, we started out with the hope and determination of an old prospector in search of gold. Jotted down on paper were our requirements of a good resort location, as best as we understood them, though perhaps our standards were too high, for many combinations of land, trees and water were to be rejected before at last we were to find what we wanted. In our wanderings we crossed and recrossed lakes, sometimes in leaky boats, or made our way on foot around wooded shores. We asked questions of woodsmen and Indians, we forded streams and climbed hills, our clothes rasped by briars as we pushed through the thickets. Yet it seemed we searched in vain. The woods had the vastness of the sea, which at times bewildered us. On bright days the sun was our guiding beacon, but when it was gray and cloudy we became confused in our directions. Old tote roads led us everywhere and nowhere, as we urged our car over their aimless wanderings, or went on foot when fallen trees blocked our progress.

Lakes having low and swampy shore lines and those with muddy bottoms had no place in our plans. Several deep-set lakes which we were obliged to reject weighed upon our conscience. Regardless of their many qualifications, we felt that precipitous banks were not suitable for resort purposes. Easy access to the water was a major factor with us. We found fish quite abundant in most waters, but so, too, found other creatures, for as we emerged from one particular lake, our feet were covered with leeches.

There was no end of prospective sites to explore, and each day soon became a repetition of the one before. We were imbued with hope at sunrise and despair at sunset. Notwithstanding, we knew that somewhere about, tall pines were whispering a message of welcome for our very own ears.

Our temporary quarters gave us shelter, and its homey atmosphere did much to dispel our growing impatience. At the end of each day we menfolk would drop on our backs complaining of our emptiness, while Lois set the table and Mother prepared food for our stomachs. Nightfall usually found us in a huddle about the kerosene lamp, its soft glow hardly reaching beyond the family circle. The oilcloth covered table became a general catchall where elbows rubbed while tongues wagged. Books, old magazines, writing materials and even tools appeared almost before supper dishes were cleared away, and when at last Mother and Lois squeezed into our circle, we made room for them and their work.

This, too, was a time for conversation, a time for free vent of feelings, for discussion and debate and not infrequently for discord. While busy hands plied their various tasks, voices would rise in defense of or against some bit of shoreline which failed to pass muster. Events of the day were relived and plans for our tomorrows were born. The final act of each day's bit of drama came abruptly when Mother blew into her cupped hand at the fluted chimney top, thus extinguishing the meager glow of our kerosene lamp.

Only in spirit could we compare our search with that of Moses and the children of Israel, for in reality they searched for 'a promised land of milk and honey'. We wanted only a promising land, one of hope and opportunity. Early in our wanderings, we had learned of a piece of lakeshore property that lay some miles west of our cabin. After considerable debate, we decided to explore its possibilities, for at least part of the journey, we had been told, was to be over a corduroy road. This would be a new experience, crossing a bog on nothing more substantial than a roadbed of poles.

"Do you think it will be dangerous, Charlie?" Flora asked. "I used to play on one when I was a child, and it was certainly something to fear."

"Well, you know as much about it as I do," I replied. "At any rate you can see that it will be rough going."

"If it's only roughness, I don't mind," she said, "but if it's going to be skiddy, let's not go. You know I'm a coward about slippery roads."

"Well, I don't know what we'll find, but with three men along we ought to be able to get ourselves out of any difficulty, no matter what it is," I replied.

"Let's go!" the boys shouted, impatient to be off.

Through the woods we traveled in silence till suddenly the scene changed. In our path lay a swamp, eerie and foreboding, wrapped in a shroud of vapor. As we drew near, a heron rose and we envied its safe crossing, as it winged silently through the mist. At first sight of the narrow ribbon of logs over which we must pass, Mother balked.

"We'll never make it," she said. Lois, too, tearfully objected, but with three for going on and two for turning back, the die was cast and we started across.

"It's like running the car onto a raft," I thought as we bumped over the first few logs.

From the window Mother could scarcely see the few reassuring inches of log ends and she shouted, "Oh, I'm scared!"

"Just keep your shirt on, Ma," Bruce said. "We're doing fine."

We could feel the logs give beneath the wheels as black, slimy mire squirted from beneath them. Slowly we crept along, getting the feel of the thing as we went. In spite of our precaution, what we feared most happened quickly. The front end skidded, dropping a wheel over the edge. Fortunately the car came to rest, and a frightened family poured out.

In the nearest woods we cut some jackpine poles. By way of leverage and a bit of cajene, we eased the vehicle back onto the semi-floating road and safely continued our journey across. Abandoning the car a short distance further on, we started out on foot, our dinner basket swinging in our midst. Birds sang about us and squirrels barked in the treetops. Through thickets of hazel brush we made our way in single file to the summit of a windswept hill where we got the first glimpse of the land we sought. Across the water, tall pines were standing on their wavering reflections. We stopped momentarily to let the cool breeze fan our faces, but curiosity soon got the better of us and we trudged on. A sudden shout from Harris, who was well in advance, brought me to his side. He was standing on a small rise, surveying a half-mile of lakeshore.

"Pa, I think we've found it at last," he said.

I did not reply, for past experience cautioned me against snap judgments, but the picture before us warranted my boy's optimism. Full of hope, we set out over a soft needle carpet beneath big Norways to make a general survey. In our mind's eye we visualized the home we had so long dreamed about, and without the sacrifice of a single big tree, we counted cabin sites quite adequate in number and spacing. Despite the virtues of the place, in the bitter end it was all to no avail. After some further investigation we definitely turned thumbs down on this wilderness retreat, for extending the entire length of the property and directly off shore we found a semi-floating bog so dense in structure it looked like solid ground. Weeds and grasses grew upon its surface, offering resistance to the winds, so that it stirred uneasily like the breathing of some half-submerged creature. Although we explored its depth with long poles, we could find no place where it rested upon a hard, sandy bottom. Only by some major undertaking could the dense mass be removed and an adequate bathing beach be made to supplant it. Though Bruce suggested hypothetical and involved mechanisms as a means to an end, we knew full well the hopelessness of it all.

Returning, we reached the corduroy road once more, and Lois and her mother picked their way gingerly on foot as we men piloted the car over the wet and slippery poles. When at last we reached our little cabin, its windows were ablaze in the setting sun.

Chapter 3

LAY OF THE LAND

Flora and I had gone to bed earlier than usual one evening as we needed sleep, but a whippoorwill outside our window had other plans for us, and we listened to his never ending serenade. Lois had already retired and soon we heard shoes scuffling on the ladder as Bruce climbed to his bed on the balcony. Harris was still on the water, trying out a rod of his own making. We had lain for a while counting the calls of the whippoorwill when we heard our daughter calling.

"Mom!" she shouted. "Come here. I don't know if this is a bedbug or a wood tick."

For a moment Mother hesitated, then without answering she slipped on her robe and took a small bottle from the windowsill. I knew she would apply turpentine to the wood tick's body, and that only by gentle pulling would head and all come free from her flesh.

"Don"t worry, Lois, bedbugs don't hold on like that. Now look close and see that little gray horseshoe on its back. That's how to tell it's a wood tick." Flora was evidently holding the wood tick close to the lighted lamp.

Once again we settled down to sleep, Mother pulling the sheet well over our heads at the sound of marauding mosquitoes. Although the whippoorwill had vanished into the night, we were again disturbed, this time by Bruce who shouted, "Pa, this is a crummy way to make a roof. How do they expect it to hold a load of snow?" From where I lay, I could scarcely see the pole rafters to which he referred but was in no

23

mood for conversation, so I didn't reply. He shouted again, "Pa, are you awake?"

"It's not likely to snow tonight, son, so why worry about it?" I yelled back in exasperation.

The boy wasn't to be put off so easily. I soon heard descending footsteps, then the scratch of a match, and his shadow darkened the living room wall. The sound of his pencil and the occasional clatter of a rule told me that stresses and strains were absorbing his mind. When I turned on my pillow and slept, I dreamed of little triangular paper trusses falling silently like snow on our cabin roof.

A good night's rest usually sent us to the breakfast table as hungry as spring bears. The crispness of morning air together with the tantalizing odor of coffee and bacon was a double appetizer that kept Mother constantly over the pancake griddle. As far as we were concerned, this was just another day, a repetition of yesterday. Flora had other ideas, for out of a blue sky, as she settled down before her own stack of cakes, she asked, "Whose birthday is it today?"

We looked from one to another in surprise, and in my confusion I could think of only Washington or Lincoln. When I saw a look of chagrin creep over Bruce's face, I understood. Mother had surely put one over on us.

"I think," she continued, "we should celebrate Bruce's birthday by staying home today. The change will do us worlds of good. What do you say, Charlie?"

Who could say no to such a proposition? Surely not I, for somehow the idea had a ring of hooky which appealed to me. And coming from one who campaigned so persistently as Mother had, it was a surprise if not a matter for conjecture. When I saw her carrying our battered old wash-boiler into the kitchen, my hastily made plans for a fishing trip vanished into thin air.

On a bench out beside the door, two galvanized tubs awaited filling, and I pondered as I carried the pails to and from the lake. Wasn't it just possible that she had taken advantage of Bruce's birthday celebration to keep us all home while she caught up with her household duties? In this way she wouldn't miss out on one of our daily trips. How else could she manage it? I hardly blamed her for carrying out her little scheme, but for her to think I had been taken in so easily, well, that was the rub. At any rate I would hold my peace until bedtime. While I filled the pails I heard Lois shout, "Pop, I've found another," and knew

24

she was searching for agates among the pebbles on the beach.

In the washday atmosphere of the cabin, Bruce kept busy with pencil and paper. Harris had driven away in the car, and only I could guess his mission. So the morning passed. Mother washed clothes and stirred pots and pans, while I stoked the fire and carried out the clothes for Lois to hang. By afternoon the wash flapped lazily in the breeze, and the bobtailed cat played at dangling apron strings. Lois and Mother were resting when Harris drew up.

"Do you want to see some striae?" he shouted. Lois jumped to her feet, expecting, no doubt, to see some strange creature her brother had captured. "You'll have to get into the car, but it's not very far," he continued.

Mother untied her apron, ready for any adventure. Bruce got in reluctantly, suspecting his brother of some practical joke. But I knew what we would see. We hadn't driven far before we stopped at the edge of a valley where we climbed out. Pointing to a big boulder Harris asked us to run our hands over its smooth surface, scored with grooves.

"This is striae," he said, "caused by glacial action. Both sides of this valley are morained, laid down thousands of years ago. There must be other rocks like this, too."

I'm sure Lois was disappointed, but when I reminded her of the great polished mountain which we had once seen, she climbed back into the car quite satisfied.

My own recollection of that rocky trail in the high Sierras had been awakened. Far up in the region of the clouds we had come upon the spoor of an ancient glacier, the one that had carved out Yosemite Valley. Before attempting so colossal a task, it had polished off a whole mountain top seemingly in a gesture of practice. We had spent an hour there in wonderment, idly wandering over its shiny surface. Bret Harte once said, "so smooth was this granite that old timers, upon its discovery, fell upon their knees to caress it." From this short lesson in practical geology, we rode home in the twilight.

Bruce's birthday cake that evening might well have come from our old oven back home, it looked so full and appetizing, and only Mother knew from whence came the nineteen small candles adorning it. It was a complete surprise, though she said I had helped to bake it when I stoked the fire beneath the wash boiler.

Our supper that evening consisted of the usual fare - pan fish, crisp and brown, home-made bread, fried potatoes and for Bruce a can of tuna fish. When Mother ushered in that cake with its crown of colored candles, it was greeted by a chorus of 'oohs' and 'ahs'. Remembering the significance of the occasion, we burst into song, 'Happy Birthday to You'. For a moment we might well have been seated around our old dining table.

"Bruce, why don't you run down to the drugstore and get some ice cream to go with it?" Harris said, as Mother laid a knife beside the cake. Everyone laughed but I thought it not beyond Flora's prowess to pull a gallon from beneath the table.

Mine was to be the first wish. I pinched the small flame gingerly, then hesitated as a thin thread of smoke spiraled upward.

"Bruce," I said, "I hope you'll be the first to set foot upon our new land."

"And make it snappy," Harris added quickly.

Lois followed, who after a couple of bad starts said, "Well, Bruce, I wish you would let me have the front seat in the car once in a while."

Harris rose to his feet to make his wish. "Bruce, I hope that by another nineteen years, you and your big brother will be running the best gol-darn resort in Wisconsin." This came as a surprise to Flora and me, for we had no such far-reaching plans for the boys. We were all attention as Mother took her turn.

"Bruce, I do wish you would learn to like fried fish, for I'm sure we will never catch tuna in these lakes."

This had been our first birthday celebration in the woods, a holiday indeed, and it boosted our morale. My earlier suspicions of my wife extracting housework from me were quickly forgotten, and all thoughts unworthy of the occasion were left unspoken. When at last Flora blew out the light, sleep came quickly.

Hertel was only a three mile trip, where we bought most of our provisions. Looking for this wayside hamlet, one might easily pass beyond it quite unknowingly. There was no schoolhouse or church spire to tell him when he was there, and if, perchance, he stopped to ask his way, he'd like as not be told that he had already arrived. Traveling on state Highway 70, the first sight was the country store standing boldly in relief against dark pine woods. Beyond this structure was a dwelling or two attended by customary outhouses. Other than a huge pile of logs in the offing, this was Hertel as first we had seen it. Joe Larrabee, standing in the open doorway of his general store, might easily shout an order for eggs to the farmhouse diagonally across the corner, but search as he would, he could scarcely see another dwelling on the horizon.

If a bit disturbed by the emptiness of the countryside, one had only to set foot within this store for reassurance, for there he would find an abundance of things seldom seen in cities. Joe's counters and shelves fairly sagged with their heterogeneous burdens. In the back, a bronze plate bearing the title "U.S. Post Office", elevated a few dusty pigeon-holes to dignified authority.

When I discovered an old barber chair in a corner, beset about with canthooks and horse collars, I asked Joe if it was for sale, but he only shook his head and said, "No, it's part of my regular setup. Do you want a haircut or a shave?" I rubbed a hand over my jaw as I asked if he was the barber.

"No," he replied, "you do it yourself."

"But what about those clippers and scissors?"I countered. "Surely one doesn't cut his own hair."In reply, Joe casually hunched a shoulder in the direction of the door.

"Wait and see," he said.

With the tinkle of a bell, two woodsmen entered and made straight for the tonsorial section beyond the overall counter. Joe was busily heaving a meat cleaver, and suddenly I developed an interest in that pile of blue denims. The taller of the two men seated himself bolt upright as his partner reached for the clippers. Ye gods, am I back in the days of Shakespeare, or could this be the Barber of Seville? Another tinkle of the bell, and I half expected to see Robin Hood come through the door clad in leather jerkin and feathered cap. I turned again towards the woodsmen–hair was dropping like verdure from a swamper's axe. Suddenly a shout of "timber" and the chair fell back to a horizontal position. Then came an interlude of razor stropping and brush rattling. In the pungent aroma of bacon, coffee, harness oil and tonsorial cosmetics, I watched until both of the lumberjacks made their exit, shaven and shorn.

'Do ye unto others as ye would that they should do unto you' might well have been a motto above that old chair, I mused as I made my way homeward. How I wished that Flora, too, had been there to witness the scene, for I would do it little justice in the telling.

Somewhere in the vast archives of Washington, D.C., buried in tomes of Post Office records is the name of Otto Hertel, and somewhere in the yellowed records of Burlington railway telegraphers is the same name. So, too, might the name of my own father be counted in both places. In the latter, the names might run consecutively, for both had been operators in the little red brick depot at Clyde, Illinois. Today, half buried by cinders, this early landmark may still be seen by suburban commuters, but the town itself has lost its identity within the industrial town of Cicero, which in turn sits in the very lap of Chicago.

As a young man, Otto Hertel had been the first postmaster of the hamlet now bearing his name. On the shores of Big Sand Lake he had built a few cabins to supplement his farm income. When Otto died, his wife, affectionately known to the countryside as Lottie, carried on operations with their son, Verne, and his wife, Dorothy, as helpers. Thus they were pioneers in the resort business. I still have a vivid memory of painting a Holstein which nearly covered the side of Otto's big barn. There it remained, defying the elements, for more than a quarter of a century, though the herd it symbolized had long since been forgotten.

Our interest in this little wayside place, then, was more than casual. It had its beginning many years back, long before our children were born. Now each trip to Hertel was in itself an adventure into the past as well as the present, and I waited eagerly each week for my turn, be it on foot or in the car.

Though we had spent many days in vain search for a homesite, they had not been without their compensations, for we learned much of the surrounding country. We knew the names and whereabouts of most of the larger lakes and had explored not a few of the smaller ones. Then, too, there were the rivers and streams that threaded their way through the wooded hills. There was the Namekagon ('sturgeon water' to the Indians) that, in its indecision to go places, repeatedly turned back upon itself, to the confusion of any canoeist who would run its course. There were also the Totogatic, Clam and Yellow, all indigenous streams and beautiful in their circuitous paths to their common water to the west, the St. Croix River.

If we found interest in the lakes and streams, so, too, had we in the world of trees about us. As a boy, my contacts had been mostly with the deciduous trees that grew about Chicagoland. Here, however, were also evergreens that held their color year round, coniferous trees with needle foliage that bear their seeds in spiral cones. Among these are the white pines, best of all for lumber, and red pine locally known as Norways. Legion jackpine that eventually find their way to the paper mills, cover the lighter soil. Not soon forgotten are the tall spires of spruce and cedar that stand boldly against the sky, nor the balsams, Christmas trees that spring up overnight into miniature forests on city lots. In dank soil of stagnant waters grow the tamarack, whose needles turn to saffron and fall to earth with winter's first snows.

One bright day in our wanderings we stopped before the remains of a deserted Indian camp beside a lake. A few bent poles still marked the spot where birch bark dwellings had stood. Recognizing the place at once, Flora said, "Daughter, do you remember what happened not far from here on one of our camping trips a long time ago?"

All ears now, Lois exclaimed, "No, I don't. What was it, Mom?"

Flora reminded her of the night we had gotten such a scare from the Indians who had lived in these very wickiups. Seems a young buck had bashed in the head of an old woodsman nearby for the few paltry dollars hidden somewhere in his cabin. In the darkness we had unknowingly pitched our tent within bowshot of the camp. As we made ready for the night there was a distant rumble of thunder and the horizon lighted with intermittent flashing. We just pounded the last stake when to our surprise we saw the flare of a newly made camp fire.

"Indians," I said, "but it's too late and too dark now to pull stakes." As we lay in our beds, I told the children the story of Grandfather's frontier days in Colorado. Though a timely tale, it was hardly one conducive to sleep. As the words rolled from my tongue, I tried to visualize the events as they really happened.

"One cold night in the dead of winter a blanketed Indian crept stealthily to Grandfather's door and knocked."

Lois had now risen on an elbow. "Go on, Pop. What did he do?" she asked, as I paused for effect.

"Well, when the door opened and your great-grandfather stood there in his night clothes, the Indian said, 'You go now. Take family. Indians come tonight. Indians kill. You friend. You go.'"

"Was that at Bent's Old Fort, when your mother was a little baby?" Lois asked, sitting up now. So on and on the tale went, until sleep had overtaken the family. By now wind was shaking the tent, and big drops of rain were falling on the taut canvas. I slipped outside quietly to loosen the guy ropes, lest they shrink and pull out the pegs. Hearing the long, drawn-out wail of a dog, I looked toward the dying embers of the distant campfire. Thinking again of our neighbors, with a sense of uneasiness, I groped my way back around the tent. Once inside, I was buttoning the canvas door when a cold, clammy hand from without thrust through the flap and fastened on my wrist. I am not a coward in the real sense of the word, but I confess to a fear that froze my bones to the very marrow. I stood speechless and paralyzed. Then, recovering my senses, I shouted, "Harris! Bruce! Flora!"

The response came instantly but not from where I expected. A familiar voice said, "Charlie, it's me. Do you hear? Let me in."

The moral to the story is this: When Indians are about and the night is dark, the household should be informed when nature calls.

There really is little for one to fear in the woods. Only the birds and animals need be frightened as they fly or prowl about in constant danger from their enemies. Even bears do not lurk behind berry bushes to snatch at humans; on the contrary they run for their lives when they see one. Nevertheless, fear is part of man's makeup, a fundamental emotion as essential as love. Fears arising from superstition are absurd and should be disregarded, but fear from danger is obviously a worthwhile emotion. Fear is our restraint against recklessness, that tends toward a saner pattern of life.

Flora once said, "I want our children to live adventurously, not dangerously." Yet even the wisdom of Solomon would be hard put to distinguish between the two, for danger and adventure go hand in hand, I told her.

One morning shortly after our arrival I watched a duckling. Yellow and soft with recent hatching, it paddled silently among the shore rushes, then quite fearlessly set out to explore deeper waters. I followed the ever-widening paths with misgivings. Suddenly there was a splash, then only concentric ripples showed on the water's surface. Such had been a victory of fin over feather, but I felt sorry for the old Mallard hen that nested in the shadow of our cabin. Had she, too, wanted her children to live adventurously, I wondered.

President Franklin D. Roosevelt once said, "The only thing we have to fear is fear itself." I think perhaps we fear most that which alone can free us from all fears, death.

Flora never called us a second time to the breakfast table. She would sit down and eat in solitude rather than surrender this longstanding prerogative. In many things she was adamant and strongminded. Certain fundamentals of her housekeeping tasks she never shirked—dishwashing definitely was one of these. Nothing short of an earthquake would induce her to leave a sink full of dishes. Washing and mending clothes and making beds were tasks she seldom neglected. She enjoyed sewing, too, though I sewed on my own buttons simply because I liked doing it. Her floors were swept with more or less regularity, but dusting she neglected, and she lacked a certain orderliness, which I consider the hallmark of a good housekeeper. Many years ago Flora said, "I want my house to look as though it was lived in." This our children had accepted as an obligation, and ever since faithfully cooperated toward that end.

We found a definite freedom from conventionality in the life we were living and we reveled in it for a while, but continued frustration was having its effect on the household morale. June was slipping into July and thus far we had little to show for our efforts. There was a general lack of enthusiasm, and our meals were hardly the noisy conclaves they had once been. When I mentioned this to Flora, her reply, though reassuring, did little to dispel my own apathy.

"It's just that the keen edge has gone from adventure. Remember, it's always darkest before the dawn," she quoted. But to me it looked as if the time was not far off when we should be obliged to compromise on one of our second-choice sites. As I write this chapter some twenty-five years later, I wonder at the smug intolerance with which we rejected many of those lovely spots. Nevertheless, not once since have I regretted a stubborn persistence that kept us always on the search for something just a little better.

Once more we set out for what the day might have in store for us. Fortified by a hearty breakfast, we climbed into our car and followed the highway for a few miles, turning into a sandy trail, leading we knew not where. The weather was fine and wild flowers were about the woods and glades in profusion. Wandering through an area of stunted oak hardly higher than our car, we abruptly came upon a river. Here the trail ended. There was no bridge to offer us a crossing. As we sat by the water, we wondered in which direction our cabin lay, not that it mattered much, for the day was still young. The trip had been unplanned, a sort of shot in the dark which we hoped might lead to something.

Finally, after much discussion, we abandoned the car and set out on foot downstream. At places shallow rapids sent shafts of dancing sunlight into our eyes. Ducks rose from quieter water farther on, breaking the silence in their hasty retreat. Once a deer leaped across our path and plunged frantically to the far side, where it disappeared into the brush.

Over fallen trees, through brush and briars we pushed in single file, those in the rear avoiding the obstacles encountered by those ahead. We came upon fresh beaver cuttings at one place, but there was no evidence of a dam, nor did we see the creatures themselves. From each high point we scanned the down-river country hoping, though hardly expecting, that the hills would fall apart to disclose some hidden lake. Had we been on the other side of the stream, we might have continued on, but the shoreline beneath our feet fell away until it merged into a tamarack swamp. What lay beyond it we did not know. Thwarted, we dropped to the earth on a sandy knoll, for it was obvious we had come to the end of this journey.

The worn wicker basket which earlier had been shunned by all was now the center of attraction and under the spell of its magic, we spent an hour in leisure. The boys lay prone on their backs, while Lois and I found our way to a spot where the bank sloped steeply into the water, where we dropped crumbs of bread to flashing bits of silver in the dark pool below. Dragonflies darted erratically over the stream, and birds sang in the tree tops. For a moment I found it a good world in which to live.

"Pop," Lois said, awakening me from my reverie, as I had quite forgotten her presence, "Who would come this far just to peel birchbark?" I looked across to where she pointed. There stood two trees of unusual size angling from a single hummock. They were easily distinguishable, for big ugly black scars set them apart from others of their kind.

"More than likely some Indian stripped those trees," I answered. "They're not very pretty to look at, but no doubt their heavy bark was used for some good purpose, possibly the covering for those bent poles in that old Indian village we saw the other day, or perhaps it was made into a canoe. Who knows? I don't blame the Indians. They were only following their ancient tribal customs, but when it is the work of vandals I really get mad."

"But won't it kill the trees?"

"I really don't know. Perhaps so, but it hasn't killed those yet," I answered.

In Indian file we retraced our steps, upstream now and with the sun at our backs. When we reached the car Flora insisted we had left it on the other side of the river. Somehow she had become entirely turned around in her directions.

Chapter 4

DISCOVERY!

The sun shone no brighter on this particular day nor did the birds sing any sweeter, we had no premonition of things to come, but notwithstanding, this was to be our day. This was to be the day of all days, when Nature in one of her generous moods was to open the inner doors of her treasure house. But she would not hurry, for we were to be lured and further seduced before she would take us into her confidence. Somewhere in the wooded hills to the north lay a beautiful lake, this much we had learned from an old and wrinkled Indian. To his intriguing description consisting of few words and many gestures we added our imaginations, and headed our sedan northward with renewed hope. However, we were stopped at a small stream swollen by recent rains.

After some discussion as to how to proceed, it was Lois who provided the answer. Barefooted and with jeans rolled up, she set forth, the family taking the cue and following as quickly as possible. From the creek we entered a thicket of aspen, and as we threaded our way among the trees, a pair of snowshoe rabbits hopped beside us as we passed. Beyond this region of ever-quaking leaves, we climbed to a higher elevation. Here the going was easier and we fanned out like a sheriff's posse over a carpet of needle and leaves. Partridges flushed occasionally from our path and shot through the trees with considerable speed and accuracy.

Coming upon pulp cutters at work, we wondered how they had penetrated so deeply into the woods with their Model A Ford. Evidently this was a family affair, for among them was a woman, stripping bark from logs with the skill of an experienced woodsman. Trees from six to twelve inches in diameter were being felled, swamped out, cut into eight foot lengths, stripped of their bark and piled – all for the paltry sum of four cents per stick, as they were called, regardless of their size. What a way to make a living.

Leaving this industrious group behind, we set out once more in a wide spreading formation. With some difficulty we climbed to still another level, where Flora and I stopped to catch our breath, but the children rushed on, each hoping for the first glimpse of the lake which we knew to be not far distant. Soon shouts burst out from here and there, and we hastened on a little faster.

Indeed the view that spread out in a panorama before our eyes was all, even more, than we had expected. The lake lay long and narrow, framed within sandy beaches. From our elevation, no part of it was lost to our vision. Fleecy clouds against an azure sky were mirrored the length and breadth of its quiet waters. Nowhere in our wanderings had bathing beaches been more tempting. Surely the spirit of the old Indian was typified in this stretch of unspoiled wilderness.

Despite the charm that lay in the ensemble before us, it, too, was to be written off as others had before it. Although Bruce objected to our hastily made decision, he had but little confidence in his own quickly thought-out scheme for the construction of a mechanical escalator. Easy access to the water still remained essential in our plans.

There was another objection. As far as we knew, there was no road to the premises, although some old trail might be made passable with difficulty. So once again, as we had on so many other occasions, we tucked the place away in our memories and turned toward our car with a good part of the day still at our disposal.

There was nothing unusual in the fact that we had lost our way, except perhaps that we had done a better job of it this time. We had eaten lunch before climbing into the sedan, but somehow the wicker basket lost its soothing magic, and we were in anything but an amiable frame of mind. For long stretches hardly a word was spoken, and when conversation became necessary, Flora seemed to be the target for criticism. I was sure she was deliberately heading in the wrong direction just to satisfy some whim of her curiosity. Although we were getting nowhere fast, she would not hear of turning back, insisting that it made no difference anyhow as we had no particular destination. In spite of Lois' tears, we menfolk continued with our bickering and backseat driving. Flora only pushed a little harder on the accelerator. When she wanted, she could be the very epitome of determination. Perhaps an episode taken from our early experiences might better exemplify this particular characteristic.

Once, many years ago, in the mountains where the South Platte rises and trout are temptingly large, Flora and I had spent a few days with a Colorado cousin, Homer Adams. From his ranch on the plains we had an exciting trip in a covered wagon to a high camp up in the rare mountain atmosphere. During the last night of our stay the fury of a mountain storm let loose and heaven poured forth its wrath. Lightning rent the darkness and stabbed persistently at the rocky battlements about us. Our beds shook and trembled, and the empty canyons echoed and re-echoed their defiance.

Like all storms, it had its end, and the early morning hours found us preparing for our return to the flat world below. To our consternation our horses, together with a mule colt, had vanished completely with the storm, leaving no hoof marks on the rocky earth to indicate the direction they had taken. Even Homer's mountain lore availed us nothing.

"Your guess is as good as mine," he said as he started out with a coil of rope over his shoulder. Before dividing our forces, Flora and I counseled each other. Then she started out in the general direction of Pike's Peak. I watched with misgivings as she picked her way over a rough plateau and soon became lost from sight among its boulders. Of one thing I was certain: should she come upon the animal's tracks she would never quit until she turned the creatures back.

Long after the noon hour, while resting from my own fruitless search, I heard a shout from far beyond a rock filled gulch. Flora sat dejected atop a boulder with the mule colt prone at her feet. When I eventually reached her side I saw a sorry picture, indeed. Though I was shocked at the ragged condition of her clothes, I could hardly believe my eyes when I saw her shoes, for what little remained of them was hardly worthy of the name.

"If you think my feet are bad, just take a look at the colt's," she whispered.

The little creature raised its head as I took one small foot into my hand to examine it. All four hooves were broken and bleeding, worn down to the very quick. No coaxing could make it rise. While Flora rested, she related the experience. Finding a few tracks here and there, she trailed them to a steep and almost impossible decent. Nevertheless, by clinging to bushes and sliding bodily from rock to rock, she reached the floor below. The solitude and stillness of the forest frightened her, but to her joy she came upon the horses. She unknowingly drove them onto the very trail over which we had come but a few days before. Cousin Homer, who had been backtracking our trail toward the plains, came to the rescue and drove our horses to camp while Flora followed with the colt. From that day to this, Flora had lost none of her determination, and now I knew the futility of further argument.

Passing an occasional farm, we finally came to a crossroad. Though it offered us a choice of three ways, Flora unhesitatingly made a turn to the right. I have often wondered if it had been the hand of Providence on the wheel at that very moment. I shall never know, but shortly thereafter we were to look upon the wooded acres that would hold within them the destiny of our family.

We saw a tiny schoolhouse tucked away in the woods, suggesting habitation, but there was no one to ask our way. Farther along we came upon a clearing of sod-bound acres. The afternoon sun fell oblique upon a weather-beaten barn, highlighting each rough board in its twisted structure. Paradoxically, just beyond a picket fence stood a freshly painted cottage, looking cozy and very much alive. Woodbine clung to its porch and lilac bushes hid its windows. Phlox, lilies, daises, pansies and clumps of peonies bloomed in profusion, and the perfume of wild roses filled the air.

All of these things were quickly put out of our mind when we beheld the shimmering water of a lake beyond a long, grassy decline. On its far shore, a mile or so across, dwarfing trees about them, was a grove of pines, tall and straight, the big boles resplendent with golden sunlight. We stood absorbed, scarcely believing. Could this be the end of our wanderings at last, or would this, too, be weighed in the balance and be found wanting? Startled by a voice, we turned to see a woman standing in the open gate before the cottage.

"Won't you come in?" she asked as she caught a ball of yarn.

"We didn't see you," Flora answered. "I guess we were too busy looking across the water."

"Well, do come in. I was just knitting a pair of socks for my grandson when I heard your car." We followed her to the low-ceilinged porch, where she pulled up a rocker for Flora.

"My goodness, there goes that little wren. Do you know, it has its nest beneath the seat of my chair. I hate to disturb it but it will be back again. Do sit down."

We introduced ourselves as we found seats here and there on the small porch.

"I'm Abbie French. I live here with my grandson, Harold," she said. Then she told us about herself. After the death of her second husband, being unwilling to cope further with the demands of the old farm, she had helped build a few cabins down along the lakeshore. From the income of these during the summer and by sewing for townsfolk throughout the winter, she managed to support herself.

In answer to our inquiries about the lakeshore property, she spoke of that "lovely piece of land across the lake" in terms that set our feet itching to be on our way. 'Lake Lipsie' she called the water and I verified the name on her map. When we had gotten our bearings and charted a route that would take us back to our cabin, we rose to bid her goodbye. The old rocker was hardly vacant before the tiny wren returned and took over.

"I do hope you're going to be my neighbors," she said, not knowing how desperately we wanted to be somebody's neighbors.

Instead of going straight home, we piled out of the car at the small school house and took to the woods. At the head of the lake where there were a few cottages, we crossed a creek and continued toward the big pines. We were torn between hope and misgivings as we trudged along. We had only Abbie French's word that the place was ideal for our purpose. Perhaps her standards differed from ours.

At the lakeshore we got our bearings once more and soon we were in the very midst of the grove. We walked about quite speechless, hardly believing our eyes. How the big red pines had escaped the woodsman's axe I could only conjecture, for they were virgin timber towering well above the second growth about them. The general lay of the land finally brought us to a conclusion that here nature had provided a unique setting. As though by design, the Norways stood within a natural amphitheater, one end open toward the lake, the rest rising gently to the surrounding terrain. In area, it was about equal to a city block. Birches dotted the inner hillside, as did oaks, aspen and popple, and as far as we could see beyond, the country was thick with woods. After scouting the forested shoreline to the north and to the south, we found it the answer to our long quest. Although the beach didn't equal the last we had seen, it was better than most and potentially what we wanted. The water was clear and shallow, ideal for children's bathing, and Abbie had vouched for the fishing.

The setting sun was a fiery ball on the horizon. A cabin here and there and a distant boat out on the water only intensified the solitude and stillness. The boys and I sat upon a log waiting as Mother stood beneath a tall pine, her head thrown back, pondering its height. Though she answered my call, she did not come until she had thrown her arms around it and shouted, "See, I can't begin to reach around it."

"Pa," said Harris, "it's just the place we've been looking for."

Even Bruce with his mechanistic mind had no fault to find. There wasn't a dissenting voice as one after another expressed themselves. Perhaps I had overemphasized the potentials of the place, as Flora said, "I'm all for it, and I certainly do love these big trees, but Charlie I'll admit, I haven't your imagination." I understood her, for it did take imagination to see the possibilities and beauty that lay hidden beneath that tangle of brush and windfalls.

"Flora," I said as we sat about the table that evening, "that natural amphitheater is the best part of the whole place. When we clean it up, we'll have a wonderful park. There's enough room for croquet, and we can put a horseshoe court beneath the big trees. Can't you just shut yours eyes and see grownups and children playing there in the shade? Teeter-totters, swings and all that?"

"No, I can't, but I'll take your word for it. I'll never forget the first time I saw you paint a theater curtain. You stood with your nose straight up against the big canvas, daubing here and there with a brush. You told me that in your pots of color were alpine mountains, a flock of sheep, a blue sky and a waterfall. Of course, I could only see the paint. Now don't expect me to visualize your park. I'm sure it will be just like you say it will."

Harris pushed a crude sketch of the property across the table, showing his idea of cabin sites, and quite independently Bruce had carried out the same general scheme on paper. Both plans called for a few cabins around the top of the horseshoe-shaped rise with others fanning out in both directions from the park to the lakeshore. No buildings of any kind were indicated within the park proper; this was to remain for recreational purpose. This idea had been my own as well.

We were busy with our thoughts when Mother broke the silence, saying, "But Charlie, suppose that place isn't for sale. What then?" This possibility had haunted me from the first, though I had held my tongue. Now that it was out in the open, we accepted the challenge.

"What if some survey line runs right through the middle of the park?" Harris volleyed. "Only half of it might be for sale then."

"And maybe the man who owns it lives in New York or California," Lois said.

"Why not China?" Bruce cut in. "All the more reason for selling, I'd say."

"Now listen to me for a minute," Flora said. "Maybe we're a little premature with our planning, but unless I miss my guess, all of this wild land is for sale. We've got the money to buy it, and now I suggest we go to bed and get some sleep. Tomorrow's another day, you know."

My Sunset

God hung a rainbow out to dry
pinned to an evening star
And the winds that wash the western sky
Frayed it near and far

But passing clouds brought every strand
To my enchanted shore
And wove a fabric far more grand
than ever been before

C.J. Palmer - 1933

Chapter 5

ACQUISITION

At the time that Abbie French had spoken of the store where she did her trading, my thoughts had been on the far side of the lake. However, Harris remembered her directions and was sure he could find his way there.

"Mr. Byrnes can tell you all about that property," Abbie had said.

We rose earlier than usual, our minds filled with yesterday's discovery. Not until our breakfast dishes were done did we climb into the sedan. Perhaps our ideas of a country store had been influenced by Joe Larrabee's emporium. At any rate when we drew up before a small tar-paper shack beside the road, we were somewhat taken aback. At least there's smoke coming from the chimney; someone must be up, I observed.

We had just stopped when the door opened. An Indian woman stepped out, her dark face turned questioningly toward us. For the moment I forgot our mission. When we entered, the roughness of the interior did not impress me so much as did the tall storekeeper himself. Arising at once, he offered his chair to Flora with marked courtesy.

"We've come for some information," I said by way of introduction. "My name is Palmer, and we are from Cicero, Illinois." At this his gray eyes narrowed as they bored into me like gimlets. Tall, thin and straight, with moccasined feet, he nearly brushed the lean-to rafters with his sandy hair. Not until I stated our business did his florid face soften and put me at ease.

"We're interested in that piece of property on Lipsie Lake directly across from Mrs. French's place. Do you know anything about it?"

"You mean the place with the big trees? Yes, I know all about that property. It belongs to a man in town by the name of Grant Ross. A mighty nice piece."

Before leaving we were introduced to his son, Charlie, who came in with a kit of carpenter's tools on his shoulder. As we stepped into our car, Mr. Byrnes said, "I hope you can make a deal with that fellow Ross, but I know he's refused some mighty good offers for that property. He knows there's nothing else like it anywhere around."

Though his words were not encouraging, we drove the ten miles to Spooner, hoping for the best. We knocked on Mr. Ross' door with apprehension.

"Well, what can I do for you?" a voice came before the door had swung full open.

"Are you Mr. Grant Ross?" I ventured.

"Yes, what can I do for you?" he repeated.

"We understand you have some property on Lipsie Lake. Is it for sale?"

"I've got a hundred and sixty acres on that lake. Come in." We followed him into his small vestibule office, where I described the property as best I could.

"Well, make me an offer," he said.

At least the land is for sale.

"We're not interested in the whole thing. I've got $500 cash I'll give you for say half of it, provided it includes those big trees."

As though he hadn't heard me, he spread out a map and

Spooner, WI

42

expounded the virtues of quite another piece of land on Mathews Lake. "And you can have it for that offer you just made," he said.

Of course we were not at all interested, but he was insistent that we see the property, even if it did lay about twenty miles north of town.

"Come back and see me, and if you don't like it I'll consider selling you what you want, but it'll be at a price, mind you." He added as an afterthought, "Better meet me in front of Benson's Store, say at one-thirty. I'll be there in my car."

Needless to say, the trip ended in disappointment, though the property was all that he had claimed for it.

The restaurant dinner that day was a treat, and over our coffee we ventured guesses as to the figure Mr. Ross would ask us. "But at a price" he had said. This was vague, indeed, and could mean anything, leaving us at a disadvantage, with little base for bargaining.

"I'll say a thousand dollars," I said recklessly.

"But Charlie," Mother exclaimed, "we couldn't possibly pay that amount, we've spent so much for the truck and other things already. We just haven't got it."

"Well, I'm only saying what I think he'll ask us, not what I'll offer in the end."

The time passed quickly enough, though we were torn between hope and skepticism. Finally a car pulled up to the curb just as the hands of the big clock across the street stood at one-thirty.

"At least he's keeping his word," I said as I rose from my chair.

"Now Charlie, the rest of us will wait in here while you do your business. Good luck, and don't be too long," Flora said as I stepped outside.

Mr. Ross opened his car door and I took a seat by his side. I could remember no other transaction in my life so fraught with responsibility as that which I faced in those crowded quarters. Notwithstanding, it was one solid hour of finagling, with my opponent always at an advantage. "My price is $2000," he would say over and over again, until my meager offer of $500 seemed no more than peanut money. I recognized the futility of it all as I watched the anxious faces through the restaurant window. Although I offered to raise the ante a little, it was of no use. Finally Mr. Ross stepped on the starter and as the motor took hold, I opened the door and stepped out.

"Say, if you've got the cash" he said, "I'll make it $1990."

I hardly needed to explain to the family, for they caught the final offer full in the face. We filed slowly across the street to our waiting car.

Our little cabin seemed even smaller than usual that evening as we went about aimlessly. Not until after supper did we discuss the day's events in earnest.

"Well," Mother said, "I think we had better start right out again as though we had never seen that Ross property and..."

"Or else go back to a second choice," I interrupted. "Personally I've about given up hope and we just must get located, for here it is July already."

"Pa, we didn't even consider that other property of Ross' we saw today," Harris said. "It was a good lake, there was plenty of room for cabins, and there was lots of shade."

"Shade, yes. Nothing but scrub oak and popple. I don't think I saw a pine on the place," Bruce said.

"When I think of living up there in the winter, well, that's just too isolated," Flora put in as she reached for her pen. "There's not even a road that goes all the way in." So the conversation went on and on until Mother called a halt.

"You've just got to quiet down while I concentrate on this letter to the folks," she said. "Maybe we'll all feel better in the morning. At any rate we can't settle anything now and tomorrow there's washing and some baking to do."

As we crawled into bed that night, I said, "Flora, you don't suppose we could ask your folks for a loan, do you?"

"Why, no, I should say not. I wouldn't think of it, Charlie, there's too much risk involved in any investment these days."

"Well, I expect you're right. I just thought it might be one way out."

Once more I was the water boy and carried pails from the lake and poured them lackadaisically into the wash-boiler as Flora set a batch of bread.

"Charlie, I wish you would go to the store for me. We're running low on food. The list is there on the table, and whatever you do, don't forget to mail my letter."

As I trudged over the hot, sandy road, I watched dragonflies dart bewilderingly this way and that, and thought their erratic flight not unlike our own goings and comings. Where would it all end, and when?

In the cool interior of the store I pushed the letter into the narrow slot as I said hello to Joe.

"How are you coming with your resort business?" he asked as he checked over the list I had handed him

"Not so good," I answered, hardly in a mood for conversation. "We haven't found anything yet. That is, anything we can afford to buy."

"Say, Mr. Palmer, how about buying me out? I've got a good business all worked up and a good home, too, for that matter." His proposition burst upon me like a bombshell and left me quite speechless. In the interim he barraged me with superlatives.

"You can handle the deal with a small down payment," he continued, taking advantage of my silence. I heard him through as I packed my knapsack with the groceries.

"Well, at least I'll think it over, Joe," I said. "I've got to do something pretty quick." But the proposition diminished in its appeal with each step toward home. It'll be something different to talk about, anyhow.

At the supper table that night I said to no one in particular, "What would you think of buying Joe Larrabee's place, store, home and all?" There was a moment of silence followed by an explosion of negatives that buried the matter beyond any further exploration.

The recent turn of events was reflected in the melancholy state of our dispositions. We had resigned ourselves to circumstances and were ready to settle at last for one of our second choice sites. Even such a compromise had its difficulties, for we couldn't get together on any one of them. However, after several days of discussion, the choice had boiled down to two. There we were stymied. I could see little advantage in one over the other and Flora was ready to settle, but Bruce and Harris held steadfastly to opposite opinions. This was the state of affairs until one day when Lois walked in with the mail.

"Here's a letter from Gram and I've got one from Kenny," she said, tossing the first one upon the table.

Flora dried her hands quickly, opened the envelope and glanced over its contents. "It's from Mother," she said as she dropped on the bench and polished her glasses. We listened with casual interest to the happenings back home, while Lois perused her own mail. But when the letter took a turn in our direction, we listened eagerly.

"The girls and I have been talking things over after receiving your last letter and we are quite concerned lest you settle on that place so far back in the wilderness. While it might make a good resort, remember you will have to live there the year around. We like your description of the Lipsie Lake property and we think you had better buy it, especially as you are so keen about it. The girls and I will advance the money."

At this point, Flora was obliged to call for silence. "Let me finish this letter," she cried.

"Although we know it is a considerable risk for you to take in these bad times, I'm sure you will see your way through somehow and we want to help in any way we can."

When the long letter was finished Flora pushed it aside and said, "Charlie, what do you make of it? Do you really think we should? You know it will be a long time before we can pay them back."

I knew she was right and knew too there would be a lot of hard sledding ahead. I hadn't forgotten our own bank's failure, nor had I determined the meaning of those mortgage papers in the tin box. Yet somehow there was inspiration in those tall pines, and good luck, perhaps, in the horseshoe hill that embraced them. I wanted the place desperately, but I hesitated to put any decision into words. Finally Bruce burst out, "Pa, you know very well what you're going to say. Why not get it over with?"

Though I felt I was slipping, I took a new hold upon myself and suggested that at least we sleep on it overnight.

"What's the use, Pa? There's only one answer and you know what it is," said Harris.

"O.K. I give up. The matter is settled, but we'll all have to share the responsibility together," I said with resignation.

The next day Lois volunteered to do the housework while Flora and I rushed to town to get things started with Mr. Ross. At the bank Mr. Appleton showed us a plot of the eighty acres in question and gave us a receipt for the earnest money we brought along. He suggested, too, that the bank's attorney clear the title when all was ready. This we agreed to, and I heaved a sigh of relief when we climbed back into the car. Our trip home over the dusty road was slow, and we talked things over in a leisurely fashion without the children to disturb us. As we neared home, I said, "Let's turn off at Byrnes' Store and see if we can find that old trail that leads to the Ross…"

"Our property, you mean," Flora cut in with a laugh. But we decided against it, as the hour was late, and there were many other things to be done.

I was surprised at the boys' confidence, for they had the truck loaded when we got home, and by nightfall there was little else to do but get a good night's rest.

Chapter 6

___

SETTLING IN

With mixed feelings of anticipation and regret, we pulled away from our little old Rough and Ready, knowing full well that not for a long time to come would we have another roof over our heads that would serve as well. We were on the march, the sedan in the lead this time, early morning sun in our eyes.

Smoke was curling lazily through the jackpine tops when we reached Mr. Byrnes' store. We waited for the boys to come up, then together turned south in search of the old trail we had been told about. We went only a mile or so when we came upon it. Though brush covered, the ruts were  easily discernible. Young pine and popple marked the winding course through the woods, and at one spot we chopped our way through a tree that had recently fallen. The going was slow. Saplings bent beneath our bumpers to rise once more when we had passed, and bony fingers reached out to rattle against our windows. This trail had just started downward when Lois shouted, "I see the lake!"

Wild horses couldn't hold us now, and over the horseshoe rim and down into the park we rushed.

For one enchanted hour we did little more than revel in the thought of possession, for we knew that the title to these eighty wonderful acres would soon be tucked away in our tin box, along with our mortgage papers and grandfather's autobiography. Nor would we spoil this day with any thought of the added obligation we had entailed. Measured in time, we had come a long way for this moment, and now found it hard to comprehend the fullness of its meaning. Here in the amphitheater setting were the big pines for which we had so long searched, the lake, the beach and even the blue sky with its billowing clouds - all these and more were ours to have and to hold. With it all came an exhilaration of spirit. Many times before, in far away places, we had felt the stir of our emotions. On the brink of God-sized canyons we had stood in awe, and we had sensed the cold bleakness of distant mountain peaks. Standing here, we felt a kinship with nature never before experienced.

With a new sense of belonging we shook ourselves into action, for the day was still young. Flora called for her cookstove, saying, "Why, it'll soon be dinner time and I haven't even given it a thought. Lois, you better gather some sticks of wood to start a fire."

Ropes were untied and canvas removed and soon her heavy cookstove was lowered to the ground. With a length of stove pipe rising from its oval hole, it stood among the trees as a symbol of habitation. Next came the ten gallon milk can filled to its brim with odds and ends of victuals. In no time at all the tea kettle, filled with water from the lake, was singing on the stove. Bedding was unrolled and hung out to air, and as though by magic, a canvas dwelling sprang from nowhere.

As we sat cross-legged upon the ground, our plates heaped with fried potatoes, Flora said, "Now there are two things I must have. First, I want you men to build me a large table, and when that's done I want some kind of a roof over my cook stove."

"What'll we use for boards?" Harris asked.

"So far as I know there's not a stick of lumber short of Dan Matson's mill, and that's a long ways back, even beyond Hertel," I replied.

"Well, let's go," he said, pushing his plate aside.

When the last piece of furniture was lowered to the ground,

Harris and I started the long trip to Dan's place. "Someday we'll have to locate a closer sawmill – we can't afford to spend all our time on the road," I shouted in my boy's ear.

The countryside became familiar as we neared the cabin we had so recently abandoned. We were not long at the mill, though we loitered to watch the big saw spin its way the length of a dozen logs. Waving to Joe Larrabee as we passed, we finally stopped before Mr. Byrnes' little store.

"I see you've got a jag of lumber on," he said as he laid out our few groceries. "Does that mean you've bought the Ross place after all?"

"We've made a down payment on it at least."

"Well, I'm glad to hear that. I hardly thought he'd sell it."

When we turned the corner and our truck rolled down the hill, Harris said, "Pa, this is the first time I ever knew you to come home with a jag on." I wondered if he caught this bit of colloquialism.

By sunset a large table with plank seats attached stood beneath the spreading boughs of a Norway pine, and close by, a tiny three-sided shack, rough and without a floor, housed Mother's cookstove, cupboard and a dresser. This was our first day's accomplishment on the shores of Lake Lipsie.

Far across the water we watched Abbie French's white cottage fade into the shadows of the night. "Was it neighbors she wanted? Well, she's got them now," I said to Flora. On their cots beside the water, our three children looked up at stars through gauze nets, while within the umbrella tent Mother and I fell asleep.

The next I knew someone was shaking my shoulder. "Charlie, I do believe it's raining," I heard Flora say. When I realized the significance of her remark, I drew on my pants, but before I'd gotten outside, the children hurried in with their cots. Surprised to find that dawn was breaking, I finished dressing and stumbled outside. There was little more I could do than throw a canvas over a few things. Then climbing into the cab, I waited dejectedly, hoping for a break in the weather. The sight of our worldly possessions standing forlorn among dripping trees somehow struck a ludicrous note within me and I laughed out loud. Lengths of stovepipe awaited chimney holes, a roll of linoleum wanted a floor. There were beds and chairs without rooms and pictures literally wept for better backgrounds. Our few pieces of machinery were huddled together waiting to be housed. Yet there was a seriousness beneath the humor that gripped me as I climbed down from my seat.

The visor-like extension of the shack roof sheltered us from the dripping trees as we stood in a group and ate our first breakfast on our own land. The storm proved of short duration and dry, thirsty sands sucked the moisture from about the grass roots. Searching fingers of sunlight crept through the foliage, and a thin veil of mist lifted slowly from the water. A pair of loons stretched their necks toward our camp and sent their yodeling laughter reverberating throughout the hills.

Exhilaration was in the rain washed air as we started out to explore our northern-most boundary. A perfect day to be alive, I felt, as the boys and I studied survey markings on an old witness tree. We were searching for evidence that would enable us to locate the exact center of the section, for then we could establish our northern boundary. But the markings proved little more than hieroglyphics to us, so I left the boys and headed directly away from the lake. If I held my course due east, I knew I would come out on the road leading to Byrnes' Store, but I was becoming anxious. Why, this is the longest half mile I ever walked, I said to myself as I stumbled along. I could scarcely see a rod ahead. Eighty acres? It's a lot bigger than I supposed, but I'm bound to reach that road sooner or later. Up hill and down, through oak and hazel brush I wove my way. Suddenly before me was a beautiful stretch of water. What, another lake so close? This will be real news to the family. I took but a dozen more steps when I heard someone shout. "Where on earth have you been, Pa," and I turned to see Harris advancing toward me. Then I saw the others at the cook shack and I realized that I had been walking in a circle.

"Oh, I've just been walking around," I said nonchalantly. Not for a long time did I rid myself of the feeling that another lake lay close by.

Our cook shack, fresh and bright, with its blue smoke threading upward and the plank table piled high with all manner of things, now became the center of our universe. When Flora could find no room for a pail of water she had fetched from the lake she registered her objections.

"It's just a shame the way you menfolk clutter up my table. What are those big wrenches doing there? And that vise! At least you can find some other place for that."

The Cook Shack

"Now, Mother, we're just laying out some tools and things to pound down a well so we can have better water," Harris replied.

"Better water! Well, bless your soul, I'll not say another word. I don't know of a thing I'd rather have."

All necessary equipment, including the pump and vise, were hauled to a site just beyond the toe-end of the horse-shoe hill. We chose this particular place because it was close to where we would erect our first building. We went down about ten feet with a post auger, then a section of pipe with a well point on one end was dropped point down into the hole, much of its length remaining above ground. Finding the iron maul too severe on the cap threads, we fashioned another from oak, then watched the pipe inch down beneath each stroke. Stripped to the waist, sweating and tanned, the boys' bodies shown like bronze as they wielded the big maul.

"It won't take us much longer at this rate," Harris said hopefully, for he had estimated the water table at twenty-five feet, and we were nearly there. When at last the weighted cord came out wet, there was a shout of "water". Hurriedly screwing on the pump section with its cylinder, I poured in a prime and set the pump handle in motion, rapidly at first, then slower as the check valve took hold.

"Here she comes", I shouted, for I could feel the water rising with each stroke. Coffee brown it came, then crystal clear.

"Well, I never," Mother said with surprise when I handed her a pitcher of the sparkling liquid. "I thought it would take all day, at least. You just don't know how much I'll appreciate it."

Later that day, the real surprise was on us. For dessert at dinner Flora brought forth two blueberry pies. "We picked the berries right here on the hill while you were working," Lois said. As if that was not enough, four golden loaves of bread came from the oven that afternoon.

We had just risen from the table when we heard the tinkle of bells. Lois shouted, "Cows; it's cows," and ran in the direction of the sound. An animal appeared through the brush, then another and another, until a whole herd stood ankle deep in the cool waters of the lake. To our surprise a roan horse came slowly plodding over the rim, its rider bent forward as though sleeping, his reins hanging loosely about the saddle horn. Here, I observed, is our first visitor, and he comes in true western style. Suddenly the roan stopped, ears forward, feet braced. With a jerk the young man came to life. His face showed his astonishment, but it turned to a smile as he dismounted and dropped the reins over the pony's head.

"Well, this is a surprise," he said with an embarrassed grin. "Are you folks camping out or are you here to stay?"

"We're here to stay, I hope," I answered, hardly sure of myself under the circumstances.

"My name is Sylvester, Ralph Sylvester. I live a couple of miles to the east of here," he said.

"And ours is Palmer," I replied.

The dishes went unwashed as Lois gave herself wholeheartedly to our young visitor and his herd. First to the cows, then to the horse, and when the cowboy asked, "Want a ride?" I heard our daughter say, "I sure do." Bruce and Harris, too, had their turn about the woods, but when it was mine I politely declined, though for what reason I hardly knew. There is something about a horse and its trappings that gets beneath my skin, and even today the sight, smell and squeak of a western saddle sets my blood atingle. Perhaps this had come from my mother's family who were all cowmen.

When the cowboy and his herd had vanished from sight, Mother said, "I think I'm going to like that Sylvester family."

"I wish you would take time to brush out the path up to the pump, Charlie. It's all I can do to get through with a pail of water."

"I've just finished putting an edge on my axe, and it's so sharp it'll do the job in just about no time flat," I replied.

"You may run into some poison ivy. I'd be careful if I were you."

For some time I had suspected the three-leafed clusters, but I had no way of identifying them. I found it fun to fell the popple saplings, for usually it took only a stroke or two to cut them through at the base. The scrub oaks were different. They were tougher. I found my double-bitted axe not so well adapted to the small growth, so I exchanged it for a heavy brush scythe which made short work of vines and hazel brush. I was looking over my handiwork when Harris stopped at the pump for a drink.

54

"Well, it looks as if someone lives around here," he said, "but I don't think you've cut it wide enough," and he reached for my axe. Popples and oak fell away before his onslaught, and when at last he stopped before the shack, I was sure he would make his way in the woods. However, the job didn't satisfy Flora. Not until we had hoed, dug, pulled and cut all suspicious vines and roots from the earth was she content.

The boys had spent considerable time getting some semblance of order about our camp. They made a temporary covering for the machinery, and tied strips of tar paper over and about the furniture. There still remained a heterogeneous lot of odds and ends, especially beneath the plank table, and to this the cook periodically objected. There was hardly an idle moment for anyone, and for the time being, the fun of fishing was relegated to an hour of necessity only.

Our meals, simple though repetitious in character, were nevertheless wholesome and satisfying. Except for chicken, no fresh meat could be had short of Spooner, for although there were deer, rabbit, partridge and duck in abundance, they could only be killed in season. We never tired of fish and soon developed a taste for the smaller variety. To this day we prefer a mess of bluegill to one of bass or even walleye. But not Bruce, who stuck to his store-labeled tuna or salmon.

Milk was a problem as it couldn't be had at the store. The herd of cows that drank almost daily from the lake might have been the answer, and I confess that I had given it a thought, but that's as far as it ever got. Eventually learning of a neighbor with a cow, a trip on foot over an old tote road became a daily responsibility for Lois. A large earthen crock sunk in the ground served as a cooler of a kind, and in it we kept our milk and other perishables.

Our daily trips to the store became short interludes of pleasure which we shared more or less in turn. On one of these, Flora and I had a visit with Abbie French.

"I just feel awful that I haven't been over to see you folks yet. Fact is, I started one day but my boat leaked so bad I had to turn back. But I've been watching you with my power glasses most every day. Seems good to have you so close."

As time passed Mr. Byrnes introduced us to customers, or told us where so-and-so lived. In this way we learned the names of neighbors, even though we hadn't met them.

The path from our cook shack to the well was taking on character, for plodding feet had worn the grass thin and a trickle of sand lay throughout its length. There is something nostalgic about a path, something that strikes a responsive note and that calls up memories. I shall never forget the one through the lush prairie grass of Illinois to the red brick schoolhouse of my childhood days. I enjoyed the way it lay smooth and cool beneath my bare feet. Nor shall I forget the one to the depot over which I carried my father's lunch pail. Now our path to the pump was maturing, one of many more to come that would eventually symbolize progress.

Each morning we washed our faces at the water's edge and each morning we swept manna from heaven off our breakfast table. Pine needles, singly and in clusters, fell about us, and only when a cone dropped into a plate of food or a cup of coffee was there any undue comment.

Usually our jobs were planned and allocated before we rose from the table each morning. On this particular day, Bruce chose to install a new universal joint in the truck. Taking our inspiration from the newly-opened swath, Harris and I fell to clearing the park with a vengeance. With axe and scythe we set to work in earnest. By bending young saplings with one hand, I found I could easily cut through their fibrous bases with one steady pull of the scythe. This was quick work, and popples tall as cane poles fell this way and that like jackstraws. The breakfast work over, Mother and Lois joined us. With gloved hands, they dragged and carried our cuttings and piled them for burning. The day was hot and we drank quarts of cold water as we mopped our perspiring brows. Noontime came and went with its needed respite, and when at last Flora drew off her gloves to prepare the evening meal, I took over her work of hauling and piling. Barehanded I pulled at fallen branches and toted brush, paying little heed to the three-leafed clusters I had been warned about.

At the table that evening, the day's work was surveyed. What a change those few hours had made. The park had taken on a larger aspect; the green pump stood out, and even the big pines seemed taller. Our eyes were further opened to the potential beauty within our reach, and we crept into bed with a feeling of keen satisfaction.

"Are you awake, Charlie?" Flora asked as I lay absorbed in my thoughts.

"Sure, I'm awake," I replied as I punched my pillow into shape.

"Well, I don't like to disturb you, but I wanted you to know that I'm beginning to see those sheep in your pots of color."

We had given Dan Matson our order for three thousand feet of white pine lumber. The boards were to be especially milled, which called for unconventional planer knives, and I knew that Dan could fashion them. He was a large and brawny man who once demonstrated his strength by shouldering a breaker plow and carrying it from the field where it had mired down, yet it was his know-how that made him an asset to his community. Typical, too, of the countryside were the men who worked at his mill. Woodsmen, large and small, they were strong and sturdy and equal to any task. Their environment put a premium on their backs. We found them always friendly and ready with a helping hand.

The place we chose for our shop lay well back over the horseshoe rim and close to the pump. The boys were all for a building larger than I thought necessary, and the matter was hanging fire.

"But Pa," Bruce said with one eye on his mother, "we're going to have to live in it till we can build a house. Mom's going to need room to get meals, and where are we to sleep?" I, too, had one eye on Flora and knew he had found an ally in his mother. Remembering the crowded cook shack, I eventually conceded and saved her from taking sides.

Safe from the weather beneath a tarpaulin and adjacent to our building site lay a pile of fresh, new lumber. While sizable trees were being felled and their stumps removed, our truck was hauling gravel from distant hills and bags of cement from town. By suppertime that day, our foundation forms in place, we filed down to our sandy beach for a dip in the lake. Finally we put in an hour of cutting and burning brush, thereby setting a precedent.

We had gotten well into our work the next morning when we heard the tinkling of cow bells once more, and soon the herd of cattle passed leisurely by, switching their tails and chewing their cuds. The boys, bared to the waist, were mixing concrete in a wooden box when Ralph dropped from his horse to watch.

"We've got a small wooden-barrel mixer you can borrow if you want," he said.

"Well, I admit we need one. We intend to get one later, but if you're sure it's all right with your folks, we'll go over and get yours."

Soon our truck was bouncing on its way toward the Sylvester homestead. I often wondered about the old cabin as we passed it on trips to and from town, and now I would have a chance to meet its occupants. What a cover for a Saturday Evening Post. Dwarfed in the shadow of a large barn was a dwelling, gray and weathered with the patina of time. Hand-hewn logs reflected an era back quite beyond my own, and the gentle hillsides about were strewn with implements of the soil. There was a pioneer atmosphere about this place that appealed to me.

I spoke briefly about our undertaking as Mrs. Sylvester stood framed in the open doorway, a kindly smile on her face. A quick glance into the interior only enhanced my curiosity.

"Why, of course you can borrow the cement mixer," was her reply to my query. "Ralph has been telling me about you folks, and I've been wanting to get over." A pair of colts whinnied, raised their tails and bolted for the regions beyond the barn as we passed through the pole gate. Yes, I, too, would like the Sylvesters.

The hand-operated mixer gave us good service when we powered it from a rear truck wheel.

Flora often criticized me for lack of appreciation of the boys' mechanical achievements, especially when they brought their handiwork home from school. With the shop nearing completion, I realized more then ever that she had been right. Both had shown unusual skill in their work and in handling their tools. They put an emphasis upon the square, plumb and level, and now a professional job was in evidence.

The rectangular workshop, thirty by thirty-five feet, was partitioned off for shop and garage. We came to disagreement once more over installation of the machinery. I wanted an overhead line shaft which meant accessibility. Bruce was adamant in his stand for one beneath the floor. As usual, the controversy found its way to the dinner table. In his dislike for argument Harris took a philosophical stand, saying it made little difference one way or another as both plans had their merits. The matter was finally settled by the toss of a coin. Tails had it and Bruce won.

"Say, Charlie, are you sure it isn't Sunday today?" Flora asked, stopping dead in her tracks. "If it is, there'll be no mail when we get there."

By a little calculation we found that it was on the Sabbath that we had finished the line shaft.

"No, this is Monday all right," I replied.

"Well, I do hope we get a letter from home. It's been a long time, it seems." With only the trees to hear, we talked of our hopes, of our prospects for the things we might reasonably look forward to.

"I'm not complaining, Charlie, but I'll be glad when I can have a few conveniences again."

"Such as what for instance?" I asked.

"Well, I've lived on dirt so long I can't wait until we get into the shop where there'll be a wooden floor, room for a table, yes, and a screen door. You know it's only the essentials I want, Charlie, not luxuries." When I reminded her of the kitchen sink, the gallons of hot water, the privacy of a toilet and bath, things we had once had, I winced at the look she gave me, sorry that I had spoken.

"Charlie, if you can't take it, just say so. We can always go back home, you know."

"Stop your kidding, Flora. Why, I've never been happier in my life; you know that. Why, it's just human nature to want to better one's condition; otherwise we'd be no different than the animals."

Indeed, the mailman had left a letter, and its contents became the subject of our conversation as we made our way homeward.

"The Hickeses are coming!" Flora announced as she dropped on a bench. This was good news, as it meant a visit from old friends. Both Howard and Ethel were teachers, and with their two children, had once been our camping companions. The real surprise came later when their car rolled over the rim and into our very midst. To be sure, it was a noisy group about the dinner table that evening as we relived old experiences and discussed things in general. When we lighted one of the many brush piles that evening, the whole camp came ablaze in an amber spectacle of highlight and shadow. When a stranger emerged from the darkness and made directly for our group, we rubbed our eyes in astonishment.

"Now what can this fellow want at this hour of the night?" I said.

We were not long in finding out, however, for no sooner did he step into our circle than he asked to see our burning permit. Of course we had none, and I told him so, though not without apprehension. I watched his face as his searching eyes studied the surroundings. Clearly highlighted against the darkness were our tent, vehicles and our new cook shack.

When he saw the pump, conspicuous in the firelight, he said, "You're evidently here to stay. Am I right?"

"Yes, my name is Palmer," I replied. "We're here from Chicago and are going to build a summer resort."

He casually brushed a spark from his shoulder, seated himself on a log, and in a kindly manner set forth the hazards of brush fires. When he had gone, I resolved that never again would this ranger have cause to regret his tactfulness. We learned that burning permits were issued at the Ranger Station in Spooner, and from that day on we never burned without them.

"Charlie," Flora said a few days later "do you realize that tomorrow is the 11th of August, our wedding anniversary?"

"Oh, oh, I'd never have remembered it."

"In fact it's our twenty-fifth, and it so happens that Howard and Ethel have theirs too, their eighteenth. Let's have a double celebration. What do you say?"

The realization that I had been married for a quarter of a century came as something of a shock, but of course I fell in with her idea, and both women started to plan a big meal. Knowing of a farmer south of Hertel who wanted to sell off his young cockerels, I set out with instructions to come home with nine of them. A chicken apiece! What a celebration, I thought.

"They'll average at least a pound and a half," the farmer said as he snatched a young one at his feet. "You can have them for a dime apiece. I've got to get rid of them before they eat their heads off."

"Chickens at ten cents apiece! Why, I can't believe it," Flora said. "Are you sure that's all you paid, Charlie?"

By one o'clock our plank table was a thing to behold with heaping platters of crisp brown chicken, biscuits hot from the oven, bowls of mashed potatoes, gravy and blueberry pie.

"Where's the fish?" Harris shouted facetiously.

As we gathered for the feast, the smell of perking coffee sharpened our appetites. We had just filled our plates when to our consternation a fitful whirlwind swept over last night's bonfire and on to the lake, peppering our food with ashes.

Chapter 7

UNDER ROOF

All things considered, this moving day was a happy one, but pulling stakes at the water's edge was not without regrets, as it meant the end of our camping days, perhaps forever for Flora and me. We would miss the enchanting daybreak hours when mist hung over the water, and the weird cry of loons awakened the stillness, that hour when we were one with the eerie world about us, refugees from reality. We were about to change this gypsy life for one of convention, more or less. The inside walls of the shop were still unlined, and its studding and rafters were conspicuous in their exposure.

"It'll be a flimsy protection against the cold this winter," I said. "We'll have to do something about it this fall."

"Why borrow trouble on our first day beneath a roof?" Flora answered.

The Shop Building

The table saw, band saw and drill press, all having priority rights, had been assigned to their several places and were permanently fixed to the floor. In one corner, on a concrete base, sat our power plant, a car motor, and in another corner was Mother's heavy range. When an old enameled sink caught the cook's eye, words of gratitude flowed.

There were cabinets and chests of drawers to say nothing of boxes and bundles stowed away under the bench. When an old oak dining table and chairs were moved in, there was little room to turn around.

By noontime the first day we had gotten some order out of the chaos. "Flora," I said surveying the heterogeneous layout, "I think we're pretty well fixed at that, don't you?"

"Well, yes, but what about places to sleep? You know, Charlie, I must have my springs and mattress if I'm to get any rest." The long work bench offered the only remaining room to stretch out, with a choice of upper or lower berths. Try as we might, we could find no space for our old bedstead, until finally, in despair, we hauled it down to the cook shack where we stored it.

"I'll promise you sleeping quarters of some kind before night, Flora. Just let me figure it out by myself."

While the Hickeses moved into the garage side, I got busy with hammer and saw. When the family finally prepared to bed down, Lois turned around a few times like a wild creature and dropped on a pad beneath the bench. Our boys, however, took themselves off to their old quarters down by the water in preference to upper berths on the workbench. Flora scanned our bed up among the rafters with a critical eye, for directly below were the sharp teeth of the circular saw.

"You know you're sleeping on the outside, don't you, Charlie?" she said. The bed was suspended from the rafters immediately beneath a rectangular opening I had cut in the roof, framing the starry heavens.

"I think that skylight's a grand idea" she said, "and that bed up there is like an Oriole's nest. Come on, let's give it a try. I can't wait." I held the ladder securely while she climbed, then blew out the light and followed. The darkness of the room accentuated the depth of the heavens, and we lay absorbed in its beauty.

"Why, Charlie, this is just wonderful. It's my first experience sleeping beneath the stars. This certainly beats sleeping in a tent."

"Are city folk keener about trees than country folk who live in their midst?" I asked Flora one day. For surely our big Norways had impressed us as no other possession we ever had. Harris was especially sensitive about trees and before felling one he would approach it almost apologetically as though it was endowed with feeling and understanding. Flora, too, had a love for trees, and much preferred a walk in the woods to a venture out on the water. Outstanding among ours were the smooth white boles of the birches. Though these belong to the hardwood family, they lack the endurance of oak and others that grow about them. Of six or eight angling birches from a common stool, two or three may be dead, although this is hardly apparent to the casual observer. On the ground, the inner wood rots quickly, leaving a tough white cylinder of bark filled with a soft spongy mass.

I was witness to a slapstick comedy in which a short length of this 'wood' played the major role. Our friend, Ethel Hickes, set out one day to catch and discipline her fourteen-year-old son. Holding up a length of birch, she brought it down over his head and shoulders with force enough to fell an ox, but of course she had been sure that it would do little more than shower him with dust.

The Hickeses were so taken with the tall Norways at the north end of our property that they made arrangements to start a cabin there for their summer vacations, which later became known as Shore Leave.

From the doorstep of the shop we could look down into the cleared area of the park. Little more than a casual glance showed the poison ivy which persisted in spite of Flora's constant grubbing. However, the vines had been doomed from the start, for she would never quit until the last vestige had been destroyed. Even with her gloves, the poison had begun to show up in the form of small blisters about her wrists and above her shoe-tops, though it was having no effect upon me.

Brushing, grubbing, piling and burning became a regular chore at the end of the day, and each freshly-cut area became an incentive toward further clearing. We were always fascinated by the leaping flames as they consumed pile after pile of brush. The mass of material would fairly melt before our eyes. Cells of pent-up sap would burst in tiny explosions, then whine away into the blackness of the night. Sometimes a spark would rocket to a spreading branch and expend itself in a moment of splendor. Brooms, wet gunny sacks and pails of water were always at hand, reminders of the fire warden's caution.

As time passed, new friendships were formed. From the north came Bob Reimer to pal with Harris, and Abbie's grandson, Harold Jewell, came almost daily from the far side of the lake. Shouting and laughter broke the stillness as the boys graded our beach with Bob's team of horses.

Then there were the Van Leeuwens: Henry, his wife Margaret, and his brother George; Hollanders living directly east of us as the crow flies, and the first of the neighbors to pay us a visit. I was troweling a patch of concrete quite unaware of their presence until I rose to my feet and there they were. Had I known then how close our friendship would become, I'm sure my handshake would have been a bit more cordial.

When we learned at last that the deed to our property was ready, we hastened to town. Although the bank's attorney attested to the validity of it, we had no means of knowing that it covered the actual acreage upon which we had already settled. Land, when surveyed by the government, is divided into square miles better known as sections. These in turn are subdivided into quarter sections and the latter into forty-acre plots. Thus it becomes a simple matter to locate one's property by legal description on a plat. But when a forty falls short of its full acreage because of a partial coverage by water, the remaining part is known officially as a government lot. Such lots within a section are numbered consecutively around a lake.

We could identify the back forty on the plat, but not the forty fronting on the lake. The lots to the north were numbered one and two, but no other numbers were given on the plan. Logic would lead one to assume that ours should be number three, but the deed specifically called for lot four.

We discussed the matter with Mr. Appleman at the bank and he suggested we see Mr. Harmon, who he said had made the original survey for the government. We lost no time in paying a visit to this old-timer, who we learned later had made many original surveys throughout the northwoods country. We found him interesting and courteous, and after an hour's painstaking search through old dusty files, he found what he wanted.

"Now we shall see," he said, adjusting his steel-rimed glasses. "I think I recall that very piece where you have settled and I don't wonder that you want it, considering those big trees and all. Now if I'm not mistaken, that lot should be number three." I was amazed at his ability to think back over the years and draw forth from his memory any intelligible idea of the place at all. "Now what was the description on that deed?" he asked.

"Lot number four," I replied anxiously.

"Now look here and see for yourself; this is the original plat. There at the lake are lots number one and two, and next is number three, just as I thought, and it's nearly a full forty," he said. "There's a mistake in that deed and I'd certainly have it changed."

Once we had passed quite out of hearing Flora said, "Whew, that was a close call. What a mess we'd have been in if we had accepted it as it was. All our work so far would have gone for nothing. And we'd have a back forty and a front lot catercorner to each other, to say nothing of losing all those big trees."

Needless to say we rushed over to see Mr. Ross and we had a new deed when we left his office. After clearing things at the bank, we hurried to the county seat to have it registered, and that night we tucked it away in our precious tin box.

In our Oriole's Nest, we were made aware of each new day by bird life in the branches above us. If perchance there was an early morning rain, we had only to reach up and slide a glass sky light into place. The resonant ticking of a big school clock on the wall was a constant reminder that we had moved indoors. The first thing to greet our awakening eyes was a long shelf of books, like a colorful wallpaper border about the room. Flora had always had a close association with books, and when we had loaded the big truck for our new venture, she hadn't the courage to leave them behind. I arranged them according to color and to suit my own esthetic taste, but her library training would have none of it.

"Who cares about the color of books?" she said. "It's what's between their covers that matters. Do you know, Charlie, I've been thinking – we've got, well, I just don't know how many volumes, but they're only gathering dust. How about letting them out to anyone who wants them? They are like people, they should circulate." I thought perhaps it might result in a few friendships and readily agreed. We let it be known at the store and by word of mouth that books might be had for the asking.

Within a few days we had our first caller, a big good-looking fellow known about the countryside as Harry. His arms were filled with books as he left, and I hardly expected to see him again for some time. Yet three or four days later he exchanged these for others. He told us he worked on the Dunham place several miles away. Perhaps he found legitimate time to read the volumes he had taken, but I had my doubts. Perhaps our library was not so helpful after all.

A more interesting episode concerning our book venture came about when two small Indian children appeared one morning as though by magic. They grinned and plucked nervously at their clothes as their black eyes took in the surroundings. They were quiet as totem poles until I questioned them. Then taking courage, the older of the two, a boy, said, "We want books."

They followed me into the shop. But it wasn't the long line of books that caught the boy's eye; instead it was the big school clock. For a time he just looked, then he expressed his amazement in one brief sentence, "What big minutes!"

I climbed up on a bench, and with Flora's help, selected two story books for the children. I pressed them into their outstretched hands and said, "You needn't bring them back; they're yours." I had always felt a sense of obligation toward this misnamed, mishandled and much maligned race of human beings and I was glad for this small chance to express my feelings. I watched them file down through the park and out of sight, but this was only the beginning, for the story has its sequel.

A few days later I had rose earlier than usual to try my hand at fishing, and stepping outside, was surprised to find a package on our doorstep. Whatever it was had been placed there in the dark of night and I hesitated a moment before taking it inside.

"Flora," I called as I laid it upon the table. She came down the ladder in her dressing gown, and together we took off the wrapping of sugar-sack material.

"Why, it's a leg of lamb, Charlie. Where on earth did it come from?"

Already I was seeing the light, and as the family gathered around I said, "No, Flora, it's a leg of venison and it's the Indian way of saying thank you."

Chapter 8

SETBACK

We had staked out our new road and were working on it one day in late August. The heat in the woods was almost unbearable and yellow-jackets were mean and irritable. As usual the boys were stripped to their waists, and their bronze skin shone with perspiration as they swung their axes.

Finding the two water jugs which lay beneath a layer of cool leaf mold were nearly empty, I hooked their handles over my fingers and followed the old trail down to the pump. I was more than a little surprised at seeing Flora sitting idly down in the park, as it was nearing dinner time and the boys would soon be along. I had the sense that something was wrong, as I worked the pump handle. The sound brought Lois to the door.

"Mom isn't feeling well and dinner'll be late today," she informed, then turned on her heel before I could reply. Though Flora had long since stopped her grubbing out the ivy and its connecting roots, the poison had spread to her hands and arms and now was showing up in blisters on her feet. However, it was her utter lack of interest in things in general that had me worried. Of late I missed that quiet hour of conversation up beneath the skylight where once she had thrilled to the star filled heavens. Only in the mornings did she seem her normal self, did her spirits rise, and this morning in particular I had gone off to work hoping for the best.

With the water jugs at my feet, I stood in indecision beside the pump. I realized that my immediate responsibility lay down in the park. I could hardly remember when Mother had been too ill to carry on. Could there be something more than ivy poisoning that ailed her? Oh well, I'll see her at dinner time, and I started off through the woods toward the thirsty boys.

Through the freshly-cut swath I could see the flash of axes at the far end, and soon came upon our crude transit. If necessity is the mother of invention, resourcefulness must be its father, I reasoned as I looked at the improvised instrument. Perched on a tripod of popple poles was an ensemble of gadgets including a small level, a spy glass and a pocket compass. For the nth time I stopped to peer through its lens toward the white shirt that hung limp in a treetop a quarter of a mile distant. We were cutting an east-west swath through the woods to join up with the county-line road. This was nearing completion, and soon the last tree, bearing the shirt, would fall. Then would come the job of stump pulling, dynamiting and grading.

At noontime I was relieved to find Flora sitting at the table, but my concern returned when she showed little interest in the food Lois had prepared. Nor did she enter into conversation. Time was when she would have thrilled at such an undertaking as our new road, but she had hardly more than glanced at the transit when we spread its legs on the floor. From the first, we had planned that she would go back home in the fall to keep house for Bruce and Lois - he would finish Junior College and she, high school. But would Mother be able to make the trip? As the time for departure drew near, I became ever more apprehensive.

Despite all the timber about us, we were hard put for an adequate source of logs with which to build the dozen cabins we had planned. Nothing could induce us to cut any of the pines about the camp or along the lakeshore. Those that grew sparsely among the oaks on the back forty were insufficient in number and too large for our purpose.

Some distance south the county-line road skirted a forty acre plot with a fair stand of timber which we understood could be secured for payment of back taxes. This would be a splendid source of building material, one from which we could choose and cut as our project required. Quite naturally we lost no time in running the rumor down. We learned that the county would surrender the title only under conditions that would guarantee payment of future taxes.

Adjoining this forty on the south was a small farm where the

Fergusons lived. Bill was quite popular in the neighborhood, and his aptness with the fiddle had made him none the less so. He had been paying rent and he wanted a place of his own. Here then was his opportunity, for I would have no use for the land after I removed the timber.

At the court house in Shell Lake, I paid the back taxes amounting to forty dollars. I then made the title over to Bill, getting from him a signed release for all the standing timber on the forty. On our way home we stopped in for another look at the place.

"Mr. Palmer," Bill said as we set foot upon a rise not far from the road, "this is where I'm going to build my house. I wonder if you'll leave a few of these jackpine for shade."

"Why sure. You blaze those you want, and I'll tell the boys not to cut 'em."

The days of August were nearly spent and the warm colors of summer were giving way to cooler yellows of autumn. From distant rice beds came the feeding call of mallards, and squirrels barked as they hoarded their winter's food. Yet I had no mind for these things. Flora was getting no better. While we dug about stumps or cut through their heavy roots, my thoughts were elsewhere. I emptied jugs to fetch more water, I returned to the shop for unneeded tools, but always found things the same.

The day came when Harris took his mother to the doctor. I hoped she would return with renewed spirit and a cure for this malady that had so changed her. But it wasn't to be. When she stepped from the car she was knee-deep in fresh bandages, and those on her arm and hands were again stained with poison. She had little to say about her seventeen-mile round trip to Dr. Hering's office. Later I settled her comfortably in an easy chair beneath the big trees where she could look out over the water.

Harris' first attempts with dynamite were hardly up to our expectations, but through his failures he quickly learned to place charges more advantageously and soon had better results. Just why he liked to fondle those little demons of destruction I never understood. Their very handling gave me a headache. He would peel back the wax paper and with his pocket knife, nonchalantly drill a hole for the detonating cap, as though it were a wax candle in his hands. The whole device, fuse, cap and all somehow fascinated him and he would dispense with his shovel whenever a stick of dynamite would do the trick.

Under some pretext or other, I had started home when an unusually loud explosion drew me up in my tracks. Though I knew it had accomplished its mission so far as the boy was concerned, its impact had done little to shake the burden from my own mind.

Far down in the park, newly-sawn boards of the cook shack stood out boldly in the sunlight. However, it was the small group of people that had gathered beneath the trees that puzzled me for a moment, and I quickened my steps. As I drew near, I saw Flora. Her chair had been turned in the direction of my coming. As I made my way quickly over the rim, Lois came running to meet me.

"Hurry, Pop! Mom wants you," she cried. Tears long withheld fell freely now as I grasped her bandaged hands.

Flora

"Charlie, I don't know what is wrong with me. I'm so sick and I need you so much," she pleaded. There was little I could do or say to comfort her, but eventually her emotional storm subsided, and she became her old self again. Beneath the trees, I sat on the arm of her chair while she unburdened her distraught mind. She spoke of her bewilderment, her fears, and the despondency that had overtaken her. I listened with a heavy heart, for I knew this was a malady beyond the relief of salves and bromides. With this unburdening of her soul came an hour of quiet and understanding in which she unfolded a plan she had been mulling over for days.

"I want to go back home at once," she said, "where I'll be under the care of Dr. Stephens, but Charlie, you'll just have to come with me. I can't face the trip without you." For a moment, I was stunned. This just couldn't be – Flora, always so self-reliant. Things seemed out of perspective. I, too, wanted something to lean on, some hand to grasp for support.

"Of course I'll go. We'll start packing at once," I replied. Little did I realize the true nature of things, the enormity of it all.

When the boys arrived quite out of breath with Lois trailing at their heels, I explained as best I could the circumstances that required their presence. With our heads together, we were soon in conference.

Though we had expected Mother and the boys to return home to Cicero in a short time, we were hardly ready for such a hurried departure, yet what had seemed at first an insurmountable barrier had within the hour been reduced to a workable plan. Lois and Bruce would return to take up their schooling where they had left off but Harris would remain and hold down the fort until such time as Mother's condition would permit my return.

That evening found our camp unusually astir with activity. Clothes were sorted, suitcases packed, and our old sedan was given the once-over for the long trip home. Howard and Ethel, too, with their children prepared to leave in the early morning, as their vacation was nearing its end.

Beneath the stars that night, as Flora lay quietly by my side, I tried to fathom the meaning of it all. Was not this but a fantasy, a dream without substance, or was it in reality the beginning of the end, the end of cherished hopes and aspirations? Only time would tell.

Chapter 9

THE SAMS

The trip back to Chicagoland with Flora ensconced in pillows seemed to never end; only ever changing numerals on the speedometer dial assured us of any progress. As daylight merged into darkness, we left Wisconsin's hills for the rolling prairies of Illinois. No shouts of 'blotto' now, no bursts of laughter as we passed over the state line. I counted the hours until the darkened horizon would reflect the lights of the great city and signal the end of our journey.

Eventually, as I knew we would, we found ourselves driving through avenues of brightly lighted homes. How tightly wedged they seemed and, oh, how welcome under the circumstances. I was struck by the irony of it all, this mad rush for asylum back to the very city we had once abandoned for its lack of security. As the passing scene changed to one of familiarity, old recollections returned, and our children pressed their faces to the windows to catch a first glimpse of someone they knew. Not, however, until our car came to a stop before the big square house on the corner was their curiosity satisfied. There beyond the window sat their own Grandmother Walker.

Our premature arrival was a complete surprise to the household. Though they had been informed of Flora's ivy poisoning, they had no idea of its extent, and to see her so swathed in bandages was nothing short of shocking. After she had been tucked into bed, her real condition was revealed and its seriousness discussed.

"Nervous breakdown! Flora? Why, that was preposterous."

"Of all people, not Flora! Why, it just can't be." Such were the reactions of the Walker family on the night of our arrival.

Nothing was left undone for the speedy recovery of our patient. Under Dr. Stephens' care, the poison quickly disappeared and with it the bandages that had so hampered her every movement. This newly found freedom of limb awakened in her some of her old self-reliance, and soon she was determined to move into the old home to set up her housekeeping for our family.

"I must have something to keep my hands busy all the time. I just can't stand it to be idle," she said.

We had always regretted the absence of our oldest daughter in our trek to the northwoods, but now circumstances gave Ruth an opportunity to play an important part in the family's undertaking. Of our four children, it was she who could now best minister to the needs of her ailing mother.

As the days passed, Flora seemed much better, and with the love and wholehearted support of her family, new hope rose within me. The time finally came when, torn between love and duty, I said goodbye to all and with the consent of her doctor, turned my car northward to spend my first autumn and winter in the north-woods country.

Instead of the solitary young man I had expected to find, I was greeted by a pair of embryo woodsmen happy and content in their seclusion. The second youth was Harold Jewell who had come across the lake with his few belongings, apparently to settle down for the long winter months to come. When he found a chance to get in a word, he said somewhat apologetically, "My grandmother has gone to town for the winter to sew, and Sam asked me to come over and stay with him."

Oh, it's Abbie French he's talking about, my mind clarified. "Well, that's perfectly OK with me," I said. "In fact, I think it's a grand idea, but tell me, who is this fellow you call Sam?"

There was a moment of hesitancy, snickering and side glances between the two, then came their confession. For some unfathomable reason, each had dubbed the other Sam. As they warmed up to the night's conversation it was Sam this and Sam that, as they told of the sawmill they had built out behind the shop and of other plans for the winter months to come.

Daylight allowed confirmation of their accomplishments. Sure

74

enough, out back was a saw mill and a winter's supply of firewood neatly ricked beneath the eaves.

"It's only a temporary outfit, Pa," Harris said. "We've already brushed out a place for a bigger mill back in the woods where there will be plenty of room for a long skidway. This'll do for the first batch of logs, but we ought to have the new mill ready for the rest of the cabins."

With keen-edged axes, the Sams and I set out one morning for a load of logs which would give our small mill its first good workout. The late September day was especially warm and with the knowledge that Flora was in good hands, I felt again that surge of body and spirit so characteristic of newcomers to the northwoods country. As the boys felled trees, I swamped them out, clearing the rough trunks of their branches and snags so they might be cut into the required eight-foot lengths. A friendly rivalry sprang up between them, and they kept count of the trees they had brought down. So keen was this competition that before long, the woods looked as though a wind storm had hit it. Obviously I was left behind in the mad race, though I could hear frequent cries of 'timber'. My running into a nest of yellow jackets hadn't helped any, and with the little devils swarming about my head, I was lucky to escape with only a single sting.

After an unusually long spell of silence I left my work to investigate. As I neared the boys I heard Harold shout good-naturedly, "You know I'm still one up on you, Sam."

I found them leaning upon their axes quite out of breath, their bare skin wet with sweat. I made my way over to Harris where I showed him the swelling on my arm. "I can't finish that big tree back there in the brush on account of the yellow jackets," I said.

He hesitated a moment, then with a wink in my direction he turned towards Harold. "Say, Sam," he shouted, "I wonder if you'll swamp out that big one for my dad. He's about all in. I'll even up with you while you're doing it."

Glad enough for a change, Harold followed me over to the thicket and made his way to the prone tree. One stroke was enough. For the next few seconds he seemed possessed of a dozen arms all fanning the air at once, then like a mad elephant he went crashing through the brush. When I reached him, he was sitting dejectedly on a grassy hummock counting welts. "One, two, three, four, five — oh, what's the use. If there's anything I hate, it's those little yellow bastards."

Logs Await the Saw

That night the heavily loaded truck stood beside the mill. The breakfast dishes were hardly cleared away next morning, when to our surprise we had a visitor. Mr. Sylvester was searching for a stray heifer, and seeing our place for the first time, stopped in to say hello. Of course his woodsman's eye fell upon our small mill and for a while he scrutinized it as though it was a bizarre creature of some kind. "What are you going to do with that thing?" he asked, a little sarcastically I thought.

Before I could reply, Harris answered. "Why, we're going to slab logs for cabins."

"Say," continued our visitor as he eyed the heavily loaded truck, "what do you city fellers know about cutting timber, anyway? You'd be better off to get someone to do it for you. Like as not, one of you'll get killed."

"Well, I'll admit we're greenhorns all right, but give us a little time and we'll get the hang of it," I said. When I spoke of our plans to build a number of log cabins, he shook his head.

"I'll believe it when I see 'em," he replied.

This was our first contact with Maurice Sylvester, though we had already met his wife and family. Over the years we were to learn that his apparent pessimism and outspokenness were characteristics to be accepted as constructive criticism rather than otherwise. We were soon to find that he possessed all the attributes of a good neighbor.

Chapter 10

KEEPING IT TOGETHER

September slipped away quite uneventfully and October with its invigorating days and frosty nights settled down quietly upon our household. Of late my mail from home was not what I had hoped for. It wasn't what Flora wrote so much as what she failed to write that made me apprehensive. Though she kept me posted on trivial matters, she said little about her own condition in spite of my queries. As time wore on, there were longer intervals between letters and when they did come her handwriting was scarcely legible. When at last one came in Mother Walker's handwriting, I tore it open in haste.

"Dear Charlie," it read, "I had purposely put off writing you hoping that Flora would take a turn for the better, but now you must know the true state of things. She is really in pretty bad shape, so much so that we have taken her to the hospital where she will be under the constant care of Dr. Stephens. She wants you, Charlie, you and Harris, and we do, too. Don't worry, but do come as soon as you can."

We found Flora propped up in bed at Berwyn Hospital. She had been counting the days, hours, and minutes until our arrival. Her soft-spoken words of greeting were strange, as though for other ears, and my heart sank as I took her thin hands in mine. I hardly recognized her. The tightly drawn skin about her face had erased all familiar lines, fever burned in her deep-set eyes and her hair was whiter than I had known.

Why had I left her? Why had I permitted that barrier of miles to come between us? I was taken with remorse, with a feeling of guilt as I looked through my tears upon the shadow of the woman who but four short months ago had set out so courageously in search of a new home, a new way of life. When emotions subsided, I sat beside her on the bed and spoke quietly of things we had accomplished, of my attempts at cooking and doing the washing. I called to mind things in which she had been especially interested, and lastly I spoke of the gorgeous coloring of the woods, the thing she loved most of all. Harris, who had slipped away from the room, returned, his arms burdened with sprays of autumn leaves gathered at the height of their glory. It was as though a curtain had risen before a fairyland, so bright and gay the walls became.

"We thought you'd like them," I said, laying a colorful spray upon her lap.

There was a semblance of a smile, then feebly brushing aside a tear she whispered softly, "Oh, I do love them so. They'll mean more to me than medicine."

Before I left the hospital, Dr. Stephens called me aside. "Your wife's recovery lies beyond the scope of medicine. There is little more we can do, Charlie, but I recommend she try psychiatry. While in Vienna, I became acquainted with a Dr. Hans Deutsch, and I have a lot of confidence in him. He is a psychoanalyst now practicing in Chicago. If you agree, I'll make the necessary arrangements."

There was little else we could do, and with promised help from Flora's folks, she started the new treatment. Dr. Deutsch spoke with an intriguing accent and his very presence inspired us with confidence. Though he made the first visit to our house, he was emphatic that his patient make the ensuing three weekly visits to his skyscraper office in the loop.

"I can never do it," Flora said with what emphasis she could muster. But she did do it. We made those trips together. Her hearing was so hypersensitive, she put cotton in her ears to cushion the sharp noise of the elevated trains. Her overstimulated mind made short work of some crossword puzzles I took along to occupy her. When we reached the doctor's office that first day, she was in a state of utter collapse, too weak to even sit up.

That hour I sat waiting for her in his outer office was indeed an eternity, fraught with fear and misgivings. Psychotherapy! What was it all about? What magic lay in the word? And what of those troubled faces about me? Were they, too, at their wit's end, waiting and hoping?

Far out over the roof tops, the blue waters of Lake Michigan lay tranquil and undisturbed. A good omen, perhaps, if only I were superstitious. Suddenly all eyes turned and Flora stood framed in the doorway. Without a word, Dr. Deutsch motioned me into his office for a conference. Flora and I made the long journey home quite uneventfully.

Subsequent trips showed gradual improvement, so that the doctor finally suggested his patient come by herself. Though fearful, Flora complied, and eventually I was relieved of those long, tedious trips to the skyscraper office in Chicago's loop. Psychoanalysis, together with love and care, was surely winning the battle.

Though recovery was slow, each day's improvement opened the door a little wider toward fulfillment of our earlier ambitions. Long since, Harris had taken off to be with his friend across the lake and to strengthen the slender tie that still bound us to our project. Although I was not informed, he was not alone in his journey northward, for at his side was Freddie Nixon, an old pal and bow-and-arrow enthusiast, who was glad enough to turn his back on the idle city.

For me, days passed all too slowly now that Flora's recovery seemed assured. With zealous care I watched over her, as did Ruth and the others. In spite of it all, periods of depression still haunted her. When fear and despondency took hold, she dreaded the long, sleepless nights most. To keep her mind absorbed we would resort to conversation. I would bring back incidents long forgotten, and call to mind dates and places we had visited. Sometimes we would play games in the wee hours of the night. Given the initials of some acquaintance or prominent personage, she would respond almost immediately with his or her name. Endurance is not without limitations, and at times my words would drift off like meaningless jargon as sleep overtook me.

On the twelfth day of January, Ruth dropped in. "Happy Birthday, Mom," she said. "Maybe this will help," and she handed her a card that read:

A BIRTHDAY DITTY FOR MY MOTHER.
Now you've come to forty seven,
Every joy this side of heaven
Has blessed your passing years,
Or so it seems.
But there's one experience coming
That will keep your heart a humming,
And you'll be ever happy,
Even in your dreams.

For we'll greet a wee new member
Sometime about September,
And oh, I hope the role of Grandma
Will fit in with all your schemes.

Flora seemed to study it beyond her reading, then a smile bent her lips and her eyes lit up. She looked up to Ruth and nodded a simple reply to the last verse. This was indeed the best therapy she could have had.

Though Harris' letters filled me with impatience, they were an inspiration to his mother, whose thoughts were beginning to reach out beyond her own shrunken horizon. I looked forward to the time when the family would function as a unit once more, when each would contribute toward that goal we had earlier initiated. Happily for me, that time was nearer than I had reckoned.

"Charlie," Flora said upon her return from one of her trips, "what do you think the doctor said today? He told me I was doing so well that he thought it best for me to take the whole responsibility here at home."

Had I heard her all right? "Does that mean it's OK for me to go back up north again?" I asked.

"That's what it means. We talked it all over. I didn't want to be mistaken again."

"But Flora, how do you feel about it? You know that's what matters most."

"Well, of course I'll miss you a lot and I hate to see you go, but I do think I'm improved enough to manage things here at this end. Then, too, perhaps Harris needs you more now than I do. You've got to go sometime, you know."

The bleakness of that February day bore down upon me as I left the city behind. For a time I wondered at which end of the journey my home really lay. With the passing miles my spirits rose and my mind went to the boys. How were they faring? Were they warm enough in that unlined shop? And what were they eating, how were they passing the long winter days? A dozen such questions assailed me.

Over the snow covered hills and through the farm dotted valleys I made my way, at times in the wake of snowplows and at others over barren windswept thoroughfares, but always conscious of the empty seat beside me. When at last I turned from the highway at Byrnes'

Store, I felt an urge to hurry, and finally upon our own new road a sense of belonging swept over me. Not until I came to the park, its big trees bathed in moonlight, did I know for a certainty that here indeed was my home.

I just set foot indoors when I found to my consternation that I had barged in on three 'Sams' instead of two, for Freddie Nixon had made it a trio. I'm sure that only my years prevented them from making it a foursome then and there. The boisterous laughter from exuberant spirits more than compensated for the confusion of names. I can take it if they can, I told myself as I climbed to my quarters that night.

When the sun touched the tree tops, I stepped outdoors to greet my first winter's day. How different from the city, how clear and crisp the air, how white the snow, and oh, how quiet the woods. How good to be a part of it, to absorb its salutary benevolence.

Out on the windswept ice the boys played shinny. Nor had they been otherwise idle, for a large pile of logs, peeled and slabbed, proved their industry. Beside the doorstep an axe handle angled from a pitch-pine stump, and cords of firewood, freshly cut, lay ready to be piled and protected from the snow. These things I had expected, but there was something else. Within a rectangular enclosure built from wooden slabs was a large cube of ice.

"What's the big idea?" I asked Harris, knowing the labor it had entailed.

"Well, Pa, you know we're going to need an icebox next summer, but if you want the real reason, I was thinking about that big ice cream freezer we brought along." We did need an icebox alright, though I confess the thought had not yet occurred to me. Where the cream was to be found for this luxury I did not know, nor did Harris.

"We'll have to scout around pretty quick for some sawdust or there'll be nothing left of that ice," I said.

As long as the weather remained pleasant, we worked outdoors, finding jobs for our axes and brush scythes. We enlarged our mill site and built a long skidway of felled timber. From a pair of long stringers that once had served as boxcar girders we fashioned the roadbed for the carriage and over its length, affixed a pair of light steel rails. As for the mill proper, it would have to wait. We had not yet accumulated necessary material, nor a source of power.

Chapter 11

DIVERSIONS

February is usually when Old Man Winter launches his heaviest attacks. This particular late February day was no exception, when marshaling his boreal forces, he struck at our thin-walled enclosure with a vengeance. The temperature had taken a nose dive in the after-noon, and sensing a cold night, we had carried in plenty of wood. With evening dishes cleared away, we started our usual session at cards, but it proved of short duration. In spite of the wood that we crammed into the stove, our fingers became too numb to continue, and though we tried to play with mittened hands, we found it was no use. By ten o'clock the temperature outside stood at thirty below, not uncommonly low in this latitude, but one should be properly housed.

Bed seemed the only solution, so I climbed the ladder and crawled beneath the cold bedding fully dressed. Never had the stars seemed so bright, but like dagger points, they stabbed to my very marrow, and I pulled a heavy mackinaw across my body. As I lay there, chilled to the bone, I could hear a roar in the chimney's throat as it sucked away our heat. Fingers of firelight danced fretfully about the walls and ceiling as though seeking a way out. Suddenly a rafter cracked like a rifle shot over my head, and I heard someone stirring below. Looking down, I saw Harris. I watched as he placed his flashlight against a window pane. Outside the beam of light crept over the rough bark of an oak until it fastened upon the thermometer.

"Forty below!" his shout came.

All three Sams were up now, fully clothed, capped and mittened. While one lighted a second lamp, another shouted, "Atta boy, we need all the heat we can get."

Not, however, until a fire was kindled in the cook stove as well, did I come down from the Oriole's Nest. Though it had been plenty cold up there beneath the skylight, down below I shivered more than ever. Within an hour the temperature had dropped to forty-five below zero, and all thought of further sleep was forgotten. Old Man Winter was surely at his worst this night, but if the Sams were worried, they registered the fact only by good-natured laughter. We stoked the fires and huddled about them, pivoting periodically lest our spinal columns freeze into question marks.

"Fifty below! Oh, boy!" Harris shouted when he had taken another look. Now we started marching around the room, stamping our feet and yelling like Indians. By seven o'clock in the morning the mercury had dropped to fifty-five below and there it hung for a few brief minutes. Never before or since have I experienced such cold. By noon, we were enjoying the comparative warmth of twenty below.

There was little real schedule maintained that winter. We rose when the spirit moved, ate our meals at the dictates of our stomachs and retired according to our individual desires. Deep snows and cold weather kept us indoors, and time had little meaning. The incessant ticking of the clock was little more than a rhythmic sound in our ears.

Throughout the weeks, I managed to keep a haphazard rendezvous with the mailman. Letters came more or less regularly, and always the news was gratifying. Flora even ventured a date for her coming, though it was too distant to create any excitement.

March came with its incessant winds and unpredictable weather. There were days when the sun's rays penetrated our thin roof boards and we needed little fire and others when a north wind sent us again to the woodpile. Crows dropped in numbers upon the snow-patched earth to hold their early spring caucuses.

With melting snow came the threat to our cube of ice and we made inquiries for a source of sawdust. Following a trail that diagonaled through the woods east of the store, we finally came upon a small saw mill. A thin veil of vapor hung over a fresh opening in a pile of sawdust that lay beyond. There was no hustle and bustle as there had been about Dan Matson's mill, no intermittent gas explosions echoing through the woods. Instead, smoke curled lazily from the stack of an old threshing machine engine. As it pulsed its power through a long belt, a stoker fed slab wood into its fire box beneath the boiler.

"Steam," I said to the boys. "I wish Bruce was here to make comparisons."

Disappointment swept the weathered face of the sawyer when I told him we wanted only sawdust. "We'll be wanting lumber later on," I said by way of appeasement. "Say, tell me, why don't you use a gasoline tractor for power?" I continued.

There was a moments hesitation. "Do you see that damned old contraption over yonder, beyond that pile?" he replied, pointing toward a Fordson tractor almost hidden from view. "Well, she still sets where I dumped her off last fall. You know, I've been a steam man all my life, and there's nothing I can't do with a boiler, but for the life of me I can't even get a kick out of that thing, much less make it run."

I'll bet I know some one who can start her, I said to myself as a plan took shape in my mind. I felt for the bulge of my check book as I scanned the Fordson with a critical eye. Off hand, I could think of a dozen uses for its power and the more I looked at it, the more determined I was to have it.

"I suppose you want to get rid of it as long as you can't use it," I said casually. Pushing aside a greasy cap, he scratched his head before replying.

"I'd sell her all right, but I'd have to have all I put into her."

"How much is that?"

"Well, I got her second hand for fifty dollars, but that don't take into account the three different carburetors I tried out on her."

Fifty dollars, I mused. Not exactly hay in my kind of a budget. In the meantime, Harris pulled at the crank for compression. A wink in my direction was enough.

"I think someone sold you a lemon," I continued. "In my opinion it's worth hardly more than junk, but I'll give you ten bucks for the tractor the way it stands."

I got only a contemptuous look in reply. After considerable bickering, however, his price dropped to forty. "And that's rock bottom," he said.

I told the boys to start loading sawdust and the sawyer took off toward his mill. In the meantime, a black cow appeared, seemingly from nowhere, and started sniffing about the pile. She was a fine looking creature even to me, who knew next to nothing about cattle. We laid off shoveling when, to my surprise, the woodsman showed up once more. Sure now that he was about to make me a better offer, I pointed to the cow and said facetiously, "And you can throw in that critter to boot."

"Well," he replied in a serious tone, "We do want to sell her." Now visions of milk and cream swept over me, and I wondered, too, if Harris was thinking of his ice cream freezer. I remembered Lois' affinity for animals and thought what a fine pasture our back forty would make. Suddenly I wanted that black cow as badly as I wanted the tractor.

"She's a black Jersey and I've got her papers."

"Oh, oh, she's a registered animal," I said under my breath.

"You see, we're going to move to town, and there'll be no place for a cow where we're going," he continued.

"Well, what do you want for her?" I ventured with reckless indifference.

"She's worth twice what I'm asking."

"And what's that?"

"If you're really interested you'll have to wait 'til I talk it over with my wife." So the stoker in overalls was his wife! As we waited, Harris pulled at my watch fob.

"Your watch, Pa, your watch. Maybe you can make a trade." A good idea and worth trying, I planned, as the man returned.

"We'll take thirty-five dollars for the cow, and that's only because we have to be rid of her."

Disregarding the ring of finality in his voice, and fortified now with new ammunition, I shot back.

"I'll tell you what I'll do, I'll give you thirty-five for both the cow and the tractor and I'll throw in this seventeen-jewel Waltham watch." His eyes popped as I dangled the big silver timepiece temptingly before him.

"I do need a watch bad. I lost mine in the woods a while back," he said as he put the thing to his ear. "Does it keep good time?"

86

"Of course it does. I'll guarantee it," I answered.

"Well, I'll have to talk it over," he ventured and started once more toward his wife. Confident now, we shoveled off what sawdust we had loaded. But when I saw a puzzled look on his face as he returned, I thought for a moment the deal was off.

"This stem won't stop turning," he said as he twisted it between his thumb and finger.

"No," I confessed, "it's not a stem winder," as I reached into my pocket and handed him the key.

"Oh," he said, grinning, "you know that tractor's got a crank goes with it, too." To my surprise, he accepted my check for the thirty-five dollars and pocketed his new watch. With the Fordson and black Jersey secured safely on the platform, the truck settled down for the journey home.

As we started, I nudged Harris and said, "Son, somewhere in the line of your ancestors there must have been a horse trader."

"You mean a horse thief, don't you, Pa?" came his quick rejoinder. This had been an eventful day to be sure. Though the cube of ice still remained open to the sun, by evening our new cow was under shelter of a kind.

Although we had eaten nothing since breakfast, I had little appetite for supper. The boys, however, finished off their corn fritters faster than I could provide them. While two of the Sams played chess that night, Harold ventured an opinion concerning our purchases. He held that the tractor was the better of the bargains, and for sake of argument I championed the cause of the cow.

"Just look at the things you can do with that tractor," he said.

"But do you know if we will ever get it to run? Maybe it's shot inside."

"Yes, but what do you know about your cow? Maybe she's shot inside, too. You know she's dry now."

"Well, you've got a point, I'll admit."

"How are you going to level that ice wall and drag your beach and plow a garden without a tractor? And look how you can pull stumps. You can't do all that with your cow, can you?"

"Maybe not, Sam, but think of all the milk and thick cream we'll have, and don't forget the cow is going to have a calf. That's something that tractor can't do." And so the argument went on, to the confusion of the chess players. Then Sam thought up a new angle.

"You haven't said anything about costs. You had to pay thirty-five for that cow, didn't you? What did that tractor cost you? Nothing but an old silver turnip worth less than ten bucks."

"Ten bucks!" I shouted. "Listen, Sam, I bought that watch on Maxwell Street in Chicago for one silver half-dollar, but I'll admit I did put in a new main spring that cost me fifteen cents. That's a grand total of sixty-five cents I paid."

The stars were bright that night as I lay in bed and thought of our new acquisitions.

A meteor dropping into our midst could hardly have disturbed the status quo of our camp more than that black Jersey. Not only were we unprepared, but my knowledge of cattle in general, and calving in particular, was less than nil. I had no misgivings about the tractor, but about a calf's layette, I knew absolutely nothing. Perhaps a mother's intuition might better cope with such things. If only Flora would come before the calf did. One thing I was sure of – we needed a permanent shelter of some kind, and at once.

Patches of snow still dotted the woods as we took off for a stand of tamarack on the Ferguson forty. Though the trees would average hardly more than seven inches in diameter, they were heavy enough for a pole barn. We found the earth too wet and soggy for the truck, so we trimmed the trees as we felled them, cut them into given lengths and carried them out to higher ground.

The wind was blustery and a storm was threatening, and when at last we got a load, the temperature had fallen below the freezing mark. We had just gotten started on the county-line road when all four wheels mired down. We shoveled and pried, but it wasn't until we unloaded all those logs that we were able to crawl from the frost boil. The storm struck with ferocity before we reached home. Tree tops threshed about, ready to snap, and the wind swept snow about in blinding blasts.

Home at last, my first thoughts were for the tethered cow and I went to fetch her as the boys set about erecting a basic shelter. To my consternation, she was nowhere about. A broken halter and length of chain half buried in the snow told the story. I set out in the teeth of the gale.

"Come boss, come boss!" I shouted at the top of my lungs, but the words got no further than my own ears. On I went, brush and low-hanging branches showering me with snow. I was just deciding to give up, at least until morning, when I stumbled upon the object of my search. The black Jersey was lying beneath the low-spreading branches of a tree, safe and sound. If there was a storm about, seemingly it hadn't bothered her at all. She was chewing on her cud and vapor was rising from her sleek wet body, and contentment resided in her soft, dark eyes. Her utter indifference somehow rubbed my grain the wrong way. I was cold and soaking wet from head to foot, and mad all through. A lesson in bovine husbandry, I had to tell myself, with our cow now safely bedded down in her new quarters.

That night the Sams, their stomachs filled and dishes done, pounded their knuckles loudly as they threw down their cards, and laughed at the wind as it whistled about our chimney. I read my last letter from Flora yet again. Then bundling up, I went outside with my flashlight for a final look at the flimsy shelter about our cow. After shaking out the makeshift bedding and laying a pole over the end of a flapping canvas, I closed the thin plywood door behind me and flashed a beam along the pathway.

Suddenly I was seized with a pain that fairly dropped me to my knees. Unable to rise, I shouted for the boys, though I knew it was useless in such a gale. I crept on all fours toward the shop, following my old tracks in the snow. Finally at the door I made myself heard, and the boys carried me in, thinking I had been injured.

"It's another kidney attack," I managed to get out. "It's the worst one I've had yet."

Stout arms boosted me to my bed when they had relieved me of my outer garments. There I was treated with hot towels and lots of aspirin, and stayed for two days and nights.

Our winter's confinement was drawing to an end. Though the wind remained cold and ice still lay heavy on the water, the urge to be outdoors heightened with each day as the warming sun advanced northward. Though little had been achieved during our long shut-in, the tie that held us to our project remained unbroken. Three new boats, painted and indistinguishable one from another, were about the extent of the winter's accomplishment. These waited outside for the ice to melt, while a fourth was in the making. Now the old worn-out skiff we had picked up would be abandoned because of its unseaworthiness.

The general utility of the shop machinery had proven itself even beyond our expectations. When the lineshaft beneath the floor responded to the starter, not only was there a sustained hum, but every dish, pot and pan above came alive and danced to the rhythmic overtone. Sawdust and sandy grit were everywhere, in our foodstuffs and our bedclothes, but we paid them little attention.

I had cut an assortment of gnarled oak limbs in the woods and salvaged a number of knotty pine slabs, and from this natural material, would fabricate doors, bedsteads and rustic furniture. Not until the Sams took themselves outdoors for good would I start on this interesting project.

Chapter 12

HOMECOMING

Springtime with its balmy days was here at last, here to stay, after many futile incursions. Birds voiced it from the treetops, geese honked it from the heavens and the lake responded in dancing ringlets upon its smooth waters. With newfound freedom we emerged from our winter quarters like a family of hibernating wood-chucks. To scan far horizons once more, to breathe deeply of the vernal freshness was indeed to live again.

To the north in a grove of slender popple, our new barn took shape. Pole upon pole it rose from the ground until by nightfall, it stood complete, roof and all. Though hardly worthy to be called a barn, the shed-like structure with its two front windows and a door would do well enough until time and circumstances should warrant

a better one. As I viewed the squat rectangle in the light of the morning sun, I was struck for the first time with the significance of it all, its real meaning in our scheme of things. We had never given a thought to cattle as a means to an end, but here we were with the very nucleus of a farm on our hands. All that was needed now was the coming calf and a flock of white chickens scratching about a manure pile to complete the picture. How had it all come about? That such a simple thing as an ice cream freezer had turned us from our original course seemed incredible. Who dare predict our future under those circumstances?

Along with fresh new greenery and bursting buds was the new life that stirred within the distended flanks of our black Jersey. I looked questioningly at the narrow door of our barn as the creature stood before it sniffing at the darkened interior within. Would she accept it as satisfactory for the birthing of her calf? How long would it be, I wondered, and would Flora never come? Of late, her letters had expressed more interest in our undertaking and she was seeing things objectively once more, a good sign in itself.

"You had better come down with the truck, Charlie," she wrote. "There are so many things to go back. While walking to Berwyn the other day I saw a large cement mixer all but buried beneath a pile of coal in a coal yard. I thought perhaps you might be interested. Surely it has been there a long time without being used and might be for sale.

"Bruce says he is going to take that tractor apart and rebuild it from stem to stern. Charlie, you might also say that is what the doctor has been doing for me, mentally and emotionally, of course. I feel like a different woman, a more satisfactory one, I hope. Perhaps this is a poor analogy, but you will get the general idea, I'm sure, but enough of that.

"Now about that surprise you have for me: better shave it off before you come down, as beards are not popular here in the city. It's my turn now. I have a surprise that you'll never guess. You'll just have to wait 'til you see it with your own eyes."

The very fact that Flora could indulge in a bit of humor was in itself reassuring, to say nothing of her general tone of optimism. How had she learned of my secret unless, heaven forbid, she had become psychic under the influence of that Viennese physician. What profound secret did she have in store for me, I could not even venture a guess.

The forms of our first cabin foundation stood out boldly against the blue of the lake, but since Flora's last letter there had been little activity about the place. The thought of that big cement mixer lying idle, rusting beneath a pile of coal while we needed one so badly, was just too much. With ten or a dozen cabins to build, it was worth looking into to say the least. Surely such an investment would be worthwhile regardless of cost.

Though the shop was a big improvement over a tent as living quarters, its dingy, crowded interior was hardly a fitting place for a convalescing woman. Could Flora take it in her condition? I had had occasional visions of a new home, but always they were based upon nothing more substantial than wishful thinking. If only we had finished our first cabin! Yet if Flora was her old self again, as she claimed, I knew she could take it, and without complaining, too. There were also others to be considered in the homecoming. Bruce would get a kick out of the tractor, and Lois would be in seventh heaven with a cow and calf.

With ever-warming days and the freshening of woodland pastures, the black Jersey paid little attention to her new quarters. Accustomed as she was now to her surroundings, she roamed the woods at will. Footloose and free, she had the run of the premises, only at dusk to return to the barnyard enclosure for a nourishing meal of mash, after which she would bed down for the night.

Increasingly anxious for Flora's return, I talked the matter over with Harris. One morning soon thereafter he was on the road to Chicago in our truck with Freddie Nixon. Freddie's going meant the breaking up of the trio of Sams and their whistling s's. They were not alone on the road, for a few hours behind came the old Studie.

"I'll be back just as soon as I can make it," I told Harold as I took off.

I was becoming so familiar with the route between Spooner and Chicago that I passed the time guessing the names of the villages, towns and cities I would next pass through. As I neared Chicagoland, my mind turned to things that lay nearest my heart. I recalled Flora's words about her being made over and her analogy to the rebuilding of the tractor. What kind of a woman will it be who greets me at the door? A new model, perhaps. I confess it was something to think about. It was not, however, until the wee small hours of the morning that I had the answer. There, framed in the doorway of our old home, was the woman I had married many years ago, the very same. If there were changes they were not apparent to my eye. A smile lighted her face and surprise shone in her eyes as we welcomed each other in embrace.

The following morning I moved about as though in a dream, hardly believing that once I had enjoyed so many conveniences. Electricity! Would it ever find its way to the northwoods? There was the radio, refrigerator and hot and cold running water. Even the carpets beneath my feet were not without appeal. Luxuries these, but not for us in our present scheme of things. My reverie was quickly broken when Flora called me to the kitchen window.

"Well, Charlie," she said, pointing into the dooryard, "There is my surprise. What do you think of it?"

I rubbed my bare chin as I looked down upon forty-odd white chickens, half grown. "And I raised them all myself," she continued proudly.

At the breakfast table she told of her experiences with a home-made brooder in the basement. She had placed an electric bulb in a pan of water and shielded it as best she could against any danger to her brood. When she went down the following morning to check, she found to her dismay a number of small corpses in the water. In their scramble for warmth, the chicks had piled one upon another and had fallen over the wire guard and drowned.

"I cried," Lois said, simulating her emotions in pantomime.

"I'll say you did, and Bruce scolded me for my carelessness," Flora said.

After the boys and I chased about the city for many needed things, we went in search of the much talked about cement mixer. We found it just as Flora had said, buried in a coal yard, as inert as the industry it accompanied. Learning that it belonged to a bankrupt contractor, I hastened to his home, and after hearing my story he gladly accepted the fifteen dollars I offered him for it. "God knows I wish I was on some such project like yours," he said as he slipped the check into his wallet.

From auctions, unclaimed freight and bankrupt sales we obtained doors, window sash, stoves, chicken wire, boxed mattresses, kitchen pumps, well pipe, shovels, axes, a lawn mower, oars, a coil of heavy rope, logging chain, kegs of nails, hardware and many other things. The last to go up on the truck platform were the two crates of Mother's chickens.

94

We took off before daybreak and as the first rays of the sun swept the morning haze from a passing landscape, Flora said, "Do you know, Charlie, I have a funny feeling when I see that big truck ahead. I feel as though we are on our first trip, still looking for a place on which to settle. Do you have that feeling, too?"

"Well, no, I can't say that I do, but I can understand your confusion, for in reality we are enacting that whole scene over again in detail, overloaded truck and all."

"All but those chickens," Lois added, pointing to the red-topped heads and long necks bobbing nervously in and out of the crates.

"That reminds me, Flora, those crates, I mean. Awhile back I had a vision of a flock of chickens scratching about a manure pile in our new barnyard, and what's more, they were white, just like yours. Maybe I'm psychic or something," I said, stealing a glance in her direction. There was no response.

"Gee, Pop, I can hardly wait 'til we get there. We're going to have a farm and a lot of animals, aren't we?" our youngest said. We saw little of the boys perched high on the truck seat. Only at lunch time or when they stopped for gas did we exchange words with them.

Bruce's mechanistic mind reflected impatience in the many questions he put to his brother about the Fordson tractor. He had just graduated from Junior College where he had finished a pre-engineering course, and now was burning to put his knowledge into practice.

"Too bad he didn't have a short course in nature study, too, everything considered," I ventured as we talked over his prospects. "Flora, I don't think he knows one fish from another, and as for birds and trees, I bet he can't tell a jay from a jacksnipe, or a birch from a beech."

"Well, you're probably right, but with that inventive mind of his, he'll find plenty to keep him busy around the shop. Anyway, I'm not going to worry about the children's futures, not for a while yet."

Lois, too, had graduated, from high school, but time had not changed her outlook upon life. Her effervescent spirit was her fountain of youth, and she had no intention of ever growing up. I was eager to see her reaction toward our cow, and especially the newly-born calf when it came, or had it already arrived? That thought struck home with a vengeance.

In my anxiety the journey seemed unending, longer by far than any heretofore. We "blottoed" at the state line as had the boys, and Lois counted on one hand the white horses she had seen on the way.

Time dragged and we were glad, indeed, when from the crest of a wooded hill we saw the small city of Spooner spread over the countryside. There was still a smidgen of light upon the western horizon when we stepped down before our shop, travel stained and weary. Upon spying the barn, Lois made off on a run, the family following at a more leisurely pace. Soon we were standing in a circle about the black Jersey who had settled down for the night. A prod or two brought her awkwardly to her feet, and it was evident her calf was yet to be born.

"What do you think of her, Flora?" I asked impatiently as she assessed the creature in the dusk of a fading day.

"Why, I'd say she's a fine looking animal, though I'm no judge of cattle, of course."

"What about the calf? Just when do you think it'll come, and what are we going to do about it?"

"Now see here, Charlie, I don't know any more about that cow than you do. She's going to have her calf in her own good time, in spite of anything you can do, so why worry about it?"

As for Lois, her happiness knew no bounds and not till darkness robbed the creature of romance and reality did she crawl to her bed beneath the bench, with her bobtailed cat. That night Harold packed his belongings, ready to take off in the morning, since his grandmother had returned and was expecting him.

Chapter 13

BUILDING SEASON

Months had elapsed since our family had gathered about the table as a unit. It seemed ages since we had counseled together. Now here we were once more and with all accounted for, eager to accept the challenge of our undertaking. Since Flora's return, the distant mailbox held little attraction for me. However, one day a letter came from a Chicago cousin informing me of his interest in our project and his plan to spend the summer with us. "You can expect me when I get there," he said in closing. How little I realized then what his coming was to mean to our enterprise. He wasn't the only one, however, for Flora's nephew was coming to spend his summer vacation. Although neither gave us any idea of the time of their arrival, we took immediate stock of our sleeping facilities – spare cots, tents and so on. Our biggest problem was not their housing, but how to provide room at the dining table.

Our garage might well have been utilized for purposes other than intended had it not been a catchall for the overflow of the shop. As it was, Bruce's tractor, or what remained of it, lay scattered about the floor, no two parts being integral. The heavy barrel body stripped of its innards stood on end in one corner, the motor, less crank shaft and pistons, rested in another. Though the big wheels leaned against an oak outside, the balance of the floor was littered with minor parts. Bruce was right in his element!

Lois accepted wholeheartedly the care of the Jersey and named her LuluBelle. When another week went by with no calf, I appealed to Flora again, though not without some trepidation.

"Yes," she responded, "I've had four children and I understand in a general way, but I wasn't brought up on a farm, you know. Now why don't you run over to see Mr. Sylvester? He knows all about cows." So the matter was disposed of, temporarily at least.

Instinctively we looked to the mellow earth for sustenance as our forefathers had done, but tearing a sizable garden spot from the  woods, we were to find, was quite an undertaking. A hundred yards or so up from the shop, beside our old rutted road, we made our assault. With axes, brush scythes, mattocks and shovels we tore our way through an acre of trees. Oaks, popple, birch and aspen fell before our onslaught. Though the soil was sandy and mellow, a tough, fibrous network of roots clung to it with relentless tenacity. Half-naked, the boys chopped trees and dug about their roots while the rest of us tugged and pulled and made the earth ready. Hoes and rakes followed in the wake of axes, and no sooner was the soil prepared than it was planted. If only the tractor had been ready, the time and labor we might have saved! As it was, many days of grueling manual effort passed before we finally turned the garden over to sun and rains for their contribution.

Mother's white chickens, though of course too young to lay, were nevertheless a source of delight to the eye, and like LuluBelle they had the run of the premises. Their marked contrast among fallen leaves made them easy targets for hawks, and at times the throaty call of a cockerel would send them scurrying for safety.

My awakening thoughts were usually of the barnyard, and while Mother stirred pancake batter, I would step out for a breath of crisp morning air. Our crude barn, crosshatched with shadows at this hour, the black Jersey waiting languidly by the gate, white chickens polka dotting the landscape – somehow it suggested a picture of frontier days that belonged in Grandfather's autobiography. Then one morning, there was something missing from the picture, for LuluBelle was nowhere about.

"Do you suppose she's gone and had her calf out in the woods somewhere, after all our work on that barn?" I asked Flora.

"I don't know but I'll keep your breakfast warm while you go and look."

I set out for the back forty in the direction where once she had taken refuge from the storm. My hunch was right as I found her there. She stood beneath the spreading branches, and there by her side was the little creature for which we had waited so long, its stilt-like legs spread as it nuzzled its mother's bag. All worry and concern on my part had been for naught; nature had taken care of everything. How marvelous! A being that only yesterday had existed in a dark and different world was now part of ours.

Lois was wild with excitement when she spied the wobbly calf behind its mother as they emerged from the forest. From that moment on, the little stranger was hers to mother and make over to her heart's content. If LuluBelle was jealous, she in no way showed it. We had failed to determine whether this was her first calf, nor did we know anything about its father, but in color, the newcomer was as blond as autumn's fallen leaves with no semblance to its mother.

"What are you going to call it?" I asked Lois the following morning.

"I've already named her," she replied as the calf sucked hungrily at her fingers. "Her name is Mollie."

LuluBelle and Mollie, I mused, wondering why she hadn't chosen Blackie and Brownie instead. I had waited long for this christening, and if it suited Lois, it was OK with me. Although Mollie's coming into our own small world had been without fanfare, it was followed daily by a rattling of pans as Mother made ready for each deluge of milk. With patience and apparent understanding, LuluBelle withstood our daily assaults until finally both Lois and I acquired the knack of milking. For days Lois went about flexing her fingers. "I'm practicing," she would say. Finally the time came when she announced her intention of taking over the barnyard as her responsibility, from pitchfork to milkstool.

"It's all ready to go," Bruce announced one day as he stood beside the tractor, wiping grease from his hands. Good news, indeed, for jobs were accumulating that required power beyond that which our backs could provide. 'Ready to go,' Bruce had said, but he had spoken too soon, for try as he would, he could not turn the motor. From across the lake, Harold had come with a pal, Bob Reimer, to witness the start. Both had watched the machine assembly with more than a little interest. In spite of their combined efforts, the crank refused to budge.

"The main bearings are too tight," one suggested.

"You'll have to tow it," said the other. The low transmission gearing was of a design that virtually precluded towing as a method of starting. Still, there was a remote chance that it might be accomplished, so it was worth a try, to say the least. With Bob's avoirdupois balanced on the rear axle, Bruce aboard the tractor and Harris at the wheel of the Chevy truck, the signal was given. There was an instant of sputtering and back firing from the tractor, then silence.

"Where there's life, you know," Bruce shouted confidently.

Once more the truck was gunned and once more there was a sign of life. After repeated attempts, the motor took hold and soon Bruce was off, bouncing down over the rim and into the park. When at last he turned the ignition off before his small audience, he said, "Pa, the steering is terrible and I'm going to have to grind valves. This thing won't pull the hat off your head."

A few days later when the Fordson was ready for its second try-out, not only had it had a thorough valve and ring job, but Bruce had discarded the steering mechanism and installed in its place a worm gear steering column from a wrecked car. When he took off this time, it was through the woods. In and out and around trees he went, barely missing stumps and crushing saplings in his path. At times I feared he would up-end, as the big iron wheels crept from crater holes. But when he returned, he wore a wide smile of satisfaction.

"What on earth are we ever going to do with all this milk and cream?" Flora asked one day as she carefully shifted brim-full pans along the work bench. LuluBelle was more than fulfilling our expectations, and in spite of the hungry calf, we were hard put to keep abreast of the milk supply. The answer came one day, at least in part, when the mail man dropped off a tall, hungry-looking passenger beside our mailbox.

Cousin Lou Arnold had been a Chicago mail carrier, with the distinction of having worn badge No. 3 among a great horde of gray-uniformed postal employees. He had lost his wife and only two children many years back, and looked forward now with eager anticipation toward a place in our family circle. Lou was a city man through and through, understanding little or nothing of country life. He was a born student, a bookworm sort, with a big appetite for learning, and incidentally, for good food as well. Architecture had been his hobby since his retirement. Although he was my senior by a few years, I facetiously called him "son" on occasion, a touch of humor that added to his sense of belonging.

We pitched his tent close by, in a grove of white birch, and there he slept, timidly at first, not being accustomed to night sounds, the call of a whippoorwill or hoot of an owl. Although we paid the Sams but a pittance for their time, Lou would have none of it. Not only did he volunteer his work, he insisted on paying for his board and keep.

By the time Lou had settled himself, Flora's nephew showed up. Teen-aged Dick Johnstone was tall and thin, and possessed of an appetite and board-inghouse reach equal to that of Cousin Lou. We added another leaf to our table in the already crowded room, and Mother laid an extra plate for this seventh hungry mouth. Under these circumstances, our milk problem diminished materially.

At the site of our new cabin, the rumble of the big cement mixer echoed throughout the woods as Lou shoveled sand, gravel and cement into its revolving drum. While Bruce and Harris took turns with the heavy wheelbarrow, I tamped the mixture thoroughly in wooden forms. As for Dick, he sweated and fussed as he bent over the handle of the small pitcher pump, no doubt bemoaning his choice of a vacation.

The day had been a hard one, especially on tender hands and little used muscles. Though there were grunts and groans about the table that evening, there was little complaining. Our work proved an incentive for further progress, and Lou, with his eye for architecture, was as anxious as I to see the completion of this cabin.

Daylight came all too quickly, and as I rose from the breakfast table that morning, I nudged Lou in the ribs. "Let's go, Son," I said. "If we're ever going to finish that cabin, we'd better get going."

Lou pushed himself up slowly from his chair, and with his hands at the small of his back, replied between groans, "OK, Charlie. I'm ready if you are." If my own spinal column was any criterion, I knew just how his must feel. As for Dick, he remained in his pup tent until noon, nor did I blame him. Time is a healer and soon blisters became calluses, and aches and pains but memories.

How Mother ever managed to provide for our hungry lot, even with Lois'help, remains a mystery. Fish were a staple, to be sure, and easy to come by, but green things were at a premium. Corn was little more than knee high, tomatoes needed another month of sunshine, and potatoes were still in the nubbin stage. Rows of string beans were beyond blossoming and welcome the day of their picking. Therefore it was left to LuluBelle to add substance to our fare, and this she did unstintingly.

"Gollee, but that's good!" Lou exclaimed as he finished off his first mug of buttermilk. Cottage cheese, too, was a dish he never tired of. We were about to take off for work one morning when to my surprise he started clearing off the table. "You fellows go on about your business," he said. "I'm going to stay and help around the house."

Although I was appreciative of my wife and her ability to carry on under the circumstances, it was Cousin Lou who really did something about it. Each morning thereafter he made it a practice to spend an hour or so helping out. Among other things, churning just naturally fell into his hands. "Here she comes," he would shout at the first slowing down of the crank. When finally the wooden paddles refused to budge altogether, he would drain off the buttermilk and marvel at the miracle he had wrought. "Green grass, black cow, white milk and yellow butter," he said on one occasion. Indeed it seemed nothing short of a miracle to us all.

In spite of Lou's help, Flora found little time for relaxation, except perhaps for an occasional hour spent in our garden. Sundays were no exception. Imagine her bewilderment when two more unannounced boarders, with their tooth brushes, walked nonchalantly into our midst. Otto and Chuck Baum, old neighbors and bosom pals of

Bruce, had hitchhiked their way from Chicago to pay him a promised visit. What to do? To be sure we had room enough to bed down an army with canvas to spare, but meals, that was the hitch. The following morning chairs were pushed aside and wooden benches substituted, and by pulling in our elbows, somehow made room at the breakfast table for these two knights of the road. Tough and tanned from exposure and empty of stomach, they mowed down stacks of pancakes as fast as they hit the table.

They had barely finished, however, when a plan materialized in my mind, and by midmorning they were at work fencing, under Bruce's supervision. Our own cow as well as stray cattle were threatening our precious acre of growing things, and the sound of a cowbell was enough to send the whole camp to the rescue, pronto. Thus these two were to prove themselves assets rather than liabilities.

More than ever now I feared Mother might give out under the load. Her determination to provide homemade bread for the nine hungry mouths disturbed me most. "It'll be the proverbial straw," I told her, but she was adamant. She would set the sponge at night with yeast foam and the following morning would work in more flour. When the dough had risen sufficiently, she would punch it down and wait for it to rise again, then shape the batch into loaves. When these were light enough, usually by evening, she would pop them into the hot oven. Finally, stoking the fire she would set the sponge for the following day.

"It's nothing short of chain baking," I said, "and I don't know how you keep it up."

"Well, I'll admit it's nearly that bad. The oven never seems to get time to cool. But you menfolk like my bread and that's enough or me." Surely there's more to psychiatry than meets the eye, I concluded.

Chapter 14

PERSPECTIVES

We had plenty of hope, ambition and energy, but of dollars we had few. Nor could we find an adequate substitute for them. Though we had vowed to borrow no more, we were obliged to do so. At every turn it seemed we were confronted with some unexpected expenditure. The cow, tractor and cement mixer, little as they had cost, were nevertheless things outside our budget. There were others also, insignificant in themselves, but when added together became matters of consequence – our unexpected trips back to Chicago, for instance.

Our first tax bill, too, was somewhat of a surprise. Not that I hadn't expected one, but somehow our few unimproved acres seemed such a nonentity within the vast sea of woods that the matter had escaped my mind until the assessor showed up. Back in Chicagoland we had sewers, water, paved roads and alleys, street lights, garbage disposal, police and fire protection, all for a minimum levy. What did we have here to warrant a tax bill of $14.58?

Mr. Byrnes at the store put me right on that score. He called my attention to things not immediately obvious, things like the teacher's salary in the small school house beyond the lake, the distant courthouse in Grantsburg with its various offices, the men and machinery who patrol the roads, winter and summer, and even the great marble capitol in far-off Madison, with its many expenses. When this tall merchant in buckskin moccasins finished with me, he fell into retrospection. Seems there was one assessor in particular he remembered who, for want of better means to get about, made his calls on foot. Over the hills and through the woods he went on shank's horses, sleeping where darkness overtook him and eating what the good people offered him. I saw no point in this tale until he finished by saying the fellow had worn no shoes, making his rounds in bare feet. I tried to imagine a barefoot assessor back home. What a sensation he would be, what a story for the papers.

Since Flora's return, we had been fortunate in renting our old Cicero home. That rental together with Lou's board money amounted to fifty-five dollars each month, a tidy sum in a penny-pinching budget such as ours. Our help was costing us little. To each of the Sams we paid a weekly wage of three dollars. Now, however, with an assured income, we raised the ante to four for the Baum boys. What with our new Chicago supply of building material, our dairy products and promising garden, to say nothing of the rent from the old home, the future looked bright, and it was hard to believe that only a few short months ago our little world had seemed on the verge of collapse.

As our first cabin neared completion it was easy to look forward to the time when ten or a dozen such units would dot the premises, when the park and bathing beach would come alive with happy vacationers. Nor was it hard to look backward and speculate on the status of our family had we not taken a chance, but remained in the decadent city. Here at least, where we initiated our own industry, there was no such thing as unemployment, no idleness for men past fifty.

With one leg hooked over a rafter, I was running my eye the length of the ridgepole one day when Harris called for my attention.

"Look, Pa, over there across the lake. See that sail? What do you think it can be?"

From my high vantage point I could see far out over the water and there it was, sure enough, a sail, bright in the sunlight. I knew of no such craft on Lipsie and I, too, was puzzled.

106

"Looks like it's headed our way," Lou shouted from below.

While the two pondered over the matter, I continued on with my checking and marking. Soon, Harris called again, "It really is headed straight for our beach, Pa. Maybe we'd better go down and see what it's all about." Our curiosity heightened as we stood in a group and waited for it to draw near.

"Can't be a Chinese junk, the sail's too clean," Harris said, laughing. All doubts as to its nationality and origin quickly vanished when Abbie French put into port and dropped anchor.

"It's such a grand day," she said as she set foot on shore, "I thought I'd pay you folks a visit. Is Mrs. Palmer home?" As her eye took in the premises she continued, "My goodness! How nice it looks with all the brush cleared, and just see that new cabin." She shook an armful of posies into the semblance of a bouquet and queried again, "Is Mrs. Palmer in?""

While our seafaring neighbor ambled wide-eyed through the park, we landlubbers gathered about her strange craft. The sail that had reflected sunlight so brightly out on the water proved nothing more than an ordinary bed sheet secured to cross arms on a popple pole. A makeshift mast rose from a hole in the forward seat of a row boat and could be rotated for tacking. The whole craft from stem to stern reflected the genius of its owner, for Abbie French was a competent soul. Not only could she wield a needle with proficiency, but also a hammer and saw when the need arose.

That night in the seclusion of our upper berth, Flora told me of our visitor's trials and hardships when first she had settled upon Lipsie. Somehow when I had heard her through, our own troubles seemed trivial by comparison.

When Abbie, with her husband, settled upon a homestead in the forested area south of the lake, there was little if any underbrush beneath the big trees and one could see far into the woods. Even so, there was no other building, no dwelling within range of their vision. Summers were spent clearing and plowing and caring for their cattle and hogs. Though she became accustomed to her isolation, she dreaded the long cold winters with their loneliness. Winter was when her husband would leave her, to carry on alone as best she could, while he sought employment in distant logging camps.

One particular winter was an exception, for an unusually early blizzard paralyzed the countryside. For days on end snow continued to fall until the violence of the storm locked the winter woods against all trespass. Even so, Abbie was happy, happy in the thought that her husband couldn't desert her now. With cattle housed and cared for and the pantry shelves well stocked, there was little cause for worry. Time would see them safely through.

Alas for Abbie and her reckoning. The old wagon trail, though impassable to the outside world, was to prove no barrier to the phantom feet of disease and death. Hardly had the storm ceased and the warm sun shone its face than this once happy little home became a place of doom and horror.

"It was pneumonia following a spell of flu that finally took him," Abbie said. Alone with death now, she waited, waited for help she knew in her heart would never come. Day and night she kept vigil beside her dead husband, hoping against hope, yet praying.

Help did come, though not from beyond the woods. It came as an inspiration, a plan that set her heart pounding. No sooner had she thought it through than she started tearing apart an old apple barrel. "Snow shoes!" she cried as she snatched up a stave. "Snowshoes! Oh why didn't I think of it before?" Tears welled in her eyes as she bound the crude things to her feet. "I can make it now, I'm sure I can."

Bundled and mittened, she tarried beside the corpse with a prayer on her lips, then stumbling clumsily over the threshold, she set off in the direction of her closest neighbor. Snow lay deep and white, covering all familiar landmarks. Only the top of an occasional post told her of the pasture fence and the direction of the old trail that ran beside it. She set out timidly, then with calculated steps, she made her way to the nearest post. There new hope prompted her on to another and yet another until finally she dropped in her tracks, tired and out of breath, but confident. Before rising, she adjusted the flimsy bindings about her ankles and tightened the wires binding the staves together.

"If only they'll hold till I get there," she breathed as she dragged one heavy foot after the other. Her rest periods became more frequent, and when she finally turned to check her progress she could hardly believe the crazy twisting trail she had made. Of more concern were the improvised snow shoes that groaned with every hard earned step. Slowly but surely they were succumbing to the heavy strain. Finally, where the woods merged into the wide expanse of open country, her fears materialized – the staves parted one from another, and Abbie sank in the snow, heart sick and exhausted.

The macabre nightmare she had left behind would give her no respite. Unimpeded now by the clumsy, makeshift snowshoes, and up to her waist in snow, she plunged ahead, each scant advance a struggle, each step a project unto itself. Again she lay back motionless, her confused mind pondering the futility of further effort. "I can't do it, I can't. I just can't go one step further," she breathed into her mittened hands. But her heart quickened when, against the horizon, she saw a thin column of smoke. On her feet now, she recognized the roof and chimney of her neighbor. Weak and bewildered, she looked down absently on the shallow impression her prone body had made in the snow.

As though in answer to her prayer, an idea came, a plan for escape. Dropping on her back, she started rolling, her face buried in her hands. A few turns at first, then more and more. Nothing could stop her now. She had hardly started, however, when the white world about her became a spinning maelstrom of woods, sky and horizons. Overwhelmed by nausea and retching repeatedly, she continued on. Finally, within the very shadow of her goal, she was obliged to admit defeat. After a few feeble calls for help, the whirling universe mercifully engulfed her in complete exhaustion.

When she regained consciousness, strong arms were bearing her over the threshold of her neighbor's cabin.

Chapter 15

FIRST BORN

Perhaps it was fortunate for all concerned that Dick had a good disposition as there were times when it stood him in good stead. Having lived a more or less protected life, he found it hard to adapt himself to unfamiliar circumstances. His lack of know-how laid him open to a lot of kidding, but his good nature took it all in stride. With his quick repartee and the support of his Aunt Flora, he was able to hold his own. To my amusement, I came across him one day off shore in a boat, leaning upon an elbow, absorbed in a book.

"Why Dick," I shouted, "I thought you were taking care of the cows. How come? Where are they?"

"Oh, they're alright; they're up there in the woods somewhere," he replied.

"But Dick, that's no way to herd cattle."

"I know, Uncle Charlie, but I'm just reading how the cowboys do it," he replied with a sheepish grin.

One particular wash day, though, was when Dick really laid himself wide open. Flora had set out the tubs and asked Dick to fill them. Glad enough to be of service he went down to the lake and returned with two pails of water.

"Oh, Dick," Flora cried from the doorway, "I meant to tell you to use well water this time. The lake is too roiled up from the storm."

"OK," came the reply, and merrily whistling a tune he walked down to the lake once more and poured back the water. Even his

Aunt Flora deserted him for once and had a good laugh at his expense.

Each member of the family, with the exception of Lois who declined, was to have the privilege of designing and drawing up floor plans for a cabin, providing, of course, they conformed to sound building principles. Now that our first cabin, Flora's brain child, was about ready for occupancy, Harris was to follow with his, then Bruce, after which I was to try my hand. Though this arrangement gave me the advantage of their experience, subsequent cabins would do the same for them.

Flora, Bruce and Charlie at Crows Nest

Flora's cabin, later called Crows Nest, nestling low among the trees, with its tan stained logs and forest green roof, seemed very much a part of the woods itself.

"Gollee, Charlie, it looks just like it grew there," Lou said, viewing it from the shop door one morning.

"Well, that's the very effect I had hoped for, Lou. Personally I think all buildings in the woods should be low with wide spreading eaves, sort of toadstool-like. Makes the trees look taller."

Maurice Sylvester's eyes widened one morning as he walked slowly around the structure. "Well, it's a pretty good job, I'll say that much, but now that you've got it built, who's going to rent it?"

"It's already rented, at least for two weeks," I replied with certain satisfaction. I didn't tell him it was to a relative who had engaged it for his honeymoon. I, too, wondered how we would go about renting it. "Oh, we'll keep it filled all right," I added with borrowed enthusiasm. In the meanwhile, Flora showed Mrs. Sylvester through the cabin, proudly pointing to this and that and explaining the layout of the rooms.

I reserved as my prerogative the addition of such artistic touches to the interior as I deemed necessary. To relieve the plainness of the front door I applied knotty-pine slabs to its six cross panels, and with a brush added a few knots and whorls to its stiles. The result was a pleasing effect, not to be had on any commercial door.

When Maurice's eye fell on a piece of slab work of unique design on the living room wall he remarked, "It's funny how those knots just happened to look like a flying duck."

"All I did," I replied, "was a little carving on the wings. The body, long neck, head and all were there to begin with. Even the eye and bill were a natural part of the slab."

Although there were a few things yet to be done, when the honeymooners arrived Flora opened the back door with a smile of satisfaction. Dick's brother, Warren Johnstone, and Pearl, his new wife, followed their Aunt Flora inside, the rest of us trailing along.

"You know, this is my cabin. I designed the whole thing, but of course the men did the work. We are all taking turns, that is all but Lois."

"Gee, what a swell kitchen! Look, Warren, a pump and a sink! And such a dandy cupboard. This is a nice work table, all covered with linoleum."

"Yes, I think you'll find everything you need," Flora said proudly.

"Well, I'll say! Silverware, egg beater, potato masher, rolling pin. Golly, you haven't forgotten anything. Even ice in the icebox."

"I'll show you how to operate the oil stove," Flora said, lighting one burner. "There is nothing to pump up or generate; you just turn it up or down like this, see! That blue flame is really hot."

"And now this is my pride and joy," Flora beamed, opening a door to expose a screened dinette porch. "I selected this corner for its protection from the lake breeze and the fine view."

"See, Warren. What beautiful woods. I can't wait for our first meal."

Back in the kitchen, we stopped for a cold drink at the pump. "Sure's better water than we get back home," Warren announced when he finished his second glass.

"Here is the bedroom," Pearl said. "This bed, Uncle Charlie, I'll bet that's some of your work. Look, Warren, it's made of birch logs! And an innerspring, too," she said, punching at the mattress.

"That's a sort of picture window there in the living room," I said, stealing some of Flora's enthusiasm. "See, the four sashes are hinged together so they fold back out of the way."

But Pearl had thrown herself on the studio couch, saying, "Don't ask me to look now. I'm going to stay right here the rest of the day.

The whole thing is simply a dream." When the Johnstones had finally inspected the screened front porch, we gave them a hand with their luggage and left them on their own.

Slowly but surely LuluBelle was surrendering her sphere of dominance to her offspring, for Mollie was growing to self-determination and independence with each passing week. Somehow she managed to keep on the loose regardless of the new pasture fence. Instead of taking off to parts unknown as her mother would have done, she preferred to hang around our living quarters, making a general nuisance of herself. To her, our footpaths were things to be defiled, and this she did with daily regularity. Mollie had the agility of a deer and the undiscriminating appetite of a goat. Nothing was sacred or safe within her reach, not even the clothes on the line. When she chewed the hem from Lois' dress, she had gone unpunished. She was a pet, immune to punishment as far as Lois was concerned.

Her curiosity got her into trouble one day when she entered Bruce's tent and chewed a lace pattern around the tail of his best shirt. Pet or no pet, Bruce was mad.

"I'll fix that calf, once and for all," he said as he set off for the pasture with a roll of barbed wire on the truck.

Lois was really scared now and to play safe, she built a pole fence about her brother's tent. Bruce's precaution, however, was all for naught, for going to his tent a few days later he caught Mollie red-handed, as it were, and she nearly upset him in her haste to get out and over the birch railing. I heard Bruce's shout and watched; I knew he was beside himself with rage.

"You dirty stinker," he shouted as he wielded a heavy club, "if I ever get my hands on you I'll kill you." Over the rim and down into the park they ran, Lois frantically shouting for someone to come to the calf's rescue. Around the big trees, past the cook shack and finally out of my sight they raced. Curiosity finally drew me to the source of the trouble, and there, to my consternation, I found that Mollie had left her calling card right in the middle of Bruce's bed.

Chapter 16

STONE UPON STONE

Dishes heaped with ice cream and plenty more in the hand cranked freezer, were our reward for one especially tough day with axes, tractor and scoop shovel. We were clearing a cabin site along the lakeshore, a hard drag, especially for Lou, and one that nearly proved his undoing. While we chopped at the base of a particularly tall pop-ple, the dead trunk broke about half way up, and spearing its way earthward, the upper portion barely grazed him. More frightened than hurt, he lay stretched out on the ground unable to see clearly until we found his glasses which the tree brushed from his face. When his color finally returned and he got to his feet, I suggested he knock off for the balance of the day. This he did, though reluctantly.

At supper time I found Lou in one of Flora's aprons grinding away at the ice cream freezer.

"How are you feeling now, Son?" I asked casually enough.

"Well, you just try to stay with me eating this stuff," he replied, taking one last pull at the crank handle.

When darkness settled down that evening and the soft glow from a lamp fell across the table, Cousin Lou rose. "I'll be back," he said as he disappeared into the night. When he returned, he had a briefcase tucked beneath one arm. What on earth is he up to now? He pushed aside the sugar bowl and made room before him. After methodically polishing his thick lenses, he drew forth a roll of blue prints and spread them out upon the table.

"Charlie," he began, fixing me in his myopic stare, "Now that we've got that cabin off our hands, I've got a proposition I'd like to make. To begin with, you folks are not going to spend the winter here in this shop if I can help it, especially Flora. I know all about the tough time you had last winter, and it's not going to happen again. I want you to look over these plans I've drawn up and make any changes you see fit. They're for only a one story house, but big enough for the family." Too utterly surprised for expression, I waited until he finished. "When I was in town last week I stopped at Lampert Yards and got a figure on costs, building materials, and so on, in round numbers. It was about $1000."

"But Lou," I interrupted, unable to contain myself any longer, "the whole thing is preposterous, impossible. Why we..."

"Never mind that now, Charlie. I know what you're going to say. You wait until I'm through. What I want now is your OK on these plans."

"But Lou, you don't understand. We haven't..."

"The money," he cut in. "Well, I have. I wasn't expecting you to finance it. I've got some money lying idle, doing nobody any good, and I don't know of a better place I'd like to spend it." Too bowled over for words now, I listened while Flora expressed herself.

"Why Lou," she said, "it's perfectly grand of you and we want you to know how much we appreciate your kindness, but we just can't let you do such a thing. You know we can move into the new cabin for the winter."

"Now you listen to me, Flora, that cabin was built for summer, not winter, and it would take a lot of fixing. Cement floors are cold. I've thought this whole thing through from beginning to end. I know what I'm doing. I drew up these plans last winter in Chicago. You see, I have my reasons. Do you think I've forgotten your long car trips to Rockford when we went to see my mother in the Eastern Star Home? Not by a long shot. And how about those times when you went there alone, Charlie? I know about them. Those are things I'll never forget."

We heard him through as he enlarged upon details that I had forgotten, insignificant things that had happened so long ago. Regardless of anything we said to the contrary, Lou was adamant in his intention to carry through with his plan. Up in the Oriole's Nest that night, Flora and I considered the offer from every angle, though in our hearts we already knew the answer. To thwart Lou now in his gesture of kindness was to deny him his cherished place in the family circle, so we rationalized, but our decision to accept, I'm sure, was not without a tinge of selfishness.

Our overall program was expanding almost beyond our ability to keep up with its many aspects. Of late it seemed that the unexpected had dictated our policy rather than any well thought out plans of our own. The black Jersey, for instance, had virtually dropped in on us unannounced, as had the tractor, and both proved to be major turns of events. Now it was a new home that was to materialize, seemingly out of thin air. If illness had been a setback in our undertaking, surely these unforeseen happenings were in a measure, compensations for our misfortunes.

Forgetting all other demands upon our time, we unrolled Lou's blueprints and after a few minor changes by Flora, we set to work enthusiastically on our new home. The site we chose was settled upon only after deliberation, for our home was to be the business center of the resort, the office as it were, handy to both incoming and outgoing traffic. The site overlooked the park and presented a panoramic view of the lake through the boles of our tall pines. This location was especially situated to catch the full impact and glamour of the setting sun that poured forth its gold at the end of each day.

Following tractor work, grading and leveling the soil, the foundation was poured. Surely the ears of the bankrupt contractor back in Chicagoland must have burned as his big mixer sent forth staccato blasts to echo throughout the woods and over the water.

Among other things set forth in the plans was a large fireplace in the living room. This called for a big three-flue chimney, and the question arose, who among us was capable of doing the job?

"Not I," said Lou. "Give me a hammer and a saw any day to a trowel." Though the boys had proven themselves artisans of a kind, neither had ever worked in stone. Obviously, it was up to me, and as a matter of fact, I would have it no other way. I consulted Harris for an adequate source of material. His outdoor activities had familiarized him with the whereabouts of certain rock formations. There were plenty of granite boulders scattered here and there by ancient glaciers, but I wanted none of these.

"Why, Pa, I know the very place," he said. "Over near Tadpole Corners, if you know where that is. There's an outcropping of quartzite there and a lot of weathered pieces out in the fields. They'll make a better fireplace than anything else you can find around here." Many people are endowed with an innate love of stones in one form or another. Perhaps it was the place of my birth that accounted for my interest in this most basic of earth's material, for I was born where the Colorado Rocky Mountains split apart to form the gaping mouth of the Royal Gorge at Cañon City.

Several trips with our truck gave me a huge pile of rock from which to choose. Though the variation of color and texture of rocks have always interested me, I never so much as cemented one stone to another, and now I itched to get started. When the heavy chimney foundation of concrete had seasoned sufficiently, I set to work. The frame of our house had progressed to a point where the rough floor of the living room lay bare and open, and this area I appropriated for my own purpose. A successful fireplace, I knew, meant more than esthetic lines and colorful stone. I was aware that good workmanship counted for little if the throat in the chimney was poorly designed. At best a fireplace is an inefficient and uneconomical method of heating, but with all its faults, it does fulfill a definite, if primitive, urge for man to toast his shins before an open fire.

With prescribed plans for the smoke shelf and proper measurements for flues and damper fittings, I went to work with zest, for here was a challenge not only to my artistic temperament, but to my mechanical ability as well. Laying out various rocks on the floor, I juggled them about according to their size, shape and color until I was satisfied as to their potential positions. Before me on the floor lay a huge palette alive with color, and about me were my brushes in the form of hammers, chisels and trowels. I had now but to paint the picture.

Each colorful stone contributed its own individuality and characteristics as the heavy chimney pushed slowly upward through the rafters and out the roof. Finally the time came when I laid my tools aside and stepped back to survey my handiwork. There it stood, solid and compact, and with the symmetry of form I had envisioned in my mind's eye. There was the raised hearth, arched breastwork with the choicest of stones, and even two small rock shelves, one on each side, repositories for my pipes, I told Flora to satisfy her curiosity. Not until we had moved into the house did I find time and inspiration to add the finishing touches that would properly set it off. Shoulder high across the breastwork I affixed a small, semi-elliptical shelf, faced with a wide band of Norway bark.

"Just the place for the glass domed clock," Flora suggested when I finished it.

Now there remained but one thing more to complete the picture I had envisioned from the start. From a steel pin well above the mantle, I hung the head of an eleven-point buck. Conspicuous against its colorful background, it added a touch of outdoors to be appreciated when snow lay deepest and a hearth fire crackled merrily.

Better fireplaces there may be, but none ever gave more pleasure and satisfaction in their making than did this one built of quartzite stone from Tadpole Corners.

Chapter 17

VALIDATION

The bird house, high on a tamarack pole, was empty and silent now; its purple martins had migrated southward. So, too, had the Baum boys, and we missed their mirth and dry humor. Somewhere on their journey homeward they had thumbed their way past the Walker car. My in-laws were on their way up to Lake Lipsie.

We left nothing undone toward their coming. Beds were made ready, cakes and pies joined the oven's bread chain, and the broom reached a bit further beneath our machinery. Even the mop came in for its first wetting in weeks.

Dinner was well over, dishes were washed, and a bowl of wildflowers graced the center of our table when their car finally stopped before our door. We all rushed out to meet them – Manora, Grace, Blanche and their mother. Mother Walker had hardly set foot on the ground when she proudly announced, "We've good news, Flora. Ruth has a baby girl."

"Then you're a grandmother, Mom," Lois shouted, before her mother could reply.

"Well, thank goodness it's come at last. Of course it isn't any surprise. We've been keeping in pretty close touch with the mail box of late. And Charlie, don't forget that now you are a grandfather."

"Holy cow, I must be an aunt," Lois exclaimed, not to be outdone.

"What have they named her," Flora asked.

"Kathleen Nancy," a chorus of voices responded.

"Kathleen Nancy Swenson. Why I like that name, but I bet they call her Kathie for short. When did she arrive, Mother?"

"Well, now, let's see. It was day before yesterday, wasn't it? I'm so confused. Yes, we got the word just before we left home. Ruth is fine. Tell me, how are you doing, Flora? You look so well." All were happy to find their old patient so strong and contented in her new environment. When the conversation turned to things in general, we took to the outdoors for a tour of the premises.

"So this is your park! How lovely!" Mother Walker said as she minced her way over the rim with the help of Dick and his mother. "What lovely big trees!"

"Yes, and just see! I can't begin to get

The Park

my arms around one," Flora said, demonstrating. The shimmering blue waters drew their attention, and they gathered on the lake shore to drink of its charm.

"Why, I hadn't any idea it was so big and so beautiful," Grace voiced. "Just see the reflection of that shore line across there – it's like a huge mirror, and this sandy beach, what a place for children!"

Their curiosity knew no bounds. Nothing of consequence was overlooked and no path was left unexplored, even one that took off to nowhere in particular. When the Balagnas, John and Esther from Farmington, Illinois, invited them into the new cabin, Flora's moment had come. No words she had ever written to them had done her brain child justice. This was now her opportunity to expound its virtues in person.

More than all else, however, it was our new home that captured their interest, and it was Lou, of course, who did the honors. Nothing would do but that he first unroll the plans and explain the layout in detail before showing them through.

"What a pleasant living room! Just see the view from this window! But aren't you going to have a ceiling?" Mother Walker asked, peering upward.

"No, you see this is a studio ceiling. It goes all the way to the ridge, but of course the rafters won't show when it's finished."

"And that fireplace! Isn't that something? Where on earth did you get all those colorful stones?"

Now it was my turn and I left little to their imagination. "Better come back this winter when it's had its finishing touches," I suggested. The kitchen and bedrooms came in for close scrutiny and comments.

"I'm so glad you're to have an inside toilet," Mother Walker remarked. "Your winters are so long and cold up here." Although the roof extended well beyond the kitchen to include a garage, hardly more than its cement floor and framework were ready for their inspection. The tour continued after we had eaten supper, as daylight lingered long and there remained much to see.

We found LuluBelle tied to a post beside the log barn, and she wrinkled her nose as was her habit when strangers were about. It was Lois' turn now and she set about her milking with the know-how of an experienced hand, the strumming of a stream of milk striking rhythmically against the bottom of her pail.

"My hands used to get awfully tired at first, but not any more," she said as the strumming changed to a continuous swish, swish of warm white liquid.

"You might know she could do it," Manora commented as Lois rose from her stool with a frothy pail of milk.

Harris was already at the mill when the family emerged from the woodland path. He had made considerable progress and was anxious to demonstrate his accomplishment. He rolled a log from the huge pile on the ramp onto the newly finished carriage.

"See," he said, "how easily it pushes on rails. These are called dogs," he continued, pointing to a pair of dagger-like points that held the log securely on its bed. "Now take a look at these calibrations – they are marked off so we can cut boards to any given thickness. Just watch while I spin this wheel. There, see, it's set for exactly one inch." His hands were busy as he answered questions, and when he satisfied their curiosity, he continued. "We're just about ready to hook up to power of some kind, but that's the rub – we haven't a motor big enough to do the job. There're plenty of old Model Ts around, but they're too small. What we really need is a six cylinder motor like the one in our Studie. Looks like we'll have to finish the house, though, before we can go ahead with the mill."

The sun was spending itself in a profusion of color over the water, and shadows lay long in the park when again we gathered indoors. Only the family was present now, and before our city folks took to their makeshift quarters in the garage, the days events were relived and reevaluated.

When Mother Walker spied our Oriole's Nest high among the roof rafters she exclaimed, "My goodness, Flora! Aren't you afraid you'll fall out of bed some night? Why, you would land right on top of that sharp saw!"

"That's Charlie's side of the bed, Mother, so I'm not afraid."

"Well just the same, I'd put sides on that bed if it were I."

Feeling the situation needed some clarifying, I ventured a reply. "Now listen, I've slept in all kinds of places, from box cars to hay stacks, for more than half a century and I haven't fallen out of bed yet. It's pretty late in life to go back to sleeping in a crib, don't you think?" Mother Walker said nothing. She just fixed me with a meaningful stare, her gray eyes sharp over her rimless glasses. She was never one to waste words. My thoughts went back to that day of our departure, to our heavily loaded truck, the group that had gathered to see us off, the handshakes, the good-byes to neighbors and friends, and to our old home. Yet it was Mother Walker's words of farewell, so pertinent and yet so brief, that had impressed me most.

"Good bye, Charlie," she had said. "I am sure you and Flora are going to succeed. You both have the cajene to make a go of it." I wondered if she was still of the same mind. Were we really making a go of it? Times were bad the country over, and unemployment was still rampant. Could Maurice Sylvester be right? Might our new cabin go begging after all? Had our financial backers any such misgivings, was the question, as they inquired about any future reservations. If so, I hoped that Flora's optimistic report might put their minds at ease.

Crows Nest

"Do you remember that Crow family from Des Moines that came right after Warren and Pearl left? Well, they're sending friends of theirs up for a two week stay. By the way, that reminds me, we're thinking of naming the cabin Crows Nest after them. The Cranes have sent in their deposit, too, and I still have another inquiry to answer. All in all we've taken in more than a hundred dollars so far, and we're not through yet. I call that pretty good for a start, don't you?"

Following a breakfast of pancakes the next morning, we continued our sightseeing, this time over the narrow garden path. We trudged in single file through a thicket of hazel brush, popple and oak, uphill and over uneven ground. Finally, where the woods fell away before the garden gate, the vanguard waited, and soon all were knee-high among our growing things. To our surprise, who should emerge from the shadowy path moments later but Cousin Lou, with a salt shaker in his hand. Lou, who only yesterday refused to lay aside his tools and join us.

"I get a big kick out of these tomatoes," he exclaimed as he stooped over and plucked a luscious specimen from its stem. "You know, they don't taste like this in the city."

Here in this acre of sun-drenched soil was earth's abundance. Here was color in profusion; reds and yellows, with shades of green predominating. Here, too, were things of the spirit not to be weighed like cabbages, intangibles not for the eye, but reminders of long hours of toil and sweat not soon forgotten.

"It's certainly a wonderful garden," Mother Walker exclaimed, "but it's just too far up this hill. I don't see how you'll ever care for it," she continued as I closed the gate behind her. On our return, burdened now with garden produce, I pointed to vines heavy with wild grapes and chokecherry trees red with ripening fruit, signs of approaching fall.

"What about the chickens, Flora? Will you be able to house them over winter?"

"No, foxes and mink have gotten a number of them already and we have decided to kill the rest as soon as it freezes this fall. Any hen house we might build this year would be such a makeshift one, it wouldn't pay."

Bruce was eagerly awaiting our return, anxious to impress his urban relatives with the merits of his tractor. Midway up a tall cottonwood he had fastened one end of his heavy log chain. Bruce was never one to fell a tree with an axe and leave its stump to rot in the ground.

"I just hate to see them sticking up all over the place," he said. Instead, he would dig and chop about its roots, then pull it free from the earth like an unwanted tooth. Preliminary to this tree pulling, however, which was to be the last act in his repertoire, he put the Fordson through various tests to demonstrate its versatility, especially with regard to its new steering mechanism. In and out among the trees he went, circling this way and that over the rough terrain. I was apprehensive lest his showmanship end in tragedy. When his front wheels suddenly leapt skyward, I held my breath, fearful of a backward somersault. But a quick release on the clutch pedal brought the front end to earth again. A bit of purposeful dramatics on his part, I surmised. Before his grand finale, he pulled up before his audience and cut his motor. How quiet the woods seemed.

"Bruce, tell me, why do you fasten that chain up so high?" his Aunt Blanche asked.

"It's simply a matter of leverage. If I fastened it down low, why, I couldn't even budge the tree. I wouldn't have power enough," was his reply. "Now just watch," he continued as he mounted his iron horse with the agility of a movie artist. Slowly the tractor started and slowly the heavy chain arose from the ground until it stood taut and angling like the jib tackle of a ship's rigging.

"Better stand back, you can never tell," Harris shouted, waving us backward. As the big cottonwood bent beneath the strain, Bruce turned in his seat to gauge its length lest its top catch him in its downward plunge. However, try as he would, the tree would not budge. Roots that had long withstood the shock of wind and storm still held fast to the sources of their strength.

"I'll fix it," Bruce shouted as he slacked off for a final pull in another direction. Meanwhile Harris got in a few quick blows at the roots with his axe and the show was on once again. With a resolute hand on the wheel, Bruce rose to the occasion. There was a resounding jerk followed by a shower of dead branches, and slowly the heavy trunk started downward.

"Here she comes," Lou shouted, well out of danger's way.

"Timber," the family shouted in an impressive display of the vernacular. It had been Bruce's show from the start, and only his quick veering to one side kept it from a possible tragic ending.

A brush pile was lighted the last night in a farewell gesture to our city visitors. When leaping flames subsided and the heavens were bright with stars, we sat around in the soft glow of dying embers and talked of things yet to come. Although we did not realize it then, we were establishing a precedent that was to continue for more than a score of years - a weekly camp fire down in the park, a festival of song and story telling.

The following morning the Walkers were off. Dick and Lois with their belongings were somehow shoe-horned into their midst, together with a basket of garden produce.

"We'll see you next spring, daughter," Mother shouted toward the moving vehicle.

When Cousin Lou also took his departure a few days later, the premises seemed deserted, especially at meal time. There were no 'gollees' of appreciation for the cook's ears, no more help with the dishes. Even the lake and streams reflected their loneliness. Labor Day had come and gone and school bells had sounded the country over, calling vacationers back again to their worlds of reality.

Chapter 18

HOME AT LAST

The clear, crisp days of fall were upon us, days we had looked forward to with keen anticipation. Now that the household was back to normal once more, Flora's duties were at a minimum and she found time for an occasional book or crossword puzzle. However, there was no slackening off elsewhere on the premises. Our new house, even with its priority, was still far from finished. As for our sawmill, so long neglected, there seemed little hope of its completion before the snows came. A score of lesser jobs called for hands too busy to respond, and for time that did not exist.

I was fitting window sashes into their frames one day when I turned to see a stranger in the doorway. He seemed undecided whether to enter or retreat and I set his mind at rest by asking him in. On a few occasions I had seen odd characters on the streets of Spooner, especially on weekends when silver jangled in woodsmen's pockets. Here now was one such, on my own threshold.

"I heard you wanted to buy logs," he ventured through a mask of lush whiskers.

I buy logs? Why, I had never thought of such a thing. His mink-like eyes fixed on mine as he waited for an answer. Perhaps he had something after all. It was something worth considering to say the least, I thought, as I questioned him about prices,

My unexpected visitor was a small, wiry individual dressed in the conventional blue denim of his calling. He looked around him with provincial curiosity and spied the fireplace, suggestive of his own rustic environment. But he was especially fascinated by the moving sash weights as I raised and lowered the windows.

"What won't they think of next?" he exclaimed, as if witnessing some new innovation. The height of his provinciality, however, came as he was about to leave.

"Say mister," he said, scanning the door yard in every direction, "where's your back house? I don't see it anywhere."

"Why, there isn't one. We've got it inside now. See, there through that door. Go in and help yourself." Had it been urgency or was it curiosity? I shall never know. No sooner had he entered the small cubicle than I heard the rattling of hinged covers followed by a bang. Out he came, mistrust on his bearded countenance.

"Looks too much like a bear trap," he shouted from the doorstep. "I'm going out in the woods."

Now that the house was nearing completion, the boys stole an occasional day's work on our mill. Flora, her mind on her new home, spent much of her time with me, making minor changes and adding touches here and there that appealed to her femininity. Her broom was seldom idle, nor the fireplace as it burned rubbish.

Our long awaited moving day approached at last, the third now since our exodus from the city. Though our manner of living thus far did have its shortcomings, it also had its compensations. There had been little convention in our carefree gypsy life down by the water's edge and we had experienced a certain closeness with nature there on a pine needle floor. This we exchanged for four walls, albeit those of a workshop. Now we were moving again, and to what purpose, what end, I wondered as I lay awake in contemplation.

Things long stored away and forgotten were now unpacked and re-turned to service. Cur-tains, bed-spreads, tablecloths and doilies came to light, and our living room rug was unrolled. Before closing the shop door behind us, Flora took one last longing look up towards the skylight.

The House

"Charlie" she said, "more than anything else I'm going to miss our Oriole's Nest." Surely she had spoken my own thoughts, for never again would we have such a view of the star-spangled heavens.

A newly driven well beneath the concrete floor of our garage was now the source of our water supply. This was the deepest of three we had driven, but unlike the others, this one was hooked up to a water system. Soon it became a family chore for each individual to contribute two hundred strokes on the pump handle each morning. From a large stock tank in the attic, gravity would bring the water down to a shiny faucet over the kitchen sink. Running hot water was still in the offing, but hot water could be dipped from the kitchen range reservoir. The toilet, notwithstanding its lack of bathing facilities, was nevertheless a much appreciated adjunct to our new living quarters. To compensate for its shortcomings we sent away for a portable rubber tub that folded conveniently for storage. We were now snugly housed, and thanks to Cousin Lou, could thumb our noses at Old Man Winter.

Autumn with its audacious coloring was spending itself in one last fling of pageantry. The intermittent whine of buzz saws came floating over the water as they bit off lengths of stove wood. Snow fences were springing up along the highways, and corn in shocks stood like Indian teepees in the fields. Nearer home, too, were signs of approaching winter. A large stack of hay stood beside our log barn, wild grasses cut earlier from swamplands beyond the county line. The scythe and pitchfork were becoming familiar tools to us.

On the cold, wet days, forerunners of winter, I had little liking for barnyard chores with their demanding routine. If only I could depend upon LuluBelle, I might spend much more time at our mill, but call as I would she would seldom respond. "Come Boss, come Boss," I would shout at the top of my lungs. From far away over the wooded swampland I would hear the bawl of neighboring cattle, but our black Jersey would only push further into the dripping woods.

A huge pile of oak, birch and popple lay out behind the house, butt ends stacked foremost, awaiting the coming saw-rig. This was our winter's supply of stove wood, insurance against sub-zero blasts that were sure to come. But woodcutting must bide its time. Our mill now had priority and had ever since the day of our moving, since powering it was now of vital importance. If we were to peel and slab our cabin logs, it must be soon, for each passing day was setting the bark a little tighter. Thus far our search for a motor had availed us nothing. Second hand cars there were, with powerful motors, but not for our kind of money. Nor were we interested in worn-out engines. Under these circumstances, our Studie came in for consideration and not a little discussion by the boys. As for me, I wanted time to think it over. Our old car was still in good shape and we needed it to get about.

"Maybe we'll start going to church or something. What will we do without it?" I asked. "Are we going to walk?"

Harris, sensing a weakness in my argument, replied, "But Pa, we always drive the truck to town anyway. You know that. It's two to one, so you might as well give up."

The vote was two to one all right, but there were other things to be considered, those deafening "blottoes" at state lines, and the many miles of service this car had so faithfully rendered. There was sentiment long come by and deeply etched in my mind. The boys had no such qualms. They continued to beset me with facts and figures until, for better or for worse, I gave the word that was to spell doom for our old Studebaker.

Chapter 19

EVERYWHERE WEST

The glowing coals on the hearth that evening were reminders of other days, as we sat about eulogizing the condemned car. Incident after incident came to mind, places long forgotten were recalled, for we were paying tribute to a vehicle that had served us far beyond the call of duty. When this Studebaker had rolled off the assembly line back in 1926, it differed in no respect from the thousands that had preceded it. A few years later, however, when it stood ready to take us on an extended vacation tour throughout the west, it had no counterpart anywhere on earth. No other car that ever crossed the Continental Divide had been better equipped to minister to the needs of its occupants, for not only was its powerful six-cylinder motor to carry us safely over desert and mountain, but strangely enough, it was to do our cooking as we went. This innovation I had made possible by casting an aluminum receptacle that fitted about its exhaust manifold, snugly as a shoe on a foot. Into this repository I put the family pressure cooker. With a steam gauge along side the speedometer, the cook had only to relax on her cushioned seat with one eye on her dinner, the other on passing landscape.

Of equal interest was the unique cooler to carry our perishables, for where would one find ice in desert country? This expedient consisted of one thin metal box within another, having water between, the whole assembly attached to the lower front end of the car. A series of tiny holes carried moisture to an outer covering of cross-stitched and padded canvas. This contrivance was nothing more than a glorified desert water bag, having room inside for meats, butter, eggs, milk and so on. Rapid evaporation was obviously the cooling agent. Copper tubing from a ten gallon uptight tank on the rear completed this system. We had only to let down a hinged panel door beside this reservoir to expose a water tap and convenient wash basin. Within the cabinet were cosmetics, towels, washcloths, toothbrushes, a mirror and last but not least, a first aid kit.

The running boards had been quartermastered into food and duffel lockers, and on top of one was a tightly rolled umbrella tent, our children's sleeping quarters. And there were still other rabbits in this hat. One had only to pull forth a pair of brass tubes, telescoped within the car's innards, unfold a thin four-leaf top, and presto, a complete dining table with neither legs nor sky hooks to support it. Beneath the hood, securely fastened, was a supplementary three burner gasoline stove to be used for breakfast and lengthy stopovers.

To cope with high mountain altitudes, a quantity of warm bedding was required, but space to carry it was at a premium. With sleeping pads and blankets for all, the result was a bedroll, staggering in size. Left to Flora, the problem was solved in unique fashion. From car-top material, she fashioned an auxiliary top having metal fasteners at given intervals. These in turn matched up with their counterparts which I had screwed into the upper framework of the Studie. The following procedure was then to become routine each morning. First the false top was spread upside down upon the ground and its inner flaps turned out. The blankets and pads were spread on this, and the flaps turned in. The whole was then rolled into a bundle and hoisted to the car top where it was unrolled into position. Finally, it became a simple matter to then secure it by matching up the fasteners. The net result was a false top as smooth and slick as the original, but some five or six inches nearer the clouds. With its seats easily convertible into a bed for Flora and me, the old Studie was nothing short of a twentieth century Pullman.

'Everywhere West' was our slogan as we set out that fine day in June, 1929 to see what we could see. We were not alone, as two other parties, imbued with a lust to travel, joined up to accompany us part of the way; the Howard Hickes family and the Warren Cropp family.

Across the wide Mississippi we went, into Hannibal, Missouri, Mark Twain's home town. At the foot of a great cliff, we made ready

Under-Hood Cooker

for the first meal from our Magic Chef beneath the hood. Although I had little if any misgivings about it, the family looked on with some skepticism as I drew forth the aluminum cooker from its nesting place. There was a general sigh of relief when they got a whiff of its contents, a delectable odor that set our mouths to watering. Mother placed the steaming hot dish on the table, and a burst of ohs and ahs followed, and even I could hardly believe my eyes. There it was, a roast of beef done to a turn and fit for a king. With its complement of savory brown potatoes, it was the envy of the entire camp. Would our cooling system serve as well? Only time would tell.

Our small caravan went on toward Kansas City, to Westport, jumping off place for forty-niners. Here we started over the general course of the old Santa Fe Trail, on occasion spying a rusted remnant beside the concrete highway. Traveling through a sea of growing wheat we finally came to the outskirts of Dodge, the city where the West begins.

At the historical site of Bent's Old Fort in Colorado we stopped long enough to pay tribute to an old pioneer, for it was here in 1863 that Barzilai Adams, my grandfather, was put in charge of the fort, then a way station on the Barlow and Barnum overland stage route. Here, too, within its thick adobe walls, my mother had been a babe in arms during the Indian uprisings that ended in the tragic Sandy Creek Massacre.

Pueblo, Colorado Springs, Garden of the Gods, all soon vanished from our rear view mirror. At Cañon City, my birthplace, we took the famous Skyline Drive and headed for the mile high bridge spanning the Royal Gorge. Not content with this altitude, Bruce and Warren Cropp got a further thrill taking an airplane trip over the great chasm.

Back at Pueblo once more, we headed southward toward Trinidad and the Cimmaron country. Down and down we went, twisting and turning our way through Eaton Pass to the floor of New Mexico far below. We pitched our tents beside the precipitous walls that cradle the Rio Grande. Perhaps on this very site, there had been camp fires of early Spaniards, later fur traders, and still later cattle-men. This was the land of Kit Carson, the Sublettes, the Bents, Jim Bridger, old Peg Leg Smith, who had done his own surgery by the light of his campfire, and a score of other indomitables who lived by their wits and died with their boots on. We found it a wild and rugged country, one with special appeal for Harris, the embryonic geologist of the party.

Taos, New Mexico was neither a town nor a city as we knew such, but a bit of the past left over for exploitation by the present. Who could describe its contrasts, its blend of the old with the new? Surely not I. We left its bizarre inconsistencies for the brush of an artist and the words of a poet and dreamer.

At Santa Fe we abandoned the caravan to better see this old town and drink in its atmosphere. Adobe architecture and antiquity! Both were everywhere about – in dwellings, the sprawling old mission and public buildings, all a part of the very earth on which they stood. The Museum housed memos of the past; ancient weapons, accouter-ments, Indian relics and crude objects from a primitive culture. Of particular interest to me was an old stage coach, its body suspended precariously upon a pair of leather traces in lieu of springs. How many times had this aged conveyance stopped before the iron stud-ded gates of Bent's Old Fort?

More than ever I appreciated the comfort and convenience of our miniature Pullman as we proceeded toward Albuquerque. At this modern little city, we were told that to leave the state without seeing Carlsbad Cavern was to see only the tent and not the show. Although this trip meant an added five hundred miles to our itinerary, there was not a dissenting vote to spoil the journey. Eastward we traveled, contrary to our original plans and the "everywhere west" slogan we had adopted. Over hot dry plains and through ancient lava beds the highway unrolled before our eyes until once more we were in the mountains. We stopped beside a cool stream to stretch our legs and replenish our water supply. Here, too, Mother transferred a mess of string beans and a chunk of salt pork from our cooler to the cooker, planning to feed her family somewhere within the normal range of cooking miles. No ice being available for their boxes, our traveling companions appropriated space in our Pullman refrigerator for their milk and butter for the rest of their journey.

With an eye on both the pressure gauge and speedometer, we

scanned the wayside for a place to eat. On and on, mile after mile, we went with the safety valve popping off at regular intervals, but nary a shady rock could we find. Finally a short distance out of Roswell, New Mexico, we pitched our tents, and our hungry but apprehensive family turned toward Mother as she raised the hood and removed the cooker. She looked chagrined as she peered into the steaming caldron. We watched anxiously as she drew forth a sample and gingerly put it to her tongue. "Phew," she exclaimed and passed the spoon on to me. The overcooked stuff was brackish as sea water, smooth as salve, but in all fairness it had a slight beanish flavor to it.

"Looks more like axle grease," Harris said. "Why not put it in the transmission?" I took the gooey stuff over to a hole in the rocks.

"For the rattlesnakes," I shouted, and dumped it in.

The following day was the Fourth of July, and we celebrated with a leisurely and quiet breakfast, then took to the road as usual. Heat waves danced before our eyes, and centipedes crawled over the pavement to lose themselves in hot desert sands. The hotter the day, the more we would appreciate the cool temperature beneath the earth's surface.

At the cavern's entrance, we joined forces with a host of other holiday tourists awaiting a signal that would send them on their long journey underground. We were a thousand strong when we finally started, and there was a guide for every one hundred souls. Halfway down we turned around. What a spectacle! As far as the eye could see, the pilgrimage came, their colorful attire mellowed in soft light from the vaulted ceiling. A multitude of men, women and children came wending their way along slowly, like a scene from Biblical days.

We stood on the bottom level, open-mouthed at the spaciousness about us. The great room was high enough to contain a modern skyscraper and seemed to house a small mountain. We diverged in all directions to explore the far reaches of the strange netherworld that lay before us. Great halls hung with alabaster drapes, pillared chambers competed with crystalline pools, and formations fantastic and grotesque greeted us at every turn.

Making the long trek back, the crowd gathered as a unit once more. At a word from the guides we seated ourselves about a great crystalline column formed by the fusion of stalactite and stalagmite, old beyond man's reckoning of time. A murmur swept over the throng when, without warning, all lights were extinguished and we found ourselves in pitch blackness. All suspense and apprehension gave way when a clarion voice rang out with the old familiar Rock of Ages. A thousand voices joined the theme song and echoed through the darkened corridors.

The trek had covered seven long miles beneath the earth's surface. The contrasting heat above seemed an inferno as we made our exodus and boarded our caravan once more. Away from hordes of sightseers, we three families headed westward toward the setting sun, our minds filled with the day's events. We stopped for the night on a hot, dry canyon floor as distant peaks faded into darkness. Harris dispatched a buzzing rattler in front of the children's tent, and scorpions took cover here and there as we lit our campfire.

Weary from the day's activities, Mother and I were about to turn in when a distant light caught my eye. "We are not alone after all," I said, and flashing a beam before me, climbed to higher ground for a better view. In the gray distance, I made out the lines of a cabin on a rocky ledge. Who would live away out here in such a lonely place? Curiosity led me on, and all too soon I found myself on the threshold of my objective, wondering just why I had come. With some trepidation I knocked on the door. I did not have long to wait.

"Come in," a deep voice shouted. Hesitantly, I turned the knob and pushed. Who should greet me but a vicious creature, its teeth bared and its claws extended.

"Here, take this critter off my hands and I'll rustle up a chair," my host directed, foisting his pet in my direction.

"No, thank you," I replied. "I'll just take that chair by the window if you don't mind." Once we were seated, he with his wildcat upon his lap, and me with my heart in my mouth, I offered a reason for my coming.

"I'm very much interested in Indian things," I said, "and I thought maybe you'd have something of the kind, living way out here as you do." The straightforwardness in my words must have struck a corresponding note of interest, for his response was immediate and his bearing cordial. Settling down in his chair, his wide-brimmed hat pushed well back, he stroked his ill-tempered pet as he related one hair-raising experience after another.

A cave man in cave country, exploring the honeycombed earth had long been his hobby. Obviously his exploits had been venturesome and not without danger, but there was one story in particular I shall never forget. Far back in the dark recesses of a cave, his flickering torch revealed the mummified body of an Indian in a sitting posture. Surrounding this ancient corpse at intervals were objects he at first thought were stones. These later proved to be human heads, the only authentic evidence of head hunting within the borders of the United States, he said, according to the National Geographic Society, who had written about the find.

Creeping things and denizens of the dark had been his companions, and rattlers beyond recall he killed in line with his precarious calling. Yet not until I heard the story of the countless bats and realized its significance did I know the truth, for this fearless mountain hermit with his exotic tales was none other than Jim White, discoverer of the greatest of all known caves, Carlsbad Caverns.

Behind us now were the Guadeloupe Mountains. Strange to say we left them with a twinge of regret, for in spite of snakes, scorpions, tarantulas and centipedes, there was a bewitching lure about this semi-arid land, and I for one meant to return. Ahead lay Texas, land of the Alamo, and beyond, Juarez, Mexico, our immediate objective. There we stopped only long enough to sample the spiced cuisine south of the border, chili in particular. "Whew," our family shouted between gulps of air and water. Never again would we abandon the offerings of our Magic Chef on such a gamble.

Back across the Rio Grande to El Paso, and on to Los Cruces, Silver City and beyond, where we met our Waterloo, for in an attempt to negotiate a shortcut to Arizona, the Cropp car let us down, breaking a rear axle. Thus far we had been fortunate in getting ourselves out of difficult situations, had even installed a new piston on one occasion and ground valves on another. But what to do now? Here we were at the bottom of the world, between mountains and hundreds of miles from any source of auto supplies.

Turn about we must, that much we knew, and within an hour our frustrated little caravan was on its way back, our Studie forward, pulling, and the Hickes' car in the rear pushing. Finally, at the junction with our old route, we stopped to consider our next move. The long, straight highway ahead, leading ever downward as far as one could see, was more than Warren could resist.

"Let's go!" he shouted, and go we did, coasting mile after mile until the earth flattened out beside a babbling brook, where for obvious reasons, we made our camp. We found it a restful place, this forced landing among willows, and the water was sweet and cool. Moreover, we meant to enjoy our stay regardless of our predicament, each according to his own dictates. However, when we gathered around the campfire that evening Bruce was not among us, nor did anyone remember seeing him during that afternoon. Though our shouts echoed throughout the valley, we heard no reply. Up stream and down, we pushed our way through thicket and over rock strewn earth, but could find no sign of him.

When at last the blackness of night called a halt to our search, we turned to the fire for what encouragement it might offer. Driftwood being plentiful, we heaped it on until our whole camp and the sky above became a beacon of light. With ears alert for the slightest sound, we waited. An hour passed, then another, as our minds conjured up every conceivable manner of mishap. A broken leg, perhaps, or a snake bite, or just being lost was bad enough. When someone mentioned grizzly bears and mountain lions, our children crowded in closer.

What the hour was I don't recall, though it seemed ages, when a grim-faced young man dragged his weary feet into our midst and dropped beside the fire. He told the old story of a mountain that had seemed so near, luring him on and on until darkness overtook him and he lost all sense of his whereabouts. Finally, stumbling upon a tiny creek, he reasoned, and quite rightly, that camp lay downstream somewhere.

With all accounted for we slept soundly enough the rest of that night, but awakened the following morning to the full meaning of our predicament - a broken axle, and what to do about it? Apparently the only habitation for miles was a small dwelling I had noticed in our search for Bruce, and with breakfast over I set out in its direction. To our good fortune, I found it occupied. At my approach, a white-bearded old man rose from his chair on the small porch. He had heard our shouting during the night and seeing our beacon light, guessed the reason for the commotion.

"Yes, there still is an occasional grizzly in these parts," he said, "and plenty of mountain cats, but not much to be afraid of."

When I finished telling him of our predicament and asked him where I might expect to find the nearest garage, to my surprise he had a suggestion. He said his son had a small shop some eighteen miles further down the highway. He could repair most anything, including cars, but of course he would have no axle on hand. There was, however, a ranger telephone, and he could call a dealer in EL Paso and get one.

"But surely no one could be expected to deliver an axle way out here," I countered.

"No, they would send it out to a place on the highway, to be given to the first tourist coming this way. You might have to wait a few days, but you'll get it eventually." There was refinement in the old man and an evident contentment seldom found in city folk. What story lay hidden away in that isolated spot I could not conjecture. Within the hour, Warren, Harris and I were on our way toward his son's place of business.

We found the wayside shop, and its proprietor, but more to the point the telephone with which a new axle was ordered. Midway on our return to camp we pulled off to investigate an abandoned old ranch house close by the roadside. The place had an air of antiquity and spookiness about it which aroused my curiosity, all the more so when I spied a weathered tombstone rising obliquely from a patch of weeds in the dooryard. "DIED BY GUNSHOT" ran the last line of the epitaph. How in keeping, as I looked around me.

Of greater interest was a half-dug Indian ruin with many pot shards lying about, evidence of burials more ancient than the one beneath that stone slab. Thereafter, our camp beside the willow lined creek held little interest for me. While others waited impatiently for some wayfaring stranger to arrive with our car part, Harris and I spent three all-too-brief days digging and searching through the tumulus at that deserted premises.

To slip the new axle into its housing was a matter of but an hour or so, and once more we were on our way. With hardly more than a passing glance toward the Petrified Forest, and farther on, the big meteor crater with its thirteen miles of extruded circumference, we finally arrived at the zenith of attractions, earth's greatest chasm, the Grand Canyon. We approached it nonchalantly and with little more than hearsay to stir our imaginations, but as we stood upon its very brink, we were speechless and awe-struck. The words of Genesis came to mind, "And God made the heavens and the earth and the Grand Canyon of the Colorado." Or was this a fanciful paraphrasing born of inspiration? "And He rested on the seventh day from all the work He made." No wonder, I reasoned, as I surveyed the breath-taking phenomenon before us. With mixed emotions, I turned aside, leaving mere adjectives to others better versed in their use than I.

We left Arizona and its spectacular scenery for our first real taste of sweltering heat. Just outside Needles, California, gateway to the Mojave Desert country, we came to an oasis. We found it a welcome spot and a place to recuperate before our final push over the expanse of hot, dry sands. Beneath its few scattered trees was a pool of clear, cool water where we loitered until nightfall. To make such a crossing in the heat of the day was out of all question. We spent idle hours alternately dipping our bodies or lying in the shade. This was to be our last bivouac together, for on the morrow our traveling companions would leave us for their several destinations.

Not until the desert sun had run its gamut of color, and darkness settled down, did we climb aboard our vehicles. Stripped to the limits of propriety, and with wet bath towels hung at our windows, we made the crossing, not, however, without discomfort and some degree of trouble, for of all places, our dependable old Studie chose the middle of this desert and midnight for its first flat tire. A hundred and fifty miles of inferno brought daylight, and with it the parting of ways. At Barstow we took leave of our friends, and our family Pullman turned southward on its own.

Though we had lived thus far as carefree gypsies, eating and sleeping where and when circumstances dictated, we were glad to accept the hospitality of civilization once more. At my brother's place in Los Angeles we sat on upholstered furniture and stretched out for a night on soft mattresses for a change. Yet soon enough we had our fill, and took to the highway again with the Mexican border our destination. Oil wells without number, orange groves, old Spanish missions and miles of coast scenery took us to San Diego, then the return, and at the City of the Angels once more, we set our sights on the Canadian border or thereabouts.

Giant Redwoods, a ferry across the Golden Gate, San Francisco's Chinatown, all were to become treasured memories, and finally, too, Yosemite Valley, rest haven for weary travelers, where we camped for one tantalizing and all-too-short week. Itinerant tramps that we were, we left the park by way of a little used backdoor route. Up and up we climbed over the high Sierras, our radiator boiling and cooling in a series of goes and stops. Through Tioga Pass we rolled and on toward the Nevada line. At Lake Tahoe we made camp. I searched for arrowheads while Flora gathered cones among the pines.

Morning found us in Carson City. We inquired the whereabouts of the state capitol building, only to be told we were standing at its very threshold, a wooden structure, of no more pretentiousness than a county courthouse back home. On to Reno with its gambling casinos, its stacks of silver and get-rich-quicks, a spectacular show but one that tempted us not a whit, and soon the city of chance and divorce was no more than a speck on the horizon.

Extinct volcanoes, ancient lava flows and beds of cinders marked our path as we continued northward. Far inland from the ocean we found the country desolate and unpeopled, but all the more fascinating for its very remoteness. There was an element of adventure in each long and uninhabited stretch, a possible breakdown or a running out of gas. Equally hazardous, too, were sharp fragments of lava that threatened our tires on the unpaved roads. Despite it all, we eventually pulled over the state line and into the small town of Lakeview, Oregon, safely and without mishap. This was a land of drought, though hardly equal to the desert country we had experienced earlier. What only a score of years ago had been beautiful lakes were now empty basins of dust and alkali. We camped beside one of these where once a steamship had passed on its regular course over a sixty mile expanse of water.

In spite of the desiccation and intolerable roads, we pushed on into the interior, hoping all the while to find a shortcut that would take us to Crater Lake, but fate ordained otherwise. Somewhere in the midst of the mountain wilderness, a sheer wall arose before us, a geological fault we guessed, blocking our way. We could not avail ourselves of the trail that skirted its base either, for smoke and falling ash from a distant forest fire ahead was a threat better left unchallenged.

Back at our starting place, we took off for Klamath Falls, this time over a well established route. Dusk was settling over the seven thousand foot elevation when at last we pulled into the public camping grounds at famous Crater Lake. Tired, travel stained and hungry, we disembarked and set about with our usual camp procedure, only to find ourselves surrounded by curious folks and plied with questions.

"From Illinois, I see. Well, so are we. What town?" Or, "How long are you staying?" or "Where are you going from here?" But the catechism ceased abruptly and eyes widened when, with a twist of his wrist, Harris exposed the Pullman's complement of toilet articles at the rear of the car.

"Well, what do you know," gushed one observer, as a stream of water poured into the fold-away basin beneath and Harris started to clean up and shave. A murmur of astonishment when, abra-cadabra, the jiffy dining table appeared from nowhere! But not until Flora pulled a roast chicken from our motor with the finesse of a magician was our audience completely overcome with astonishment and we were bombarded again with questions.

"Say, tell me, where can I get one like it?" "You mean to say you made it yourself?" "Do you have a patent on it?" On and on, the questions continued.

All thought of mere man's handiwork was quickly forgotten when we peered into the blue, blue depths before us that next morning. How marvelous Nature's accomplishments, how diversified her objectives, and how adequate her tools. Carlsbad's great labyrinth carved by subterranean water, the meteor from outer space that had punctured the earth's surface near Winslow, that keen silver blade that was still cutting its way in the depths of the Grand Canyon, and now this. At some remote period, the earth had literally blown its top in one grandiose display of internal dynamics and nature had hidden the scar forever within the depths of azure blue waters.

We took leave of our fellow campers the following morning to survey the deep-set lake from a mountain road that encircled it. For miles our view was screened by enormous clouds of yellow butterflies in some strange erratic flight, a phenomenon in itself, as finally the atmosphere cleared.

Following our exit from the park, Grant's Pass was but a hop, skip and a jump for the agile Studie, but we did not reach this interesting city until the following day. The pristine beauty of the Rogue River, its rocks, rapids and foam-flecked water demanded a tribute we were glad enough to render.

Chapter 20

SLOW RETURN

The apogee of our long journey was now behind us, and though home still lay thousands of miles in the offing, the thought of its staid and snug environment rose to disturb our itinerant minds as we rolled through apple orchards of the Willamette Valley. With a long and straight run now before us, Lois and the boys fell to reviewing the many weeks we had spent in the open. They dwelt on the unpleasant things they had experienced, trivial incidents that would soon escape them - intolerable desert heat, camps we had made in the rain, the windstorm that flattened our tents, and atrocious detours. Nor had they forgotten the clouds of mosquitoes and crawling, creeping things that were a part of camp life. They remembered, too, their mother's acute attack of neuritis that had robbed her of so many miles of enjoyment.

As never ending orchards swept by, they called to mind happenings I had long since forgotten, yet at the mention of the Hickes' car accident, I came alive, for unlike the broken axle incident, this one had a near tragic ending. It had happened back on the Kansas prairie when an exploding cylinder showered the Hickes' windshield with hot oil and enveloped their car in a cloud of steam. Believing her time had come, Ethel jumped, landing head over heels on the pavement. Camp was immediately established and their engine torn down while the men scouted the countryside for a new piston. The following day turned out to be a scorcher, and with no shade and amidst a scourge of black flies, we set about to make amends.

While the women prepared dinner, Howard lay beneath his motor at work with his wrenches. Without warning, his vehicle slipped from the jack. Panic stricken, Ethel ran about exhorting us to hurry. After what seemed an eternity, the car was hoisted and Howard crawled out, frightened but unscathed. There was rejoicing in the camp, but a telltale grease mark across his forehead was reminder enough of what might have been, as it bore the imprint of the oil pan that had pinned him to the earth.

Adversity and misfortune soon resolved themselves into happier thoughts, however, as visions of the past presented themselves with kaleidoscopic change. Ancient Taos with its bizarre display of color, its white-sheeted Indians and their adobe living quarters, the Grand Canyon of the Colorado, God's masterpiece, and Yosemite's never-to-be-forgotten "Hello, Camp Curry, hello Glacier Point" – "Let the fire fall!" I could see once more that great shower of sparks in the magnificent drop of a flaming bonfire to the rocky shelf below. And I, too, could see the lurid sun through the haze of smoke as we rolled down from the high Sierras on the margin of a forest fire.

The children's hour of fact and fancy took on a mundane note as they generalized on more personal aspects of camp life; night sounds they had accustomed themselves to, keen odors of outdoor cooking, and their mother's proficiency with a Dutch oven over a bed of glowing coals. The very thought of gingerbread or hot biscuits was enough to set my mouth watering.

Lois recalled with no fondness for the memory, an event at a camp at the edge of the desert. It had seemed an isolated spot, and following dinner, Lois stole off to a nearby spring to bath. Fully immersed in the cool waters, she was suddenly stuck by the approaching lights of another car entering the area. She screamed for Flora to bring her a towel, and momentarily, Flora headed off to answer her plea. As Lois reached out, Flora offered our budding beauty a tiny face cloth, a bit of humor lost entirely on one in the limelight.

Though little emphasis had been put on the Studie thus far, in all fairness it must be said that with its manifold accessories, it had functioned beyond our expectations and under all circumstances. yet like its occupants, it was beginning to show signs of wear, especially its rubber. Rear tires that were new when we had adopted our "Everywhere West" slogan were now full of cuts and bruises.

Moreover its motor seemed tiring from the long mountain pulls to which it had been subjected.

Eugene, Salem, the capitol, then on to Portland just in the nick of time, for here we were obliged to purchase and mount a new tire. Over the line into Washington to add another state toward the fulfillment of our slogan. At Vancouver we turned about and soon found ourselves in Oregon once more, drinking in the beauty of the Columbia River landscape. We rolled on through its wide, scenic valley until the DesChutes beckoned us to stop beside a great granite boulder, where we ate a meal of pork and beans steaming hot from our cooker. A gentle breeze stirred through the tree tops, and we found the place so cool and tempting, we decided to make camp. Smoke was soon rising lazily from a driftwood fire where Flora was preparing to do the family wash. What better place than this to give the tired old Studie some needed pep, a thorough valve-grinding job.

So the hours passed with clothes drying in the breeze and tools rattling beneath the hood. But the day that had started so delightfully was now showing ominous signs. The bright sun turned to a murky ball, barely visible through foreboding haze. With unbelievable suddenness, a sand storm was upon us, fairly blasting the car, filling every nook and crevice, and finding its way into our bedrolls and foodstuff. It's an ill wind that blows no good, and later, with Mount Hood's distant peak aglow in the new morning sun, we set about in search of arrowheads. Those we found were each poised upon its own small pedestal of sand, thanks to yesterday's gale. They were little gems of Obsidian, just begging to be picked up and appreciated.

Continuing eastward, our thumb-worn map directed us once again into the interior of Oregon, somewhere in the vicinity of the John Day River. We were soon following a highway bearing that same name, and with Boise, Idaho our immediate destination, gave the car a good tryout.

"I will never eat another Idaho spud," I vowed to Flora after a long pull through a muddy detour beyond the city. However, before nightfall our roving Pullman was spiking the mountain air with the tantalizing aroma from a roast of pork and a mess of halved native potatoes. As we drove into a secluded nook to prepare for the night, we were surprised when a stranger pulled along side and stopped. "Oh, oh, the sheriff," I said, as the spirited Studie had really been rolling since its overhaul, but his quizzical smile quickly dismissed all concern of speeding.

"Say," he said, sniffing the air, "would you mind telling me what I've been smelling for the last twenty miles, like a restaurant or something."

Visions of Yellowstone rose as our pepped-up motor hummed along through rain and fog the following morning. Would we camp that night along side Old Faithful, or would weather and road conditions call a halt short of our goal? The incessant swish of windshield wipers continued throughout the day, and when the hour came to charge the cooker with victuals, Flora was reluctant, though she realized it was strictly her responsibility. Time was unyielding and finally she stepped out and raised the hood. An oncoming motorist, seeing a gray-haired lady out in the rain tinkering with the motor, slowed down long enough to glower at the menfolk within.

There was no letup in the weather when we crossed over into Montana and finally into Wyoming's National Park. We pitched our tent among the many others and waited impatiently for the Cropps and Hickeses to show up as was the prearranged plan at our parting.

"Rain, rain, rain! Three days of it and no letup," I said to Flora impatiently as I donned my waterproof clothes.

"Where are you going?" she asked as she laid aside her book.

"I'm going over to the hotel for a dozen fresh eggs. I'm going to put 'em in a pail and I'm going to boil 'em in that hot hole over by Old Faithful."

"But Charlie, you can't do that. You know very well the rangers won't permit anything in any of the pools."

"I know, but the rangers don't like the rain any more than I do. They'll be in somewhere where it's dry."

The sight of "Isaac Walton" sitting nonchalantly out in the rain beside a boiling pool, rod in hand, was hardly orthodox, to say the least. Nevertheless, to a few who dared the weather that day, the scene was real enough. The perforated pail with its precious contents had hardly settled beneath the surface than a motorist slowed down to stare unbelievingly, then pass on. A car door slammed and I looked up to see another approaching on foot, incredulity written all over his face.

"You mean to say you're fishing in that boiling water?" he inquired in Scandinavian singsong. A quick glance toward his car confirmed my suspicion – Minnesota license plates. I'll just spoof him for the fun of it.

"Well, why not," I replied, tightening my grip on the pole. "Just under that boiling water there's a cold mountain spring, alive with trout. Takes a little patience, that's all."

Curiosity now possessed him, and as he moved in closer he asked, "How many have you caught so far?"

For a moment he had me, then remembering the old story I replied, "If I catch this one and two more, I'll have three."

Still credulous, he turned up his collar and said, "I think I'll stay till you get one."

Heavens, the eggs! Had I fallen a victim to my own trickery? I pulled out my watch. Ten minutes – whew! Oh well, what's another minute or two. The big hand swept around the dial all too swiftly as the Minnesotan looked on questioningly.

"Say, what's the idea of the watch?" he queried.

"Well, you see," I hesitated, groping for a reply, "when I hook one I pull him up into the boiling water and hold him there for five minutes and he's ready to eat."

"Now I am going to stay," he said with emphasis.

Fifteen minutes, sixteen, seventeen! Oh what the heck, they're petrified by now anyway. Out came the pail, squirting water in every direction. One look was enough. The big Swede took off. As I trudged homeward through the drizzle I could hear his exhaust burning up the highway.

In spite of the weather, nothing of consequence within the park was overlooked, from gurgling caldrons of mud to the ethereal beauty of Yellowstone Canyon. While we were gathered at Artist's Point below the falls, an osprey struck the water with a splash then rose and passed over our heads. A little old lady by my side, seeing a large trout clutched in its eagle-like talons, gave vent to her pity.

"Just hear that poor fish scream," she said.

On to Cody, Wyoming, Buffalo Bill's town, thence northward to the Big Horns. Up and up and ever up the Studie labored, its radiator threatening to burst with every hard earned mile. Higher and higher we climbed over the little-used ranger trail. Whose wild idea was this, anyhow, this hairpin trail to the clouds? Part way up we came to an abandoned Model T, cramped closely against the inner wall as though fearing to peer over the ledge into the depths below.

What to do? To back down was unthinkable, to continue on impossible. Or was it? An estimated twelve full inches of earth insured us against a quick trip to eternity. Should we chance it? Was it worth it?

Up the road, the rest of the family watched breathlessly as I inched our Studie past the derelict. None the worse for the delay, they clambered aboard to continue the trip to the summit. Some months later in a review of our trip, Flora wrote, "It was an unimproved road seldom used. The grade was terrific. We went up in first and second for sixteen miles, and there were precious few places to pass if one had to. The turns were so sharp in places as to make our hair stand on end, but oh, that view from the top! The panorama was simply glorious, absolutely different from anything we had seen. The country over which we had traveled at least the day's journey lay at our feet like a dream, and the beyond, lost in blue haze."

We were on the very edge of a great rolling plateau, almost detached from the world below, but any such illusion was quickly dispelled when we came upon a band of sheep and a lone herder. Evidence of his aloofness lay in the miles of uninhabited grassland from which an occasional buffalo skull stared blindly up as we passed. Time has brought change, and today a U.S. highway bisects the tableland, assuring a safe passage to all who attempt its crossing. No longer do macabre reminders of the old west stare up from its grassy plains.

Soon Sheridan, with its ghosts of Phil Kearney and Red Cloud, was behind us and the Black Hills of South Dakota lay ahead on the horizon like a distant smoke screen. Mount Rushmore, that great shrine of democracy - what would it be like? We had just joined the small group assembled there when there was a blast, and an avalanche of debris came rattling down the mountain side.

"Jefferson's eye," remarked a ranger indifferently as he lighted a cigarette.

Foremost on the great escarpment was the striking finished visage of Washington, Father of our Country.

150

"Tall as a five story building," our informer added.

The proportions were so staggering as to be quite incomprehensible, and as we climbed aboard to leave, we resolved to return some day to see the finished work. Surely no monument to freedom would be complete without the countenance of Abraham Lincoln, the Emancipator, and who, we wondered, would peer out from that inner niche when we returned? Would it be Adams, Jackson, Grant, or maybe Teddy Roosevelt?

The memory of Calamity Jane and Deadwood Dick added nothing to the spirit of the great shrine as we passed their final resting place on our way to Deadwood City. Eastward now, past the Badlands and into open prairie country our roving sedan rolled on. Our faithful Studie had crossed its last desert, climbed its last mountain. Now like a tired old horse sensing the end of its journey, it quickened its pace over the flat countryside.

We resigned ourselves of late to a matter-of-fact acceptance of the part our Studie had played in ministering to our comfort and bodily needs. Now, however, as seas of ripening corn and fields of golden stubble fell away, we began reviewing the vehicle with due appreciation - its cooling system, how well it had functioned, the jiffy table, the compact and versatile toilet service with its running water, the quartermastered running boards, the Pullman sleeping quarters. Nor did we forget the curiosity and interest it had aroused along the way. Mostly, however, it was the unorthodox cooker that held our thoughts, and we recounted the many good things that had come from beneath the hood.

Our retrospection came to a quick end. There was a thud, and as I applied the brakes, a shower of feathers flew past our windshield. On the cooler beneath the radiator lay a sage hen, plump and fat from the stubble fields.

"Chicken today! Who'd have thought it?" Harris exclaimed as he plucked away at the remaining plumage.

"And eighty miles till dinner," his mother continued as she added vegetables to the car's contribution. Not content with being chef only, the Studie would be caterer too, keeping the pot filled. My contention that the old car had actually leaped a foot or so to snatch the bird from the air only drew a contemptuous look from Flora, but then she never did have any imagination!

On our arrival in Minneapolis, we bought another rear tire. Then like a family of yokels, we took in the sights until we finally stopped in front of a Chinese restaurant, where we parked. People stared in wonderment at the spectacular vehicle with a buffalo skull fore and a pair of elk antlers aft. Little did they realize the oddities that lay hidden within the intervening space. Weeks of outdoor living had given our family a gypsy look, and as we sat around an ornately carved table, we felt strangely out of place. The tantalizing  odor of exotic dishes, however, soon dispelled any self-consciousness and whetted our appetites. For once we were anxious to forego the offerings of our magic cooker for those of a Chinese chef.

We continued over the Mississippi, hundreds of miles north of our previous crossing. We were soon in the land of lakes, the beautiful forested country of northern Wisconsin. We pitched our tent on the familiar shores of Big Sand Lake and fished for walleye, bass and northern, then finally took off on the last leg of our journey.

In Milwaukee, we received change from a ten dollar traveler's check, the last of fifty such we had purchased at our start. We arrived home by sundown of the same day, broke financially, but rich in a wealth of knowledge and experience. Three whole months of fun and adventure, each day an unforgettable lesson in natural history.

We had traversed seventeen states and camped in most.

E V E R Y W H E R E   W E S T

Surely we had fulfilled our slogan, thus ending the great saga of the old Studie.

Chapter 21

MILL TIME

Our mail box, though a mile and a half distant on the highway, was nevertheless an important part of our institution. The postal system was our only link with our city friends and relatives, two of whom were our own daughters. Although we could drive to our box quickly enough, which we did most of the time, Flora and I preferred to walk when time and weather permitted. An hour so spent was a change, and hardly a week passed that we did not take the hike. We would set out with knapsacks and walking sticks, sometimes through the woods, but more often over our new road to the county line road, thence on to the store and our destination. The whir of duck wings overhead, the sight of a hawk soaring high in the heavens, fresh tracks of a buck in the sand, finding an agate or any one of a dozen such things might influence the trend of our conversation.

Of late Flora's thoughts were mostly on her new grandchild, and when fortune favored us with a letter, she would read it aloud as we trudged slowly homeward. But Ruth's letters were always brief, and with their perfunctory endings, left far too much to the imagination.

"I'll just have to see Kathie with my own eyes to know what she really looks like, I guess," Flora sighed as she finished reading one.

Lois' letters on the other hand were full of humor and revelations in themselves. She left nothing unsaid that might be of interest. Living now with her grandmother and three aunts, she was taking a course of study at the Art Institute. Her creative mind together with her unusual dexterity fitted her well for a career in art. Since her kindergarten days she had shown cleverness in the use of both color and modeling clay, and now her letters confirmed our faith in her future. Pages long, they were often accompanied by sketches of the subject matter.

"If only the trend toward modern art with its misrepresentations, distortion, and general ugliness doesn't catch up with her, she'll make a go of it," I told Flora.

Mother Walker was the source of our really newsy letters. She wrote of church and school activities, of births and deaths among old friends, of social events, always ending with an account of the family doings.

We did not subscribe to a newspaper, because somehow newspapers belonged to that sordid city environment we had so recently escaped. Nor did we have a radio that first year – there was the matter of our budget to be considered. The excitement of our venture, the strangeness that lay everywhere about us, were enough in themselves to keep our minds occupied.

There seemed an interrelationship between all our undertakings. Projects were not entities unto themselves, and seldom were there ends that could be tied off as finished. Each achievement had a way of calling for a sequel. The Jersey demanded a barn and fenced pastures. Cabin sites were inaccessible without roadways to them, and now with winter in the offing, there was no place to store our garden produce.

"Charlie, I just can't put up with this any longer," Flora bewailed as she rolled cabbage and squash beneath the bed. "I'm at my wit's end. Just look at my kitchen shelves – they're running over with canned goods, and those potatoes, onions and carrots on the garage floor, they'll freeze there. You know that. We've got to have a root cellar, that's all there is to it."

I realized the futility of further delay and we set to work digging into a hill behind the house, but as fast as we threw it out, the fine bank sand ran back down into the hole. The result of a half day's shoveling was an excavation about eight feet across at the bottom and sixteen at the top. In this concave pit we built a rectangular room of upright logs resembling a frontier stockade, then filled in around and on top of it. Wooden steps led down to a double thickness door and here in this dark interior we stored our garden stuff, safe enough against winter's freezing temperatures.

With little else than chores on the docket, we tackled our mill in earnest and with clear conscience. The heavy Studie motor together with its transmission was installed as a power plant, and the day of tryout was close at hand. Our conversation about the dinner table had lately developed into a lingo of mechanics and power, gear ratios, leverages, dynamics, RPMs and so on, until Mother balked.

"You men just wait till Lois gets here. We'll talk of nothing but selvages, biases, pinking and appliqués," she snapped back. But I knew better. Though much we said was Greek to her, she was keenly interested in our discussions and listened with more than average feminine understanding.

Processing the logs was to become a major part of our overall program, and though we had somehow managed enough for our first cabin, with a dozen or more buildings yet to be built, we looked to our new mill as a time and labor-saving institution.

The source of our raw material was the vast forest of jackpine that had proliferated in the cut-over country. Though most immature trees find their way to paper mills, much of the larger timber is milled locally into lumber. Jackpine is a low grade timber, about on par with the sucker in the fish realm. Its bark is shaggy, drab and unattractive. Nevertheless, the forests are fast growing and seemingly inexhaustible, a constant source of revenue for the woodsman. Spring cut logs are best for peeling, for when the sap has risen, the bark slips off easily. Left unpeeled, however, logs set their bark a little tighter each succeeding day. Winter cut logs, on the other hand, cling tightly to their shaggy coats and require a sharp edged blade to pare away the bark. This procedure leaves long strips of inner bark of reddish brown, not unpleasing to the eye. Heavy stands of jackpine grow straight and tall and sparse of limbs making it ideal timber for log cabins, averaging about three eight-foot logs to a tree.

A mountain of this timber now lay on the long skidway waiting to be slabbed on two sides, peeled of bark, washed clean of sap, then dried and stained a golden brown. Our thirty-inch circular saw close by looked businesslike and ready to go, the cutting edge of each large tooth bright and keen from recent sharpening. We had gotten it along with its arbor at a farm auction in a package lot of rusty junk. It spun easily now, its bearings set firmly in a heavy buttress of concrete. Though the day had witnessed the finishing touches on our mill, darkness and hordes of mosquitoes took over, postponing its initiation, much to our disappointment. Around the fireplace that evening, impatience was written on every face, like that of children awaiting Christmas day and shiny new toys.

The morning sun crept over the tree tops, touching first the uppermost tier of logs, then sending fingers of light here and there about our mill as though searching for some imperfection. This was a day in our calendar that could mean much in the march toward our goal. Old Sol was not our only visitor on this auspicious day, for ironically enough our good neighbor, Maurice Sylvester, was on hand, having followed our progress with more than a little interest and some skepticism.

Pointing now to the direct hookup we had made between the saw and motor, he advised with emphasis, "You fellers'll never get away with it. I've worked around a lot of mills in my time, and I've never seen one without a belt. Why, there's not enough flexibility, anyone

will tell you that."

"Maybe you're right, Maurice, but you know there's got to be a first time for everything," I countered.

"See that gearshift lever?" Harris cut in. "Well, that means we can shift into any one of three speeds from low to high. And take a look at that big universal joint – that'll give us all the flexibility we want."

There was no reply, but with a jerk of his hand our neighbor set the big saw spinning, then stepped back to check it with a critical eye.

"Runs true enough," he said, "but I'd like to see it in action."

"Well, it won't be long now," Harris said as he sank the dogs into a shaggy-coated log on the carriage.

Beyond the mill, in the dark shadows of the woods, I could make out the body of our old Studie, quite worthless and forgotten. Its chassis lay in the hazel brush, stripped of every nut, bolt and removable part. Touched now by the mounting sun, the aluminum cooker drew my attention, calling to mind the part it had played on our long westward journey. Was this then the grand finale of it all, the end of our camping days, our trips to far-away places? Had I not been too hasty in my giving in to the boys. But there was little time for soliloquy now.

"She's ready to go," Harris shouted.

As Bruce bent over, crank in hand, I remembered how well the motor had performed on the road. Would it do as well now, pinned as it was to the earth? There was a moment of suspense until it took hold, then it idled with the old accustomed purr. Would it carry through when under a load, or would it sputter and stop for want of power? We would see.

"Try her first in low," Harris shouted from his stand at the carriage. Bruce carefully shifted gears, then easing out the clutch, he opened the throttle. The saw started to turn, and built up in crescendo until it reached a sustained hum. A smile of confidence now lighted our master-craftsman's face as he prepared for the all-important test. Slowly the butt end of the first log approached the whirring teeth, then the woods awakened to a high-pitched whine as the saw bit its way throughout the length of the log.

"Now try her in second," Harris shouted as again he bent to push the carriage over the strap-iron rails. Once more a surge of power came, and once more a golden slice fell away from the prostrate log. Yet the real surprise came, and with it not a little satisfaction, when a cut was completed in high gear, with evident ease and smoothness. The two lower gears might well have been eliminated, as we were never to use them again. Though the initial tryout of the mill had performed beyond our fondest hopes, Maurice preferred to withhold his opinion till later on.

"Wait till you've finished all those logs there in that pile - that'll tell the story," he said.

Processing of logs proved a long and tedious job. After being slabbed on two sides they were rolled onto the peeling ramp to be stripped of their remaining bark. From there they continued on to the dunking tank where they were scrubbed in hot, sudsy water. Now bright and free from sap that would otherwise mildew and turn black, the logs were stacked in aerated piles to dry. This accomplished, they were then colored a light brown with a creosote stain, simulating the shade of fallen leaves. Following this final touch, the logs were hauled to the building site and stacked according to their variation in quarter inch sizes.

We spelled each other about the mill, acting as sawyer, rolling logs about the ramp, peeling, or washing them. There was plenty to do, and we were glad enough for Flora's help, as she insisted on doing a great portion of the washing. Later when Lois came, she helped her mother. Flora said one day, when I thought she was overdoing it, "I'd rather scrub logs out here beneath the sky than floors in the house." The job of mixing the pigment to the right color quite naturally fell to me, and like Flora, I too preferred it to other work such as chores about the barn.

To stand idly by and watch the goings on about a busy saw mill, to see and hear heavy logs go thumping down the ramp, to see them respond so easily to every whim of the woodsman, to catch the rhythm of it all, is indeed a fascinating experience, and all the more so to the uninitiated city dweller. Our mill was but a toy in comparison to such an institution. Ours lacked a power-operated carriage that shuttled back and forth under control of the sawyer, or a roof overhead for inclement weather. It had, however, many things in common, for instance the whine of the saw that echoed throughout the woods and the omnipresent odor of freshly cut timber.

Chapter 22

FETCHING LOGS

Our boys, with a couple of pals, had driven over to the Ferguson forty for a load of logs that had been previously cut and lay ready for hauling. With the promise of a busy day ahead about the mill, I had kindled a fire beneath the dunking tank when to my surprise, I heard the truck returning. Surely, I thought, they couldn't have loaded in so short a time.

No sooner had Harris stepped from the cab than he started berating our neighbor to the south in terms hardly befitting his even temperament.

"Pa, when we got to the forty, we found barbed wire stretched across the road. I thought that was funny so we went on down to Ferguson's house to see what it was all about. Will was there with a couple of fellows and he told me that you had no right to any more of that timber, that it all belonged to him now."

"That's right, Pa. He was pretty ornery about it," Bruce broke in.

When I heard them through, I realized there was trouble ahead. Better take it easy, there're generally two sides to every story, but the more I considered the matter, the more worked up I became.

While the boys waited, I took off to talk over the matter with Flora, as she was familiar with all the circumstances surrounding the deal. Out came our old tin box, and from among its papers she drew forth the Ferguson contract. Together we went over it, searching for some irregularity, some loophole that would justify his action.

We could find nothing, nor was there any time limit set for the removal of the timber. Mad through and through, I started back.

"Now don't you go and fly off the handle, Charlie. They're neighbors, you know. Just hold that temper of yours," Flora admonished.

Fortified now with the contract, I climbed aboard the cab and stepped on the starter. The boys stood behind, on the platform, legs spread and leaning on their axe handles for support. I wanted no trouble but that timber was mine and I meant to have it. I had seen fights in movies, woodsmen against woodsmen, over just such matters, though I was sure nothing like that would happen even if the boys were in a belligerent frame of mind. I would keep the peace but be firm in my demands. However, the sight of those tightly stretched wires only heightened the tension on my overwrought nerves.

At the Ferguson place the boys jumped from the truck, axes in hand, and we made for the small porch where Bill and his men were evidently awaiting us.

"Bill," I shouted angrily in spite of my good intentions, "how come that barbed wire is there on that forty?"

"Say Charlie, you've got no more claim on that timber and you know it; your time has run out."

"Says you! Since when has my time run out?"

"Since right now. You've had all year to cut that timber and haul your logs. Why didn't you do it?"

"Because I didn't have to, that's why. You know very well there's no time limit in that contract. I'll take that timber any time I want some and I happen to want some right now."

"Oh, no, you won't! That forty belongs to me, and everything on it. I've got the deed and that's that."

"OK, Bill, just take a look at your copy of the contract. That'll put you straight once and for all."

"I never had any contract."

"Oh yes you did," I shouted, pulling mine from my pocket and waving it before his eyes. "Here, this is my copy. Listen to what it says. It's dated Sep. 27, 1933, and says, 'Received of C. J. Palmer the sum of forty-two dollars, being payment in full for the standing timber of all kinds on the property described as follows: The NW Quarter of the SW Quarter of Sec. 18, Twp 39, Range 13 west. It is further understood that the seller, Mr. Ferguson, shall haul out all logs to a place where they may be loaded onto a truck, said work to be included in above price. Signed, W. D. Ferguson.' Tell me, Bill, did you hear anything about a time limit in that contract? You bet you didn't. Now take a gander at that signature. It's yours, isn't it?" There was no reply. Slowly Bill rose to his feet and rolled up his sleeves.

"That's right, Fergie, come on down from that porch 'n I'll show you who owns that timber."

I turned to see Harris peeling off his jacket. "Put it back on, son," I said, "there's not going to be a fight here if I can help it."

"Well, Pa, I just can't take any more of that stuff he's handing out."

Bill, too, was sticking to his guns and was ready to accept my challenge, but my quick intervention staved off any brawl. Realizing the futility of further argument, I turned toward the truck, the boys at my heels. The barbed wire fence proved no obstruction to our pent up anger, and soon the militant woodsmen were expending their energy swinging their axes.

The trouble did not end there, for the following day a car rolled in over our new road and stopped before our shop. The man at the wheel was a stranger, and I wondered why he had come.

"I'm Bob Willis," he said as he slid from the seat of his Model T, "Deputy Sheriff of Washburn County. Your name is Palmer?" he questioned as he sized me up.

"That's right, my name is Palmer."

"Well, I'm here to warn you not to cut or haul any more timber from the Ferguson place."

"Now hold on. Not so fast, Sheriff; there's another side to this story. That timber belongs to me and not to Mr. Ferguson," I continued.

"Why, he showed me the deed to that property just this morning. That makes it his, doesn't it?"

"Well, not exactly. Here, just take a look at this," I said, handing him the contract I still had in my pocket.

There was a look of incredulity when he looked up from the paper, and pointing to the document he said, "Do you mean to tell me that's Bill Ferguson's signature?"

"It sure is, and you can verify it any time you want to go to the trouble. Now listen to me – I paid the back taxes on that forty and gave the land to Bill. I retained the timber rights, as you can see. He told me he was sick of paying rent and wanted a place of his own, and I was helping him get it. That's all there is to it, believe it or not."

"Well, that puts a different slant on the matter. Do you know he's putting it in the hands of a lawyer? He sure has got his nerve. I suggest that you run in and talk it over with Glenn Douglas. You know, there in town."

"But why should I run in? If he wants to see me, let him come out here."

"Now see here, Mr. Palmer, you don't want to get involved in some long, drawn out legal case. Keep it out of court if you can. Anyhow, see Mr. Douglas and show him that contract, that's my advice. You'll be going to town soon, no doubt, and that will be time enough."

There was little else talked about that night. I still insisted that the burden of proof lay on Bill, and the boys shared my opinion. Flora, on the other hand, saw it differently and agreed with the sheriff, which meant some amicable settlement out of court. Some few days later I stopped in at Douglas and Omernik's law office, though somewhat reluctantly.

"Yes, I did want to see you, Mr. Palmer. I'm glad you came," Mr. Douglas said when I had introduced myself. "Bob Willis tells me you have a contract with Mr. Ferguson, giving you title to the timber on his place. Is that correct?"

"Yes."

"May I see it?" I handed him the papers, hoping he wouldn't scrutinize my poor attempt at legal phraseology. When he finished reading he said, "Does Mr. Ferguson have a copy of this contract, Mr. Palmer?"

"He sure had one," I replied, then I told him my side of the story.

"Well now, if you'll excuse me, I'll get Mr. Ferguson here. I know he's in town and I think I know where to find him."

When they entered Bill seemed surprised to see me and with hardly more than a nod in my direction, he seated himself.

"Now, Mr. Palmer, will you repeat in Mr. Ferguson's presence the story you told me?" the lawyer asked. I did so and when I finished, he turned and said, "Is this all true, Mr. Ferguson?"

"Well, I guess it is, all but that part about the contract; I never did have a copy of that. I supposed Mr. Palmer had only a year to get the timber off the place."

"Is that your signature?" the lawyer asked, holding up the contract so Bill could see it.

"Well, it looks like it is. I guess it is, but really don't remember signing any such paper."

162

"That will do," Mr. Douglas said, and rising he went into an inner office. I heard a typewriter clicking while Bill and I sat waiting. Presently the door opened.

"I think this should be satisfactory to both parties concerned," he said as he handed us a typewritten agreement as follows:

AGREEMENT

Whereas a dispute has arisen between C. J. Palmer and W. D. Ferguson concerning the timber located on the NW Quarter of Section 18, township 39 north, of range 13 west, in Washburn County, Wisconsin, and

Whereas the parties to this agreement have agreed to settle all disputes, claims, and mutually release all causes of action which either party may have or claim to have against the other,

IT IS HEREBY AGREED AS FOLLOWS:

1. C. J. Palmer is to have all jack pine, Norway pine, white pines and tamarack of all sizes now standing or being on the property described herein, which timber is to be removed from the property herein described by not later than June 1, 1935, and any timber remaining after that time shall belong to Mr. W. D. Ferguson.

2. That all other timber, standing or being on the property herein, described, shall belong to W. D. Ferguson.

3. That either party may have free access to and on said estate, and particularly, C. J. Palmer shall have right to make use of the north gate as an entrance to said property.

4. That W. D. Ferguson shall have the right to cut wood belonging to him at any time, and shall have the privilege of cleaning up the brush left by Mr. Palmer in cutting trees.

5. That any timber in trees belonging to and cut by Mr. Palmer which is swamped out, is to be taken by Mr. Palmer, and anything that Mr. Palmer does not swamp out is understood to be left for the use of Mr. Ferguson.

IN WITNESS HEREOF, said parties have hereunto set their hands and seals this 8th day of November, 1934.

In presence of:

Glenn R. Douglas	C. J. Palmer
Isabel Pike	W. D. Ferguson

I read the document over carefully. June 1st to get the timber. Well, why not? I'd have had it off before that anyhow. There wasn't so much left. Then, too, what if Bill had actually lost his copy of the contract? What if he was really honest in thinking my time had expired? Maybe Bob Willis was right after all. "Better keep it out of court," he had said. Swallowing my pride, I affixed my signature alongside that of my neighbor and pocketed my copy.

Some time later I ran into Bill.

"Say Charlie," he said "you haven't forgotten that promise you made me that day we got the deed fixed to that property, have you?"

"What was that, Bill? I can't say I remember."

"Why, you promised to leave a few big jacks standing for shade where I'm going to build my house."

"So I did, but I really had forgotten. You just blaze the ones you want, and I'll remind the boys not to cut them."

Time has confirmed the logic of my action. For many years the Fergusons remained our good neighbors to the south. And though the tall jacks have long since succumbed and the house stands empty, there is an air about that place which awakens my memory as I drive past on my way to town.

Chapter 23

THE HUNT

Old timers tell of deer being scarce in the days of the big timber. Now, however, vast thickets of underbrush, acres of slender popple, seas of scrub oak, and dense dark stands of jackpine that have since taken over provide ideal cover not only for these timid animals but for all manner of wildlife.

Fishing is allowed from early spring till late fall, then one may drop his line through a hole in the winter ice if he is so minded, but the nimrod who would hunt deer must confine his sport to a few days in late November. The Conservation Department is responsible for the preservation of wildlife and they prescribe the time and conditions under which deer may be taken. In the minds of a few who exist mostly upon the natural resources of the country, such laws are subservient to their innate rights to eat venison at any time they see fit. Jackpine farmers subsisting on poor sandy soil are not above taking a little government veal now and then, and one can readily understand their logic. When I hear a shot reverberate throughout the woods, I realize that some distant neighbor, or Indian perhaps, is living up to his convictions. But God help the bootlegger who kills for profit, for if he is caught, no one else will.

For one in the recreational business, he is sure to be barraged with endless questions about these beautiful creatures. Mounted heads in our cabins seldom fail to arouse interest and not a little comment.

"Did you shoot that deer yourself, Mr. Palmer?" "Are there many deer around here," and "Where can we go to see them?" Dozens of such questions may be expected each season.

Every deer hunter has his own repertoire of stories and he is always ready to inflict them upon any and all who will lend an ear. Ask him about his greatest thrill, though, and chances are he will reply, "Why, it was the time I shot my first buck."

Though I have taken my share of deer over the years and have forgotten most of the accompanying circumstances, a few still remain outstanding in my mind. Having hunted only small game on the flat open prairies of Illinois, my first deer hunt in the woods of Wisconsin was an occasion of magnitude, and like all such experiences, anticipation played no small part in it. While Flora sewed bright red patches on my hunting togs, my mind was on the morrow. I slipped my 30-30 Winchester from its oil-stained cover. The feel of its smooth walnut stock, the soft luster of its blue steel barrel, the smell of gun oil - the whole bewitching ensemble fired my imagination until I was deep in a jungle of thought.

"I do hope you get one, Charlie." The words exploded like bullets bringing me to my senses. "You know we need the meat" Flora continued, "and it'll be such a welcome change. Fish and chicken, chicken and fish; I'm getting tired of them."

"Well, if I don't have any luck, maybe Harris will. The Sylvesters and Nortons really know their stuff. I doubt if there're more deer in the Moose Road country than there are right around here." I threw my rifle to my shoulder several times to get the feel of it. Tomorrow, I thought, its small peep sight will frame my first buck.

"I'm going to get up before daylight to do the milking. You had better keep LuluBelle in the barnyard, just to play it safe," I said to Flora pulling off my shoes.

"I'll get your breakfast before you go, Charlie, and do be careful. I'm so afraid of those stray bullets."

In the breaking daylight brittle leaves crunched as I took off through the barnyard. Better work upwind, I thought, but could sense no movement in the air. I slipped cartridges into the magazine; one, two, three, four, five, and pumped one into the chamber. If I get that many shots today I'll be happy. With an itchy trigger finger, impatient and overanxious, I found it hard to hold back. At the pasture fence I checked the safety on my rifle and tried for a silent crossing, but the taut wires squealed from post to post as my weight bore down on them.

Outside my own domain now, with my eyes and ears open, I pushed along an old deer trail. In and out of underbrush, through open glades, beneath low-hanging branches, up hill and down, the sylvan path led until I was confused as to my whereabouts. Suddenly a shot rang out, then another and another in rapid succession, resounding beats of a gavel opening deer season -- the wilderness was alive with hunters, both individual and in gangs. What direction this firing came from was hard to tell - ahead or behind, it made little difference.

Before me lay a low-spreading bed of sphagnum moss. Though it looked foreboding it proved safe enough, its fibrous growth springing beneath each step as though one were walking on a mattress. The few symmetrical balsams that had taken precarious root reminded me that Christmas was in the offing. Once more I took my stand on higher ground, my little-used leg muscles sore, and sweat trickling beneath my heavy jacket. From this elevated position the view showed the highway far to the north and the cranberry marsh where I had been recently, to borrow a breaker plow. To the east a thin line of smoke threaded upward against a crimson sky. Someone about in the store – Charlie, maybe, or more likely his father, for Charlie would be deep in the woods with Keith Kimball and his party.

Bang! Bang! Bang! Bang! A barrage of shots near enough to startle me. Then shouting. From where? Yes, up the highway there beyond the creek, two hunters. Maybe I'll get a shot. Better check my rifle. Two more red coats emerged and I watched till the whole party took to the woods again, evidently empty handed. How could anyone mistake a man for a deer, I could not help but wonder, recalling the many accidents recorded annually. Boy, it's getting cold. Better dance around a bit…Wait, what's that noise? Only a woodpecker there on that charred stump.

There was shooting now in the direction of our own back forty. Must be Fergie and his gang making a drive. Should have stayed near home. The distant, drawn-out bawl of LuluBelle. Was she safe, there by the barn? Everywhere there was desultory shooting; the country was alive with hunters, and deer, too, if one could judge from the noise. I could even distinguish larger calibers from smaller, and at times the sharp snap of a percussion cap could be detected before the heavier rumble. Black powder.

As yet I had seen neither hide nor hair of any critter, much less a deer, and my patience was wearing thin. Shifting concentration to an apple that Flora had slipped into my pocket, I stomped my feet, swung my arms and hunched my shoulders to keep warm. This manner of hunting was all strange to me. Several times I drew bead on an imaginary target. Would I get buck fever, or was that a lot of hooey?

Seems like every one is getting a shot but -- Bang! Bang! Bang! Very close. My thumb searched desperately for the hammer, and my heart pounded as I scanned the dense gully at my feet. Suddenly the alders exploded and a buck bounded out, and just as quickly the big rack of horns disappeared. I hadn't so much as raised a finger.

"Did you see him go by?" Startled, I turned to see a hunter on the spoor of his kill. "I hit him all right; there's blood on the grass," he shouted once more, his eyes to the ground.

I followed, my gun at half-cock - maybe he'll lose the trail, and I'll get a shot after all. But the further we penetrated the dense cover, the more frequent the splotches of blood, and the less my chance for the coup de grace. Finally, at the creek beyond the bed of sphagnum moss, I came upon both the hunter and the hunted, a ten-point buck. Evidently it had been too weak to cross. As to the former, he told me that we had shared the same hill top, his stand being but a bow shot from mine. Though he knew of my presence, I had not known of his.

Flora had eaten her lunch by the time I reached home. She listened quietly to the account of my morning's failure, then voiced her feelings as she set coffee before me.

"If you'd only done this and you'd only done that, you'd have brought home the bacon. Well, it's not too late yet. What do you say we go out together this afternoon? I'll drive the deer and you do the shooting." Not a bad idea, but I had some qualms as to her staying power in the tangle of brush she would encounter. Standing at the mirror in improvised cardinal patchwork, her silver hair tucked well beneath her woolen tam, she looked no different than the average nimrod that afternoon.

"Now I can hike to the store any time without being scared to death. But Charlie, are you sure I don't need a hunting license with this outfit?"

"Just don't get caught with a gun in your hands and you'll be OK as far as the law is concerned."

High hopes of thick venison steaks imbued our minds as we

closed the door behind us and headed across the barnyard. While I shoved shells into the magazine again, Flora forked hay to LuluBelle. We parted company, she taking off for the new road while I moved northward through the woods for a predetermined position on our back forty. Beneath a large Norway I took my stand, here to await the results of her drive. Chickadees hopped nervously about, scratching here and there among the dry leaves for food, a red-headed wood-pecker hammered close by and overhead a whining crow voiced indignation when discovering my hideout. Surely Flora was on her way through by now.

Gun in hand I waited expectantly, alert to every sound and move-ment in the thicket before me. The wait seemed like hours. I was about to abandon my stand and go in search, when the snap of a twig brought me around pronto. There she was, red tam and all, disheveled and worn and approaching from an entirely unexpected direction. While we munched apples, she related her experience. Try as she might, she had been unable to keep her bearings in the sea of underbrush about her. While I fumed and fussed over my stand, she was off in some other quarter trying to orient her position with the rest of the world. Though she had played her part with purpose and the tenacity of a hound dog, it was all to no use. The closest she ever came to our quarry was several bedding-down places recently aban-doned. Except for that fever-keen thrill of anticipation, the afternoon proved unrewarding, and sundown found our family larder as bare as proverbial Mother Hubbard's cupboard.

However, the season was yet young. The following morning I was deep in the woods once more, determined more than ever to catch up with one of the many antlered creatures I had seen during the sum-mer. If yesterday's noisy barrage was any indication, I knew that by now a tawny carcass hung in many a neighborhood dooryard. Nor was Byrnes Store any exception, for there by the highway, for all to see, was a big buck, suspended tail down from a tree limb.

As for me, however, ill luck continued to hound my footsteps. Trails that looked promising enough developed nothing more sub-stantial than hoof-prints in the soft earth, and brush filled ravines contributed nothing larger than an occasional partridge or rabbit. So noontime of my second day found me hunched over my coffee in anything but a genial frame of mind, quite ready to admit my failure as a deerslayer.

Back on the open prairies of Chicagoland, my hunting had been confined to small game with a scatter gun or a .22 rifle, and I had been successful enough. Here, however, in the wooded north country conditions were different. Could I adapt myself to the change. Could I handle a 30-30 Winchester with the proficiency of a smaller caliber, and would that malady known as buck fever stay my trigger finger at the critical moment?

"I'll tell you what," Flora exclaimed, startling me from my reverie. "You go out alone this afternoon and stay until dark; I'll do the milking for you."

Had I heard her correctly? "You'll do the milking?" I exploded. "Why, you've never so much as laid a hand on a cow, much less milk one."

"Well, I can if I have to. I've watched Lois, and you remember she nearly filled the pail her first time." Far be it from me to object, I thought. Maybe she would take over sometime when I wanted to go fishing.

"Well, it's OK by me, and thank you for your offer, but remember, Flora, you asked for it."

Funny what a full stomach will do for one's morale, I mused as I stepped outside. My confidence now told me I could hit a peanut at fifty yards. At our pasture fence I aimed at an imaginary buck as it bounded across the road before me. Beyond the gate a few paces brought me to my destination, a prone oak felled by the wind. Surveying the near surroundings proved it was a perfect place for a stand. I stomped the noise from brittle leaves beneath my feet, placed my watch conveniently on the rough bark, and with elbows atop the heavy bole, started my long vigil. A stone's throw distance a well-defined trail diagonalled across the pasture to parts unknown, and on this bit of spoor, my hopes were pinned.

Not a breath stirred in the treetops, and only an occasional shot echoed in far off hills to disturb the midday quiet. The woods were so still, the only sound was the ticking of the dollar watch at my elbow. One thirty; a long wait till dark but worth it if only I can get a shot or two. Two o'clock. More shooting now, but nothing near my own field of operation.

Two thirty! By now I had familiarized myself with every detail within range of my rifle. What at first appeared a squirrel's nest of leaves later proved to be a pair of partridges on a limb. Further along a fire-blackened stump took on the semblance of a standing bear, and my pulse quickened when later on a rabbit hopped leisurely from the brush as though to tempt my marksmanship, a reminder for me to check my rifle. Yes, I had pumped a cartridge into the barrel all right, and the hammer stood at half cock. And so the vigil continued.

Three o'clock! Three thirty! And still nothing doing. Was this day to be a repetition of yesterday? Was ill luck still dogging my footsteps? The monotony of inaction set me to pacing to and fro with the measured beat of a sentinel.

Four o'clock! Back on my stand, my egotism waning with each minute of the dying day. Four thirty. I heard the distant and muffled sound of a closing door and then a long drawn-out bawl from LuluBelle. Flora was on her way to the barnyard. She'll do well to finish milking by dark.

As the soft horizons of dusk closed in, the futility of my long vigil swept over me with a vengeance. I slumped over the prone trunk to acknowledge defeat, when with startled suddenness came a snort at my very back. I swung about to see a buck wheel and take off. With shaken nerves I managed somehow to cock the hammer and jerk the gun to my shoulder. Would darkness rob me of a shot? To my astonishment, there, not ten rods distant, the creature stood, his head turned to indulge his curiosity. Though scarcely able to draw a bead, I let go. What a great disappointment as when with a bound, he cleared the pasture fence, hardly more than a phantom shadow.

Despite my failure to connect, the ludicrousness of this situation somehow struck my funnybone and I burst out laughing. With my heart still pounding, I wondered which of the two had been the more frightened, hunter or hunted. The irony of it! A big buck virtually breathing down my neck and nothing to show for it. What will Flora say?

There was more to this incident than met the eye, however, for a strong odor hung about the place, an odor so strong as to be quite obnoxious. Sudden fright, no doubt, had over-actuated the creature's musk glands, a situation I was never to encounter again in all my years of deer hunting.

"I'll get you tomorrow," I said as in my mind's eye I saw once more the antlered specter melt away in the darkness.

Still amused by the humor of it all, I told the story to Flora, leaving nothing to her imagination.

"Well, that buck's not the only thing around here that stinks. Just you take a whiff of my hair," she exclaimed, lowering her silver tresses in my direction.

"Phew! How come?"

"Well, you know, I didn't have sense enough to cover my hair when I did the milking, that's how come. I had my head up against that smelly cow for more than an hour. You can hunt all you want, Charlie, but there's one thing for sure – from now on, you're going to do all the milking. Now I'm going to take a bath if you don't mind."

Beneath the covers that night I reviewed the afternoon's fiasco with true perspective. If only I had chosen my stand on the other side of the tree, or on the other hand if only the buck had come from the other direction. Better still if he had come in the light of day, how different my story might have been. So I rationalized, with no end of 'ifs' to establish my reasoning.

The thought of my watch there on the rough bark was a reminder that I had forgotten it entirely, had left it behind to tick the night hours away. With the morning's milking done, I set out before breakfast to retrieve the neglected timepiece, taking my rifle along, just in case. Arriving at the pasture fence where last I had seen the buck, I was drawn by curiosity to the roadside. Had he left any tracks in his hasty retreat.

Sure enough, there they were, etched deeply in the sand, and what's more, to my astonishment they showed evidence of a wounded animal. One hind leg had dragged, plowing a furrow across the roadway. That shot in the dark, had it actually found its mark? Was there a crippled deer somewhere in the woods, suffering, awaiting death perhaps? I regretted yesterday's rashness now and determined to do what I could to make amends.

Flecks of blood on the grass and leaves only spurred me on as I entered the woods. I had hardly set foot on the trail however, when I found myself face to face with a real live buck. Startled out of my wits, I froze in my tracks and watched him turn aside and disappear in the brush. I hadn't so much as raised a hand, though its white flag was discernible for some distance. Buck fever? Well, perhaps. Anyhow, the creature was too fast for me or I was too slow for him.

Chagrined by my obvious panic, I started in pursuit, hoping for a lucky shot in some open glade further on. I had no more than left the trail when again I stopped short in surprise, for there at my feet lay yesterday's buck, still and cold...He had dropped not far from where he'd been hit, and the dark stained area beneath his sleek body was evidence enough of a fatal wound. I realized the importance of dressing out a deer, or any other edible creature, as quickly as possible. This one had lain unattended overnight. Was our family to forego the needed venison under the circumstances? Not if I could help it.

This was my first deer, my first kill, and any thought of abandoning so much meat was unthinkable. Head downward upon a knoll, the creature had bled profusely. Furthermore the night temperature had been considerably below freezing, reason enough for my decision. With a pounding heart and a shaky hand, I dressed out the carcass, and with bloodstained hands, dragged it to the roadside. What a rack of horns; better still, what a store of red meat for the winter months to come.

Such is the saga of my first deer, an insignificant incident beyond our domain, perhaps, but one of importance to our family who had come to the wilderness for livelihood.

Chapter 24

THE JOURNEY

Thanksgiving time was at hand. We counted on our fingers the material blessings that contributed toward our happiness and welfare. Some of these we had earned, to be sure, others we had not. Benevolent hearts had opened on our behalf, and even nature had been overly generous in her giving. It was a time of acknowledgment, of retrospection, of thanks for things accomplished, and, too, a time for one big sigh of relief.

The trees were bare now and we could see deeply into the woods, a slinking fox, perhaps, or a roosting partridge on a distant limb. Snugly housed as we were, we paid little heed to winter's early threats of storm and cold. Biting winds leaving their evanescent trails of white only heightened our sense of security. Mostly the days were bright and sparkling, and so calm that an occasional voice could be heard from over the frozen lake – Harold's perhaps, or his grandmother's. The hard earth, too, gave added resonance to our mill saw, its intermittent whine reverberating clearly throughout the woods.

With the first fall of snow came a vastly different world, one fresh and invitingly new. Things were no longer what they seemed. In the thicket beside the mill lay the old Studie body, silent and inert as a tombstone, its angular lines softened now by a mound of white. No pathway led to its resting place. Only the lacy trail of tiny rodents disturbed its smooth and sparkling mantle, as a family of big-eared mice had commandeered its plushy interior for their winter quarters. Although the Studie motor had found a permanent spot in our plans, no such place could be found for the rusting tonneau. Even Bruce, with his inventive mind, was at a loss to put it to some practical use. Time and resourcefulness would one day find need for the abandoned body, of that I was confident. To what purpose I could not even venture a guess, and perhaps it was just as well.

If the family of kangaroo mice were warm and comfortable beneath the snow, so too were we in our new quarters. No more turning pages with mittened hands, no watching the night through in outer garments. Our hikes to the mail box were less frequent now and Flora reacted only mildly to the charm of the fresh winter landscape. Of late, the beauty of the woods, the angling birches, naked oaks, the evergreen of the pine drew little comment from her. Her mind was elsewhere, her thoughts upon one thing that lay nearest her heart. Tunes seldom heard since our children were small now accompanied the hum of her sewing machine as she stitched tiny garments. We had no picture of Kathie, though Lois included sketches in her letters. Even a three-dimensional likeness modeled in clay did little to stay a grandmother's curiosity. The time had come when only the feel of soft baby flesh would satisfy her maternal longing.

Much as we enjoyed our new house, we men were obliged to spend many hours in the shop. With the sun's rays upon its thin roof boards and a good oak fire in its stove, we were comfortable enough. Wheels and pulleys which had lain idle much of the summer now spun once more. Time now was a commodity to do with as we pleased. With no schedules, no deadlines to meet, we found opportunity for creative expression and the development of new ideas, especially along the line of cabin construction.

"Pa," Harris said one day as he poked about in a pile of scrap metal beneath the bench. "We've got to have a better way to square our log ends. They don't fit against the uprights like they should. I've got a rough idea for a jig I'd like to see carried out." This came as no surprise to me. Since building Crow's Nest, the matter had been uppermost in my mind. For perfect cuts, to say nothing of good workmanship, it was obvious that a saw-guiding device of some kind was necessary. To this end, then, we set to work.

Within a rectangular framework of oak, Harris built a bank of drawers, storage places for various tools and equipment, and upon this sturdy base we fabricated a rig made of steel. Along the bench's eight foot length, Harris countersunk a slotted iron channel which he had previously calibrated into inches and fractions thereof. Sliding in this slot was a moveable tail block that could be locked at any desired calibration. An adjustable head block slotted for a crosscut saw not only assured us perfect right angle cuts, both vertically and laterally, but also acted as a clamping device to hold the log in position. To accomplish this, we made use of the steering wheel and column from our discarded Studie body. A single spin of the wheel actuated a countershaft which brought both head block and clamping dogs, made from motorcycle connecting rods, simultaneously into play. This device was the result of composite thought and effort, providing not only precision end cuts, but exact log lengths as well. Since all horizontal wall logs were to be laid up between slabbed uprights, the value of such a contrivance was obvious.

The short winter days passed quickly enough for our busy hands working in the shop. For Mother, however, it was different. Alone in the house with her thoughts, the days seemed long as Christmas time drew near. She missed her absent family. There was Ruth, her eldest, and now baby Kathie. She tried in vain to conjure up a picture of Kathie in her mind. She also missed the companionship of Lois with her exuberant spirit and willing hands. Though Lois' letters were bits of her real self projected into our midst, they did little to fill her vacant place at our table. Our children were maturing. Lois in particular was growing up, maturing in spite of herself. Her every mention of Kenny was a reminder that some day, all too soon perhaps, she, like Ruth, would take on the responsibilities of matrimony.

If I knew Mother, however, her spell of loneliness was but a seasonal one of short duration. Her thoughts of the Christmas holidays with only two of her children about, and neither her mother nor her sisters, were nothing short of heartsick, but she would get over it.

Lazy snowflakes were drifting slowly down one day when Harris entered and tossed a letter on the table. "It's from Gram," he said as he brushed white flakes from his shoulder.

"Good! A letter from home!" Mother said with fresh excitedment. We followed her into the living room as she tore open the envelope, Christmas seals and all. Seated about the open hearth we listened to news of the neighborhood we had known so well, news of school and church, and the doings of old friends. But toward the end, at the mention of Christmas, we sat up and took notice.

"Now as to your coming down for the holidays," Mother read loud and clear.

"Hey! Read that again," Harris directed.

"I'll say," Bruce echoed.

"Now you just wait 'til I finish," Mother cut in with a raised hand. She continued, "We must have some kind of understanding about your plans for Christmas, for if we are to send our package, we must know in time. Manora is planning for you at the table and we want to order the turkey. With you folks, we are figuring on about twenty, that is including a friend or two. You won't disappoint us, I know, though it may entail some inconvenience on your part."

For a while no one spoke; we just looked at one another. Lois had come up on the train to spend her Christmas vacation with us, but the thought of gathering the entire family in the Walker house still tugged powerfully upon us.

"Well, what do you say, Charlie?" asked Flora at length. "Do you think it's at all possible?"

Though in a way I had anticipated this very situation, for a moment I was at a loss for an answer. "Flora," I said finally, "I don't want to be a crepe hanger, especially around Christmas, but you know yourself the idea is preposterous. It's impossible. In the first place, we haven't a car to travel in. And as for railroad fare, well obviously that's out."

"But Charlie, there must be some way to make it come. As for me, I won't give up till we've exhausted every possible means of getting there."

"There's only one solution so far as I can see and this is for you and Lois to go down on the train," I said. "The boys and I can make out OK while you are gone."

"Don't be ridiculous. You know very well I wouldn't go a step unless we all go."

"Well, I'm sorry, but I don't see any other way out."

After a moment's hesitation Flora continued. "I've got a lot of things for Kathleen, little things I've been working on for a long time. I suppose I'll have to mail them now."

"Who's Kathleen? Oh, you mean Kathie."

"Shame on you, Charlie Palmer, you're not funny at all. Don't ever let Ruth hear you talk that way. Now tell me, am I to wait forever to see that child?"

Thus far the boys had kept silent, but now Harris ventured a possible solution. "Pa, why can't three of us crowd into the cab of the truck, and two of us ride back on the platform. We could take turns, you know. Except of course Mother."

"Yes, and freeze to death," Bruce expostulated. "Do you know how cold it was here last night? Fifteen below, that's how cold. Now listen to me.

I've got an idea. Why not put the old Studie body on the truck platform and we can all go down?"

"In style!" Harris laughed.

Mother's wistful face lit up with animation. "Yes, why not? It's a splendid idea," she exclaimed. "We'll start getting ready tomorrow."

The next few days were busy ones. While sorting and packing went on inside, the cow and calf were driven over the wind-swept highway and housed in Sylvester's big barn. A pathway was then shoveled to the sedan body, and its white blanket swept off. Though we found it in fair shape, there were acorns in the mohair pockets and rodent nests in the glove box and seat springs. Chipmunks had moved in with the mice, and the interior smelled like an animal house at the zoo. But the glass was unbroken and the seats comfortable as ever. Beggars can't be choosers, I mused, as I brushed and cleaned the soiled upholstery. While the boys slowly inched the resurrected body up a plank skidway to the truck platform, I drained our water system in the attic, for on the morrow we would be on our way. Bruce worked into the night fashioning a re-route of the truck's exhaust pipe to pass it through the floor board of the Studie to provide at least some heat.

When darkness settled down that night, a strange looking vehicle stood beside my bedroom window. Irrespective of its exotic appearance, I knew it would be comfortable, yes, and warm, as Bruce had run the exhaust pipe from the truck engine up through a heater in the sedan body and out through the rear.

I thought the boys would never stop their wisecracking.

"Mom, aren't you ashamed to be seen in such a cockeyed contraption?" Harris asked with a wink in my direction.

"Well, I do think we had better get started before anyone is up in Spooner," she replied.

"Say, Pa, what kind of a license will we need, a truck or a car?" Bruce asked.

"Looks like the Studie made a forced landing," Harris quipped.

"Sure does. It's one up on the Chevy," Bruce continued. And so on and on went the smart aleck remarks, addressed mostly to Mother until finally she weakened.

"Well, I confess we'll be a sight, but the real rub is at the other end. What will our old friends and neighbors think when they see us piling out? Prodigals coming home, maybe."

"Who cares what they'll think? I don't. We can drop you off before we get there, Mom, and you can thumb the rest of the way if you want."

"Well, after all, Harris, I guess I'd ride home in a wheelbarrow if it was the only means of my getting there."

Thoughts of a Yuletide in the big Walker home filled our minds with happy anticipation. The levity of the early hours, however, turned to nervous tension as last minute preparations were made for an early start. Not until the lamps were out and the quiet night settled over our household did I appreciate the real meaning of our decision. Surely as a family we had earned this holiday, a respite from the never-ending quest for security. Mother, however, more than the rest, looked forward to the big event with eager impatience, for it was to mean the fulfillment of her fondest dreams.

Yet how little our understanding of fate. I was awakened in the night by a feeling of distress. This mounted steadily into unbearable pain. Though I held my tongue, my writhing awakened Flora. Hot applications did little to relieve my agony. The boys were up now, counseling with their mother.

"We've got to get him to a doctor. I'm sure it's another kidney attack. If only we had a phone," I heard Flora's voice. "It's nearly twenty miles to Doctor Hering and I don't know how much further to a hospital."

Sick as I was, I understood our circumstances. Yes, it was a kidney attack and a most severe one. But there was reassurance in that strange conveyance out by the doorstep. Vaguely, I knew that the old Studie body had come into its own at last.

The accoutrements of a makeshift ambulance were assembled. Mattress, woolen blankets, hot water bottles, heated flatirons – all went out the door into the blackness of the night. Dressed in a plaid woolen mackinaw with breeches to match, I was carefully maneuvered out the door and up into the sedan, onto the waiting mattress. Fortified with a bottle of aspirin, Flora acted as a nurse on the long journey. And what a journey! I shall never forget it.

Dawn was breaking as we pulled up to the Hering home in Shell Lake. A few sound knocks brought the good doctor to his door. We shall never know what passed through his mind when, in the weird gray light he beheld the hybrid vehicle, half this and half that. One thing I knew, never was a hypodermic needle more appreciated. A shot in the arm soon had me on my feet.

In the doctor's living room, comfortable and relaxed on his couch, the absurdity of our situation suddenly swept over me like a wave. On the way to Chicago for the holidays? Huh! With mixed feelings, I took in my surroundings; the medic there in gown and slippers, his discerning face and thin hands, a column of smoke rising from his cigarette, and that gray dawn still at the windows. Was not the whole thing a nightmare? I knew better - the diagnosis was real enough, and there at my side was my family, faces drawn with anxiety and concern. Now that my pain had subsided, I felt guilty. I wanted to apologize, to get up and go home. The doctor had other ideas.

"Here, take this pill and go to sleep," he said, as he handed me a glass of water and a tablet.

"But doctor, I'm feeling OK. We're going to Chicago for the holidays." The doctor pushed aside the curtain and peered out. "You say you're going to Chicago? In that thing?" he said, pointing toward the window.

"You see, doctor, we..."

"Well, you're going to take a trip all right, Mr. Palmer, but it'll not be to Chicago. You're going to the hospital in Rice Lake."

When I eventually awakened, I was again in pain and somewhat confused as to my whereabouts. I heard Flora's voice, and the boys, from an adjoining room together with the rattle of dishes. I was back once more in the Hering home. While the doctor had been out on a morning call, his good wife had prepared breakfast.

Rice Lake lay some twenty miles farther on, but with the doctor's sedative I made the journey with a minimum of discomfort. The sun was high when we arrived at the hospital entrance, and nurses stared in wonderment at what they saw - a collision, no doubt, the vehicles still fast together.

I was admitted and told I was to wait for a Dr. Dawson who would make the diagnosis. In the meantime I was shorn of my heavy plaid woolens, given a hospital gown, and put to bed. The boys, tired of waiting, left, saying they would return after seeing the town. Lois stayed with Flora, wearing a look of concern that hadn't left her face from the moment everyone had been awakened the night before. Though I was suffering once more, the high iron bed was a relief from the ever-bouncing truck with its incessant noise. I nodded in and out of sleep until well toward noon when the doctor showed up and took me in hand.

"He is a fortunate man, Mrs. Palmer," he said when he had finished his questioning. Me fortunate, lying here in a hospital bed, our Chicago trip shot to pieces? How?

"Well, just what do you mean, Doctor?" asked Flora. "Won't he need an operation?"

"I can't say yet, but the hospital has just acquired the latest thing for diagnosing this trouble, and it will give us the answer, one way or another, without any guesswork."

I was soon on a table where a tiny light bulb was inserted into the affected area. The instrument was equipped with an eye piece through which the doctor could recognize any foreign substance that might account for the pain.

"Well, Mr. Palmer, I think we can get you straightened out in a day or two without any cutting. There seems to be no stones, nothing but a granular sand we can manage without surgery," he advised as he rose from the instrument.

Back in my bed, I recounted the whole procedure to Flora. Of course she was elated, as were Lois and the boys.

"At least there's some hope of our making the trip after all," I said encouragingly.

Two days later they came for me, all packed and ready to continue on to Chicago. I watched impatiently as they pulled into the driveway. Not until then did I get my first objective view at our means of travel. When Dr. Dawson saw it he shook his head.

"Better take the train," he said, "you'll be better for it."

We had a family huddle on the spot, after which the boys drove Flora and me to the depot, then continued on in our contraption southward with Lois. Flora used Lois' return ticket, and the cost of my fare, we rationalized, was little enough when compared to the expense of an operation.

When the truck finally rolled into the drive in Cicero some ten hours later, Lois climbed out of the Studie body complaining she was colder than she had ever been in her life. Somewhere on the later part of the trip she felt she had to get away from her brothers, and took to the Studie body with a sense of adventure. As she warmed up in the house, she found the soles of her shoes nearly burned through, as she had rested them directly on the exhaust pipe in her attempt to keep warm! But here we were, all together for Christmas once again.

Chapter 25

SOFT BARRIERS

Home for Christmas! It seemed incredible. The joy and excitement of the occasion, its music, gifts, bountiful table and all was verily a dream come true. How bright the lights and joyful the merrymakers. Gathered in the big square house on Christmas day were the Walkers, Johnstones, Swensons, and now to help them celebrate, their country kin from the northwoods. How good it was to see Ruth and Ed once more, and as for little Kathie, she more than filled her grandmother's cup to running over.

But as all good things have their endings, so came the day of our departure. One January cold gray morning we climbed aboard our makeshift conveyance for the long journey homeward. Within its pumpkin-shell compartment Mother and I settled ourselves in silent retrospection as the boys piloted the truck over familiar avenues of our old town. The festive glamour, fellowship and family contacts - what was Flora's reaction to it all? Was she weighing it against her own provincial way of living? Had the happy holiday in any way altered her perspective, and had it changed her mind? I wanted to know.

"Flora," I said hesitantly, "now that it's all over and we will soon be home, just how do you feel? Are there any regrets, any misgivings? Would you like to go back there and live once more?"

The light from a street lamp swept her face as I waited. "Why, Charlie Palmer! Shame on you for asking. You know very well how I feel. Why, I wouldn't trade my new house in the woods for the best one in Chicago."

We followed in the wake of snowplows through cities, towns and hamlets, over drifted and wind-swept highways until at long last, between the distant hills, we saw the lights of Spooner. Thus far, our return journey had been uneventful in spite of the hazards of winter driving. At Byrnes Store things were different, for a hostile providence stopped us in our tracks. One look at the county-line road verified our growing apprehension. The snow lay deep and undisturbed over its moonlit length. The last mile of nearly five hundred, unplowed and impassable. What irony!

The store windows proved a welcome beacon and we gladly  accepted its bid of hospitality. As we stood around the sheet-iron stove berating our misfortune, we heard a loud "Whoa" from outside, followed by stomping feet. Who could it be, out with a team at this hour? The door opened, and to our surprise there stood Bob Reimer, bundled to his ears and in felts. His face lit up with a smile as he greeted us.

"I saw that rig out there and I knew it must be you folks coming home, but didn't expect you back so soon." He became serious now. "Looks like you're going to have some fun getting in."

While the boys and their pal were looking over the situation, Flora and I listened to Mr. Byrnes' recollection of a certain family who, snow-bound, had carelessly been caught without food in the house. We got the point of his subtle innuendo, and when the boys entered once more, the counter was heaped with staples.

"We are going to break a trail down to the house," Bob said. "My sled will cut its way through the drifts, and I think maybe your truck can follow in the tracks. You better wait inside until we get back," he continued as an afterthought.

However, Flora demurred. "Why, I haven't seen a team of horses hitched to a bobsled since I was a girl in Michigan," she exclaimed as we followed the three youths out into the crisp, sparkling night.

As we watched the boys climb into the hay-filled box and settle themselves for the short run, I too was a youth again, back in the days of horses, sleighs and jingling harness bells.

Bob stood for a moment, his feet widespread, reins in hand, while he surveyed the long white stretch between the trees, a silken ribbon in the moonlight. We heard his soft "chirrup" and the creak of leather as his team bent to their task, and they were off, spreading the fluffy barrier before them - but not for long. Another loud "Whoa," and the spirited creatures slowed down, then stopped on the crest of a hill. Once again the team laid into their collars, belly deep now in drifts, but easier going where the snow lay on the level. For the team it was stop and go, dip and rise, until sleigh and all were but a dot merging into the shadow of the woods.

We waited anxiously, toasting our feet by the fire, or out scanning the fresh-broken trail for their return. Finally they came, the horses stepping willingly enough now, their heaving flanks steaming, their distended nostrils sucking at the crisp air.

"We'll give them a good rest," Bob said as he threw blankets over their sweating bodies, "then we'll have another try at it. Only this time you can all follow behind in my tracks."

When the time came to mount the truck, I found Flora settled snuggly in the hay beside Bob.

"Why, I wouldn't miss this for the world, Charlie. Better crawl in too," she said, extending a helping hand.

Though it was fun there in the hay behind the horses, it was a struggle for the boys in our truck, for they were obliged to make frequent use of their shovels. We found it was a cold house, indeed, that welcomed us, colder inside than out, even though the boys had kindled the kitchen fire on their first trip in.

"What do we owe you, Bob?" I asked over our coffee.

"Why, nothing at all," he replied. "You folks helped me buzz my winter's wood, didn't you?"

Christmas holidays were over.

As Harris and I mushed back over yesterday's hard-earned trail we found the going anything but easy. I determined then and there that another winter should not catch us so unprepared. A pair of snowshoes or even skis – what use we might put them to right now. There would be plenty of times when snowshoes would more than pay for themselves. Winter would then be a new world to explore, a new field of adventure and fun.

We stomped snow from our boots at the store's corner, then set out east over the wide, recently plowed path. We were on our way to the Sylvester place where we would find LuluBelle and her calf comfortably housed within their spacious barn. Since I first set eyes on the timeworn place, I had a yen to investigate its cabin, to look into every nook and corner. What lay behind those weather-beaten logs, I could only guess; a wooden churn, or an old spinning wheel? Who could say?

We closed the pole gate behind us and pushed through the barnyard, hearing the soft crunch of snow beneath our feet. If there were cattle in the barn, they were conspicuous for their silence. Before us stood the small log cabin, picturesque beneath its blanket of snow, with only the smoke that rose above its ridge telling of its occupancy. Would it be Maurice, head of the family, who would answer my knock, or Walt, to whom the boys had taken such a shine? Or Charlie, maybe, with his repertoire of wisecracks? Possibly Ralph, who on his cow pony, we had encountered down by the lake? Who would open the door?

As we stood waiting on the step, we observed a web of paths running this way and that over their premises to the big barn, distant hog pen, hen houses and chip-littered area of the woodpile. From inside we heard a rustling sound, then creaking hinges, and in the doorway stood Mrs. Sylvester. Not until the door opened did I realize where Walt had gotten his eternal odor. Following her greeting she shouted in the direction of the barn, then turned and invited us in. The small room came alive as tongues loosened. For the moment I was absorbed in my surroundings. In the center of the floor was a stack of firewood, evenly ricked and ceiling high between two pole uprights. Beside this stood a cast iron range, conspicuous for the array of foot gear and mittens suspended above it. In an open cupboard beyond were dishes that might better be in a collector's cabinet. From the knick-knacks on a corner whatnot, my eyes moved to an old brass-bound powder horn and how perfectly it looked against the log wall background. Adding to the pioneer atmosphere, three deer rifles hung on pegs driven into as many ceiling beams, and ears of seed corn dangled from their braided husks beside the guns. While the others were absorbed in conversation, my prying eyes continued their search. Not, however, until they fell on a shadowy object beneath the attic stair did I break into their noisy palaver.

"Where on earth did you get that antique spinning wheel?" I asked, pointing toward the corner.

"Antique nothing!" Maurice exploded. "Here, take a look at this," he exclaimed as he pulled up his pant leg. Long red underwear! Was I seeing things?

"Nell carded the wool herself from our own sheep, she spun it on that wheel, then dyed it and knitted me two suits." There was pride in his eyes as he went on, "And do you know, Mr. Palmer, I was offered ten dollars for one after I had worn it a year. Do you think I sold it? Not on your life."

Incredulously I turned toward the distaff side of the house. "Yes, that's true," she confirmed, and I knew it was.

By the time we finished our coffee and doughnuts, the afternoon sun was a blood red ball upon the horizon. Mother would be waiting and wondering. At the barn LuluBelle wrinkled her black nose as though I were a stranger. Surely, she can't have forgotten me in so short a time. She sniffed inquiringly at the snow before venturing beyond the threshold. Molly, upon being turned out, took off at top speed, Harris' heels plowing furrows behind her.

When we again closed the pole gate, it was with a better understanding of the Sylvesters. I turned for a last look at the old cabin. What a story it might tell! They had raised five of their own and two grandchildren within those walls, and under circumstances far more adverse than our own.

Skies remained overcast with temperatures varying but a few degrees. Each succeeding day found the snow a little deeper, and lines of demarcation slowly vanished. Woods, lake and farm were soon beneath winter's heavy blanket. So silent and gradual had been the transformation that we failed to comprehend its meaning. The trail we had broken vanished and our truck was immobilized. Only our eyes could carry us beyond the compass of our feet. The few paths converging at our doorstep marked

the extent of our goings and comings. Thanks to our thoughtful storekeeper, we were not without food; there was hay and fodder aplenty for our cattle as well. Shop, barn and root cellar remained accessible, though days would pass before our distant mill would turn once more. Eventually the leaden skies gave way to the sun and the naked woods became a network of light and shadow.

Though darkness came early and our nights were long, our fire-side hours were seldom spent idly. There were always gloves and mittens to mend, and at times, shoes to be soled. Saws needed filing, and we were never without a keg of bent nails to work on. When Mother tired of her rug making and clothes mending, she would spend an hour reading to her family, a practice that was to continue over the years.

The sun's bright rays quickly changed our little world into a fairyland of dazzling beauty. Crows Nest was now a Swiss chalet, its wide-spreading eaves heaped with snow. From our window we could see a huge marshmallow down in the park where the cookshack had been, and beyond that, a vast expanse of unbroken white.

"I don't mind being snowed in as long as there's plenty to eat and no one gets sick," said Flora. "To tell the truth I rather like it, but I'd feel a lot better if only we had a telephone."

This, too, was my own reaction, for in its very novelty there was adventure of a kind. "At least, it's a lot more fun than being snowed out," I replied, remembering our recent experience.

As days passed and the gravity of the situation became apparent, our smugness turned to apprehension and finally to anxiety. Though we had worked to good advantage in the shop and even accomplished some things at the mill, there still remained one important job, one quite impossible under the circumstances, that of the harvesting of next summer's ice. Each hour of delay sent the frost a little deeper and meant added labor. Already the ice was beyond the 16 inch depth common for sawing and handling. Short tempers and mounting tensions sharpened our tongues, until even Mother succumbed to the long spell of confinement. After a fortnight of tolerance and understanding, she gave vent to her own true feelings.

"Now listen to me, Charlie," she exclaimed with a petulant toss of her head. "We can't just go on like this forever and do nothing about it. I've written two letters home now and there lay both of them. What do you suppose they're thinking back there? Now you and the boys stop your bickering and get those letters off. I don't care how, but they've got to go."

"And that's an order," I added in her own terse way of speech. Yet it wasn't until a third envelope lay sealed and stamped beside the others that anything was done, and it was Harris who did it. The weather moderated in a January thaw, and my mind was on our distant mailbox. As I got ready for the hike, I felt a tug at my knapsack and turned to see Harris.

"Pa," he said, "I'm a lot younger than you and my legs are longer. I can make it to the store and back in half the time it would take you."

Though at first I resented the implication, I finally agreed. Perhaps time was catching up with me after all. I reluctantly handed over the sack and Mother's three precious letters and wished our youthful carrier luck as he started on his mission. As I watched him drag one leg laboriously after the other through the drifts I recalled the beginning of the challenging motto to which the postal service was dedicated; through sleet, snow and rain...How fitting, I thought, under these particular circumstances. I turned back to the shop, to duties better suited to one of an older generation.

Dusk was erasing evening shadows when at last Harris returned. Anxious as he was to relate his experiences and tell of the news he had picked up, he was obliged to wait until his mother read the letters from home.

Our tenuous tie with the outside world was welcome, indeed, but did little toward solving our greatest problem, the immobility of our truck. To our surprise and delight, however, we were not long in suspense. Hearing a commotion outside, we hastened to investigate, and who was it but Bob, the good Samaritan, shouting to his horses. There he stood, reins about his body, his hands upon an ordinary farm plow. He was scanning the furrow left behind him. When we finished with our greeting and exchanged a few neighborly words, he told us his plan.

"I'm going to make another furrow on the way out at the width of your truck wheels," he said, and with that he was off. He was barely out of sight when Flora, sensing the end of her long imprisonment, exclaimed, "You know, Charlie, I haven't seen another woman in weeks. I'm going to the store. Even the sight of a squaw in skirts would do wonders to my morale – I'm fed up with this man's world."

Bob's day didn't end with the trip out. Not until he had plowed a road down to the lake and out upon the ice did he head for home.

Chapter 26

WINTER YIELDS

Before the days of electric refrigeration, harvesting ice was practiced on both a large and small scale. The railroads, taking advantage of this free crop, stored up thousands of tons each winter for the safe transportation of perishables. Countless families the nation over also depended upon this cheap and abundant commodity provided by nature. As for the recreational business, at the time of our coming, every resort of any consequence had an ice house capable of holding at least fifty tons, and no cabin was completely furnished unless it had an icebox.

Like the logging business, cutting and storing of ice was work that called for technique and tools quite alien to our city-trained hands. Nevertheless, we approached this task with the same assurance we had when we built our mill. A saw was a saw, we reasoned, whether it cut through wood, steel or ice, and except for minor differences, was subject basically to the same rules.

What a thrill it was to find myself beyond the confines of my own bailiwick once again, to feel the surge of freedom and scan distant horizons. Around me lay unblemished snow, limitless and sparkling in the sunlight. Conditions were ideal for the job, as the temperature stood well above freezing when we started to work. Harold had plodded his way across the lake to give us a hand, making it a crew of four.

When the drifts had finally been pushed aside, we stood in a rectangular space of clear, green ice. A portion of this we then scored into a checkerboard of squares according to the number and size of cakes we required. A hole was now needed in which to start the sawing. If you have never chopped a hole through twenty-four to thirty-six inches of ice, you had better not attempt it with an axe. You will need not only a keen edged, long handled chisel, but plenty of staying power as well. Better still, get hold of a modern motor powered ice auger such as are used by ice fishermen of today.

To learn the thickness of our ice, an axe handle was let down into the hole until its head slipped beneath the under side. Sixteen inches would have been sufficient, but this was late February, and the ice had reached

its maximum. Soon the two Sams were spelling each other over a long, heavy toothed saw, puffing, sweating and wise-cracking as was their custom when working together.

"They use a two-man saw on trees, Sam," said Harris with a twinkle in his eye. "I wonder why they don't use them on ice?"

"That would be all right with me, only I'd want my choice of end," was his reply.

So their tongues waggled until the first tier of cakes were sawed and afloat in their narrow channel. Most material expands with heat and con-tracts with cold, and water is no exception to this rule, but strangely enough on reaching the freezing point, water reverses the process and expands. Thus heavy cakes of ice float, as they weigh about six pounds less per cubic foot than water. To land these floating blocks with tongs and send them skidding away over the slick surface was a trick I soon learned, and rather liked to perform. As for Bruce, the back breaking job of loading and hauling had fallen to him. With cakes weighing better than a hundred pounds each, however, it was more than he could man-age alone, and we all gave him a hand when necessary. With Bob Reimer's sled loaded, he would take off over the ice and frozen hills to our half-finished ice house. Within its four walls the cakes were then stacked in layers, all cracks and crevices packed with snow, and the whole mass cov-ered with sawdust.

All things considered, we found the job of ice cutting to be clean and invigorating work, but we were to learn over the years that it was not without incident and provocation. What a surprise awaited us one morning when returning to our location, we found the whole area completely submerged. Unwittingly, we had left a half-day's cutting around the hole. Poor judgment and the weight of the heavy cubes had accounted for the mishap, a lesson not soon forgotten.

Temperatures, too, were factors to be considered in quarrying ice. Sub-zero weather was not only a threat to our bodies, at times it played havoc with our equipment as well. The long ice, saw if left inactive in its narrow slot, would freeze in almost instantly, requiring chopping out, a tedious job indeed. The same was true with circular saws, powered with their model T motors. In such bitter weather the ice cubes would become extremely brittle and would break easily in their han-

The Ice House

dling. Conversely, with the thermometer standing well over freezing, the cakes would honeycomb in the sun's rays becoming soft. This would render them useless for summer storage.

Out on the windswept ice, there was always the danger of accident. The ever enlarging hole lay like a pitfall to the unwary, where a careless step or slip of a foot might plunge one into a frigid bath. As for me, I usually wore ice creepers on my boots while working about the hole. Though such dunkings were infrequent, when they did occur they were memorable occasions that called for laughter and kidding over the winter days to follow. Perhaps the most frequent casualties were crushed fingers. A heavy moving cube contacting another might injure a foot or a hand, so powerful the impact.

When our last cube was finally loaded and Harold and the boys had taken their leave, I tarried a moment beside the open hole and peered into its jade-green water. What a strange world it was there beneath my feet, how dark and how opaque its sky. Far back under the hole were fighting bass, walleye, northern and countless pan fish. They were awaiting the summer to turn their dark world into sunshine once more, when they would rise to the colorful lures of vacation-minded fishermen.

As our cabins increased in number, we quit cutting ice and purchased it for a cent or two a cake from the Christner boys who made the harvest their winter's business.

The proverbial winds of March blew steady and warmer as the days lengthened into April, and suddenly it was spring once more. Billowing clouds brushed their shadows lightly over the awakening earth or darkened it as quickly to deluge it with rivulets of water. Raucous crows gathered and scolded from the tree tops. To plant our feet upon the bare earth once more and drink in the tonic of springtime was indeed a therapeutic experience that kept me outdoors hours on end. For weeks Flora had poured over her seed catalogs - now she rattled the small packets impatiently as she awaited the day of planting.

"Charlie, what's become of my wheel cultivator?" she shouted one day as she scanned the brittle remnants of last year's garden.

"Like as not it's where you dropped it last fall," I replied, not without a certain satisfaction. "It's not the garden I'm worrying about so much as the pasture. That fodder we got from Moorheads ... well, it's about gone, and our cows hardly touch what's left of the swamp hay. We're going to have to spend some money, like it or not, if the grass doesn't show up pretty quick."

While warming sun mellowed the sandy leaf mold, we fell to the many jobs winter had left in its wake. Our manure pile had risen to roof level behind the pole barn, awaiting spreading before the garden could be plowed, and to our dismay we found the popple fence posts on the back forty rotting away at their bases, many of them already down. A whole new pasture fence was needed. There seemed no end to the things that should be done.

Despite our workaday schedule, we somehow managed time to appreciate the magic spell spring had thrown about us. While following a wooded path over a late spring snow, I was surprised to come upon an area completely peppered with tiny black specks. Quite naturally I was curious, and taking off my leather mitts, knelt down on them for a closer look. As I focused my eyes upon an individual mite, presto, it disappeared, nor was it obvious how or where it had gone. Another and another vanished into thin air as I continued to watch. They were easily discernible against the bright snow, and they disappeared and reappeared intermittently. Of course they were tiny creatures of some kind not visible after their explosive take-offs. Grasping a handful of snow where they were thickest, I went into the house and examined a single specimen beneath a microscope. I was amazed to find no wings. Instead the tiny body was suspended between two powerful hopper-like legs. How could such a small being could survive the sub-zero temperatures? Perhaps they lived through winter in the scaly bark crevices of certain trees. I called them snow fleas for want of a surer name.

Once a cochineal bug, no larger than a flax seed, stopped me in my tracks, for I had thought it much too far north for this tiny creature to live. Its brilliant red coat against the drab earth had attracted my attention.

"Take a close look," I said to Flora. "It's the cardinal of the insect world, and it's used extensively in Mexico for making edible dyes. Remember those old peppermint sticks with red stripes? Well, the color comes from many of these little fellows like this one."

There are tiny lizard-like creatures that slither in and out so quickly among the rock piles. My first attempt to catch one left me with only a wriggling tail between my fingers. I learned this was but a ruse of nature for its protection, since soon enough a new tail would grow. A skink, Harris called it.

The rhythmic sound like that of a clock held my attention one day as I put my ear to an unpeeled log in the barn wall. Tick, tick, tick - it continued without interruption. This sound was the so-called death watch making its macabre predictions. Not being superstitious, I knew no one was about to die, but that an inch-long larva was snapping its hammer head against the inner side of the bark.

Among the small things that intrigue me in the woods is the tree toad. It's heard more often than it is seen. As its name implies, it is a climber, especially of trees, but any surface, even glass, will support the tiny suction cups on its toes. No larger than a half-dollar, it has a green back but its real wealth of color and beauty lies in the golden splotches on its underside. Its trill is bird-like and so elusive it is almost impossible to trace its source. The cool interior of the pump beside our shop became the favorite haunt for one particular toad, and it would plop out with the first rush of water. To satisfy my curiosity, one day I carried the little creature over the rim and down through our park to the water's edge. However, the following morning there it was in my drinking cup once more.

There are hummingbird's nests with pea-sized eggs, tumble bugs that push heavy dung balls with their hind legs, snapping beetles that do acrobatics, and swarms of May flies that come in June. These are nature breaks that make our work more interesting.

Perhaps more obvious are the hibernating creatures, gophers, chipmunks and other rodents that reappear in the spring. Groundhogs come from beneath the barn floor to survey the bright new world from their haunches. Hardly a day would pass that our eyes weren't drawn skyward by the honk of passing geese or whir of duck wings.

Of the several varieties of birds that had remained with us the winter through, I think the partridge intrigued me most. Indeed, its drumming, if nothing more, sets it apart from other feathered creatures. Softly and slowly it starts as in a dirge, then increases in tempo and volume to a resounding roll, but it's the sudden, abrupt stop that transfixes me, for the bird's head might well have been shot off. I came upon a drumming bird only once, and stood dumfounded, watching and listening to it beat out staccato notes. Quite often in the spring, partridge would feed in our park and I never tired of watching the strutting cock showing off before some demure and uninterested hen. Not far beyond the log barn I came upon a nesting partridge. Its simulated injury, though meant to mislead me, only guided me the quicker to its woodsy retreat. I counted thirteen eggs that morning, though within a week all had hatched. Later on, at my approach, the young ones would squat to become part of their surroundings. To a prowling fox or sharp-eyed hawk, they were nothing more than dried leaves or bits of grass.

When flushed, partridges take off with amazing speed and choose some patch of blue sky as an avenue of escape through trees. Thick woods are no impediment to their flight, and they hit small targets of light with the speed and accuracy of bullets. This very characteristic sends scores of them to their death each season. Many such casualties have occurred on our own premises over the years. Seeing daylight through two aligned windows and mistaking it for a clear passage, they strike the window head on, smashing screens and often glass. An outstanding example of such impact happened one day when no one was about. Upon entering the shop I was surprised to find glass scattered over the floor. The mystery was quickly solved, for among the tools on the work bench lay a feathered corpse. Not only had the impact torn the wire screen from its moorings and shattered the glass, but it had broken two wooden stiles as well.

Such instances were to multiply as our cabins increased in number. One in particular is worthy of mention. Though the bird in question lived to fly away, it left in its wake not only a few feathers, but a ludicrous bit of comedy as well. Bruce, baching it at the time, and thinking there had been an explosion, rushed to the living room window. There beneath the casement, supported by thin ice on our big minnow tank, lay the quivering body of a game bird.

"Oh, ho! There's my dinner," he shouted, and rushed to lay hold on it. But the reviving bird had other ideas. To this very day, Bruce's face displays chagrin as he recalls the lunge, or better still, plunge, that sent him headlong through the thin ice. Imagine the picture he presented as he crawled, wet and bedraggled, from the tank, a fistful of feathers in place of his dinner.

After the vernal equinox the rains came, and with them green and succulent grasses. Ferns pushed their curly heads through the dark leaf mold, and arbutus, hepatica and anemone dotted the woodland floor. Wintergreen shone once more with new luster. The ice had gone in one final assault upon our shore. Translucent slabs had buckled into tent-like formations, then vanished like magic in the rays of the sun. Winter left a heavy ridge of sand and gravel along the water's edge. "An ice wall," Bob said, and with his scoop shovel and team, he leveled off the beach area. "It's something you'll have to contend with every spring," he advised.

The crystal clear water lay quiet and inviting. Walleyes were done with their spawning, and now bass were lying in close to shore. The eerie call of a loon reverberated throughout the hills, music night and day. Not only did the moods of spring make us mindful of the wildlife about us, it turned our thoughts to our own barnyard creatures. Mollie was nearly a year old now and had abandoned many of her hoyden ways. Good breeding was showing in her trim feet and straight back though she was unlike her mother in color. Vague stripes, indistinct as water marks in bond paper, were developing on her flanks. Would Lois recognize in her the little creature she had so reluctantly left behind? More important was the fact that her mother was about to freshen once more, and we would again be swimming in milk and cream.

As I sat enjoying my supper one evening after an inspection tour of our pasture fence, Flora brought up a subject the family had had under consideration for some time.

"Charlie," she said, "I still think we are foolish to go on as we are with only one cow when we have so much pasture. As it is, we have more than enough milk for ourselves but not enough to sell. With another cow we could take cream to town and really make it pay."

"Flora, that all sounds fine, I'll admit, but what are you going to use for money? Cows are high in the spring, you know."

"That's all true enough, but I've been doing some thinking lately. We've got a little saved up, you know, and with that check we got from the bank adjuster back home we could —"

"Could what? Why, that check wouldn't pay for a pig, much less a cow."

"Now Charlie, just let me finish, then you can have your say. Remember now we're going to have income from two cabins before the summer is out, and that'll mean a lot toward our budget."

"Yes, and don't forget those two cabins will be needing milk and cream, too, Pop," Bruce added in support of his mother.

"And while we're on the subject of pigs, Pa, why not buy a couple? Think of the garbage from the cabins. Why, we could feed 'em for practically nothing."

"Pigs! Now you want pigs? Let's see: there's LuluBelle and Mollie, that's two and the calf that's coming, that makes three, and if we buy another that makes four, and now you're crying for pigs. Say, tell me, are we in the resort business or are we running a second-rate farm or something? I'd like to know."

We took the matter to bed with us that night and carefully weighed the pros and cons. If truth were really known, I too wanted another cow as badly as they, and pigs as well, for that matter, but it was simply an insurmountable economic problem that stood in my way. Suddenly I was brought erect by a shout from Flora.

"I've got it," she cried, loud enough to waken the household.

For a moment I was confused and I could not think. Then I remembered the cow.

"Charlie," Flora went on, softly enough now, "I'm sorry if I scared you, but I really have the answer. It's as simple as ABC. Somehow I had completely forgotten those two ten dollar deposit checks on Crow's Nest reservations. We can cash 'em at the store tomorrow, and with the rest, we'll have more than enough to make the deal."

The next morning I remembered a poster I had seen tacked up in Byrnes Store. "There's going to be a farm auction over near Hertel," I announced to the family at the breakfast table. "It's not 'til another week, but maybe it would pay to look into it right away. What do you think?"

"I'd say it's a good idea. Maybe we can talk to the farmer into selling us a cow beforehand. Anyway, it's worth trying," Flora exclaimed. "Better not wait."

The boys agreed and so within the hour, Harris and I, well heeled and with out heads in the clouds, were on our way. As our lumbering truck covered mile after mile of familiar landscape, I became apprehensive. Perhaps we were acting too hastily after all. Should we not have waited until the auction as others were doing? My thoughts went back to that early spring day when we came back with the black Jersey tied aboard. In my mind's eye I once again saw the sawyer and his stoker wife, the veil of vapor over the opened sawdust pile. I could hear again the soft smooth running of the steam engine, and lastly the Fordson tractor - what fun it had been loading it. That had been a day, indeed. Well, with a good approach, a loose tongue and a little finagling, today might become a memorable one as well.

We found the farmer a resolute soul, however, a man of few words and not at all inclined toward bargaining. Furthermore he was totally unimpressed by the color of my money. Reluctantly, he showed us a cow.

"She's not much to look at," he said, "and she won't bring much at a sale, but she's a dang good milker, and that's the gospel truth." Except for the price he quoted and his closing remark, "take her or leave her," there was little else from his lips.

A tinge of regret accompanied us home that day. Indeed there was little to gloat over. Each look at the animal tied aboard only lent more credence to the thought that I had bungled my responsibility. How I had ever fallen for such a creature was beyond my understanding. A Guernsey, the farmer called her. To me she looked more like a museum piece, a throwback from some long extinct line of grass eaters. In all fairness, however, there was that about her underparts that reminded me somewhat of a cow.

"Pa," Harris said peering through the rear window for the nth time, "I think that fellow saw us coming. Why didn't we bring Maurice Sylvester along? He sure knows his cows."

"Well, it's too late for that now, Son," I said. "Maybe the old girl will look better after she's unloaded." But the farther we went the more my heart sank. What would Flora think, and the neighbors, and Lois when she came? We had scraped the bottom of the barrel, and for what?

Within our barnyard enclosure the creature ambled slowly down the ramp with the assurance of an animal used to being hauled about. While Harris made her fast, I took off through the woods shouting for LuluBelle, glad enough to be absent when Flora showed up. Upon my return, she was there with Bruce, both staring wide-eyed at our purchase. With the two animals now side by side, I stepped back a few paces, to make a comparison. LuluBelle looked neither this way

199

nor that, chewing contentedly on her cud as though no other creature were about. Apparently it was beneath her Jersey breeding to acknowledge the presence of so ill-bred a creature of the Guernsey kind. I took in her familiar lines and weighed them against the angular form of the new-comer. I found little resemblance. Upon the hammer-like head of the Guernsey, one horn stood erect, the other drooped languidly downward as though frost bitten. Her gnarled joints only accentuated the cant of her legs and her long comedian-like feet reminded me of Charlie Chaplin.

Yet with it all, the Guernsey had her redeeming features. Her bag was overly generous, so much that her back sagged beneath its weight. Then, too, there was an extra teat, thrown in, no doubt, for good measure. Added to this, she was quiet and well-behaved, and her eyes were truly bovine, soft and liquid, as though she was about to burst into tears.

"Certainly she's no Venus de Milo, Charlie," Flora said, breaking her silence. "I do hope she's a good milker. After all, fifty dollars is a lot of money, especially right now."

"Well, we'll soon find out," Harris shouted as he shook out a fork of leftover swamp hay.

After we ate supper, I settled down upon my stool, a pail between my knees. I reached apprehensively for the nearest teat, then another and quite before I knew it had both hands going in a perfect rhythm. My spirits mounted as the foamy liquid rose higher and higher.

"She's a dang good milker," the man had said and so she was. When I straightened the kinks from my back and hefted the pail, I turned to Flora.

"And she'll do better when the pasture comes along."

Chapter 27

EMERGING SUCCESS

Each day brought us a little nearer to the realization of our dreams. Though logging, mill work and cabin construction were fundamental in our undertaking, there were days on end when nothing was accomplished along these lines. Barnyard chores in themselves were time consuming. More than anything it was the unexpected, the minor jobs, which made any set schedule quite impossible. The small patch of grass where Harris had tried the lawn mower proved an exciting challenge, for in it we saw the potential beauty which lay in our park area. Slowly we were conquering the perverse wilderness which had hemmed us in.

June brought vacation time again. Decadent cities the country over were stirring, if only temporarily, and schools were pouring forth hordes of happy children. Employed and unemployed alike were feeling the urge to travel. For weeks they poured over maps and brochures, and now the time had come for them to set out for some remote lake or other watering place. How often we, too, had felt this yearning to splash in the crystal waters of some woodland lake or stream. Man's predilection for water is not unique - it's inherent in his very makeup and possibly stems from his aquatic beginning. Was he not once a creature of the sea and still drawn to water as though by a magnet?

We were now putting out the welcome mat for all vacation minded grownups and children. Who would be first to set foot upon it but

Lois, bursting with enthusiasm. She was still unpacking when Cousin Lou showed up, and good-natured Dick was not far behind. All three slipped into their respective places like feet into old slippers.

Our new home, of course, was the first topic of conversation. How did we like it? Had we kept warm enough? Did the fireplace smoke? This was Lou's hour and his face reflected his satisfaction. He was to find a long table in the garage portion where the old Studie had been. Mother had commandeered this room as she could find no other place large enough to feed her growing family.

Of course it was the cattle and not the house that got Lois' undivided attention. "Don't tell me that's Molly!" she said. "Why, she's as big as her mother, and how come those stripes? They weren't there last fall." After one long look at the new Guernsey she turned and said, "Pop, are you sure she's a cow?" After a moment's hesitation she went on. "What have you named her, Pop?"

"Now that's strictly up to you, Lois. You named LuluBelle and Mollie, you know."

"Well from what Mom wrote, I thought I'd call her Jezebell, but now I think I'll call her Anabelle."

The Guernsey was responsible for much of our table fare now, and to hear Cousin Lou's, "Gollee but that's good," was like hearing the birds sing again. Those words were to become a familiar cliché, an expression of appreciation for not only dairy foods but for Mother's cooking as well.

The boys had given much time and thought to the layout of their respective cabins. Both had taken drafting in school, and now their plans had a professional look. Their work on Crow's Nest had shown unusual skill, amateurs that they were.

Lou's architectural training had not included log cabin construction and being a creature of rote, he was puzzled as to how to proceed. "Where do you measure from?" he asked one day as he plied his six-foot rule along a wall. The logs are all so different in width."

Harris liked to work with wood and his painstaking care was evidenced in all his undertakings. Bruce, on the other hand, much preferred steel. Machinery fascinated him and micrometer precision was almost an obsession with him. Harris had chosen a site well down the hill from Crow's Nest, a secluded spot, and though set back among the trees, it presented a picturesque view of the lake. We had poured the foundation in early spring, and now the walls were built high. The new jig had more than proven its worth; not only was it a time-saver, but now all log ends fitted squarely against uprights.

The new season was upon us and Crow's Nest was filled to capacity. Once more our sandy beach was alive with splashing children, and from all indications it would remain so through most of the summer.

Bruce hitched his iron horse to the cement mixer and hauled it to his own site overlooking both the park and the lake. Lou preferred to remain with Harris, and I took off to give Bruce a hand. Working there close to the water would be especially fun. Ducks were flying overhead and a soft lake breeze stirred throughout the pine needles. What a contrast, to the city life we had put behind us. Here incentive took the drudgery out of labor, and there was adventure in every swing of an axe or turn of a shovel.

I set to work that day little realizing what strange things nature might have in store for me. While leveling the earth, the heavy scoop had torn through an old, rotten log, scattering fragments over the whole area. Some pieces stood on end, others lay in shreds along the lines the tractor had moved. There was nothing strange about this — we had plowed through buried logs before. Instead, it was the pungent smell of dank earth that interested me, and the grubs and beetles we turned up. Lightning played on the horizon when finally we trudged homeward, tired and hungry. With darkness came a distant rumbling to remind me of a tool box we had left open. Reluctantly I started for the diggings, shuffling over the uneven ground lest I stumble.

The night air was soft and fireflies blinked in the tree tops. There was no hurry, for the storm was still far off. Dubiously I felt my way on toward my destination. Suddenly I was stopped. Before me lay a spectacle of phosphorescent beauty. By all appearances I stood on a mountain top, and there in the valley below lay a city, its tall buildings aglow, its thoroughfares a network of lights. Beyond lay the more subdued residential district, its diffused pavements highlighted by an occasional movie facade or shopping center. Spread over the valley floor were church-spired towns and villages, some bright with festive splendor, others obscure in the dim distance. Little imagination was needed to see the city's airport beneath the blinking lights of a firefly on the shadowy horizon.

I had discovered the phosphorescent property of rotting wood, a delicate chemical balance bestowed by nature. Capturing and carrying the sun's light well into the darkness, it conveys both mystery and beauty. Was there no end to nature's resources, I wondered.

LuluBelle had been missing for two days, and search as we did, we could find no trace of her. From lake shore to county line we combed the woods without success. Though we came upon places where deer had bedded down, there were no signs of our absent cow. Her absence meant only one thing - she had had her calf. Quite to our surprise she showed up that evening, and more surprising, she was alone. She had hidden her offspring in some secluded spot, a trait her ancestors had followed for generations. Flora saw her coming and thought the calf was somewhere beyond the garden. At the barnyard the Jersey stopped only long enough to finish the box of grain she knew would await her. Then she disappeared into the gathering dusk quite before we could collect our wits.

"When she comes tomorrow night I'll be in the garden and when she goes by, I'll sneak along behind."

"And me, too," Lois exclaimed. "I want to be first to see that calf."

Sure enough the following evening LuluBelle showed up as expected. When she had her fill, she started off as though with an objective in mind. Little did she know when she passed the garden, sharp eyes were watching her. Silent as Indians the watchers fell in behind, certain now their strategy would soon pay off. They had gone only a short distance, however, when the cow turned in her tracks. Seeing them she started feeding leisurely as though she had reached her destination. When she failed to go on, it was plain the whole thing was but a ruse to throw possible followers off the track. She had no intentions of divulging the whereabouts of her calf.

Thus far our time had been wasted. We had learned nothing from last evening's vigil, and now at the breakfast table we laid further plans. LuluBelle showed up, but later than before, and while she munched her grain, Harris hid himself down by the blueberry trail. Flora slipped behind an old stump, Lois dropped in a hollow behind a clump of birches, and I peeked out from beside the shop. Nevertheless, the cow was suspicious when she left the barnyard. As she passed the shop she sniffed the air. Dusk was settling and her black bulk would soon be lost in the darkness. She moved slowly over the rutted road, then suddenly stopped and threw up her head, ears forward, all attention. Softly at first, then louder, came the bawl of a calf, and with it LuluBelle set out on a dead run. She passed Lois, her tail straight out, her heavy bag swinging from side to side. Harris had to dodge to let her pass, then he set out full speed behind her. He hadn't far to go, for in a secluded glen he came upon her. There, too, was the calf, legs spread and busily sucking.

"I sure put one over on her that time," Harris said as we gathered about.

"You put one over?" I asked. "What do you mean, you put one over?"

"Why, it wasn't the calf that bawled. It was me."

That evening Harold came over and listened as we told our parts in the drama, or was it comedy, of the cagey cow. After a game of checkers the two Sams fooled around with an old phonograph, playing The Man on the Flying Trapeze until my patience was nearly exhausted. Finally they settled down at the table, our thumb-worn Sears catalog before them. This big book, second only in size to Mother's dictionary, and appreciated for its utilitarianism, served us in many ways. It accompanied us to auctions as a guide to values, served as a reference work on design for feminine apparel, and even served as a medium for a family game. If carelessly dropped it would usually open to the building material section. The boys seemed interested only in a casual way as they thumbed through its pages. Suddenly Harold's face lit up with an idea.

"Say, Sam," he burst, whistling his s's, "how about sending for a couple of these? I've always wanted one but never had the nerve.

If you'll wear one I will. What do you say, huh? Here, read what it says."

Harris bent over the fine print and read aloud; "Ten gallon cowboy hats, made especially for Sears by a leading manufacturer. 100% wool felt, blocked to hold their shape, Shipping weight, 2 lbs. 9oz. Each $3.98."

After a moments silence he said, "Well, I don't know, Sam. I just spent three bucks on canvas for that old canoe and I'm about broke."

Obviously the final word hadn't been spoken. The boys pondered a long time over the intriguing display, their voices hardly more than

a whisper. Then Harris, suddenly remembering his quarterly of twenty-five dollars was about due, got busy, and soon a stamped envelope lay sealed beside the catalog.

"How long do you think we'll have to wait?" Harold asked as he rose to go.

Honey Bird

Harris' cabin was about ready for occupancy, and without waiting on ceremony, he named it Honey Bird. Over at Webster we had gotten eight French doors at a bankrupt sale of mill stock. They were heavily constructed of bird's eye maple and cost us but two-fifty each. "Just what I've been looking for," Harris said when we were told of the sale. Now two pairs of these doors hung between its screened front porch and living room. When folded back, the result was one large room open to the cool lake breezes. From here, one entered the kitchen between two short log newel posts, and on either side of the kitchen were the bedrooms, with a maximum of privacy. It was a pleasing layout with every square inch of space utilized. Bedsteads were of white birch as were the table legs, contributions to the rustic atmosphere of its interior. The cement floor had been enameled red throughout and a colorful linoleum lay in the living room.

"I wouldn't mind spending a week or two in it myself," Flora said as she closed the door behind her.

Though the cabin stood a neighbor to Crow's Nest, it had little in common other than its low-spreading roof, and even that was different, for Honey Bird's eaves and gable edges were rounded. Harris had accomplished this by using a quantity of six-inch wooden disks that had lain around waiting for just some such purpose.

We had just gathered our tools when a family of tourists off the highway took possession, expressing their delight over their find. Their happiness was no greater than ours when they settled up for a two-week stay.

Completion of the new cabin called for a celebration, and Mother provided it in the form of luscious strawberry shortcake, drenched with LuluBelle's thick cream. To top off the day, the two Sams planned a trip out on the lake. There was nothing unusual about the boys going fishing together, as Harold, though not working for us, was a constant visitor. But this was a special occasion, the initiation of their long-awaited ten-gallon hats. Down the hill and beneath the big trees the pseudo cowboys ran, giggling self-consciously as they headed for the beach. Instead of a couple of waiting horses, they made for the overturned canoe.

"We'll give it a good tryout," Harris said as he stowed away rods and tackle box in the newly re-covered canoe. I steadied the wobbling gunwales while the two settled down into their places. Then with a shove, sent them on their way.

"We're going after a big one this time," Harold shouted over his shoulder.

"Well, good luck," I shouted, "and hang onto those hats."

For an hour or so the rest of us loitered about. Lou and I pitched a few games of horseshoes, the others stretched out lazily on the grass, oblivious to time.

Our quiet time was broken by a shout, and we hurried to the beach to greet the returning fishermen. What a sorry looking pair of wet and bedraggled cowboys! The wide brims of their hats hung limply over their ears like sunbonnets, and they grinned sheepishly as they stepped onto dry land.

"Why, you're soaking wet!" Flora cried. "What happened?"

"Did you tip over?" Lois asked.

The size of the fish they were dragging got my attention. Hardly knowing whether to laugh or complain, they started toward the house, the tail of a big dogfish dragging through the grass. Hot coffee soon loosened their tongues.

"What do you think that fish'll weigh, Pa?" Harris asked as he pulled a dry sweater over his head.

"To heck with the fish," Harold interrupted, "I'm out four bucks. Just look at that hat," he said, slapping it over his knee. "Show me that catalog again. They're supposed to be waterproof, aren't they?"

"Well, I can't say as to that, Harold, but they're supposed to hold ten gallons of something - it might as well be water," I replied.

We finally got a detailed account of the debacle. Down at the south end of the lake the big fish, in striking, had tangled with some lily pads. By careful maneuvering, the Sams had managed to get him out in the open. Here they played him with a taut line and what skill they possessed. Eventually, when Harold was about to gaff him, a sudden gust took his prize hat out to sea. Needless to say, his sudden lurch to save it sent both into the water beside their overturned canoe. Finding the water only chin-deep, Harris, his reel still spinning, pulled in his fish before he made for shore. In the meantime, Harold rescued the canoe and, more importantly, the two mail-order pieces minus their starch. To this day the tackle box still remains where it sank on the bottom of Lake Lipsie.

Chapter 28

THOSE BEFORE US

The old diagonal road whose sandy ruts marked the trail of earlier days no longer bisected our park, for we had turned its course to serve not only Harris's cabin but those that would come later. Though we begrudged the time spent pulling trees and burning bush, we knew that roads were as essential as the cabins they served. With grading for cabin sites, leveling cradle knolls, uprooting trees and plowing our garden, much of the earth's surface had been disturbed, and I kept a constant vigil for anything unusual Which might be turned up.

Buried in the sand at the base of a Norway, I came upon a steel knife blade of Indian origin. This came to light with a shovelful of earth. Our garden netted me a couple of arrowheads, too, and others had shown up on the inner hillsides of the park. Many years ago Abbie French unearthed an ancient flintlock rifle, or what remained of it after a century or so of rust and decay. These things did not come as a surprise to me, as both Indians and whites were choosy in their camp sites, and the lay of the park, adjacent to a good spring as it was then, was an ideal spot. My greatest surprise came when an old rusty cast iron tea kettle turned up, without a cover and filled with earth. Two bullet holes pierced its side, a target for some woodsman's gun it seemed. What was it doing a way out here? Later, when the edge of an old stove lid caught my eye, I began to suspect that we were not the first to settle on these acres. Subsequent diggings unearthed fragments of old dishes, a white porcelain doorknob, a cast-iron lamp bracket, a buttonhook and other things.

The shoreline in front of Honey Bird bore further evidence of earlier times. A rectangular hole in the hill side, we learned from an old-timer, was the site of a steam boiler for an old saw mill, probably before the turn of the century. I tried to picture those early logging days when our lake was filled with logs. I found it hard for me to believe that others had actually lived here before us, but was aware in this country, the wilderness takes over with a fast and relentless hand when man's activities cease. We later learned we had chosen a site on the old 1912 Phelp's place. Only our long table with its plank seats attached remained beneath the trees as a reminder of our earlier days, as we had wrecked the cookshack to salvage lumber.

Bruce spent many overtime hours on his cabin and regarded the results with satisfaction, as well he might. A heavy log truss across the living room not only lent charm to the interior, but was so constructed that a few turns on a nut would give rigidity and strength to the  ridge pole. Perhaps this had been an unnecessary precaution, but Bruce considered the low pitch of its roof and the heavy snow loads it might be required to bear. At any rate it symbolized the extent to which he was wont to go in all his undertakings. No one was surprised when he called his cabin Air Pocket, for aeronautics had long interested him. Like Honey Bird, his was also a two bedroom cabin. (Eventually however, we were to enlarge it to three.) At the cabin's completion, the season was half spent, and it seemed but yesterday that we had poured its foundation.

We got a cream separator at a local auction. The bid started at five dollars, and a little old lady raised it to ten. My raise of another fifty cents was the last. "Sold to that man with a necktie," the auctioneer shouted, and I got a look of disdain from my competitor. I'm sure that her meager raise indicated the true state of her purse, but I, too, was counting my pennies.

Lou took a firm grip on the handle and started out slowly, then cranked faster and faster until the crescendo from the spinning disks settled finally into a sustained hum.

"Gollee! It's like pure gold," he said as he compared the trickle of cream with the bluish-white stream from the other spout. The mechanism of this acquisition puzzled him, and when it came to assembling the complex system of cupped disks, he was totally at a loss and called for help.

"Why, it's simple," Flora explained. "There's a system to it. See those numbers stamped there on the disks. They run consecutively. They're the key to the whole thing."

Lou peered through his thick lenses until the demonstration was finished. More than ever he was enjoying his place in our family circle. His zest for work, inside or out, was unending and contagious, even to Dick. Unlike Dick, however, Lou hardly knew how to play. He seldom went out on the water, and as for fishing, he was totally ignorant. Coax as I would, I could never get him into a bathing suit.

He preferred an indoor sponge bath rather than subject his ungainly anatomy to the public.

The first to occupy Crow's Nest as paying guests had been a nephew and niece, and Flora's folks had been among our early patrons. Now our own daughter, Ruth, and her husband, Ed, came for their first northwoods vacation. With our little grandchild, Kathie, they were occupying Honey Bird, with lots of room to spare. The Walkers, too, had come again and were in Air Pocket. It was like a family reunion when we were all gathered for a picnic down in the park. Sometimes I wondered if we could have made a go of it without so many relatives, not forgetting 'Cousin' Lou.

Of the few remaining jobs that needed doing before our help took off for the city, our pasture fence was the most important. At the store, I brought up the matter of fence posts, thinking Mr. Brynes might reach out and put me straight with a little of his jackpine philosophy.

"I'm having trouble keeping my cows at home. They're always getting through our pasture fence and wandering off." This was a good start, I thought, but Mr. Byrnes only bored me with his gimlet eyes and volunteered nothing. He stood with his hands on the back of a tilted chair, a moccasined foot on its lower rung.

"I'm going to build me a new fence," I went on. "I want to run a lane down to the lake from my back forty. I don't think the cows are getting enough water." Still no response.

"I've got jackpine aplenty on my place and oak and popple, too, and I can get plenty of tamarack, as well. What would you suggest I use for posts?" This was a direct question, one he could hardly ignore. He moved slowly around the chair, then settled himself.

"There was a fellow I recall, lived over on the Hanson place. Had a nice stand of cedar he cut up into fence posts and when he had sold the lot, said he was a hundred dollars to the good. Later on a storm sent his cattle through his own fence, and he found two of them dead, mired down in a swamp. Had to borrow money at the bank for more." At this point he turned a speculative eye in my direction. Had he made his point? "Popple's no good," he went on, "and tamarack, but you can't beat cedar; it'll pay off in the long run."

On my way home, I pondered the homely wisdom of this man who spoke in parables.

This had been a good season in many respects. Patrons left with a promise to return, we had made progress on our building program, our dairy herd had expanded, and best of all, Flora seemed none the worse for her long siege at the cookstove. What a wonderful week it had been with our four children together once more, and as for Kathie, Flora clung to her 'til the very last. Both Lois and Dick left with the Walkers, and it took only Cousin Lou's farewell handshake at the depot to send us home depressed and in little mood for words.

A golden sunset drew Flora and me to the water's edge where ripples were dancing in colorful profusion. As we stood absorbing the beauty, the sound of distant drums came over the water. "It's the Indians," I said and we dropped on a grassy knoll to listen. On the evening breeze came the soft thump of tom-toms. "They are gathering wild rice," I continued. We had once been witness to this historic event, and as the unique music reached our ears, we recalled the picture vividly.

On the shore of a lake hardly more than a bow shot beyond Lipsie, the Indians had gathered as their ancestors had done since time immemorial. They came to harvest the crop nature so abundantly provided. On foot and in old cars they came, individually and by families. Canvas tents stood among the trees, clothing was draped over bushes, and blankets were spread about on the ground. From beneath blackened kettles, smoldering embers filled the air with nostalgic smell of camp life.

Except for dark-faced youngsters, their mongrel dogs, and a few aged and infirmed, the camp was deserted. All able bodies were out in canoes and old boats. With deft hands they drew in the long stems and flailed out the ripened heads onto blankets. All day long they poled and flailed, leaving an occasional head untouched for further propagation as their forefathers had done.

With their return, the camp came to life. The grain was poured into a kettle over smoldering coals, and after roasting, was put into a rawhide receptacle into which stepped a moccasin clad buck. Gripping a pole tripod for balance, he started a weird shuffling dance to the beat of tom-toms. Not until the chaff was loosened from the kernels did he stop his rhythmic gyrations. Time now for the last act, that of winnowing. As the grain was tossed into the wind, my mind went back to Bible scenes of ancient Israelites in their fields at harvest time. How small the harvest seemed when the precious kernels were finally poured into a cloth bag. In direct contrast, however, was a modern touch - a young mother who poured orange juice into a nippled bottle for her black-eyed papoose.

Only a touch of crimson remained on the horizon as we ceased our reminiscing and retraced our steps homeward.

Bruce seldom left our premises unless the trip concerned business matters. On the other hand Harris took advantage of every opportunity to scout about the woods. Although he never shirked his work, somehow he managed to keep in touch with the things that earlier attracted him to the outdoors. He liked to hunt with his bow and he was especially proud of his steel-tipped arrows because the broad heads were of his own design and were stamped from a die of his own making.

His targets were usually rabbits, though crows, too, came in for their share of misses. I have seen them turn in their flight in answer to his mimicking call and swoop down within shooting range. During the crisp fall days of deer season he would take off, full of confidence, only to return at sundown, empty handed, with a dozen alibis. "I'll get one yet, Pa. You just wait and see," he would say, and somehow I believed he would. Perhaps it was the silver medal he won as runner-up in the intermediate division of the National Archery Contest held in Chicago four years prior, which inspired my confidence in him.

A fat groundhog got in the way of his arrow one day, and he half regretted having shot it. As he dropped it at my feet, he said, "I'd just missed a good shot at a buck and I was pretty sore when I saw this critter beside his hole. Anyway, his hide will make me a good quiver. I'll decorate it with arrowheads." He frequently brought home rocks that appealed to his fancy. Among them were chunks of banded sandstone, blocks of quartzite, granite boulders, glacial striae, nodules and calcite crystals from a distant cave.

"Pa, did you know there were volcanoes here in Wisconsin at one time?" he asked as he rolled a heavy chunk of lava from the truck one day. Years later when geology was his profession rather than his hobby, he brought me a slab of marble which he got at a small abandoned quarry hidden away in the rugged hill country of Ashland county, the only marble quarry in the state.

"You know the capitol building at Madison?" he said. "Well, the rotunda is built of beautiful marble from all over the world, but there's not a single piece from our own state. If I were the governor I'd surely do something about it."

My own hobby since boyhood had been collecting Indian things,  and Harris added materially to the number of hatchets, celts, ceremonial pieces and thousands of arrowheads that made up my collection. He came home one day with a bushel of large quartzite quarry blanks. All were in unfinished condition, found in Silver Mound, a famous Indian quarry site in Jackson County. They needed only a secondary chipping by the experienced hand of an Indian to make them into useful objects.

On the periphery of a hill overlooking the Yellow River, we found a large conical mound, and though others before us had recognized it as a burial place, we were sure no one had recognized the long crescent-shaped upthrust of earth nearby as the work of ancient man. Mature trees and thick underbrush hid its particular characteristics, and within the chord of its arc we found a number of small button shaped mounds. Sometime later in its vicinity we discovered kitchen middens and ancient tepee holes, all of which indicated that at one time, sizable Indian village, possibly of Sioux, or even earlier origin.

With the passing of time, the diversified leanings of our children became more apparent. Harris, like his father, found interest in things that had once been, in the unfolding of nature's past, but for Bruce retrospection and the past had no being - his sights were only on the future. As for Ruth and Lois, they, too, were as far apart as the poles. We could only wonder what the future had in store for them. We wanted our boys to go on with their education as Lois was doing, and they in turn meant to see their parents established in the resort business before striking out for themselves. Harris had finished Junior College before our coming, and Bruce had gone back to complete his last term at the time of his mother's illness. Under the circumstances we could do little planning and perhaps it was just as well. In the meantime, the boys were getting a practical education that would stand them in hand, whatever their future calling.

Chapter 29

DOWN A LAZY RIVER

For a long time Flora and I had talked of a trip down the Yellow River, and now that day had come at last. With most of the fall work behind us, we loaded our equipment on the truck platform and with a clear conscience, took off for the three-mile trip to Couche's bridge. Upon our arrival the boys unloaded our duffel, wished us good luck, and returned home. The day had been tailored for just such a trip. No wind stirred the half naked trees that marked the course of the water. Aquatic plants trailed their long tresses lazily in the current, and downstream in shallow waters of the bend, sunbeams danced on wet boulders.

We had chosen my duck boat in preference to Harris' canoe, and now that it lay tied at our feet, it looked small and inadequate in the brown water. A squat box holding our lunch, a cushion for Flora, two paddles and my shot gun were the extent of our equipment. We hardly pushed from shore when the current swung us end for end, and not until we reached the bend did we straighten to face downstream. We went along almost without effort, dipping a paddle only now and then to keep our course, passing beneath low-hanging boughs where brown leaves fluttered down to join us on our journey. Resigned to the whims of the current, our low-riding craft seemed a very part of the stream itself, and we skirted each shore alternately, as though searching for some hidden outlet. Only the sound of rippling water disturbed the silence about us. What a time to forget our yesterdays and tomorrows and live for the day only, in rhythm with the water, woods and sky.

A horned owl, perched high on a limb, turned its head slowly as we drifted past, its big eyes scrutinizing us. With each bend in the meandering stream new vistas opened before us, and wooded hills seemed to threaten our further progress. Concentric rings on the surface of one particularly shaded pool sent my hand in search of a rod that wasn't there. Later we came upon a small island, and while we hesitated in a choice of channels, a doe and fawn splashed to the safety of the denser shoreline. On and on we went until finally our appetites called for a halt. At the foot of a tall weeping willow, we stepped ashore and climbed the steep bank. It was good to straighten our backs and exercise our legs after such close confinement.

While Flora laid out lunch, I took in the surroundings. Somehow they seemed familiar. Then I knew – it was here we had stopped on one of our earlier treks in search of a homesite. There on the opposite shore were the same angling birches, leafless now but their black scars ugly as ever. Further on was the quiet pool, unmoved by the eddying current, into which Lois and I had dropped bread crumbs. Although I had come to know much of the country which we trekked across earlier, this discovery came as a surprise, stirring our minds to reminiscing.

"I'm sure Lois would not have forgotten those birches," I said.

"I wish she was here with us now. Two years is a long time for her, but I'm sure she'd remember," Flora suggested.

"Just think back at the many things that have happened since that day we ate our lunch on this very spot."

"I wonder if we'd have had the courage to go on if we'd known then what lay ahead, my long spell of sickness and all."

"Who knows? Maybe it's just as well we can't see into our future, but somehow I think we'd have gone on, don't you?"

"Charlie, I don't want to spoil this wonderful day by talking of such things, but while we are on the subject of my illness, why, I think you should know that it has resulted in a re-education for me, a costly one perhaps, but it has given me a new sense of values, a new perspective on many things. If the family, too, has benefited by it, why then it was worthwhile. At the time, I thought it the most devastating thing that could happen to anyone, but the way I feel now, well, I believe it was the most valuable experience of my life. A nervous breakdown is no disgrace, and what's more, I think there are few people, sick or well, who wouldn't be improved both physically and mentally under the care of a psychoanalyst. When you go back into your past, you understand why you have become what you are. Old prejudices lose their grip on you."

I didn't reply. I wanted time to think it over. Never before had she talked so freely of herself, of her inner feelings.

The breeze had stiffened – we heard it in the tree tops. Further on down river we felt its force on our backs as though to hurry us on our way. Soon we encountered a large tree lying directly across our course, fresh earth still clinging to its mass of upturned roots. There was room for the low-riding boat only to pass beneath, so we approached it slowly, not wanting a wetting. Once alongside the big trunk we both managed to climb atop and hold on as the duck boat slipped beneath. Then with continued caution, we dropped back into our places and continued on our way.

The sun was losing its warmth and the breeze had stiffened to wind proportions, brittle weeds and dried pods rattling in our ears as we brushed past them. The character of the stream was changing - no longer could we see its sandy bottom, nor were there any more rapids with foam capped rocks to dodge. The high banks that so long had cradled our stream now vanished, leaving the current to find its own way through a tangle of weeds and cattails. Here red-winged black-birds flaunted their brilliant splotches as they clung precariously to crisp waving stems.

Quite suddenly, we found ourselves within a sea of wild rice, windswept acres of undulating grain. How insignificant we felt in its midst, and apprehensive, too, for we were floating over a netherworld of sucking silt where my paddle could find no bottom. This had been our destination from the start. We were in the duck waters of Rice Lake, and taking up my gun I sat forward while Flora paddled slow-ly through the rice. Mud hens moved before us in jerky motions as though walking upon the bottom. Ducks arose occasionally, calling loudly as they climbed into the wind. But their keen eyes kept them well out of range of my gun.

"What's that big post doing way out there in the middle of nowhere?" Flora asked, pointing with her paddle.

"Why, that's a pile," I replied. "You can see others there farther on, all in a line. They're what's left of an old logging boom. During the early days, a chain of logs, fastened end to end, held fast by those poles, reached along the lake to keep the logs in the channel. The river was dammed farther down and the water was higher than now. Just imagine this whole area packed tight with logs held in by that boom."

"When I was a girl in Evart, Michigan, a big log drive would come down the Muskegon River every spring, and we all rushed down to the bridge to see it coming. My, it was exciting to see the men with their peaveys jump from log to log to break up the jams. Of course this is a small stream compared to the Muskegon, so it would have been a much smaller drive here. Where would the logs go from here?"

"I suppose they would go into the St. Croix River and to a saw mill at St. Croix Falls, or they may have gone on to the Mississippi for that matter. Say that wind is really getting stiff," I shouted as we turned our course northward through a stretch of open water.

I was about to reach for my paddle when Flora pointed to a lone duck coming down with the wind. He was directly overhead when I fired and fell obliquely with the speed of a bullet. Although we had heard the splash, it was some time before we saw the green head against a drab tangle of rice stems. Yet the fun of shooting was giving way to apprehension as the waters roughened.

"Not much chance in this weather. I'd better get a couple of those rice hens and call it a day. We've really got to get moving if we're going to get home by dark," I shouted as I slipped more shells into the gun.

Finally with a bag of three birds we started back in earnest. With the waves breaking over our bow, we were forced to veer our course toward the low lying shore. We skirted it in comparative safety until we came upon the mouth of the creek for which we were searching. Hemmed in by trees, the little stream was a welcome haven. However, we were running against its strong current and it pressed us hard, making us dig deeper with our paddles and apply them with more vigor than ever. We worked our way up the narrow channel until we emerged into a marshland. Here a pair of mallards took to the air within easy range, and taking aim with my paddle, I clucked a barrage of shots with my tongue, and smiled as the birds winged from my sight. The shores closed in once more and soon the channel was too narrow to use our paddles. Flora used hers as a pole, while I, ankle deep in my high-tops, pushed from behind. Beyond this short bottleneck we came to our first portage of the day, if a low plank bridge can rightfully be called such. Here we drew the boat from the water and braced ourselves against the wind as we peered toward home across the waters of Lake Lipsie.

"So near, and yet so far," sighed Flora wearily as she held out a blistered palm for me to see.

This would be the last leg of our journey and a safe one, we hoped, but it would call for more courage and skill than we had yet been obliged to show. The wind that had been at our backs earlier, was now to strike us full in the face with greater force. Flora stood gazing across the water.

"Are you afraid?" I asked. In answer, she only tucked her gray locks the tighter beneath her cap and reached for her paddle.

"It's really dangerous," I went on. "You know we can walk around the shore line if you want; it's longer but it's safer."

"Charlie, do you think I'm going to spoil this whole trip by walking the last mile? Well, I'm not, and I'm not afraid, either. Let's go." Wisdom may be the better part of valor, but it doesn't always work, especially with a stubborn wife. We got away from the shore but not without difficulty.

"Keep her nose right into the wind," I shouted. "It'll take us close enough to the dock." We kept our course fairly well by shifting our paddles from time to time.

"If it doesn't get any worse we'll make it OK," I shouted, but just then a mounting wave struck us head on, drenching the front deck and breaking against the narrow gunwale.

"Hold on to your paddle; if you lose it, we're goners," I warned.

"You hold onto your own," I heard over my shoulder. I turned to see my wife applying her paddle with no more concern than had it been her kitchen broom. "Why, I'm not scared," she said, seeing the worried look on my face.

"Well, you better be. If the waves get any worse we'll be lucky to make it half way across." I was provoked by her evident indifference to our predicament. But we kept on and soon the seaworthiness of our tiny craft built up my confidence and I thought better of my wife. After all, she'd been a good sport and companion throughout the trip.

"Looks like we're standing still. I don't think we've gone a foot in the last half hour and I'm almost worn out. Can't we take a rest?" My own back and arms ached, but to stop for a moment would be to swing into the trough of the waves, the very thing to be avoided.

"Line up one tree against another over on the shore and you'll see we're moving all right" I shouted back encouragingly.

"You know I can't swim, don't you, Charlie?" Oh ho, she's taking things seriously at last, I thought. However, I knew I was mistaken when she again shouted, "If we do turn over, which are you going to save, me or your gun?"

"That's not funny," I flung back at her.

"Don't forget that you traded my good dining room table for that gun, and did it when I wasn't even home. It must be worth a lot to you."

Oh, what's the use, I thought, and took her ribbing in silence. Progress was slow, indeed, but quite safe as long as we kept a straight course and even keel. At last, in the lee of our own big trees, we saw the worried faces of our boys turn to smiles.

Chapter 30

MONEY MANAGEMENT

What little understanding we had of the resort business we had gotten from our friends, the Hertels, who had coaxed us from our tents into one of their housekeeping cabins on their Big Sand Lake farm. We spent a part of a summer there helping out with the work. Our natural liking for the outdoors made the time pass all too soon, and from those few short weeks came the inspiration that brought us here. Now that we were on our own, we realized how little we actually knew about the resort business. We had jumped into the sea to learn to swim, as it were.

In this country, where the recreational business was rapidly becoming a major industry, competition might well have resulted in our cabins being empty. Under the circumstances what little success we had achieved thus far we attributed to our unique setting; the natural lay of our park, the sandy beach and the eye appeal of our rustic log cabins.

We had considered an American plan resort with its potentially bigger returns, but had never seriously gone into the matter. Somehow the responsibility of feeding people had little or no appeal, especially for Flora, who was spending time enough over her cookstove as it was. Then, too, times were hard. They were especially so on those engaged in the American plan resorts, as many could testify. Not a few of their patrons had gone over to the more moderately priced housekeeping type of resort, especially where sizable families were concerned. They made that sacrifice rather than have no vacation at all. Now many were finding a new freedom within the new environment. Here they could choose their own food and eat at their own convenience. When the crappies were biting, best there was no bell to call them to dinner. Dress and etiquette became personal matters within the family, and children were free to romp within their own four walls. Certainly there was that never ending chore of cooking for the housewife and mother, but even this might be lessened by inviting along some congenial friends who would be glad to share the work for a breath of country air.

We soon learned that twelve weeks at full capacity was about the limit of expectation, in fact more than average. This was due not only to a belated opening of the bass season, but even more to later closings of city schools. Generally speaking, Labor Day marked the end of our season. There were always a few early, as well as late, comers who are eagerly welcomed and appreciated by proprietors, the meringue on the pie, we would say.

The Park

Our cabins were doing better than we had hoped, considering the hard times. Thus far, advertising had cost us not one cent, for our patrons were simply telling their friends about our place. Yet the time was coming, we knew, when publicity would be a factor in our budget. With ten full weeks of reservation in Crow's Nest and a total of twenty eight weeks in all, including both Air Pocket and Honey Bird, we had done well enough. This represented a meager income to be sure, when compared to city wages, but how many were getting city wages, especially family men of my years?

We weren't complaining – we were content with our accomplishments. Two years was hardly enough time to erase memories of the hopeless inertia of the big city we had abandoned. Here work was a personal prerogative, not a fickle whim of economics. What's more, we arrived at the second milestone of our undertaking with full stomachs and a sense of newly-found freedom. There was no whistle to start our working days, no time clocks to punch. Yes, we labored hard and long, and we were over our heads in debt, but we were our own bosses, making our own decisions, and all remuneration was our own.

Although fishing sends thousands upon thousands of vacationers into this part of the country, there are other interesting and worthwhile things for those so minded. Furred and feathered creatures may be seen and appreciated by exercising a little patience. Hikes over wooded paths and canoe trips down meandering streams are added features, and no rod and line is needed to breathe the invigorating air or bathe in sun and water. What a pity the pageantry of October's colorful woods is missed by the average vacationer. October nights are cold and woolen blankets are needed, but the days are nearer perfection than at any other time of year.

"When the work's all done this Fall." What fitting words for the month of October and how meaningful, especially for country folk. Although our work is never done, late fall days are restful and pass in a more leisurely manner, and time is ours to do with as we please. Autumn is simply springtime grown to maturity.

A lot of credit for our independence was due to our garden and cows, for most of our living was coming directly from the premises, with no middleman's profit. With the sale of cream, cousin Lou's board money, a few dollars from boat livery and the monthly rental check from our old city home, we were doing well enough that we faced the approaching winter full of confidence.

But if we were content, Dame Fortune was not. Her crowning gift came as a surprise when we found a check for $300 in the mailbox. We could hardly believe our eyes. This money came from the sale of a building lot which I despaired of ever selling. What a godsend it proved to be, for we were virtually out of building materials and cabin equipment. We might have purchased these locally, but being acquainted with Chicago's bargain centers, preferred to make the long trip, for it would result in saving at least fifty cents on every dollar spent. The result of this timely windfall was a planned shopping trip for both Harris and Bruce sometime before the snows would set in to interfere. There was the heterogeneous merchandise of Chicago's Maxwell Street, bankruptcy sales, daily auctions, sales of unclaimed freight, and the newspapers were full of factory closings. By and large it was a buyer's market, though hardly a safe and sure one for the uninitiated.

"The boys have been with you enough times to know their way around," Flora assured, "and it'll be good experience as well as a vacation for them."

With our augmented capital, we decided to purchase logs directly from pulpers in the woods. There we could select only the best and straightest of their cuttings. Furthermore, all logs would come with their bark peeled and ready for our dunking tank. At a price of only twenty five cents per standard eight-foot length, regardless of girth, we could not afford to do otherwise. Longer ridgepoles and rafters we would have to select for ourselves before cutting.

We had finished the mill work, and now tackled the job of fencing the wooded back forty, our truck loaded high with cedar posts. Our old pasture fence was in a sad state of repair, and with nephew Dick gone, our cattle had become a constant nuisance in the attention they required, especially at watering time. We dropped posts off at regular intervals as we wound our way through the trees. Wire was removed from old posts, new holes were dug and old ones re-dug. With the driving of the last staple, further problems confronted us. The old log barn was becoming too small and was unsanitary with its damp, rough floor. A new and larger structure was necessary. We got an order off to Wards for four new steel stanchions and individual drinking cups and hauled cement for the new floor, now more convinced than ever that our cows had become a permanent asset to the place.

Preparation for the long winter months in this northern latitude is analogous to the hoarding of acorns by squirrels. Though the former is based on reasoning rather than instinct, survival is the aim of both. Equally as important as food is sufficient warmth, and how fortunate that fuel in the form of wood is so abundant. No one in this country need go cold if he possesses an axe and saw.

Like the harvesting of ice, wood cutting, too, has advanced beyond the stage of hand tools. Portable saw rigs, powered by old car motors, particularly Model T Fords at the time of our coming, had taken the drudgery from this task. Neighbors got together as their forefathers had done at bees, and now as then, they exchanged labor rather than donating it. It's a job that requires strong backs, good team work, alertness, and a maximum of caution. A spinning saw has no conscience - it cuts wood, bone, or flesh with equal alacrity and is a constant threat to life and limb, especially so if snow or ice is underfoot.

Our boys were anxious to get started on their shopping trip to Chicago, but there was still our wood to put up. We had practically finished the new barn, and now that the Sylvesters had offered their services together with their saw rig, we rushed to get the stanchions and drinking cups installed before they showed up. Although Bruce had intended building a rig of our own, as yet he had nothing more tangible to show than a sketch on his drawing board.

"I've got to wait 'til I get a welding outfit before I can go ahead," he explained.

On a beautiful fall morning, our neighbors drove into the yard with their saw rig. Flora was disappointed to find only men.

"I was hoping your wife would come along," she said to Maurice.

"Nell's over to Nortons helping out today. One of the young'uns is sick, I guess. Where did you get that?" he asked in the same breath, pointing to a stack of wild hay beside our barn.

"We cut it over in Conner's swamp, south of the cranberry marsh. Anything wrong with it?" I asked.

"Nothing, except it'll never last you through the winter. Better get some good fodder to go with it, that is, if you're expecting any milk."

Our new barn was hardly conventional with its drop siding exterior. Then, too, we had painted it to match the house; in fact it looked more like a human dwelling than a place for cattle. Although it was considerably larger than the old log structure, it was nothing compared with the

Lois in the New Barn

227

big Sylvester barn. Regardless of its exterior appearance, its interior was snug and warm. The row of stanchions and drinking cups gave it a modern air. We made underground connections with the house water system so there would be no more carrying heavy pails through the snow. Perhaps the most sanitary feature of these new quarters was its concrete floor with a manure gutter the width of a scoop shovel, which could be flushed with a hose. LuluBelle, Anabelle and Mollie were still in their stanchions when we entered. The odor of hay in the mangers, the fresh, clean smell of white-washed walls, the calf in the corner pen, and sunlight pouring through the windows contributed to a pleasant atmosphere of the place, and we were proud of it.

Taking little notice of these things, Maurice Sylvester stepped over the gutter and stood beside Anabelle. He ran an appraising eye over the bony creature, felt her udders, then straightened and said, "You boys needn't worry much about that cow. You got your money's worth alright."

Walt and Charlie were generous enough with their words of approval, and if there were things not to their liking, they kept them to themselves. Walt's even temper and ever-ready smile had made him many friends throughout the neighborhood. The fact that there were three fingers missing from one hand in no way handicapped him - he was equal to any task the rough country might ask of him. With his brother, Charlie, and his father, Maurice, they had sawn wood on most places about. Now we had a crew of six individuals, half of them experienced men.

The wood to be cut lay in one huge pile consisting of tree trunks and poles of all sizes, an accumulation from our road building jobs, windfalls and cabin site clearings. They lay with their butt ends toward the waiting saw. My job was that of off-bearer, and it was up to me to dispose of the chunks as fast as they fell away from the saw. This meant lively hand work, especially when cutting poles of small diameter. Across the saw from me stood Maurice, the sawyer, whose job was obviously what the name implies. The balance of our crew were free to move about and responsible for feeding a continuous chain of poles to the saw. At times, all four would be needed to lift and handle some especially heavy log. This was hard work that required strong backs.

"Let's go," the sawyer shouted as he pushed the first pole end against the spinning teeth. Zip! Zip! Zip!, and the chunks were mine

228

to throw away as fast as they dropped into my hands. No sooner did the pole jog its way through the saw than another took its place. It was gang sawing at its best. With a man or two constantly tugging and pulling at the big pile, there was no let up in the stream of firewood that poured forth from my hands. Only when heavier cuts were made, when the logs required rotating while being sawed, did I find time to pick up smaller pieces that had inadvertently dropped at my feet.

Old car motors are unreliable things, ignition and carburetor trouble being common, and belts slip off their pulleys. As a rule, such stops are welcome interludes which provide time for a smoke or a story or two. The rig may then be moved forward to keep pace with the vanishing pile of tree trunks. With each fresh start, the jobs were rotated, until by day's end, each had had his turn as sawyer and off-bearer. The saw rig's path is intermittently dotted by mounds of sawdust, the pile of poles had vanished, and a mountain of sixteen inch firewood now stood between us and the cold months of winter.

The boys had taken off for Chicago, and Flora and I found ourselves alone on the premises for the first time. This was a new experience and a taste of what we might expect in the not too distant future.

"What am I ever going to do with all this bread?" Flora asked as she slipped four big loaves from the oven that afternoon. "I should never have baked so much. I'll have to remember there's only two to cook for now."

At breakfast the next morning, Flora said, "Do you realize, Charlie, that this is how it's going to be when the boys are gone for good?"

"We're going to miss them all right, but with the cabins finished and the resort on a paying basis, we'll make a go of it somehow," I replied.

Remembering the deep snows of last winter, Bruce had build a snowplow prior to his departure, and he had gone to the limit in workmanship and design. I watched it take shape as each narrow board was bent to fit the heavy V-shaped framework. He was nearly finished when I said, "Why, Bruce, it looks like a steel plow and it's big enough for a locomotive. Don't you think it's too heavy for the tractor?" But he kept right on shaping the narrow strips until the thing stood ready to go, wanting only snow to prove its worth.

I, too, had recalled the deep snows and those shut-in days, and had prepared with a new pair of snowshoes. Roads were enough for Bruce to navigate, but I wanted a wider range to explore. My new acquisition was of Indian make and design, fashioned from white ash and rawhide, decorated with woolen tassels.

"They're too good to wear outside," Flora said, and I agreed, putting them away with my collection. A handful of arrowheads traded with a second-hand dealer soon brought me another pair, more sturdy and conventional, and like Bruce, I waited anxiously for the first fall of snow.

While walking from the store one day, we heard a car approaching behind us.

"I hope they don't offer us a lift, Charlie. I'd much prefer to walk."

"Maybe it's the boys with the truck," I suggested and turned to see. "No, it's a car – better step aside and let it pass." As Flora had feared, the vehicle stopped, but to our amazement instead of a neighbor, it proved to be Bruce at the wheel, wearing a big smile.

"For goodness sakes! What's happened? Whose car have you got?" Flora asked after her usual mother's greeting.

"It belongs to Harris. He's following somewhere back there with the truck. Do you know, Pa, this baby's got power. She went almost to the top of Baraboo Hill in high before I had to turn around to keep the gas tank higher than the carburetor."

On the way home we listened to his story. Harris had heard of a widow who was left with a Model T Ford which she couldn't drive. He found it jacked up off its tires and in good condition, and she offered it for quick sale as she was about to move. The price was only twenty-five dollars and Harris bought it with his own money.

"But it's for family use," Bruce said as he applied the brakes at the shop door.

Soon afterward, Harris arrived. He had stopped for a bite to eat, regardless of his brother's desire to keep on going. The spacious platform of our truck was piled with much needed things, the sight of which reminded us of the good fortune that had made them possible. There were window sashs, doors of various types and sizes, lengths of steel pipe, kitchen sinks, well pumps, stoves, furniture, galvanized screening, kegs of nails, boxes of hardware, tools for the shop and garden, and many other things.

The following is a partial list of the material as taken from an old account book showing costs that prevailed at that time.

24 eight-light casement windows	$24.00
20 four-light barn sash	$5.00
2 doors @ $2.50 each	$5.00
1 30" mill saw	$5.00
50 ft. of 6" canvas belting	$3.00
2 cant hooks @ 25 cents	.50
2 garden hoses	.50
10 window locks	$1.00
1 5' Diston saw	$1.00
2 long-handled shovels	.80
2 used doors	$1.00
1 brush axe	.25
1 pound stick of 50/50 solder	.30
4 kerosene lamps	$1.60
100 lineal feet of 36" galvanized wire screen	$6.75
2 3 lb. double-bit axes	$2.50
1 1-1/4" pipe stock and die	$1.25
1 wheel barrow	$2.00
1 porcelain sink	$5.00
10 lengths of stove pipe	$1.50
3 elbows	.30
1 brush scythe	$1.25
1 screen door	$1.25
1 9x12 linoleum	$3.75
5 used doors	$3.75
50 feet of logging chain	$10.00
3 pitcher pumps	$4.95
5 brooms	$1.80
200 feet 3/4 inch rope	$3.00
1 keg 100 lbs. spikes	$2.25
10 rolls 90 lb. Mule Hide roofing	$12.50
1 doz. hacksaw blades	.60
6 gal paint	$6.00

Some of these items were shop worn, others represented unclaimed freight sales, while others were second hand. As an indication of local prices, the account book shows that we purchased 5,150 ft. of rough lumber for $62.75, and had it planed at a cost of $14.00. We also bought 2500 ft. of finished clear white pine lumber for $42.50, or at the rate of $17.00 per thousand board feet.

The boys trip had been successful both from a material and an educational standpoint. We were anxious now to put the things they had gotten to use.

Chapter 31

BEST LAID PLANS

The days were cold and clear and our thermometer registered around the zero mark nearly every night. Although the snowplow stood in readiness, the weather remained uncooperative, and Bruce spent his time in the shop learning to weld with an acetylene torch he had picked up in Chicago. I, too, was waiting for the weather man; I was anxious for my first trip on snowshoes.

In the meantime, I tackled the mountain of stove wood out behind the barn. Flora volunteered to rick it up as I split it, which was fair enough. To get the feel of a new axe, I spit on my hands and struck at a few smaller chunks, splitting them where they lay and swinging leisurely wherever a round end presented a good target. Although I was hardly equal to either of the Sams with an axe, I had learned a lot and could usually hit the same place twice. What's more, I could still count five toes on each foot. Finally, I shed my jacket and began the job in earnest. I passed up many chunks from old windfalls and purposely avoided the especially knotty pieces as being too tough. Those were left for the fireplace. I found splitting wood to be interesting and clean work, and comparatively easy when circumstances were right. A series of hard freezes conditions the chunks for easy splitting, for then they pop open like overripe watermelons, especially those cut from green oak.

Unlike the smell of blended sawdust around a mill, the odor from each variety of wood, when freshly split, has its own aromatic characteristic. The pungent odor of oak is tantalizingly pleasant while I swung my axe, but a close-up whiff is sharp and much too acrid for my nostrils. Popple may be bland and quite odorless, but in a state of moist decay, its odor becomes the quintessence of the woodpile, the delicate incense too vague and elusive for description. A blaze, not an axe is needed to coax the fragrance from cylinders of white birch, and there is no smoke I would rather smell.

Equally interesting are the birds that invariably keep me company at my task. I know them to be the same little chickadees that gather each morning at our doorstep for tidbits. As the chunks fall, sharp eyes search for small white grubs that drop from frozen crypts in the wood. When I stop for a rest, they flutter about excitedly, sometimes alighting on my axe handle or even on my cap. Although wood splitting is hardly classified as constructive work, it's an interesting chore nevertheless, and many cords of ricked wood, when under cover, leave one with a sense of security.

At long last a real storm with a night wind whipped snow about the woods and over our ice-bound lake, getting Bruce out of bed with a vengeance.

"Just what I've been waiting for," he said as he peered at the clean new world outside.

Breakfast over and a promising sun above the tree tops, our family set out over the mill path in the direction of the plow and Bruce's proving ground. Deep drifts ribbed the narrow corridor through the trees, and Bruce considered their depth appraisingly. As we approached, we could scarcely see the tractor, hidden as it was behind the bulky snow covered plow. While Harris wielded a broom, Mother and I warmed our hands around a steaming kettle of water we brought along at Bruce's suggestion.

"Do you want to make a bet?" Harris challenged his brother. "I'll bet you'll never make the shop with that heavy outfit."

"Hand me that kettle," Bruce said, not deigning a reply. He poured hot water over the intake manifold and around the carburetor, then pulled a few times at the crank. To my surprise the motor started, and after a few spells of spitting and coughing, settled down into the even throb of a well-mannered engine. Bruce dropped into the iron seat, then quickly rose shouting, "Oh, boy! That's worse than sitting on a cake of ice. Did anyone bring along that cushion? Here, throw it. OK, here she goes," he shouted over the blast of exhaust.

Gripping the wheel, he shifted into low, then eased out the clutch. The plow's wooden nose started slowly forward as Bruce gave her the gun, but it didn't go far. Midway into the first drift, all forward movement stopped and the tractor started to skid sideways. Try as he would, he could not hold to the road. The plow simply pivoted while the tractor slid sideways into the brush.

"I was afraid of that – I don't get any traction," he said when he had shut-off the ignition.

The reason was obvious, even to Mother when it was pointed out to her. The parallel cleats on both wheels ran diagonally across the treads in the same direction. In short, the tractor was equipped with two left-hand wheels, a matter of not much consequence in soft earth but a definite handicap on frozen ground. Instead of one set of cleats countering the side slip of the other, they worked together as a pair to literally screw the Fordson off the road. Bruce, I was sure, would come up with a solution of some kind, good or bad. We talked it over on our way back to the house. Harris suggested changing the cleats on one wheel, but that was out, for they had been welded on.

Flora had a thought. "Why don't you put one wheel on backwards?"

"How very simple!" Bruce retorted. "You know it can't be done. I'll tell you what, I'm going to load those wheels; they're not heavy enough."

"What are you going to load 'em with? All the heavy rocks are frozen down," I replied.

"Just wait and see," he replied. "I've got an idea."

The following morning the tractor was again ready for a tryout. Now each of the big wide wheels weighed about a ton for they were solid with ice from rim to hub. This had been accomplished by loading them with slush and sand and subjecting them to overnight freezing. Notwithstanding the length to which he had gone to accomplish his end, the result was no different than on the previous day. The outfit remained where it was.

I was in an 'I told you so' state of mind. "What do you think – will he give up now?" I asked Flora that evening.

"Not if I know Bruce," she replied. "He'll not quit until he has to." She was right, for he spent the next day bolting on a set of auxiliary rims which we had picked up at an auction. Though they were standard Fordson equipment, their application to ice packed wheels was another matter, especially in freezing temperatures. Fortunately the cleats on both rims were at right angles to the tread and would give perfect traction with no slide slip effect.

By all the rules that crown patience and perseverance with success, the boy was deserving of a medal, but this was not to be, for though he had added weight to the rims as well, the outfit was unequal to the task required of it. Bruce finally acknowledged defeat, a thing he rarely did, taking out his vengeance upon the drifts with an old grader blade attached to the front of our truck, resulting in the expense of a new universal joint.

Bruce's Folly we dubbed the plow, and it lay in the brush beside our road for years thereafter, a trysting place for rabbits and a roost for birds.

Snowshoes, with their simplicity of construction, their lightness and symmetry of design, never fail to fascinate me. Like the bows of ancient archers, they have come down through time with virtually no change in their basic form and make-up. And like the bow, snowshoes have rendered mankind an invaluable service. To the great fur trade that opened the northwest for the white man, they were indispensable, and even in this day of mechanization, nothing better has come about to replace them. I find it incredible that such reliance should be placed upon a few ounces of wood and a bit of woven rawhide.

There was no comparing the simplicity of my snowshoes with the complex vehicle that Bruce had built, though both had virtually the same objective. To be sure, a plowed road to town had its advantages, especially in emergencies. But so, too, did the broad surface of the snow, with its short cuts and its freedom of range. With snowshoes, last winter's paths had lost all meaning. The barn, shop and mill would all be starting points rather than the limits of my treks. The white expanse of our lake and wooded hills beyond were no longer inaccessible places but now open to this age-old means of travel.

A lot of short trips about the premises to taught me the tricks of snow-shoeing, and I encountered my share of nose dives into deep drifts. Crawling out and rising again with my webs still intact and without the aid of sky hooks, was no small achievement. Nevertheless, to choose some distant objective and reach it over the surface of deep snow I found to be a new and thrilling experience. My first trip through the woods to the store and back really bolstered my ego, and I was determined that Flora, too, should soon have her own equipment.

We awakened one morning to find snow up to our windowsills. It was a good day for indoor activity, and I set to work nailing soles on a pair of hightops.

"Charlie, come over to the window and see the snow. It's nearly up to the eaves of that cabin there," Flora exclaimed.

"That's not all snow. There must be a hill under it," I said.

"Well, I don't remember any hill there. I'll bet it's all snow," she insisted.

"I'm sure there's a hill, but there's only one way to find out and that's with my snowshoes. I dare you to strap them on and find out for yourself." To my surprise, she took me up on the challenge. Her curiosity had accomplished more than all my coaxing, for thus far she had promised to join me in my fun only when she had snowshoes of her own. Now, being eager to prove me wrong, she accepted my challenge.

I adjusted the straps to fit her shoes, and held the door open while she waddled clumsily out of the house. With my face pressed to a window pane, I watched her place each foot before her with deliberation and forethought until she reached the nearest Norway pine where she halted. She looked back smiling, proud of her achievement. Full of confidence and with arms swinging, she set out again with a quickened pace toward the mound of snow. She made it without mishap, much to my chagrin, but had barely reached its summit when suddenly she vanished from sight. When I saw her again, she was thrashing about, though upright, with a show shoe in each hand, shoulder deep in a drift. Her disheveled hair was whiter than ever and framed a face of surprise and consternation.

"Well, what did you find out?" I shouted through my laughter.

"That's for you to find out," she flung back at me.

Chapter 32

RURAL CHRISTMAS

The check that had sent the boys on their shopping trip to Chicago had incidentally brought about unplanned changes in our daily routine. Not only did we have a car in which to run about, but among other things, we had gotten a radio, too. It was a battery set, to be sure, but a radio nevertheless. We had gotten along well enough without one, but after a few week's contact with the outside world, our ideas changed and we became addicts of the airways. By judicious choice of programs, we managed to listen regularly to news items, Ford and Glenn, Amos and Andy, One Man's Family and Major Bowes Amateur Hour, with only a minimum of trips to town for battery chargings. In addition, a few periodicals now found their way to our mail box.

Winter being the time for self indulgence, Harris added hockey to his pastimes and this obviously broadened the scope of his acquaintances. He and his friends chose a small, secluded lake, hardly more than a pocket in the woods, for their sport, but it meant a lot of snow removal nevertheless.

As might be expected, Bruce spent much of his time in the shop experimenting with his welding equipment. Although we were in no immediate need of a saw rig, he built one. He used inch and a quarter pipe which he bent and fashioned to suit his fancy. One day as I watched him puddling liquid metal beneath the acetylene-oxygen flame, he said, "Pa, I'm not learning this just to be a welder. It's necessary if I'm going to carry out a lot of my ideas." The versatility of this newly acquired torch opened up so many fields of endeavor for Bruce that his hands were unable to keep pace with his mind. He filed away ideas for future development, and hardly a week passed that a drawing of some kind was not added to his collection.

Flora usually spent any idle winter hours over books and magazines, often reading aloud to the family in the evening. The discovery of some old unworked crossword puzzle was always a challenge she could not resist.

Before the arrival of our radio, we had seldom been conscious of the date. Even the day of the week had been inconsequential. The calendar held little significance for us. Back in our old home town, we had gone to church with some degree of regularity, and the children's attendance at Sunday School had been a matter of course, but here in the woods things were different. Church was twelve long miles away, winter weather was cold and the drifts were deep. During the summer months time was pressing, and the days and hours were precious in our march toward success. Was it not the scriptures that said that the Sabbath was made for man and not man for the Sabbath? Did not the Bible admonish man to do good on the Sabbath? Who, then, was to distinguish good from evil? To provide a roof over one's head or to plant a garden – were these evil things? Thus did we rationalize, did we make excuses and assuage the family conscience. How many times had I said we would start going to church next spring, next winter, next fall, or after the cow freshens, or the next cabin is finished? So the months lengthened into years, and habits that had once been fixed became no more than promises to be broken.

Sunday was no different from the day that preceded or followed it. On one occasion when we had needed material, we made a special trip to town with our truck and were surprised to find the lumber yard closed.

"How come?" I inquired of the druggist.

"Why, they're always closed on Sunday," he replied.

In those early days, our Post Office address had been Ferron Park, Wisconsin, which meant little so far as any park was concerned. Nor did the fact that we lived in the Town of Rusk mean that there was actually a town, a cluster of houses so named, for there was not. The title merely referred to a unit of self-governed land synonymous with the township in Illinois. This whole country was very sparsely settled. Our school district which comprised an area of seven square miles, could boast of but seven children, three of which were Indian youngsters. Though we could not see the schoolhouse from our shore, we could hear its bell, and its nostalgic tolling never failed to bring back memories of my own childhood days.

"Just think Charlie, only one child to every square mile," Flora said one day. "Why, back at J. Sterling Morton in Cicero there were more than nine thousand students, counting all departments. I wonder how many there were to the square mile there?"

Having no children of school age, our interests lay elsewhere until an occasion arose to alter that situation and make us more school conscious, if not civic-minded. This came about a few days before Christmas when, to our surprise, we had a visitor in the person of the young school teacher. She lost little time in acquainting us with the purpose of her visit.

"Mr. Palmer," she said when introductions were over, "I've come to ask a favor of you. You see, we are preparing our Christmas exercises and we need a Santa Claus."

Surely she can't mean me, but as her eyes scanned my midsection appraisingly, I knew I was mistaken. She gave a lengthy dissertation of her plans, and the part I was expected to play in them. The matter seemed settled in her mind, and I hadn't the nerve to disillusion her openly.

"Well, at least I'll think it over and I'll let you know in the morning," I said.

"Why the very idea, it's ridiculous," I said when she left. "Let her get someone else. There's Charlie Byrnes or Ole Morud. Anyway, I'm not going to do it."

"Now Charlie, don't be too hasty. It's the very least you can do. Why, it's your civic duty; you owe it to the community. Of course you're going to do it." There was a ring of finality in Flora's words that could have but one conclusion, and I acquiesced, but only with a compromise and a lot of face saving argument.

"You'll have to help me with a Santa Claus suit of some kind. You know you can't just go up to Byrnes Store and buy one, don't you?"

"Now let me see. Suppose we use a suit of your old pajamas, those white ones will be just the thing. I'm sure I've got some red dye somewhere about the house. I think it's a splendid idea. What do you say? And don't forget, Charlie, we brought along that old make up box of yours. It's up in the attic."

"That old metal box? Why, I'd forgotten all about it." The recollection brought back the many times I had had a part in some amateur

241

play. Fingering through its contents, somehow I caught the spirit of make-believe and could see myself now as Santa Claus. After all, wasn't Charlie Byrnes too tall and Ole Morud too thin for the part? Among the various shades of grease paint that had melted down and run together there were mustaches, blond and brunette, and a bulbous nose with a wart that recalled a tramp outfit I once had assembled. There were rouge and powder puffs, and finally I produced a Russian beard, black as a crow.

"How'll this do for Santa Claus?," I asked facetiously as I framed it about my face.

Flora had gotten an idea and she lost no time explaining it. "Why not go over to Sylvesters and pull some wool from one of their sheep? You know you can make a perfectly scrumptious beard if you want to."

Well, why not? It'll be fun, I thought, and soon was on my way in the Model T. At the approach to our neighbor's place, I searched the pasture for some sign of the creatures with their heavy winter coats, but none were in sight. Fortunately for me, I found them corralled in one end of the big barn, and with Mrs. Sylvester's permission, gathered more than enough wool, but what a time I had doing it.

As I entered our kitchen door, I heard the familiar pulsing of the treadle sewing machine, and found Flora busy with my pajamas and bands of cotton batting.

"Whew, how you smell, Charlie!" she said. "Go and change your clothes."

I spent the next hour or so washing and cleaning dirt from the fleece, and finally the oily mess from the kitchen sink. Once the long fibers had dried, they responded nicely to a comb and brush, and what a Santa Claus beard they turned out to be. Soft, fluffy and snowy white - whiskers that might well have been the envy of rabbi, priest, prophet or patriarch. I was really proud of my accomplishment.

Though I had passed the small white schoolhouse a number of times, I had never set foot beyond its threshold. As I approached its door with my make up in a gunny sack, I felt nervous and apprehensive. I wanted to turn back for I was still a stranger to most of my neighbors. But with my family urging me on, I took courage and entered. In the half lighted vestibule was a water bucket on a wooden bench, winter jackets hanging from hooks, and for a brief moment I recalled my own boyhood days. The classroom beyond took me back to an era even beyond my own memory. Here parents and friends had gathered, Indian and white alike, to see their children perform. They sat shoulder to shoulder on newly sawn planks, patiently waiting.

The place was crowded and overly warm, and the odor of barnyards eked from rough shod feet and overalls. Kerosene lamps in cast iron brackets shed soft light upon eager faces. I immediately sought refuge behind an improvised curtain. Bed sheets with safety pins for rings were arranged to slide on a taut wire across the stage. Within my hideout I could peek beyond the curtain without being seen. In the dim light I saw a walnut organ, and beyond were school desks of various sizes, filled to overflowing. To me it was a picture, quaint and primitive, yet I knew that from just such an environment a President had once come. In fact, Lincoln might have envied these children's desks, their bell, kerosene lamps, and especially their books. I couldn't help wondering if the students at J. Sterling Morton, with their many advantages, were any happier, if they were as appreciative of their opportunities.

As I applied my makeup behind the curtain, my mirror reflected the wide eyes and grinning faces of the cast of pupils. Soon beads of perspiration burst through my grease paint, and bewhiskered as I was, a pillow stuffing my belt, I felt I would suffocate.

Finally the program opened, and as the curtains parted, I cringed further back into my niche behind the overheated stove. I listened to a song by the school children and recognized the Indian lad and his black-eyed sister as those who had come to our place for books. Pete sang in a monotone, never varying the pitch of his voice, and what he lacked in melody he put into volume. I knew this was his last year in this little school and wondered what lay ahead for one of his race and upbringing.

Through the long program I tried to forget the heat by calling to mind Christmas gatherings long past. One in particular, when a Yule tree candle had set fire to my beard, did little to relieve my discomfort. The memory of tinsel and colored ornaments made me aware of the fact that no tree was in evidence here, here in the very land of spruce and balsam. As a matter of fact, there was no place for such a tree; a good sized one might have filled the room.

At long last, the pupils had performed their parts and only a duet off stage remained to be sung before it would be Santa's turn to appear. There was much shuffling of feet and shifting of positions on the benches as two missionary ladies prepared to sing. Could I possibly hold out? To make matters worse, no one had remembered to draw the curtains together, and I was trapped in my little oven. Although I turned constantly to escape the heat, I was slowly roasting like a chicken on a spit. Sweat stood out in beads about my red nose and I could even feel it trickling down my back. Would those women never get started? Then I heard the soft notes of an organ prelude. Won't be long now, I told myself. Fresh hope stirred within me and I took one last look in my mirror. Ye gods, that heat – it was ruining my makeup. Both ends of my mustache had curled tightly about my nose, and my long white beard – it was already creeping toward my chin. If those women don't hurry I'll be a total wreck. Half way through the duet, the organ faltered, then stopped altogether and so did their voices. Good! They've broken down and they're through. But no such luck. Someone held a lantern before the music, and they were off once more. There seemed no end to verses.

Now it was a race between time and my whiskers. Finally, after the last note of the recovered organ, and with a "Hi" and a "Ho!," prompted by distress rather than joviality, I burst forth, pack upon my back and a smile upon my face, as though blown in on a wintry blast from the North Pole.

"What a flop I made of it," I said to Flora that night.

"Why, I thought you did splendidly, especially the wisecracks you made as you handed out the treats."

"Well, maybe so, but it'll be a cold day when I play Santa Claus again," I said, wondering if she had gotten my point.

This was to be our first Christmas in the woods. Ever since Ruth had been born, our family had enjoyed this gay holiday in the big Walker house among relatives and friends. Our children had grown to expect it – it had become a matter of course with them. To keep this family tradition inviolate, we had, on the last occasion, made the trip against odds and in quite an unconventional manner. The time had come at last when tradition must bow to the inevitable. Circumstances had altered things and though we now had a Model T at our command, we decided to stay home and celebrate in our own modest way.

We would certainly miss the long table at Grandmother Walker's, heaped to overflowing with good things to eat, and especially would miss the happy faces gathered about it. And what of that morning session of opening gifts when all eyes would be fixed on each recipient as he or she in turn tore away the colorful wrappings. We would miss those "ohs!" and "ahs!" and that facetious refrain, "no 'preciating, no 'preciating" from the onlookers, themselves anxious to open theirs in turn. Then, too the group singing in the parlor around the old piano, the good fellowship, cordiality, the spirit of kinship and unity that accompanied it. The First Noel, Silent Night, Little Town of Bethlehem, Away in a Manger—time honored carols these, hymns that stir the imagination. Could it really be Christmas here without a song fest?

Yet happiness is where you make it, and after all, I told Flora, it is from our own northwoods that the trees and greenery come which carry the Christmas spirit to the Walkers and their city counterparts. Here, then, where the trees are ever green and the snows ever white and sparkling, we had decided to spend our Christmas. There would be a Yule log upon the hearth and embers to shed their warm glow over the room and stockings stuffed with candy and oranges.

To provide a bounteous table, Mother had only to go to our root cellar for vegetables. In place of a turkey we would have wild duck, Mallards taken from a large earthen crock where they had been put down in home-rendered lard. Not as traditional, perhaps, as turkey, but their savory and plump bodies, stuffed with wild rice and well browned, would be a splendid substitute. Lastly there would be my birthday cake with its all-too-many candles.

Christmas parcels had already come by mail, stirring curiosity. Opening them here would be without the usual noise and fanfare, but there would be no lack of appreciation. We would miss our relatives, young and old, and there would be no singing of carols, but thanks to our radio we would not be without Christmas music entirely.

So reluctantly, but with determination, we broke a family custom of long standing and remained in the woods for the holidays.

> Beneath a heap of Christmas snow
> On Lipsie's ice bound shore
> Our low roofed cabins scarcely show
> a window sill or door
>
> For Old Man Winter's in them now
> with legion imps of cold
> To lay siege and take a vow
> To drive us from our fold

But Palmer's clan is inside too
Where birch logs crack and sing
And send their challenge up the flue
to scoff at Winter's sting

And as we gather round the board
To fill the inner man
If we forget to ask the Lord
To bless those out the clan

The wishbone from our turkey's breast
This joyous Christmas time
Will make of you our Yuletide guest
In thought and verse and rhyme.

C.J. Palmer

Although snow fences along the highways had almost vanished from sight, our county line road remained passable despite drifts that lay across it. Our Model T took snow in stride, forging ahead like the thoroughbred it was. We were moving in the general direction of Couch's bridge spanning the Yellow River. The Bert Moorhead farm lay over white open fields, where Marcia had last been hostess to the club, and it was good to know that our friendships were slowly expanding. Flora had joined the "Homemakers," and I was driving her to a meeting.

The Clyde Brown place occupied a goodly acreage of fertile valley land cradled by wooded hills. Today it was Opal's turn as hostess, and broken drifts at their entrance meant that we were late in arriving. Through careless driving, just as we were about to turn in, we found ourselves hopelessly off the road in the ditch. Though Flora might easily have continued in on foot, she chose to remain to help, though it was quite evident from the start that our car was stuck beyond its own power to get out. We pushed and shoveled but each wheel spin only made matters worse. We were taking a breathing spell when Flora pointed to a rig slowly approaching.

"Maybe that'll pull us out, Charlie," she said.

"Maybe, if it can get enough traction," I replied, getting our tow chain from under the seat. The closer it came, the stranger the outfit looked. It seemed to be only crawling over the snow. Finally, to my great surprise, we recognized it for what it was, a yoke of oxen drawing a farm wagon. On its seat was a lean, all-weather type of man, not unlike Lincoln in face and limb. Acknowledging my greeting with hardly more than a nod of his head, he stopped his creatures beside our stalled car. As though this had been his initial objective, he unhooked his oxen and hitched them to our front bumper.

Surely this was an apparition, my own grandfather's ghost, perhaps. There were no words, no commotion, only the clank of chains and metal as he worked. At his signal, the beasts lowered their heads and dug their wide, horny hooves through the snow and into the frozen earth beneath. Slowly the Model T started and continued to move until finally it stood free from the drifts and ready to go. With little ado, this wayside Samaritan took his leave as silently as he had come, with a nod and a wave of his hand in acknowledgment of my appreciation.

Although many old trails throughout the woods had outlived the oxen whose slow, plodding feet had etched them in the soil, a scarce few such creatures still exist, remnants of a past era. The wide spread of their cloven hooves, together with their stolid disposition, make them ideal creatures for work in swampy places where horses are apt to thresh about and mire down. On our way home from town one summer's day we came upon a yoke of oxen ditching a black bog for drainage on the Charlie Edward's place. We found it was interesting to watch the beasts as they pulled their feet from the sucking silt of the swamp, exhibiting hardly more concern than had they been on higher ground.

The strangest, most fantastic of all vehicles I ever encountered came as though from the land of make-believe. I came upon it a short way out from town, in the form of an old Model T coupe, minus motor and windshield. A jackpine pole served as a wagon tongue, and on either side was a beast of burden. On its upholstered seat was the individual whose bizarre mind had conceived the device, and brought it into being. Strange as the conveyance and its occupant were, stranger still was the means of its locomotion, for on the gee side of the pole a horse was hitched, and on the haw side, a cow. Surely it was one for Ripley.

Closer to home and within our own school district, where policy required the transportation of children, a strange looking vehicle showed up, one that intrigued Flora in particular, appealing to her sense of humor. With the transportation contract going to Johnny Wiesman, he set to work with saw, hammer, and not a little provincial resourcefulness to construct a rig suitable for the purpose. Upon a pair of horse-drawn bob sleds he built a squatty enclosure from heavy paper cartons, studding each joint, hit or miss, with shiny metal disks that reflected the sunlight. The enclosure was bare of windows, and of paint for that matter. The means of exit and entrance were one and the same, a curtained opening at the driver's seat. With plenty of hay on the floor, it was snug and comfortable for its short trip, even in the coldest weather. What a far cry from big modern busses that now transport children to and from their various places of learning.

Aside from the ridiculous and the unique, there was in our town one particular conveyance that was renowned for its antiquity. Unlike the many ancient model cars that have been rebuilt for show purposes only, this old Ford truck had been in constant service for well over thirty-five years. Each time I watched it chug slowly past the store, I marveled at its stamina and thought surely I had seen it for the last time, but this had been so for many years. Winter and summer alike, over unpaved roads and forest trails, the old truck had hauled logs for the Kemp brothers, and though their mill had long since vanished, the old Model T continued on. Its wood spoked wheels and small, thin tires never failed to attract attention, but more significant was its phenomenal performance record. On weekly trips to town, the old truck reflected austerity from radiator to tail gate, in keeping with the very nature of the bachelor brothers within. Time had woven a web of tradition about this old Model T and the backwoodsmen who nursed it along for nearly four decades.

Chapter 33

BEYOND WORK

Spring rains were frequent now and all nature was responding to the rays of the sun. Our cattle were losing their shaggy coats and taking on a new sheen as succulent grasses became more abundant. Birds were busy mating and bursting into song, and fish were seeking shallow waters within their own environment for their seasonal spawning. Spring had come at last and before we realized it, May had slipped into June and another busy season was upon us.

Into this state of affairs came our three city standbys - Lois, bursting with enthusiasm as she gathered up the four loose ends of her milking job, Lou with equal gusto claimed immediate priority to both the separator and churn, and Dick gladly accepted his new role of handy man, having surrendered his job of cowboy to the new fence. Though many things were unpredictable, there was one thing we could count on, for as surely as spring followed winter, so did calves appear with equal regularity. Even Mollie had given birth to a calf.

"What are you going to call the next one?" I asked Lois as she settled down on her three-legged stool.

"Well now, let's see, we've got a LuluBelle, Mollie's Daisy Belle and Annabelle. I know what, I'll call her Isabell."

"Well that's OK with me, but what if it isn't that kind of a calf?" I replied.

Quick as a flash she came back with, "Oh, that's easy, Pop. I'll call him Isabull."

Our new barn, the growing herd and the very barnyard, all were taking on an aspect that surprised us. Our patrons were showing an ever-mounting interest in the farm atmosphere of our place. They would come around at milking time just to see Lois milk, or the cows as they filed from the barn. On one occasion a little girl who had been watching as I cleaned out the concrete gutter rushed up to her mother saying, "Mommy, now I know where manure comes from." As for us, we appreciated the quantity of milk and cream our patrons consumed.

Shortly after the arrival of our city helpers, we added two pigs to our domestic menagerie – Tom and Jerry we called them. They were as alike as two wieners side by side. We allowed them the freedom of our premises and they soon became tramps. A few grunts at a cabin door usually brought them grub of some sort. With these handouts and the accumulation of garbage from the premises, they needed little attention. Furthermore, they would require no winter feeding, since after the fall crop of acorns, they would be converted into pork and lard for our table. Lou, to my surprise, took a lot of interest in the porkers. "I'd sure like to have my feet under your table next winter," he said as he watched them wallowing in the sandy soil. But alas, Tom sickened and died, and we were sure it had eaten broken glass in the garbage.

Bruce was by and large a serious worker, his mind set to planning and hands to tasks leading to our goal. It surprised me one afternoon to find that both had been diverted for some mischief. Nor was he alone in the diversion, for it seemed Harris had planted the seed of it. My first awareness came at the conclusion of their efforts, in the form of an explosion the likes of which I had not heard in forty years.

Apparently Bruce had been talking to Harris about a plan to someday obtain an acetylene generator for his welder. Harris contributed the fact that the gas was easily generated by simply adding water to carbide pellets, and the seeds were sown. On one trip to town, they had managed to procure a small supply of carbide to 'test'. Later, some water and matches showed it was indeed a simple matter to generate the flammable gas. From that point to their little project was not much of an effort.

Bruce borrowed one of our stout milk cans, boring a small hole near its base. Into this hole he had screwed a spark plug. Harris found a spare ignition coil, and with the addition of some wire and a battery, they were ready for the final exam. Bruce pulled the lid off the can, poured in a small handful of the carbide pellets followed by a cup of water. The lid was replaced and tapped to a secure seal. The wire was attached to the spark plug, strung a distance away, and connected to one side of the coil. When the battery was ready for connection to the other side of the coil, both hunkered down. The wire was touched to the coil terminal and a hundred feet away, a small blue spark pulsed inside the can. The lid exceeded all expectations in altitude and the shot was heard all around the lake. As the lid nearly faded from view, the boys were all laughs at their success, but sobered quickly when they realized they could hardly predict where the three pound galvanized stopper would be returning to earth. Both let out running through the woods as if being chased by a bear.

This was the topic of discussion for the night, and as stern as I presented the dangers of such a prank, I could not help smiling inside – the whole thing reminding me of a quite parallel project I had done at the age of eighteen. My friend Art Whitney and I had gone out west to be cowboys. At ranch after ranch, we found the reality that rookies like us were not needed, but we pressed on. After dozens of disappointments, we were finally offered jobs by one owner. We quickly learned, however, that far from the sought-after life in the saddle, we were to be sheep herders, simply watching the flock on foot in a remote area of his ranch. And to make the situation even worse, we would not even be together, but each tending separate far-flung flocks.

This turned out to be one of the loneliest times of my life, supplies dropped every couple of weeks, and nothing at all to do. I wished a coyote would come prowling, so I could at least shoot at him. I carved a lot, even making a small skull from a die, using two of the dots as the eye socket locators. Finally, in frustration, I sifted through the junk aboard the wagon in which I slept. I found a short length of pipe and caps for each end. An idea was born. For many nights, I pried open the rifle shells which had as yet seen no other use. I emptied the black powder into the pipe until it was nearly full.

The next evening, as my fire settled into deep red coals late in the night, I pulled my device from a pocket. I wondered how far away Art was, and if he would wonder what the noise had been as I dropped the pipe into the embers and beat a hasty retreat. The calm night was ripped by my small piece of pipe, a short but definitive departure from the boredom that had induced me to build it. I had made a bold statement.

I spent the next three days rounding up the sheep which had scattered in panic, a second break from my typical boredom.

Lou had grown up under circumstances wholly different from my own. Somehow, he had missed the things that had so enriched my own boyhood days. He had had little opportunity for play, and knew nothing of hunting or fishing. Nor did he cherish any memories of long hikes or of an old swimming hole. For him there had been no days at hooky, no wild adventures. Instead, work and study had been his lot, with but few hours off for fun. His many years as a Chicago mail carrier, together with his yen for learning, left little time for the things that lay beyond the city's horizons, and now, a babe-in-the-woods, he was at a loss to evaluate his surroundings. Though he was older than I and we were poles apart in our thinking, our very differences seemed a bond that held us together. Only where work was concerned did we meet on common ground.

One hot day in July, as we were nearing knock-off time, I said, "Lou, how about a nice cool dip in the lake before supper? What do you say?" I had put this question to him on numerous occasions but always to no avail, and was wholly unprepared for his reply.

"Gollee, Charlie! Do you know, I've a good notion to try it," he said as he mopped his face with his handkerchief. Hardly believing my ears I gathered up the tools quickly lest he change his mind. For three seasons I had tried my best to coax him  into the water, and now at last he had acquiesced.

As a boy I never bothered much about towels or soap or even a bathing suit for that matter, and things hadn't changed much since then. If Lou was to be favorably impressed, things must approximate the conveniences of a bathroom as nearly as possible. I was considering the matter when Lou came from his room, a bath towel and cloth folded neatly over his arm and a bar of soap in his hand.

"You know, Charlie, I haven't got a bathing suit. Can't you scare one up for me?" I couldn't, and for a moment I thought the whole thing was off, but then got an idea.

"I'll tell you what, Lou. We'll go along the shore line past that old shaggy Norway that's fallen into the water and go in naked. No one can see us there for sure. Now what to you say, huh?"

"Naked!" he shouted. "Me go in naked?" What thoughts lay behind the stare he bestowed upon me and what influenced his thinking I'll never know, but I took heart when he said, "Well, Charlie, I'll try it this once if you say so, but you're sure no one will see us out there?"

Behind the screen of the prone tree, I stripped off my clothing and waited as Lou prepared for his first bath beneath the open heavens. Brushing aside a few imaginary obstacles from a grassy mound, he eased himself down. Removing his shoes and carefully tucking in the laces, he placed them side by side upon the ground in proper relationship, one with the other. Now came his socks and garters to be neatly folded and deposited with his footgear. His long trousers followed, whose legs he matched meticulously, crease for crease. As he folded his striped shorts with time consuming care, I was reminded of our old swimming hole shout, "The last one in is a horse's hind end." Finally and at long last, he stood upright, unabashed, naked as Adam.

"Oh, my glasses," he exclaimed, and taking them off, laid them upon the neat pile at his feet. With a parting touch as though to say 'now you stay right there till I get back,' he straightened up. "I'm as good as blind now," he said reaching for my hand. His lean, white body and long, thin legs were accentuated by his nudity and quite in contrast to my own short, rotund form. Without his thick lenses, I hardly knew him. He winced with each shuffling step as, hand in hand, we made our way down to the water's edge. The lake lay smooth and inviting as he gingerly tested the water with the tip of his toes.

"Wow, but that's cold!" he shouted.

"Now listen, Lou. Just take it easy and don't get excited," I said, gently pulling him in. "It's a little cold at first, I know, but you'll get used to it."

At knee depth he stopped. "This is my limit," he said, and so it was. But there would be another day, I thought. As I doused him with water he squirmed and shouted, but when I lathered and sponged his blue-white shoulders and back he chortled with satisfaction, "Gollee, but that feels good."

Hardly a day passed thereafter that this performance wasn't repeated, although I could never coax him beyond his original stopping place. As the days became progressively warmer, our dips were more appreciated. But a time came when, to my surprise and regret, he absolutely refused to go near the water and reverted to his old custom of sponge bathing in the privacy of his room. Nor would he venture any good reason for his change of mind. "Oh, I just don't care about it any more," he said when I queried him. But I knew better - there was a reason even if he refused to divulge it.

For many days, the water beyond the old prone Norway lay undisturbed while we hammered, sawed and sweated. Imagine, then, my utter astonishment when one day at quitting time Lou said, "How about a dip in the lake, Charlie?" just as though nothing had happened.

"Well, why not?" I fairly shouted, as I was flabbergasted. "You go ahead, Lou, and get your soap and towel and I'll meet you down at the tree." Sure now that he was about to take me into his confidence, I waited while he disrobed, but he said nothing. Maybe he'll open up in the water, I thought, as we made our way down the sandy embankment.

"I'm alright now, Charlie," he said, taking his hand from mine. With this I hurried out for a quick dip myself. I was surprised when I turned and saw Lou entering the water backward.

"Why, Lou," I shouted, "what in the world is the matter with you? Are you afraid someone is going to steal your clothes or something?"

"No, I'm not afraid of that, Charlie," he said. "I may as well tell you all about it, but I'd rather face the shore while I talk, if you don't mind. When I was up at the store one day, Mr. Byrnes told me all about Abbie French. He says she has a pair of powerful binoculars and that she scans our shoreline every evening to see what progress we've made, that's all there is to it."

"Why Lou Arnold, you old Adonis!" I shouted. "Shame on you for a whole month. Abbie French, of all women!"

Chapter 34

OH THE STORIES I COULD TELL

Surely no other sport lends itself to braggadocio and a glib tongue than does fishing, with its tall tales which grow taller with each telling. Though golf and baseball have their thrills and boastings, a hole-in-one can never become two holes-in-one, nor can a home run be stretched into a five-bagger, but a five pound bass caught today may very easily weigh six tomorrow and seven by the end of the week. Indeed, what would fishing be without its flights of fancy, its potential extravaganza and its bombast? Hardly more than an indulgence, I would say.

Although our weekly campfire gatherings have brought forth many a fanciful tale, it is the true stories that have the greatest appeal, and to our family doctor goes credit for one of my favorites. His profession had taken him into every nook and corner of the countryside, over corduroy roads, through logging trails and across windswept waters. Incidents ranging from comedy to tragedy had been part of his vast experience, and the following is one of a few which he volunteered to me one day in his office.

Two city lads had gone fishing out upon the broad waters of Shell Lake. They were doing well enough at casting until a flying plug inadvertently caught one of them full in the face. With the colorful bait dangling from a lobe of his nose like some aboriginal pendant, the lad had become excited.

"Now take it easy, don't rock the boat," his buddy shouted. "I'll crawl over and take it out."

But it hadn't been that easy, for in his frantic attempt to free his pal, an adjoining barb penetrated the ball of his own thumb. Ye gods and little fishes, what to do now? How the two ever made it to shore is still a matter of conjecture. Dr. Hering had been at his upstairs office window. "I saw them coming," he said. "They were headed my way down the main street of Shell Lake, the one thumbing the nose of the other to every passer-by."

Although we usually depended upon nephew Dick for much of our humor, it was left for his brother, Ralph, to do the unconventional when he caught his first fish. While working in the park, I was astonished to see a fish fly up in the air, then plummet back to earth. Several repetitions of this strange performance quite naturally aroused my curiosity and I took off for the beach. There was Ralph at the water's edge bending over a bass, scrutinizing it as though it were some exotic creature, and poking it with his finger.

"Why, Ralph," I said, "what on earth are you doing, throwing that fish up like that?"

"Well, you see, Uncle Charlie, I'm just seeing if it's dead. We want to eat it for dinner and I've been killing it."

Then there is always one about beginner's luck, such as this one. A man and his wife, having just arrived at the lake, were anxious to get out on the water. Stepping into his boat, the husband was about to push off when his spouse yelled, "Wait for me; you know I'm going along, too."

"Oh no, you're not. I brought you along to do the cooking," was his caustic reply, and with that, he shoved off.

"Would you like to come with me?" a woman who had overheard the dialog asked. "I'm no fisherman, but there's a line hanging over the end of the boat."

Of course she would, and soon these two were in the wake of the crabby husband, chatting together like old friends. For the rest of the story, I am obliged to rely on the words of old George Hart, an Indian guide who was out on the water at the time.

"Two women were in a boat when they passed me," he said. "They had no poles and I didn't think they were fishing. I paid no more attention until I heard someone screaming and when I looked,

I saw only one woman in the boat. I hurried over to help and then I saw the other women. She was flat down on top of a big pike, yelling her head off."

The two of them had literally hauled in a fifteen pound Northern on the dangling chalk line. Rowing in to shore, they proudly flaunted it before the astonished husband who was bemoaning his own bad luck.

Despite many years spent in a fishing camp, I am obliged to return to my boyhood days for my own prize fish story. On a warm June day in Chicagoland, back before the turn of the century, three boys might have been seen trudging toward the Des Plaines River, their bare feet clinging to the smooth steel rails of the Burlington tracks. One of the trio you have already guessed, the others were my brother, Wallace, and a boyhood pal of mine. Where the railroad bridge crosses the river, we left the open right-of-way for the cool shade of a wooded path that followed the course of the stream. Finally arriving at our favorite water hole, we cut willow poles, tied on lines and cast them in.

Luck was somewhere else that day, and soon my buddies were prone on their backs, their caps pulled over their eyes, dead to the world. The water was temptingly cool to my feet as, step by step, I made my way toward a large boulder mid-stream. Here I dropped my line and watched it drift down with the eddying current. I'd show those sleepyheads how to fish! Although I had spit on my hook and had patiently waited, luck had not returned. I was envying the boys their nap when suddenly I felt something strike at my big toe. Strange to say, through the green water I could make out a big bass, fanning its tail, evidently in preparation for another attack. Though I dangled my worm temptingly before its mouth, it would have none of it, but pushing it aside, made another formidable onslaught. I had only to wiggle my toe for repeat performances.

Determined now to catch the creature, I took to the shore where I bound a long shank hook along side my great toe. Once more I took a stand beside the boulder where I had seen the man-eating fish. Nor had I long to wait. The creature struck while I was off balance, and I floundered helplessly about, shouting all the while. Had I caught the fish or had it caught me, that was the question. By backing out, dragging my quarry along, I finally made shore where two google-eyed boys were waiting to assist me with outstretched arms, expecting nothing short of an alligator.

Evidently I had invaded the pebbly spawning ground of the fish, and its attack had been motivated by rage rather than hunger.

The generous spacing of our cabins provided an individuality and a maximum of privacy our guests. This, with the spaciousness of our park, were features that never failed to impress chance visitors as well as our patrons. These things

accounted for much of our repeat business, and heretofore advertising had cost us next to nothing. However, ten weeks was practically the extent of our business—Labor Day was virtually the end of our season. Another new cabin each year clearly called for some advertising venture. The Indian Head Country, Inc., an association of which we were a member, took a booth each spring at the big outdoor show in Chicago. To make use of its services, we would need literature to dispense, so we decided to put out a brochure. The final product was the result of the combined ideas of our whole family and we felt very proud of it.

Campers seldom visited us, though when they did, we charged them only a nominal fee. We had been campers ourselves, and appreciated their many problems. Our lake shore was slowly filling up, and we had about decided against allowing further camping. However, one day an inquiry came concerning a camping place, and influenced by past memories, we broke down and wrote the party that he might come. We quoted him a price of five dollars for the week, including the price of a boat.

The day of their arrival came and with it a man, his wife and two children. Attached to their car was a trailer and a boat piled high with duffel.

"Oh, what a swell place to camp," the man said as he started unloading.

"I'm afraid you can't camp here in the park," I said, "This is our playground." I found them a good spot close to the water where they pitched their tent and settled themselves comfortably. When the newcomer next showed up, I was working down on the beach.

"Say," he said, "I want to settle what I owe you."

"OK," I said, "that'll be five bucks."

"But that price included a boat, didn't it?"

"Why, yes, of course," I replied with some surprise.

"Well, what do you get a day for your boats?"

"A dollar a day."

"I'll tell you what, Mr. Palmer, as long as I brought my own boat along, I think you should cut that price to two-fifty." Though I needed every cent I could get my hands on, I thought perhaps he, too, was in hard circumstances

"Well, I guess that will be all right," I said. He laid two ones on my outstretched palm, and opening a purse, counted out the balance in dimes and nickels.

An hour later he accosted me again. "Mr. Palmer, can I use one of those cane poles there in the grass?"

"Why not? That's what they're there for," I answered.

"You know, I bought one at that store back there. I'm sure going to take it back." It began to dawn on me that I was dealing with no common camper. Nor was this the end of his niggardliness, for shortly thereafter he said to me, "Does the game warden get around here very often?"

"Sure, quite often," I said, getting his meaning.

"You know I just hate to pay for an out-of-state license. I was wondering if it wouldn't pay me to take a chance." So now he would beat the state, too.

The following morning, while dumping a fresh batch of minnows into our tank, our camper approached with a minnow pail. Aha, this is where I'll get even. I'll charge him plenty for his bait.

"Well, what kind do you want, chubs, crappie minnows or some of those big ones down there?" I asked.

"Well, Mr. Palmer, I really didn't come to buy minnows. I thought maybe you'd let me have all the dead ones floating on top." Ye gods and little fishes, I was ready to explode. Instead, I calmed down. The customer is always right, I said to myself. Anyway he'll be gone in a few days and I'll never set eyes on him again.

The story has a sequel, however, for some dozen years later I was awakened by an early comer.

"I'll be right out," I shouted from my window as I jumped into my pants. A car stood beside the house, filled with children, and a loaded boat on wheels was attached behind. A man and his wife were stretching themselves from a long journey when I greeted them. Although I had been greeted by name, I thought nothing of it.

"Are you folks looking for a cabin?" I queried.

"Oh, we never take a cabin. We prefer to live close to nature. We'd like to pitch our tent on your lakeshore close to Honey Bird," he said.

Suddenly my eyes were opened and I recognized the tight-fisted camper of earlier years. Yes, he wanted to live close, period. Now, I said to myself, is the time to settle an old score. Seating myself on our stone wall, I said, smiling, "Here, sit down. I want to tell you a story, if you don't mind." So I related in detail the story of a cheap camper who had once spent a week on our premises. I omitted nothing of consequence and finished by saying, "Never since have we taken in campers."

Chapter 35

NEW FRONTIERS, OLD BOUNDARIES

With cabins filled to capacity, the new diving raft the boys had built on steel barrels soon became a popular rendezvous for the younger people. Toward the end of each day when the two Sams and Bruce were aboard, the fun was at its height. Each plunge into the deep was accompanied by noisy vibrations of the long plank and shouts and laughter that followed. Yet none of this was for Cousin Lou, who would peer longingly over the water toward the noisy group.

Canoe jousting, too, became part of those early water sports.

Rival jousters, their long, padded lances poised, their seconds at the paddles, would charge each other like knights of old. Usually a sound jab on the head or body of an opponent would result in an overturned canoe, often a two team wetting, and the hills would resound with laughter.

Most unique of the boys' handiwork was a diving helmet made from a small oil drum. This was weighted down with lead and padded to fit snugly over the head and shoulders. A small rectangle of glass provided an area for vision, and a forty-foot flexible hose provided air. The device was simple, and safe enough – in case of an emergency, one had only to flip from under and rise to the surface. With one Sam at the tire pump in the boat, and the other tending the hose, Bruce made the initial dive. He had chosen a site near the inlet, the deepest part of our lake. While he scouted the silty bottom of the hole, we followed his movements by the clusters of bubbles that rose in his wake. When both Sams had had their turns, I took mine, in shallower water, and on a sandier bottom.

"How did you like it down there?" Flora asked when I told her about it that evening.

"Once is enough for me," I replied. "It might do when there's nothing left upstairs to explore."

"Couldn't be you're getting old, could it, Charlie?" she replied, stealing a glance at my graying hair.

One afternoon, Lois had decided to try out the diving apparatus, and enlisted Dick to man the pump for her. They rowed over to the deep waters near the inlet, and Lois jumped into the water beside the boat. Dick set the helmet on her shoulders, and moved to the pump. Lois let go of the side of the boat and descended into the cool, deep water. At first the mystery of the new sights and experience were consuming, but after a few minutes, she found it harder and harder to breath. She jerked on the hose, a predetermined signal for more air, but things only got worse.

Lois finally slipped out from under the helmet and made for the shadow of the boat above. As she broke the surface and gasped for a full breath, she pulled up to look into the boat. Dick sat at the pump, hardly moving the handle, as he watched a boatload of three girls passing slowly by. "Dick!" Lois shouted, and he turned to see her head above the edge of his boat. Instantly he began pumping furiously.

Less than a week later Lois found her payback opportunity. Harris had captured a large snapper turtle. We were always eager for some meat in our diet, and this would be a treat. As I butchered our find, Lois found that the heart of the turtle, kept warm, would continue beating for hours. Not only did she have a fun afternoon surprising folks around the place, opening her clasped hands to reveal the pulsing organ, but come suppertime, she placed it upon Dick's plate, covering it with an inverted bowl. Dick, late as usual, lifted the bowl and stared at the undulating thing on his plate in disbelief. Only when everyone could no longer hold their laughter did he realize it wasn't his dinner.

Soon it became evident that Harold's frequent visits were prompted by other than our water sports. During the Walker's long stay, he seldom missed a day on the premises. Strangely, too, Dick's sister, Marian, was finding a new interest in things that could be mutually shared, and with who better than the visitor from across the lake. Though this Sam's upbringing had been more or less provincial, he was uninhibited where girls were concerned, and to my knowledge this was not his first amorous adventure. While working here, he had frequently taken off to some secluded spot where he would open his lavender scented mail and dream away his noon hour.

Our immediate thoughts were not so much on a potential nephew as they were

Lois

on the probability of another son-in-law. Lois was nearing the end of her schooling and would soon be obliged to choose between marriage and a career in art. She had invited Ken Huth up to the lake for an all-too-short vacation, but it was long enough for us to learn the direction of our daughter's future. For them it had been an unforgettable week, indeed, one when Cupid had been unrelenting with his bow and potent little arrows.

In love as in life, not everything goes quite as planned. One afternoon as Lois was raking near Crows Nest, with Ken and Flora working nearby, she ran into a hornet's nest on the ground. The hornets attacked her, and she ran screaming and swatting. As she ran past her mother, Flora ripped off Lois' blouse as it was obvious the little yellow devils were up and under it. She had nothing else on beneath it. In the end, most of her twenty-two stings were under her shorts, and Lois later had to lay across Flora's lap as she pulled out the stingers. For the next few days, Lois ate standing up.

To see these young folks developing so rapidly and to find them on the very brink of maturity drove home, as nothing else, the realization that time was rapidly passing. Added to this was the knowledge that Harris would soon leave to take up his education where he had left off. This had been a hard decision on his part, for he had not intended to go until our tenth cabin had been completed. Foreseeing this, we had rushed the preparation of two more cabin sites with their concrete floors, and took over and remodeled the Hickes' summer home on our northern boundary, thus adding one more to our complement of finished cabins. This we named Shore Leave, and with its four bedrooms, was to prove a favorite cabin over the years to large families.

Despite our practice of strict economy, there were times when we found it expedient to let down the bars, to forego budgetary restraint, as was the occasion when we purchased a small portable electric light plant. This was a simple piece of machinery requiring only a kick of the starter to set the generator going. With its 300 watts of 110 volt electricity, it proved a boon for overtime work in the shop. Although we heard rumors of an expansion of the Rural Electrification Association (REA) program, nothing ever seemed to come of them. Compared to our gasoline lantern, the new generator, using the same fuel, provided astoundingly better results. We had been without electricity for so long, we had quite forgotten its great convenience.

Of profoundly more importance than our new lighting system was the telephone that came quite unheralded. Unlike our radio, this now was a two-way link with the outside world. We had only to turn a crank, lift the receiver, and converse with Ruth or Lois, or take reservations for our cabins. Surely our little world was expanding.

Our small herd of cows was increasing and, in spite of poor forage, was more than paying its way. As for our garden, though it had been an exceptionally dry summer, things remained to be harvested, thanks to water we had hauled from the lake. Beyond rows of drying cornstalks, vegetables rooted in the sandy soil waited gathering, squash lay hidden among their

Roof Tree

own twisted vines, and watermelon, Bruce's delight, was slowly ripening in the sun in a race with the first frost.

All things considered, this season had been one of accomplishment. We had done well on our building program, completing two more cabins. Honey Bird had proved so popular that we repeated its design, this time with French doors leading into a large front porch. Birch Hill cabin overlooked the park and faced toward the lake on a low, birch covered hill. Roof Tree was finished by mid-season and had been steadily occupied since. It also had two-bedrooms, but was of somewhat different design. The large, many-windowed living room was virtually a sun parlor, open to the lake on warm, clear days, yet cozy on cold or rainy ones. The path out to the lake led through a small grove of stately Norways. Roof Tree and Honey Bird were in a more secluded part of the resort; those around the park were for folks who wanted to keep one foot in civilization.

Each shortening day brought us closer to the end of our resort season, when the last vacationer would depart and the park and bathing beach became silent and deserted. Autumn in the woods is a going away time, when the birds, flowers and leaves, disappear. Even the sun is well along on its equatorial journey. To me, it is the most beautiful time of the year, though moody and melancholy at times.

The noisy family of martins beside our doorstep had already deserted their lofty quarters, and we missed their throaty quarrelings. Our friends and relatives, too, had taken leave. Finally the day came to close the door behind our last vacation straggler, and we did so with mixed feelings of satisfaction and regret. However, any sense of well-being or contentment was short lived, indeed. For like some ominous storm cloud in the night, adversity of disastrous proportion arose to threaten the very foundation of our undertaking. Sickness and misfortune had hounded us before, but from these experiences came no answer to the problem that loomed before us.

I was working on the roof of Shore Leave cabin. Its vantage point, at the turn of the lake, was a good view of the sweep of shoreline that curved beyond our own property line. This was an ideal piece of frontage belonging to Mr. Brede at the head of the lake, and I knew that someday he would build upon it, though I had little thought that the time had actually arrived. About to climb down, I saw a man approaching. As he stepped into the open, I recognized him as Jack Bearhart, a full-blooded Chippewa Indian of my acquaintance. Jack was a capable sort of fellow who could turn a hand to any job in the

Shore Leave

woods, be it felling trees, spudding pulp, or general work about a saw mill. He frequently sold me axe handles which he whittled from white-ash saplings. Industrious as he was, he found plenty of time for hunting and fishing.

Now Jack carried neither gun nor fishing pole; instead over his shoulder was a surveyor's rod and beneath one arm, held a bundle of newly-cut stakes. His backward glances told me the surveyor, too, was coming, and I kept an eye in that direction as my curiosity was growing with every moment. Nor had I long to wait, for soon the brush parted and the surveyor, as had Jack, made straight for the cabin. Daris Conner, part Indian himself, gave me the facts as he understood them from the plat he carried with him.

"This is only a tentative run," he said. "We've got to do some brushing before we can start on the survey." With his next breath he asked, "Whose cabin is this?" The question was asked with such directness that its import was obvious.

"It's mine," I answered, not without apprehension, since now I was beginning to understand.

For a moment he was quiet as though pondering the situation, then pointing down the line towards Roof Tree and Honey Bird, he asked, "Those yours, too?" Not till then did the full meaning of his questioning strike home, and with sickening impact. Should my assumption be correct, the survey was about to deprive us of a large portion of our lake frontage.

Although we had taken the precaution against settling on the wrong forty when first we came, somehow through negligence or per-haps procrastination, had failed to have a survey made of our own. While Mr. Brede and I had consulted together and had been satisfied as to the dividing line between our premises, neither of us had taken into consideration the sliver of a remaining forty, the great portion of which lay under water. This was the property in question. And now a new line was being run to definitely ascertain the boundary between our holdings. Little else was talked about that evening, and by quitting time the following day we knew the worst.

Beside the highway, a mile to the north, stood the first driven stake, a vital point upon which so much of our future depended. Then the others, over the angling creek, on through beds of sphagnum moss, southward over hills and through the woods to the center of the section, where a marker was placed. The line continued on from this point, now approaching Shore Leave. With bullet-like precision it passed directly through the center of the cabin as if this had been its target from the first. But fate was not yet content with this finding. On our bathing beach, beyond where the waters lap the fine sands, stood the last stake, driven like a dagger into the very heart of our enterprise.

Certainly we could not and did not accept the findings as final - instead we took the matter up with old Mr. Harmon who had made the original government survey and had already rendered us invaluable service.

"Now let's see," he said, scratching his head. "If I remember correctly, there should be a witness tree very close to the center of that section, and another not far from the creek up there on the highway beyond Byrnes Store."

That he could recall these details after so many years and distinguish them from the scores of other surveys he had made seemed nothing short of phenomenal. The first mentioned tree was quickly recalled, for it was a big Norway over which we had often puzzled. Close to its base and on a barkless area, a code had been inscribed which to us was but meaningless hieroglyphics. Of the last tree, we knew nothing. Though he at first refused to entertain any idea of a new survey, due to his age, as the past unfolded before his mind, his determination weakened, and each recollection became a challenge he could not resist.

The following morning, we gathered where the creek crosses the highway, hopeful if not expectant. After noting the newly established line, Mr. Harmon pointed towards the remains of a long decayed stump.

"That," he said, "was a standing tree when I ran that survey many years ago, but it will do us little good now." A rod or two away stood the first stake of Mr. Conner's survey, bright and new in the sunlight.

When Mr. Harmon finished with his survey, we found the difference sufficient to put Shore Leave in the clear, but though it saved us a few final feet of lake frontage, to all intents and purposes the initial damage still remained. Furthermore, in the eyes of the law, one survey was as valid as the other, and Mr. Conners' stake still remained where he had driven it at the water's edge upon our beach. We didn't know what to do. A fence along the lake, no matter how shortened, was unthinkable. Mr. Harmon, with the wisdom of experience and an understanding of our dilemma, suggested a way out.

"I'll talk the matter over with my friend Daris, and together we'll suggest a compromise of some kind with Mr. Brede. That narrow strip of lake front will do him no good. After all, it might just as well have been tacked onto your property instead of Mr. Brede's when I made the original survey. There are meander lines involved, too, in which the state is interested. I'm sure he will be glad to settle with you for a minimal sum."

In this country where decay and age, and even the woodsman's axe are a constant threat to witness trees, where timber barons of old purposely overshot their cuttings and established false boundary lines of their own, it is little wonder that highways are crooked, and surveyors and lawyers are always busy over adjustments and compromises.

So the matter was finally settled. What had seemed like a mountain at the time, and indeed it was, seems only a molehill with the telling now, many years later. I paid Mr. Brede the sum of $225 for the wedge of frontage, and together with our surveyor's fee, it just about canceled out the $300 I had gotten earlier that season from the lot sale.

An exceptionally dry summer had left its mark upon the entire countryside, but of more consequence was the state of our own premises. The woodland grasses, despite their shade, were wilted and poor, and our cattle pressed hard against their wire enclosure for the few green blades beyond reach of their tongues. Even deep-rooted clover, so recently come to the park, had succumbed early to the drought, leaving our park seared and brown. By Labor Day the birches were bare, and slender aspen were dropping their leaves in profusion. Birds had long since forgotten their songs, and even fish in their fluid environment had somehow sensed the earth's dryness and refused to take our lures. All nature seemed stinted and grudging. Each day was a repetition of the one before, with cloudless skies and heat waves dancing over highways and open glades.

Affecting our morale even more than this was the knowledge that Harris was about to leave, about to sever ties with the family enterprise to which he had given so much of himself. Though we knew from the start that this day would surely come, somehow it was here all too soon. Not until he himself had spoken of his desire to go did the real meaning of it all bear down upon us. Earlier one evening, at the supper table, he broached the subject.

"Pa, don't you think you and Mom can get along without me now? You know, if I'm going back to school, I've got to get started pretty quick." Too moved for the moment, I remained silent, waiting for his mother to reply.

"Well, son," she said, "Of course we want you to go on with your education, but what are your plans? How are you going to make ends meet? You know we can't do much to help you, don't you?"

"Much? Why, about all we can do is give you our blessing," I added.

"To tell the truth, I haven't any definite plans, but I'm sure I can get a job of some kind. That's the way you did it, wasn't it Mom, when you went to college? It's the tuition that bothers me most, but I've already written the aunts and I'm sure I can get a loan from them."

"Get a job? Why sure you can get a job," Bruce cut in. "The sooner you get started the better. Of course we'll get along without you." The optimism of youth, with the whole country virtually idle.

So the day of departure came. We watched our eldest son as he gathered his few belongings - a mandolin, his archery equipment, a handful of books and his clothing. As he stood ready to go, a smile on his face, our hearts sank within us. A handclasp for Bruce and me, a hug and kiss for his mother, then he was off. With lumps in our throats, we followed the course of his old Model T as it carried him from sight over the sandy road he had helped create, painstakingly blasting out the stumps. Gone, now, was that happy disposition which had made fun out of so much of our work.

Chapter 36

DANCE THE DANCE

I always prided myself on my ability to do things with my hands, and now for the first time in my memory, I had a job to do that had me stumped. It was a simple thing, requiring the simplest of tools, but I had neither the know-how nor the desire to begin. To put it bluntly, I had to kill a hog. Shooting the creature would have been easy, but I had been advised against it. Fortified with a bulletin from the Department of Agriculture entitled, "How to Butcher a Hog," I whetted my knife to a razor edge and made ready for the ordeal.

Flora, quite conveniently, took herself down to the lake, out of hearing. "I'll help you when the killing's done," she had said. Tender-hearted Bruce, who considered the whole thing nothing short of murder, reluctantly promised to give me a hand. "Call me when you're ready," was his reply.

While flames licked at our huge iron kettle, I prepared a dunking barrel, laid out a couple of hog scrapers, a hay hook and an assortment of keen blades. The proposed victim to this heinous plot lay basking peacefully in the sun, not a care in the world to ruffle his composure. I imagined myself over the prone body, my knife poised for the thrust into the soft pink flesh of this unsuspecting creature. For the moment, my courage failed me. Could I possibly go through with it after all? Again I settled down to study the anatomy of a hog. There it was, plain as day, the diagram setting forth the heart and proper point of penetration. The more I read, the simpler it all seemed, and with each paragraph my courage returned, my confidence mounted. Why, there's little to it, I thought. I better get started.

Vapor was rising now over the kettle and tiny bubbles were bursting on the surface – the water was scalding hot.

"Bruce!" I shouted as I laid a cautious thumb on the edge of my knife. Jerry still lay on his side, but at my shout, he lazily opened one eye and grunted a sleepy greeting as though to say, "How's garbage today?" With that, my nerve faltered and my heart sank. Who could stick a knife into so unsuspecting a creature? Not I, to be sure. Jumping over the fence, I took off for the Norton place, my conscience easier and my mind made up.

"Why sure, I'll stick your hog," George said when I explained my dilemma. "There's nothing to it when you know how." Bruce, guessing my mission and hearing the truck return, had, like his mother, found things that needed doing elsewhere, and only Jerry was on hand to welcome us.

"Now I'll grab him by the front foot and throw him on his back. You straddle him and hold him down while I do the sticking," our neighbor said, matter-of-factly.

"OK," I replied, and in a jiffy was astride, holding Jerry's front legs wide apart and feeling like an accessory before the fact.

"Hold him tight," George shouted, as he plunged the knife hilt-deep into the soft flesh. "Now grab..." His sentence was never finished. As the blade was withdrawn, a stream of blood caught him full in the face, blinding him. I, too, had gotten my share.

"Get me some water, quick," he shouted. "I can't see." Instead, I took his hand and led him into the kitchen, to the sink. "You know," he said as he dried his face on a towel, "I've stuck a lot of pigs in my day, but that's the first time that ever happened to me."

With the guilty feeling of an accessory after the fact, I started back to the scene of the crime, George at my heels still rubbing his eyes. But there was no corpus delicti about, only a crimson trail that led into a hole beneath the haystack. Here George dropped to his knees and peered into the dark cavity.

"Go get that knife," he shouted, as he wriggled his way in.

When I returned, Jerry was squealing like, well, like the stuck hog that he was. As for George, he, too, was contributing to the turmoil with a barrage of choice invectives. Out in the open now, a quick coup de grace, and the bloody ordeal was over and past.

Although we settled in the Town of Rusk, most of our friends lived in the neighboring Town of Evergreen across the county line. This was one community among a few that could boast of a town hall. Except on election days when the Stars and Stripes designated this provincial structure as a voting place, a passersby might easily mistake it for an abandoned schoolhouse. Austere and boldly obtrusive against a background of evergreen and popple, its padlocked door and shuttered windows reflected anything but hospitality.

Contrary to appearances, there was more than met the eye in this wayside gathering place, for at times it was the very epitome of friendliness and joviality, as we were about to learn. The occasion was a dance, an old-fashioned square dance such as our forefathers had known.

Although we passed by the place many times on our way to and from town, this was to be our first look at its interior, our introduction to a new facet of social life in this community. With some trepidation, and not a little curiosity, we stepped from our truck and hesitantly opened the door. A few early comers, strangers to us, were grouped about a huge box stove, some with backs turned and others with hands outstretched to the warmth. We felt conspicuous and out of place, and as we scanned the interior, kept one eye on the door in eager anticipation of the arrival of friends. A long table bearing an old ballot box stood on a low platform, wooden benches were stacked about, and a pile of cord wood hugged the wall beyond the stove. The yellow glow from kerosene lamps fell across the keyboard of an antiquated piano, softening its toothy smile.

Stamping feet interrupted our survey and returned our attention to the door. To our relief, in came the VanLeeuvens, arms filled with firewood and victuals, their smiling faces aglow from the cold weather. They were quickly followed by the Wisners who lived close by, she bearing a hot dish and he struggling with a big milk can of water. And so they came, the Moruds, Moorheads, Comstocks, Nortons, Sylvesters, Dunhams, Greenfields, the Schreibers, the Clyde Browns and half the countryside, until I thought the place would burst at its seams.

There was no sham here, no pretense. Denim was on a par with serge, calico with rayon. How different from the conventions I had known, where clothes had been circumspect and a matter of social propriety. Here, however, where hightops served as dancing shoes and trousers cuffs as ash trays, was a total lack of formality, a freedom from restraint, characteristic of homespun and tallow candle days.

Suddenly I was awakened by a voice: "One more couple here! One more couple!" sounding loudly over the gaiety and banter. Conversation ceased now, weather and crops were quickly forgotten. "One more couple," the voice rang out again. There was a scuffling of feet and scraping of benches being dragged as the floor was cleared. When Ralph Thomas pounded the ivory keys and Bill Ferguson sawed at his fiddle, the festivities started in earnest.

"Honor your partner and lady on the left!
All join hands and circle left!"

"Why, that's Walt Sylvester calling," I whispered to Flora as a whirling group spun by. Rhythm was in their step and a wild, primitive harmony in every movement.

"Balance all! Swing your partners!
Left allemande! Once and a half and right and left grand!"
directed the monotone chant, the meaningless calls.

"All Greek to me," I said.

"Sashay!
Do-se-do, a little more do!"

"Buckskin moccasins on a puncheon floor,
Swing once and a half and then some more."

On and on they went until time and sheer exhaustion brought it to a halt. Though I appreciated the fun and frolic of the square dance, I never learned the controlled pattern nor the meaning of its sing-song directions. On several occasions, when I managed to clown my way through, the wall-flowers burst into laughter. The footwork was just too much for me.

When it came eating time, however, with the emphasis on stomach and not on feet, I was on familiar ground, in my own element as it were. Even before the dance was over, the tantalizing smell of perking coffee

Evergreen Town Hall

excited my salivary glands and put a keen edge on my appetite. "Come and get it," was a call I could readily understand and appreciate. Food from country kitchens and wood-burning stoves was good and abundant, and I never failed to join that line with high anticipation. Was it through custom or reticence on the part of the women that the menfolk were invariably first to march around the table with their trays? Who knows? At any rate, this was etiquette as we found it in the northwoods.

Not every gathering involved dancing – sometimes the entertainment was cards. Though these were less hilarious affairs, formality was still at a minimum. Leaving for such a party one dark winter's evening, Flora admonished as she stepped out with her potluck, "Now Charlie, you blow out the lamp, and for goodness sake don't forget our card table there by the door. I'll turn on the headlights so you can see." Following her instructions literally, I quickly found myself groping in the dark. Finally finding the table, I set out for the car beside the shop.

"What in the world are you doing with that thing?" her voice came out of the night.

"With what?" I replied, stopping short in the glare of the headlights.

"Why, that folding bathtub!"

As time passed, better lighting was provided. Aladdin lamps followed the ordinary kerosene variety, then came the more stable gasoline lantern with its less fragile mantle, proving more satisfactory than anything before it. It was left to Bruce, however, to make the greatest advance of all when he wired the main room of the Town Hall for electricity. Of course, that necessitated hauling our light plant to and from the town hall gatherings. On one particular occasion when our truck skidded from the slippery highway, we arrived an hour late to find all was darkness within, folks patiently waiting. "No oil in the emergency lamps," they said.

Today a tall R.E.A. transformer pole stands beside the building, a symbol of even better lighting not only for the town hall, but for a grateful countryside.

Chapter 37

RECOLLECTIONS

Harris' going deprived us of a first-rate workman, and left us afoot once more, except, of course, for the truck. The Chevy was becoming temperamental and undependable, especially during the cold months of winter. As a matter of fact, it had one particular point of weakness ever since our Wisconsin arrival. How many universal joints we had installed over the years I have no idea, but I shall not forget a few times when their installations were anything but fun. In the sub-zero weather, only a quickly built fire by the roadside made the job possible at all for cold hands and stiff fingers. We would take turns upon our backs, beneath the chassis, pounding, twisting and making the necessary adjustments as frigid steel bit to the very bone. Being caught without the necessary spare was doubly tragic, for then nothing but a long hike would get us going again.

We found ourselves in just such a circumstance one day, miles from any source of supply, Spooner being the nearest. There was nothing to do but to take off for town, leaving Harris and Bruce to make the best of it until my return. Helped along by a stiff north wind, I made the first leg of my journey toward Highway 70. At the junction with County H, I was lucky enough to thumb a ride into town. I was not as fortunate on the return trip, though my articulate thumb finally brought me again to the crossing, with a few miles to go. I buttoned up my collar and leaning into the head wind, plodded along, shifting the heavy part from hand to hand. What would Flora be thinking by now?

"What took you so long, Pa? We've been looking up that road for hours," Bruce exclaimed, as the rag wrapped joint dropped heavily on the running board.

"Yes, and we're about froze," his brother added, dancing before the fire. Sensing a hot meal in the offing, they were under the chassis in a jiffy, busy with the installation. I could hear them blowing on their fingers as they twisted and turned the line shaft. Finally a shout from Harris - it sounded ominous.

"Pa, do you hear? You got the wrong part. Do you hear? The wrong part. It must be for a different model." Oh no, it can't be, I thought as I swung down from the cab. It just can't be. But it was.

Like so many vexing situations that have a way of eventually righting themselves, so it was with the matter of our getting about, for quite unexpectedly we fell heir to a car when Flora's sisters purchased a new one and offered us their previous model. The acquisition was another Chevy, but a sedan with upholstery and comfortable springy cushions. Though not new, it was sturdy and economical, especially considering its age and the odometer reading. Other than making a trip to a point midway between Spooner and Chicago, it had cost us not a penny.

"A little good luck for the credit side of the ledger for a change," I said to Flora on our way back.

"Maybe so, but now I have to learn to drive all over again. I'm so used to the three pedals on the Model T."

"You're not complaining, I hope," I replied.

"Well hardly. We're certainly fortunate in getting a car of any kind. Pretty fine sisters I've got." Of late, fortune and misfortune had gone hand in hand, black ink and red alike showing with equal regularity on our books.

The marginal land about the big Wilkerson swamp had lain dry and parched throughout the summer. Where once had been water, now lay an area of ill-smelling silt. Even the muskrats had

abandoned their reed thatched houses, and ducks no longer dropped down to feed among the rushes. Of greater concern were the acres of wild grasses upon which the drought had put its devastating mark. Where last fall there had been tons of wild hay, free for the taking, now was a withered and worthless crop beyond all hope of salvaging. For the first time since our coming, we were obliged to lay out cash to see our stock through winter. Crop shortages had sent prices soaring, corn fodder was scarce, and ordinary hay was ten dollars a ton. We had to have it regardless.

"Maybe we better sell a cow," Flora said, "or better yet, sell them all." Despite it all, springtime was to find our little herd still intact.

North of our place, beyond Byrnes Store, lies the Midwest Cranberry Marsh, a wide open area that drains into our lake. Here cranberries are grown and packaged for a nationwide market by an industry of trade name proportions. This garnet-like fruit, once gathered wild and prized by the Pilgrim fathers, has become traditional over the years as a fare for both Thanksgiving and Christmas holidays. Today, however, cranberries are a year around commodity and may be had out of season frozen, canned or in tasty cocktail form. What housewife today would attempt a turkey dinner without serving these piquant berries in some form or other? How well I recall my mother's cranberry pies, their colorful filling showing temptingly through an open latticework crust. Surely everyone has seen cranberries in bags, but how many have seen them in bogs?

The marsh is what its name implies, a low-lying bog area of perhaps seventy or eighty acres. This is gridironed into rectangular beds by earthen dikes and a series of canals and ditches. The low spreading plants with their evergreen foliage and tea-like leaves require painstaking attention. Unless associated with the business, one has little understanding of the preparation and unceasing vigilance that go into making a successful crop.

An abundant supply of water must be available at all times for flooding purposes, as protection against frosts which may be encountered even in late summer months. Spring blossoming is the critical period, since an entire season's crop may be ruined overnight. During this time, ears are alert for weather reports and eyes scan thermometers by flashlight. Temperatures at the marsh only a mile or so north, vary as much as ten degrees lower than those taken on our forested ground.

When we first came, the harvest was done by manpower. This presented a most colorful picture, where Indians and whites alike worked side by side, knee deep in water, hip deep in boots. Slowly and rhythmically men swung their rake-toothed containers, plucking the floating berries from their long tendrils. Truckloads of berries moved over the dikes to the drying yard on higher ground. Here they were mechanically freed from clinging vines and left to dry in crates stacked high in block-long tiers. Next they were moved into the warehouse for final processing.

From hoppers on the upper floor, the berries found their way down through a unique system of polishing and sorting devices. Most interesting was one that made each individual berry responsible for its own destiny. Sound berries, being resilient, bounced over a hurdle to safety, while duds continued on to the refuse heap. Conveyor belts then carried the successful jumpers past sharp eyes and deft fingers of women for further and final sorting.

In recent years however, harvesting has been mechanized. Rakes mounted at the sides of tractors pluck the berries which are then dumped into trucks and hauled to a modern cleaning machine where they are freed from stems and leaves before being processed and sacked.

What is a good crop? General manager, Charlie Lewis' response; "Why, in a good season, we can expect something better than four-thousand barrels of berries."

When the last of the crop has been safely harvested, a well-earned period of relaxation ensues. Yet even winter brings one last routine task, because frequent floodings have washed away protective sand from around roots. When the winter flooding has frozen hard, trucks loaded with fresh sand move onto the beds to dump it atop the ice, where it is ready to sink about exposed roots with spring's thaw.

One fine Sunday in late Fall, Flora and I had driven over to the Marudes; we had been invited for dinner and an afternoon session at the card table. As we rose from a good meal, Ole, supervisor of the marsh, stepped outside, casting an eye toward the heavens. This was nothing uncommon, for the nature of his business had made him weather-minded. His remark when he came in again really surprised us.

"We're going to get a snow and it won't be long coming," he said as he closed the door behind him.

"But Ole," Flora said, "it's too early for snow and the sun is still shining." We settled around the table again discussing past storms and glad to be housed comfortably in Morud's new home.

Soon Ole rose again from the table and glanced at the thermometer outside. "The temperature's dropping," he said and went to the basement. We heard him stoking wood into the furnace while we dealt out a new hand.

"Better switch on the light before you sit down," Ethel said, "We can hardly see the score card."

Ole had just taken his seat when a blast of wind struck the house and shook the tree tops into a frenzy. We dropped our cards to look out upon a rapidly changing world. Far across the marsh we watched driving snow erase one, then another, of the many diked cranberry beds. Slowly the big concrete block warehouse melted away before our eyes. A gray blanket swept the windows and we could no longer see out.

We dealt out hand after hand and counted our scores that afternoon, little realizing that a tragedy was being enacted not far beyond the cranberry marsh. The gruesome nature of it struck me more forcibly when I found the victim to be a neighboring resort owner. It was obvious there were no eyewitnesses, for the very elements had seen to that. Yet a fair account of the storm that had snuffed out a life may be drawn from the meager facts and filling in by imagination.

Returning home early, Mr. Carsons had taken his gun, and followed by his small dog, jumped into his boat and pushed off from shore. From his home beside the water, he had a commanding view of the lake and no doubt saw ducks settling down as he had many times before. This was Sunday and he still had a few hours of leisure. No hurry, he thought, for the weather is good and the birds are down for the night. He eased on his oars as flock after flock dropped from the sky.

Only the dog in the narrow bow of the boat seemed anxious as he whined and fidgeted in anticipation. A mile or so and they would be in his old blind among the tall reeds. Occasionally a whir of wings sent his hand toward the gun, forgetting that he was still in open water. A light breeze now rippled the surface and he no longer could see the luxurious plant life beneath his boat. A few birds rose from the water and his dog stood stiff-legged and trembling as they passed well out of range overhead. Not far to go now, he thought, as he searched the horizon for familiar landmarks. But now, small waves broke over the bow and his dog lifted one foot then another as though the water burned his feet. For a moment the man rested on his oars, rubbing his eyes as though to dissipate a cloud that obscured his vision. It would not rub away.

With the first realization that the sun had blacked out, he turned to look over his shoulder. He saw it now, just as a heavy gust of wind peppered him with snowflakes. He'd seen the lake whipped into fury by summer storms and he wanted no part of it under these circumstances. Quickly he set his prow toward home. He was sure he could make it all right, just a steady pull and he'd be there before the worst of the storm would strike. Slowly he watched the trees fade away as he pulled at the oars, his back working hard against the storm. "We'll make it all right," he kept saying to his dog, "we'll make it." But he knew he was dealing with the long arm of Old Man Winter reaching out prematurely for his first victim.

With each blast of wind, his small boat rode the crest of a wave and he dared not change his course. He wondered if he was making any progress for he no longer could tell. Just a matter of endurance now. His bared hands were cold and he dared not even look at his blistered palms. Suddenly, as though the sky had dropped about him, the storm broke in all its intensity. Stung with buckshot blasts of snow, he covered his face momentarily. Without the guidance of his oars, the wind turned the boat, and it pitched wildly in the jagged waves. One oar jumped from its pivot and disappeared.

"We'll never make it now," he whispered as he dropped to his knees beside the dog.

Chapter 38

WINTER FRIENDS

Of that happy-go-lucky trio of Sams who had whistled their s's in the subzero temperature of our shop, only Harold remained. He had come around the lake on this particular evening with a proposition which had materialized in his mind since his last visit. Even before seating himself, he launched into his subject.

"Say, Bruce, do you want to make some dough this winter?" he asked enthusiastically. His approach was so abrupt and startling that, for a moment, there was no reply.

"Well, to tell the truth Sam, I haven't seen any of that stuff for so long, I wouldn't know it if I saw it. But go on, what's the catch?"

"My dad says he knows where we can cut all the Christmas trees we want for nothing. Why don't we take a big truckload down to Chicago and sell 'em?"

The matter was discussed, pro and con, as light from our fireplace danced fitfully over the living room walls. A proposition better suited to Harris' disposition, so I wondered how Bruce would react to it – Bruce with his little regard concerning the almighty dollar. I was surprised, then, when his answer came in the form of a counterproposal.

"I'll tell you what I'll do, Sam," he said. "I'll furnish the truck and gas if you'll furnish the trees. I mean, you go and cut 'em and bring 'em back here. I'm just too busy right now, but I know Chicago pretty well, and we'll go down together and try our luck at selling 'em."

Harold eventually pulled back into our yard, red-eyed and his clothes stained with pitch.

"Well, it looks like you struck the jackpot, Harold. All those trees! Have any trouble?" I asked as he dropped from the cab.

"You said it! I got the trees all right, and plenty of 'em, but never again, not for me, not alone anyway."

"Why, what was wrong, Sam?" Bruce asked, stepping from the door. "Did someone give you the hot foot, or did you have to pay for the trees?" Not until his feet were beneath our table and his hands about a cup of hot coffee did we get the whole story.

"No, Bruce, those trees didn't cost me a cent and I wasn't chased out by anyone, not exactly. Say, Bruce, that was the lonesomest place I ever was in my life, away out there in the middle of nowhere. The place was so scary, I couldn't wait till I got those trees loaded. Everything went alright until it got dark and I was in the tent eating my sandwiches. I heard a howl away off somewhere in the woods, but that didn't bother me much. Then another, closer this time, and I knew it was wolves. Later, when I was in bed, one let out a howl that sounded right outside the tent and I grabbed my axe, and ... Well I pulled the covers over my head and waited. I got to thinking. Believe me, I crawled out of that little pup tent and made a dash for the truck and slammed the door."

"Don't tell me you slept sitting up in that cab all night," I said.

"Well, with that noise, you wouldn't call it sleeping exactly, but you bet I stayed there 'til morning and light enough for me to see."

As the boys left for Chicago a day or so later, Flora added a few words of caution and advice to mine. "Tell Ruth we'll be down just as soon as you get back, and we hope it'll be a boy this time."

In Chicago, the boys headed directly for the big produce market on Randolph Street. Though their trees were freshly cut and had every appearance of being first-class merchandise, they were turned down repeatedly by one dealer after another.

"You'll never get rid of that load around here," the last merchant said. "Why, there'll be hardly a needle left on them by Christmas time. Now if they were balsam instead of spruce, I would take the load myself. Sorry!" It was a blow to be sure, and after further futile attempts to dispose of their wares, the boys headed for the Walker home, dejected and out of sorts.

They had nearly reached their destination when Bruce burst out,

"Say, Sam, I've just got an idea. There's a place over on Ogden Avenue not far from here they call Al's Auto Graveyard. He can sell anything. I bet he'll take a chance on the whole lot. What do you say we go there?"

"Let's go," Harold shouted. "We've got to get rid of this bunch of trees even if we have to give 'em away for nothing."

When they pulled away from Al's Graveyard late that afternoon, scores of wrecked cars and the high board fence were hidden from view by a forest of spruce, fresh and fragrant as the northwoods itself.

The boys had no sooner returned and related their experiences than Flora and I set out for Chicago in the Chevy. Other than a new cut-off here or a stretch of new pavement there, it was the same old trip over Wisconsin terrain. As our speedometer checked off the miles there was plenty of time for reflection.

"Charlie," Flora said when we were well on our way, "Just what do you make of the boys selling those trees the way they did, knowing about the needles? Do you think they did the right thing?"

"Now, Flora, you're leaning over backwards again. Of course they did the right thing. To begin with, those dealers made it sound worse than it really was, on purpose. Spruce makes a perfectly good Christmas tree providing it's freshly cut and those were. They don't last as long as balsam, I'll admit, but those trees won't shed their needles before Christmas. I bet those dealers would have grabbed them up if balsam hadn't been available. And what did they get for the lot? Seventy-five dollars! Why, it should have been twice that. Take out the cost of gas and oil, wear and tear on the tires, to say nothing of the time for cutting and loading – no, there was nothing wrong with that deal."

"Well, I just didn't feel right about it at first, but I guess what you say is true. Anyhow, it was a good experience for the boys, something they won't soon forget."

We stopped off at Madison, of course, to visit Harris. As prearranged, we met him at Price's Restaurant where he waited on tables. Following a belated dinner and an hour of conversation, we took our leave, knowing he, too, would soon be on his way down in his Model T.

With darkness settling over the white countryside, we turned on our lights to join the ever mounting parade as we neared the city. Contrary to our expectations, we found Chicagoland much alive, its holiday spirit manifest far and wide as we passed through one suburb after another. We passed through miles of decorative street lighting. Everywhere, Christmas was apparent, in lighted windows, in Yule trees ablaze with colorful bulbs and dazzling tinsel. Despite the spectacle before our eyes, we knew the fallacy of it all. An ember on an ash heap, a flash in the pan as it were, for the depression was unrelenting.

Ruth's baby came on December 29th, and they named him Robin, Robin Swenson.

"I did so hope he'd come on Christmas, your birthday, Pop," Ruth said almost apologetically. In the scope of a lifetime, how could she think the exact arrival day of such a joyous grandchild would be a matter of concern? Our first grandson!

On our return home, to our surprise we found our roadway open and cleared of snow. How different a homecoming than when horses were needed to get us in. To this day, the county continues to plow us out to our very door, thus taking much of the sting out of Old Man Winter's long lash. On a cold winter's night when I'd be awakened by a rumbling sound like that of distant thunder, I would shake Flora.

"Wake up," I'd shout. "Walt's coming. Put on the coffee pot."

I jumped into my trousers and checked the thermometer outside the bathroom window. Whew, eleven below! How can he take it? Yes, and at three-thirty in the morning. What an ungodly hour to be out working. The rumbling grew louder, and the windows rattled as light flashed across our bedroom walls. Outside, bundled against the cold, we marveled at the ease and facility with which our neighbor handled the great machine as its piercing light drew nearer. As though by its own volition, the great wing blade rose to avoid a tree, then settled back once more to roll the snow aside in one great furrow.

As we drank our coffee, we heard the throb of the idling Diesel, and soon Walt was off again, but not alone, Bruce by his side, thrilled by the exhibition of power he witnessed. Not till he hiked back from the county line did we blow out the light and crawl back beneath our covers.

When the sun had coaxed the mercury to a tolerable reading, Flora laid aside her book and we strapped on our snowshoes in high anticipation. Shuffling clumsily over the threshold, we were momentarily blinded by the glare of the outside world.

"Where are we going this time?" she asked as she adjusted her sunglasses with mittened hands.

"As if I know – we'll just follow our noses, I guess."

Like a pair of fat ducks, we waddled side by side down the hill, through the park and paused at the lake's edge only long enough to tuck in a dangling strap. Although we were sure of the ice, we set out cautiously, wind rippled snow crunching softly beneath our rawhide webs. Flora's snowshoes were long and narrow with turned-up toes, mine were Indian made, short and wide. Occasionally we turned around to scan our crooked trail and mark the intricate pattern of our gear in the snow. We were not experts, to be sure, but had mastered the long hip swing that took us places. Soon we were dwarfed by the vast expanse about us, endless sky and a spotless desert of wind-blown snow.

"Here are some tracks," Flora shouted. "Can you tell what they are?"

"They're mink," I said, reaching her side. "See, the prints are in diagonal pairs. They're headed the way we're going."

"How can you tell? Maybe he's going the other way."

"That's easy when you know. Now just follow me and don't walk on the tracks." On we went, a little faster now that we had an objective. "He'll probably hole up somewhere on that far shore or in some spring-fed swamp where we can't follow."

"Then you think he'll go all the way across?"

"It looks like it now. Anyway, we'll soon find out." With each awkward stride Flora's curiosity mounted. We were about to set foot on shore when to my astonishment the trail turned sharply and took out over the snow-covered lake once more.

"Now just why do you suppose he changed his mind?" Flora inquired.

"Could be it's a lady mink," I replied. A moment of silence followed her disdainful stare.

"But really, Charlie, why do you think the mink changed its mind?"

"Well, the answer was plain enough, back there in the snow. Didn't you notice the distance between his jumps? The critter was plain scared by something."

"What do you think it could have been?"

"Why it could have been a fox, or a bobcat, or even a stray dog. Who knows?" But Flora's interest lay not in conjecture. Once more we diagonaled back across the lake, slower, but with purposeful steps. We had hiked nearly two miles now, and where the trail entered a small tunnel of buckled ice along our own shore, we settled down for a rest.

"Reminds me of lace," Flora remarked as she pointed out the delicate tracery of field mice before the opening. But we were interested only in the creature we were following. After peering into the jade green interior of the ice fold and finding it empty, we discovered tracks emerging from the other end. Now we dragged our heavy feet through a patch of brittle rushes, ice crystals crunching beneath our webs.

"What's that pile of stuff over there?" Flora asked. "Looks like a manure pile."

"Why, that's a muskrat house. Don't tell me you've never seen one before! When I was a boy, I used to stomp on them and watch the critters scamper out beneath the ice."

"Here he goes," Flora shouted, taking up the trail again. Where a pine covered promontory deflected our course, the mink's tracks made a beeline toward a small dark object out on the ice. This turned out to be nothing more than a chunk of wood beside an ice fisherman's hole.

"Now how do you account for that little side trip?" Flora asked as we followed his trail back to the shoreline once more.

"Maybe he took it for a meal of some kind, but more likely his curiosity just got the better of him. Most animals are curious - they investigate anything strange to them. This makes some of them easy to trap. Remember those coons in our garden, how that broken mirror I used was their undoing?" Things changed quickly, for now our quarry's trail led directly up a steep brushy embankment and into the woods.

"This is where we quit," I said. "We can never make that hill on snowshoes." However, Flora would have none of it.

"You don't think I'm going to give up now, do you? Why, that mink's as tired as I am, and I bet he's just over that hill a little ways."

"Now listen, I've followed plenty of mink when I was a boy. I know there's no use going any further. He'll hole up anyway, and you'll never see hide nor hair of him."

"Now Charlie, do you object to satisfying my curiosity?" There was a ring of determination in her voice. It brought back recollections of her sliding down that Colorado mountain. Oh, what's the use?

"Well, have it your way," I said, "but we'll have to shed our snowshoes if we are going to climb that hill."

We pulled our way up the steep bank, grasping at brush and young saplings and finally on top, sank into the soft snow beside the trail for a well earned rest. Then we started again, into a brand-new environment, hours, no doubt, behind the creature we were following. Unlike the even traveling on the lake, here the going was hard. Through ravines and over crater knolls we stumbled, pushing aside low hanging branches and stopping frequently to adjust our foot gear. A fox's trail now joined that of the mink and I wondered which was the hunter and which the hunted. Perspiring and tired, we came upon a morass of buck brush and swamp grass. Here we dare not follow, as the sound of trickling water told me of hidden springs and danger ahead. Even Flora was obliged to admit defeat, though she did so reluctantly.

"Well Charlie, I guess this is as close to a mink coat as I'll ever come," she said, turning in her tracks.

We returned back over our own trail, climbing step by step to higher ground once more. Here in an open glade, we dropped onto a log and shook the clumsy snow shoes from our feet. Too tired to take in the quiet beauty, we sat in silence, our perspiring backs hunched toward the afternoon sun. Rabbit tracks were everywhere, and mice and moles had featherstitched the snow about a blackened stump.

"Charlie, do you realize we haven't seen a living thing so far, not even a mouse.

"Well, that's hardly true. Remember that big owl an hour or so back? But do you know, we haven't heard a sound of any kind, except of our own making?" I countered.

"Well, that's not the whole truth either. I was sure I heard a train whistle when we were leaving the house."

"Could be, but that was ten miles away and it doesn't count."

Struck with a sudden idea, Flora said, "Now suppose we sit perfectly still and see if we can hear the least sound of any kind." Without replying, I settled into a comfortable position and tried to control my breathing.

"Ready, go!" she signaled.

I could hear not a thing, not even the rustle of a leaf. Profound silence sucked at my ear drums, becoming unendurable. I turned to see Flora cupping her ears. If only the lake would groan or a bluejay call. Suddenly, a silence-shattering whoop from Flora, and what a relief.

"Come on, Charlie, let's put on our snow shoes and go home. It's getting late and I'm hungry."

As we shed our outer garments that evening before the fire, our only tangible reward was a bluejay feather stuck rakishly in Flora's cap, but we were possessed of an inner feeling of satisfaction that would send us to bed with the assurance of a sound night's sleep.

Chapter 39

ORIGINAL RESIDENTS

To the uninitiated, our winter woods may seem surprisingly destitute of animal life. One may travel for miles without so much as seeing a creature of any kind. Yet the bewildering pattern of tracks left in the night is evidence enough that they do abound. Man's eternal quest for food and fur may account to some extent for these nocturnal habits, but it is the instinct for survival that has driven them to spend a great portion of their lives beneath the earth's surface. Should by chance the frozen earth suddenly erupt, disgorging its winter tenants, the result would be astonishing. Furred creatures, large and small, reptiles and amphibians, it would present a picture not unlike the Biblical story of Noah and his ark.

I can think of few animals indigenous to these parts that spend their lives entirely above ground – deer, of course, and also the larger squirrels. Even the bobcat, porcupine and coon may on occasion forsake their windswept tree shelters and hide themselves in some safe and warm earthy pocket below. How revealing it would be if, through some Walt Disney magic, one could spy into the earth's dark recesses, into the warrens of a rabbit, the feather-and-bone strewn dens of a fox, and the long, long tunnels of a mole.

The smallest of furry creatures on our premises is the shrew. Interestingly enough, one of its species is said to be the tiniest animal in all the world. Several times I have come across them, their little snouts twitching as they blindly snoop about. A tiny body, hardly larger than a thimble, once lay dead upon our kitchen floor. According to our naturalist friend, Karl Kahmam, shrews have voracious appetites and will die within a few hours if sufficient food is not forthcoming. Their diet consists mainly of grubs, larvae and worms.

Closely related to the shrew are moles. During summer months they drive long tunnels just beneath the earth's surface, pushing the dirt in their path upward. Their powerful forelegs are veritable shovels and their tunneling accomplishments are prodigious. One scientist commented on a hundred yard tunnel dug in a single night: "To do a proportional amount, a man would have to make a tunnel fifty miles long and large enough for him to crawl through, in a similar space of time." With magic lenses, one might follow such a mole tunnel in the early spring and find within a grass lined pocket, a number of newly-born moles, pink, naked and with eyes that will remain forever nearly blind.

What camp would be complete without the friendly little chipmunk. With tails erect, these small rodents scurry about, their bright eyes ever alert for some morsel of food. Their lack of fear endears them to our patrons, from whose outstretched hands they accept tidbits. Outstanding characteristics are their overstuffed cheek pouches and their erect tails. Regardless of the latter, many of our patrons mistake common striped gophers for chipmunks. Though we miss the friendliness of these creatures during the winter, we have their counterpart in the friendly chickadees which take their place.

Our park is a squirrel's paradise until an occasional dearth of acorns sends them off to better pickings in the neighboring cornfields. One winter's day I counted thirteen squirrels on a large, enameled metal sign lying flat just outside our window. When a saucy bluejay dropped quickly into their midst, there was slipping and sliding as big tails took off in every direction. Once a black squirrel moved into our park with the rest but it never became friendly. More striking still was a pure white specimen, an albino which I saw off in our woods.

Recognized especially for its ferocity and lack of fear is the weasel. It's a wanton killer. As winter approaches, its brown coat turns white, except for the tip of its tail, which remains a contrasting black. Known then as an ermine, this lithe creature hunts the woods, hardly discernible against the snow. There are few killers in the forest, meadows or marshlands so feared by the rodent world. Even a large woodchuck is not immune to its attack, and a whole roost of chickens may be destroyed overnight by a single weasel. Flora once watched one stalking a gopher in our barnyard, and so intent was it on its kill, it paid her no attention, though she might easily have crushed it with her foot. Ernest Thompson Seton tells of an eagle being shot, having the white skull of a weasel still attached firmly to its neck.

Related to the weasel, though much larger, is the marten. Their fur is known as sable. I have seen but one, and that some miles distant from our place. There are the otter, fisher and mink. All have characteristics of the weasel and all seek a livelihood with fang and claw.

Mink are frequently seen, and we follow their tracks in the snow while muskrats carry on their business of house building along our shoreline. On our back road I once watched a battle between a mink and a large muskrat. Neither paid me any attention, so preoccupied were they in combat. Quite naturally I expected the mink to win for, like the weasel, it is fast and furious. The muskrat, on the other hand, is slower and of a more peaceful disposition, perhaps because of its diet, which is mostly vegetable. Which of them was the challenger in this battle I did not know, but both were equally courageous as they rushed at one another. They seemed a single ball of furry fury, rolling about the rutted roadway. Several times they drew apart only to come together again with mounting rage. After one such bout, the muskrat managed to sink its long incisors into its adversary's throat. Hardly believing my eyes, I watched until the mink ceased its struggling. I am sure the outcome of that battle had been an anticlimax as far as nature's plans were concerned, but it suited me.

I know very little about the otter and fisher, for I have never seen either in their wild state. Hearsay has it that the otter responds to kindness and makes a first-rate pet. From all indications it is a fast swimmer, and who hasn't heard of otters cavorting on their steep snow or mudslides. I once came upon an otter slide at the far end of our lake.

A creature with which we live in friendly relationship is the woodchuck or groundhog. He is strictly a vegetarian. I came home one day to find one sitting on his haunches beside my back door. Quite fearlessly, it watched my approach as if to say, "Now who are you and what do you want?" If by chance I were to see this fellow basking in the sun on the second day of February, I would be reminded that his predictions are about as dependable as the weatherman's.

The skunk is a much maligned creature – too much I think. The many years I have spent in the woods have taught me not only to respect him, but through some mutual understanding, to like him. The bold white V on his black back stands for anything but vicious, as there was never a more docile animal. He goes about, always minding his own business, never flaunting the power he packs in tiny glands beneath his tail. 'Leave me alone and I'll leave you alone' is his motto. Although he chooses inhabited areas for his own environment, he does so at the prompting of his stomach, not for any desire to be neighborly. Our contacts with him have been frequent and occasionally ludicrous.

We had gone to bed one night when Lois was awakened by a thump, thump, thump. She called Bruce, who, clad only in his shorts, hurried outside. There in the bright moonlight stood a skunk, its small head caught in a salmon can. Completely blinded, it bumped headlong into every object in its path.

Bruce, at a loss to know just what to do, shouted, "If only he had his other end in that can," but feeling sorry for the creature, he stooped directly in its path and with open hands he waited. He grabbed the can quickly and gave a jerk. The sound was like a cork pulled from a bottle.

"What did the skunk do?" Flora asked.

"I don't know, I didn't wait to see," Bruce replied. But the skunk had gone its own phlegmatic way, saving its malodorous scent for a more warranted occasion.

I stood beside our house one morning with my 22 rifle, ready to shoot a pine squirrel which persisted in disturbing a nesting robin, when out of the corner of my eye, I saw a skunk ambling in my direction. Unmoving, I held my ground. Finally, after sniffing my shoes and pant legs, the fellow looked up questioningly into my face, and satisfied, moved on. Who could betray such implicit confidence? Surely not I.

Like the skunk, the porcupine that abound in our area are creatures unto themselves. They are peace loving and slow to wrath, expending as little energy as possible in pursuit of their livelihood. Despite their apparent listlessness, they are a match for anything with claws or fang, regardless of size. As an inert ball on the upper branch of a tree, a sleeping porcupine has little fear of the voracious wildcat in the crotch below. He knows well enough there will be no blood letting to stain the white snow beneath. Woe betide the unsuspecting dog that tackles a porky, for it will come from the struggle with lips, tongue and throat stuck full of quills. Some distance north of us, I counted seven of these living pincushions in a single day,

If we hope to eat our own succulent ears of corn, we are obliged to be ever alert for marauding raccoons. Some curious instinct seems to tell them exactly when our corn is ripe, since we see no sign of them beforehand. Their raids are usually family affairs, and the damage they can do in a single night is devastating. Fortunately, these ringtails are easily trapped. Two wooden crosses still stand at the head of our garden, testimony to a pair I caught in a single setting. Our grandchildren care for the graves, for they remember those sad, expressive faces which looked into the barrel of my rifle.

Both the red and gray fox of our woods keep the furred and feathered creatures constantly on their guard. They are death to our game birds, and no bounty would be too high if through that means, the country could be rid of these marauders. One day a red fox with a partridge between his jaws jumped directly in front of my car. Realizing the danger, it took off down the road. I stepped on the gas and was about to run it down when it dropped the bird and made for the seclusion of the woods. Yet it wasn't to be so easily thwarted, for when I returned a short time later, the bird had disappeared, retrieved, no doubt, by the fox. Survival of the fittest, nature's law, seemed overly harsh one day. While I stood at the store, a fox dragged the lifeless body of a fawn across the road only a few yards distant. Even to old-timers, this was a new indictment against this creature.

I am always amazed whenever a beaver is trapped in our immediate neighborhood. I marvel that this much sought fellow ever survived the early fur trading days, when he was basic to the economy of our country. Old trading post records are replete with accounts of white man's whiskey being bartered for prodigious amounts of beaver pelts. Somehow, the beaver managed to survive. Their strong flat tails and long incisor teeth are tools. These, together with their spirit of cooperation, have made them engineers of no mean ability. Before man hacked down his first tree with a stone axe, beavers had felled and cut them into lengths. Making use of these sections, together with sticks, stones and mud, they constructed dams. Once winter's ice covers the pond thus formed, they release the water, leaving a translucent ceiling. Under protection of this, they carry on their winter's activities. Are beavers endowed with a sense of prescience, do they go about their work with discerning minds? Or does blind devotion to instinct prompt them in their undertakings?

Although the timber wolf may still be found infrequently, his number have shrunk materially in the last few decades. On rare occasions during deer season, a hunter may bag a single one. They are never seen in packs. Strangely enough the timber wolf is being supplanted by the prairie wolf or coyote of the western plains. Hunted as they are now, from the air, these animals are finding a new security in forested areas.

To be sure, we always have the badger with us – is not Wisconsin called the Badger State? I know of no animal of comparable size that is built so close to the ground. One would have to look to the reptile kingdom for its counterpart in this respect. Of many animals which burrow into the ground, the mole excepted, perhaps none is better adapted to subterranean existence than the badger. A prodigious digger, this animal seeks its food the hard way. Small mammals, ground squirrels, gophers, mice and insects seem a meager reward for the badger's incessant spade work. The twenty long claws beneath its low-slung chassis are capable of throwing up a veritable geyser of earth as its body sinks slowly out of sight. The badger prefers open countryside rather than the root webbed earth of the woods. Because of its close affinity with the underworld, it is seldom seen by man.

Though once there were others, deer are now the only wild animals, save a rare moose, that leave cloven imprints in our sandy soil. Stories about deer never cease to interest our patrons. While working for me one season, Billy O'Mara, a native of our bailiwick, told me of a deer he had often seen, but never without the company of a big snow-shoe rabbit. A bit skeptical, I determined to see for myself. I cautiously approached the field in question. Sure enough, Billy had been right, for grazing there together in close companionship, like a pair of old workhorses, were these two animals, differing extremely in size. Nor was this but a happenstance, for united by some bond of friendship known only to themselves, these wild creatures were frequently seen together throughout that summer.

During the first few years of our coming, we had a dog to which we were very much attached. When it died, we had every intention of getting another, but in the meantime were surprised to find how much closer wild things came to our premises. Partridges nested but a stone's throw from the house, ground hogs showed themselves frequently, and chipmunks, gophers and rabbits took over our dooryard.

What a thrill we got one evening when out of our living room window, we counted seven deer pawing for acorns. Nor was this a passing visit, when for several evenings thereafter, we watched them, their graceful bodies silhouetted against the snow. We have never since owned a dog, much as we would have liked one.

Is there a man or boy living who does not prick up his ears when the word bear is mentioned? Strange as it may seem, these shy denizens of the woods are being seen more frequently as the years go by. While driving to the store, Bruce, with two of our grandchildren, surprised a bear at the side of the road, too interested in tearing apart a large ant hill and licking the insects from its forepaws to see their car coming. Hardly a year passes without some neighbor having a new bear story to tell. Although I have tracked bear over our own road and down to our cabins, I have had no luck with a big bear trap, though once I caught a partridge in it.

"Maybe it was an educated bear," Flora suggested, after seeing the creature's tracks go around the sign I had posted before the set trap, 'BEWARE OF BEAR TRAP!' Such notice is required by law for the protection of roving pedestrians.

There is a generally belief that bears hibernate. This, however, has been challenged by good authority. Body temperature is the determining factor as to whether a creature is in hibernation or simply enjoying a long winter's sleep. The body temperature of true hibernators drops to near freezing, which is not the case with the bear, as cubs are born during the winter, and it is doubtful that these could survive without the warmth provided by their mother's body. To bring the metabolism of a true hibernating animal back to normal takes hours of shivering and shaking. During hunting season it is not uncommon that a bear is driven from its den without so much as a minute or two into which to shake itself into wakefulness. I saw a bear in the woods one Fall that had been routed from its quarters by approaching hunters. She had run a mile before being shot down, and had shown no signs of lethargy.

I have purposely withheld to the last my account of a creature which I have had not the slightest personal acquaintance. So incredulous are stories about its wicked sagacity, I wonder that they are substantiated by good authority. The fact that we have usurped what was once its hunting ground is reason enough for my including it, the wiliest of all creatures to inhabit the northwoods, the wolverine. In no way is it to be confused with the wolf, for in reality, it's the largest of the weasel family. The wolverine resembles a small, dark bear, at least in pictures I have seen. Perhaps it's just as well that his kind is rapidly becoming extinct, for as someone has said, the wolverine is the arch criminal of nature's underworld. Its three and a half feet of overall length is packed with venom and hatred, augmented by sagacity and devilish cunning found in no other animal. Bears give it a wide berth and it is hated by white man and Indian alike. There is nothing in the woods that it fears. Unobserved, it will stalk a trapper, spring and sabotage his traps, eat his bait, devour his catch, and continue on to the last trap. Not satisfied with this, the wolverine will steal his clothing, his blankets and even furniture from his cabin, only to destroy them in a fit of rage. Oddly, its fur has been prized as neck trimmings, especially for use where it is subjected to human breath, since the hair will not frost up as with other furs.

We became so familiar with all of our woodland friends, I was always surprised when our city-based patrons asked about them as if they were totally foreign. In fact, these furry friends were the true residents here, but we so enjoyed sharing their domain.

The shop became the real center of our winter activity. Here we would stoke our oversized stove with oak and jackpine, and despite thin, unlined walls, would manage to keep comfortable, although there were times when we were obliged to abandon the place for the warmth of our house. More disagreeable than the cold was the awful smell of so-called creosote, a black tarry liquid that ran down the stovepipe and filled the place with its sharp, sickening odor. Though others somehow accustomed themselves to it, I could hardly tolerate it. A sheet metal pipe stuck through the roof, a hot stove stoked with green wood, a cold winter's day and you have a perfect setup for the distillation of this stinking stuff. Though ours was a vitrified chimney, it did little to remedy the situation.

Usually we teamed up on some project or other, but where my own cabin was concerned, I worked alone, carrying out my own ideas. With the line shaft humming beneath the floor, I could move from one job to another, ripping, crosscutting, grooving or bandsawing, as the case might be, turning out partitions, window frames, doors and rustic furniture.

My logs lay over by the mill, all slabbed, stained and undercover, together with the long heavy ridgepoles. Down near the lake lay the new foundation, a green pitcher pump barely showing above several feet of snow.

Of all the phenomena of winter, none strike me more forcibly than do the moods of our lake. For days it may lay quiet beneath its white covering, then suddenly awaken to vent its feelings in agonizing groans that echo throughout the hills as though a menagerie of nether beasts existed beneath the cap of ice. At times, even the weight of a man may be enough to start a hollow boom that goes resounding over the frozen expanse, diminishing in volume and pitch until it finally dies away in the distance with a drawn out whine. Usually it's a change of temperature that sends the lake into spasms, and leaves its surface scored with countless fractures. Someone overhearing this eerie sound from a distance, and not knowing its origin, may be at a loss to account for it, as witness the following episode.

While deer hunting in the Bear Lake region, our neighbor, Claire Wisner, was surprised when he saw four men approaching at a dog trot. "What's the hurry?" he asked as they halted before him, quite out of breath.

"Haven't you heard that pack of wolves?" one exploded.

"There it is again! Just listen to that," another shouted.

"That? You mean that rumbling sound? Why, that's only Bear Lake sounding off. It's the ice expanding with this change of weather. Nothing to be afraid of," the old timer advised.

There are no flagrant colors in the winter woods, only the somber green of conifers and warm siennas of the still clinging oak leaves. It is the ruby-red sunrise that we look to for extravaganza, when tall pines are silhouetted against a flaming sky and lavender shadows crisscross the snowy landscape.

The woods, too, may be capricious, when overnight, caught in freezing mist, stark and naked trees turn into things of crystalline beauty. Upon such rare serendipity, we awaken to a fairy world of burnished armor and scintillating jewels, and stand before our window and marvel at the transformation and sheer loveliness of it all.

Chapter 40

HOW IT'S DONE

Winter's long sleep was over at last. Once more the ice was gone from the lake and our woods were vibrant with bird calls. Orioles came in the wake of robins and stormed our park in numbers. Cloud shadows brushed the warming earth, and hawks, riding high upon updrafts, captured my imagination. The scene had been the same last spring, and the one before, and as far back as I could remember.

Taking hold once more meant corralling vagrant thoughts, and a new submission to discipline and order. Soon the ring of the axe and whine of the mill were familiar sounds that accompanied family industry.

Yes, spring was here once more. This was evidenced by the awakening of nature about us, and more significantly, by the depleted condition of our bank account. We were learning that the resort business, not unlike the spring bear, comes from winter's long seclusion poor and thin. Though we had vowed to borrow no more money, here we were nearly broke again, and in need of working capital.

Back in our little Rough and Ready quarters, when we had decided it was imperative that we go further into debt to purchase our property, we had considered our mortgage money as quite sufficient for current expenses. Though we practiced the strictest economy and were frugal in our spending, each spring somehow found us in straightened circumstances. How many times we carried a lunch to town in lieu of eating an appetizing meal in some restaurant, how little we spent on needed clothing. Why, we simply did without, except for overalls, work shoes and the like. Despite our penny-pinching, we could never quite operate on a balanced budget. Furthermore, the source of our borrowings had its limitations, for city school teachers were being paid in tax warrants, and these were not readily negotiable even when discounted. Yet we were obliged to swallow our pride and turn again to our hard put bankers for another loan.

With inquiries now coming in regularly and the receipt of an occasional deposit, we felt stronger justification for our whole undertaking, and took new courage. Even the choice of our site seemed vindicated, regardless of what it had cost. Flora found satisfaction in corresponding with strangers who somehow heard of our resort. Her replies were the reflection of her own pride in our place. They were prompt and enlightening, and usually brought results. Little did she know what a time consuming task letter writing was to become.

Although we were only amateurs from the standpoint of experience, we were constantly being asked about the resort business. Our patrons wanted to know about the winters, the wildlife about us, the cost of cabin construction, and even about the Indians. A few individuals, however, were serious in their queries, having in mind, no doubt, the time when they, too, might settle in the northwoods.

Nearly every season brings us at least one curious person, come to study our type of construction, and many cabins throughout the countryside stand as testimony to this curiosity. We were especially surprised one day when we came upon a resort that looked strikingly like our own. The proprietor proved to be none other than an old patron.

Certainly there are many ways of building a log cabin. The old-fashioned notched corner type is without doubt superior from a purely esthetic point of view, but finding an artisan with the know-how and patience for such construction is quite another thing, for log-notching is slowly becoming a lost art. This type of building calls for longer and larger timber which is hard to come by these days, and lends itself poorly to versatility of design. As far as interiors are concerned, there is no appreciable difference between our cabins and those of the notched corner type.

For the benefit of those nature loving individuals who look forward to the time when they, too, might build a summer home on a wooded shore of some lake or stream, I submit the following treatise. With as little technical detail as possible, it represents the construction of Wigwam, my own version of a three bedroom cabin, and the seventh of our undertaking.

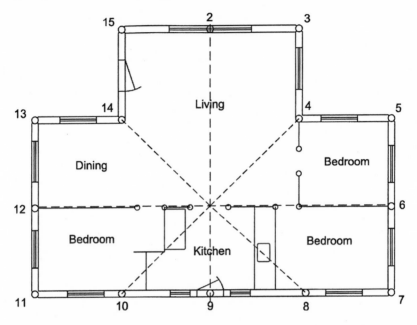

The long dashes shown on the plan represent ridgepoles, the shorter dashes are valley rafters, and the numerals designate uprights—vertical logs. Windows are shown as tight parallel lines and door openings by the swing of the door. Obviously corner logs are slabbed at right angles and all others on opposite sides. These include the horizontal or body logs which are slabbed at predetermined widths, the heaviest ones forming the lower tiers. Number 2 upright, you will note, is intersected by the front picture window. The lower portion, therefore, stands only three tiers high, while the upper one extends to the ridgepole above the 8 foot wide window opening. The upright over the back door extends from the log above the door to the ridgepole at the roof peak.

Windows are the casement type, 42-inches high, and are hung in pairs with the exception of the front, which is 48-inches high and consists of four sashs, hung in two pairs which fold back. All openings have log uprights on each side into which the plank frames are nailed.

The distance between all upright log faces is exactly 8-feet, each section constituting a so-called panel. The advantage of panel construction is obvious, for it has the versatility of a set of children's building blocks,

and lends itself admirably to any desired floor plan, large or small. Furthermore, 8-foot logs are readily obtainable from pulp cutters in the woods, and may be slabbed to order at any local saw mill.

For adequate drainage purposes, all logs, including the uprights, extend two inches over the cement foundation. Though the section of the wall shown is self-explanatory, the following will help clarify it.

On the fourth tier of logs all around (third tier in front) the window frames are set with their log uprights, and the intervening spaces beside the windows are finished with stub logs as follows; four slabbed at 7-inch-

es and three at 6-inches, totaling 46-inches in all, equaling the height of the frame. Over the window openings, two more full length logs are laid, the top one being the plate. The top or plate logs extend out

three feet past the walls to receive the overhanging eave rafters.

All horizontal logs are blind toe-nailed into the uprights from the top slabbed side, as the wall progresses in height. The plan shows that the roof consists

304

entirely of four gables. The ends of these gables are laid up with progressively shorter logs, then sawn down to the predetermined pitch
of the roof. This was accomplished with a two-man saw and guide
boards nailed both inside and out.

At this stage, the structure is tied together with 6-inch round
poles in the following manner: from upright 14 across to 4, from 4
over to 8, and from 10 to 14, these tie-pole ends being notched in.

Next came the framing of Wigwam's roof. The heavy ridgepole
running from uprights
2 to 9 is 32-feet in
length, having a 12-
inch diameter butt. The
cross ridgepole reached
from upright number 6
to 12. This is in two
equal pieces and is
joined at the intersec-
tion, its total length
being 40-feet. All are of select Norway pine.

There being no ceiling to cover the rafters, instead of using standard 2 x 6 lumber, poles are used for eye appeal. These are slabbed
on the top side to receive roof boards, and are notched into the top
plate logs and over the ridge log at 26-inch intervals.

The last job to be performed is chinking the logs, for regardless
of how long they have lain, they are sure to shrink when laid up in
tiers. For this task, common plumber's oakum is used, driven into
place with any thin, wide steel blade.

So much for the general exterior construction. Detailing the interior of Wigwam, plate-high partitions are fabricated in two sections,
one above the other and of differing construction, to provide visual
detail. The lower portion consists of 12-inch pine boards, beveled on
the edges and set upright into grooved 2 x 4's, both top and bottom,
containment in the grooves requiring no nailing. The top section consists of 1/4-inch thick plywood paneling, also set in grooves. This
procedure results in partitions having both sides alike.

Instead of paint or stain, the hot flame of a blow torch was
applied lightly and evenly to both top and bottom sections. The
resultant color was a sepia, with the grain of the wood etched in variation and each knot presenting its own individuality. It is a color that

goes well, indeed, with the stained log walls. All three doorways into the bedrooms are arched, as is the wide kitchen opening between log pedestals.

Wigwam

Having a hand wrought metal arrow for a latch and a rawhide draw string with a deer horn handle, the heavy front door presents a pioneer charm that recalls earlier days. Rustic furniture throughout promotes this theme. One bedstead in particular is unique, its head made from a buggy wheel, sanded and varnished and having a white birch sapling tire. Of course there is a buck head with a rack of horns hung above the archway, and an eighteen-pound northern hung on an adjacent wall makes a conversation piece with lots of outdoor appeal.

A large buffalo skull, a memo of our camping days in Wyoming, gives a final frontier touch to the exterior of this cabin. Well up in the front gable, beneath the wide spreading eaves, it provides a choice nesting place each spring for a family of robins.

A common job done uncommonly well, I beleive, viewing this structure from every angle, a blending of art and mechanics.

Chapter 41

INEVITABLE CHANGES

Cousin Lou had gone to California for an indefinite period. "I'll be back again," he said. But as dependable as old Lou was, it was a promise he would never fulfill, for one spring, word came of his sudden passing. Lou gone! Why, it just couldn't be. Wasn't he one of the family, a very part of our institution? Yet there it was, a telegram in so many words. How we missed him, especially at our table, with his appreciative, "Gollee, but that's good," his helping hands about the kitchen, cabins and mill. Even more, we remembered his benevolent spirit, his thoughtfulness for others. I missed him more than the rest, the close companionship that had existed between us. Only time could heal this hurt.

There were now seven cabins virtually completed: Crow's Nest, Air Pocket, Shore Leave, Honey Bird, Birch Hill, Roof Tree and Wigwam. Although we had never set a definite objective, somehow the number fifteen had persisted in the back of my mind. Lately, however, circumstances had altered my perspective, and now such an ambitious program seemed unlikely. Perhaps ten cabins would come nearer our ultimate number, twelve at most, especially if Bruce should pick up and go, as there were indications of that. Harris had set a goal of ten cabins before leaving us, but he had had to settle for six. Schedules, we were learning, were next to impossible to maintain, and predictions undependable.

Although we had given thought to hiring outside help, there was always our budget to be considered. Not until we remembered Pete Hart from across the lake did we really do something about it. We first met Pete when, as children, he and his sister showed up one day asking to borrow books from our library. I remembered him as the Indian lad who had sung Christmas songs in monotone at the school exercises. Seven intervening years had matured and added stature to this Chippewa youth, and now he was doing odd jobs here and there to earn a living.

Pete's father, George Hart, half Potawatomi, spent most of his time about the lakes and streams acting as a guide to fishermen. Pete's mother was a full-blood Chippewa squaw. We met her frequently at the store and grew fond of her. Though she greeted us with never more than an expressive smile on her broad, brown face, she occasionally communicated with us through her children, in her native tongue. In response to my inquiry, her brother, Jack Bearhart, replied, "No, he can't talk a word of English, only Chippewa." Later I learned that it is characteristic of Indians to refer to the feminine gender in masculine terms.

In her early years, this young mother had chosen a few white friends to visit. Taking along her sewing, she would sit the afternoon through in silence, her hands busily stitching buckskin moccasins. When she finished her visit, she would arise, bestow a warm smile upon her hostess, and go her way. Many years later, Flora learned that Mrs. Hart was a patient at our local hospital.

"Let's stop in to see her when we go to town this afternoon," she said to me.

We entered her room with a potted plant from the florist shop, hardly knowing what to expect. Propped up against her pillow, she seemed much older than when we had last seen her. She blinked her eyes as we drew near, as age had impaired her sight.

"We're the Palmers from out at Lipsie Lake," I said, bending over her bed. A smile of recognition broke over her wrinkled face as she took my hand in both of hers. As Flora held out the poinsettia, tears welled and fell to her pillow, a wordless expression of appreciation. Suddenly, as though her tears had washed away her inhibitions, she burst out thanking us in fluent English. Nor did she stop there. She told us much of herself, the many children she had raised, how pleased she was that Pete had worked for us, and finally of her illness. It was a revelation, having often conversed with her over the years only in signs, or through her children.

Pete could give us no more than a day or two each week, but this arrangement was satisfactory, at least for the present, for it was commensurate with our means. Though it was a long hike from his home overlooking Rice Lake, he didn't seem not to mind, and seldom failed to show up when we expected him. He was a good-looking lad, and there were occasions when girls on our premises eyed him with other than traditional interest. But Pete's response was usually negative, no doubt due to his bashfulness. At our dinner table he was extremely shy, never speaking until spoken to. Flora soon learned his favorite dishes, resulting in the frequent appearance of potato salad on our menu.

Pete's good demeanor inspired our confidence, and as time passed, we depended on him more and more. About the garden, barnyard or park, he more than earned the dollar a day he asked as wages. The small plot of grass Harris had mowed in the park was gradually expanding under Pete's care, and elsewhere about the place, brush piles were accumulating. We had cut a wide swath through scrub-oak brush from the garden down to the lake for better air drainage, as a preventive against early and late frosts. Though we had lit the rain soaked brush piles one morning, they did no more than smolder and smoke.

"Pete," I said after dinner, "better go over and check those brush piles. The wind's coming up." He had been gone but a moment when I heard him shout, and by the time I reached the door, he was coming on the run.

"Fire," he shouted, "the woods are on fire." Realizing the enormity of the situation, I took off to find Flora, the only remaining help on our premises. I shouted her name as I passed one cabin after another, until finally at Roof Tree, the door opened and there she was, a dust cap over her hair.

"What's the matter?" she asked.

"The woods are on fire," I exploded. "Grab a broom and come on."

The fire had already jumped the road and was licking its way on an ever-widening front. Pete, in desperation, was flailing at the flames with his jacket when Flora and I, already winded, set at it with our brooms. Beat and sweep as we might, the fire kept on expanding. Areas once considered out, kept flaring up until it was evident we were fighting a losing battle. Fortunately, it was only a ground fire, with the wind taking it out of range of our buildings, but to burn out forty acres of woods was in itself catastrophic.

Just when things looked blackest and we had paused in utter exhaustion, help arrived. The Conservation Department had been alerted by the nearest fire tower, and now here they were, water containers strapped on their backs. They seemed in no hurry, there was no rushing about, as they matter-of-factly worked their hand pumps along the forward margin of fire until only a blackened area remained to remind us of our own impotence. Unless one has had a like experience, it is hard to understand the tremendous amount of energy expended in so short a period.

Shortly after Pete had come to work for us we had word of the passing of our nearest neighbor. There had been other deaths over the years, when money left at the store for flowers was the extent of our obligation. This was different - it was closer to home and a matter of deep feeling and sentiment. Death had come to our little store, where we had first stopped for information, and laid its cold finger upon our friend and neighbor, Mr. Byrnes. Years before our arrival, his small establishment beside the road had been the stopping place for white and Indian alike, a place for the exchange of news and a convenience to the few scattered settlers. So it had been for us and for our patrons since our coming.

His homely words of wisdom subtly dispensed along with his wares is how we would remember our wayside merchant, and miss him, too. How often I had listened with interest to his tales of earlier days, the stories of his own struggles, long hikes to town on foot, the gunny sacks of fish he carried on his back to exchange for medicine and needed things for his family, his unceasing battle against the elements, sickness and impoverishment. Our own endeavors seemed insignificant in comparison. There had been little that was frivolous about Mr. Byrnes; on the contrary, he had a certain dignity of demeanor that had commanded respect.

I considered it an honor to serve as a pall bearer, and in so doing, paid my last respects to this neighbor and friend, this jackpine philosopher who spoke in parables.

Chapter 42

EMBERS

Late in July we finally opened the doors of Wigwam for its first customers, but our concentration in completing Wigwam had pushed aside other needed projects. We would wait on starting of another cabin until we caught up with them. We had a croquet ground and a horseshoe court down in the park for some time. Now we went ahead with the construction of a shuffleboard. It lay almost as smooth as glass when Bruce finished troweling it. A teeter-totter and a set of swings completed the playground equipment.

Off to one side of the park, where our old cook shack had stood, we held our weekly Thursday night campfires. They took a strong hold on our patrons, and they would be disappointed if rain prevented them. I started by piling an accumulation of brush and branches on an old pitch stump, torn from its moorings in the woods. This activity was usually a signal to the children who would leave their swings and sand castles on the beach to ply me with questions.

"When are you going to light it, Mr. Palmer?" "Please, will you tell us that scary Indian story again?" "Are we going to roast wieners or marshmallows?" After a dozen such questions, they would scamper off shouting, "Campfire tonight! Campfire tonight!" As darkness settled over the park, Flora and I came down the hill, loaded with chairs, blankets and mosquito sprayers.

"Here he comes! Here he comes!" we could hear children shout. There were no elders around as yet. Some were doing the dishes of belated fishermen, others were awaiting the signal from the big bell upon our roof top. There being no wind, I would light the old stump with but a single match, its pitch being tinder enough. Soon the big tree trunks stood out boldly in the light, and even images of boats riding at anchor were reflected in the water.

Now people would come, singly and in groups, men carrying benches and women blankets and scarves. Children would settle them-

selves on the park seats they had gathered or sprawl out on blankets. The time had come and a semicircle of interested faces awaited the opening ceremony.

"Will that good-looking fellow sitting on that end seat please stand," I'd say, pointing my pitchfork in his direction. All eyes turn as I continued. "Now will you please tell us your name, place of birth, home town, what you do for a living, and be sure to mention the cabin you are in." With few variations, this was the opening procedure of our campfire gatherings. Each in turn responded to the ritual, which inspired a spirit of friendliness and good fellowship. Occasional witticisms drew laughter, and timidity vanished in the merriment.

A songfest followed introductions, and in this I was wholly out of my element. Should my request for a leader go unheeded, well, somehow I struggled through. Usually folks are reticent where their voices are concerned, but each song inspires more confidence, and it wasn't long before we were in the spirit of the thing. Solos and duets were not uncommon and over the years we have listened to many fine voices; church soloists, barber shop quartets, and once, the clear notes of a radio artist.

312

Then it was time for story telling, the hour the children had waited for, but it belonged to adults as well. I was quite at home during this session, and from my own varied experiences came the inspiration for many of my tales. What a background for story telling - a lazy fire, eager faces, a crescent moon and the eerie cry of a loon far out over the water, a perfect setting for an Indian hair-raiser, a western, or that big one that got away.

One of my favorites was what happened to Harris and me in the first years of our settling on Lake Lipsie. We shared an interest in Indian lore which was plentiful in the area, and had heard of some burial mounds not far from our place. After work one afternoon, we ventured off on foot to see what we could find. We found the mounds, but digging well into the evening, we could find no artifacts inside, and in our enthusiasm, let the darkness climb upon us. When finally we surrendered and set off for home, we found that darkness had covered our way and we quickly became lost. To make matters worse, lightening began to punctuate the night sky. At last we saw the glow of a window, and set off in its direction.

Upon arriving at the source of the light, we found it to be the smallest of shacks, but with the storm driving us forward, we knocked at the door. A moment later, the plank door opened slowly, with an eerie creaking, and the orange light inside fell across the jagged face of a large, mean-looking Indian whose dark eyes surveyed us menacingly. It was hardly the shelter I had hoped for, but as the wind whipped up behind us, I explained that we had become lost, and needed shelter for the night. The expressionless Indian said nothing, continuing to drill his black eyes into us. Then his head nodded and he pulled the door open a bit more. The shack was tiny, and there seemed little room to even sit, let alone sleep, when our silent host pointed upward. I looked up to see a trap door just above a ladder leaning on the wall. With some reluctance, Harris and I climbed the ladder, pushed open the door and climbed into this storage area under the roof. We found some furs and as we settled down for the night, flashes of lightening through the small window at the end of the gable and the image of our host below did little to induce sleep despite our weary bones.

Dawn was breaking through the little window when I heard noises below. I was awake in an instant. Suddenly the trap door began to open. Little by little, I could see the rugged face profiled in the window as he rose higher and higher. But it was not until the dawn light bounced off the blade in his hand that my heart nearly stopped. I watched frozen with fear as he raised the knife slowly over me, then with a swift hack, he slabbed off a large piece of bacon from the hock tied above us, looked at me and said, "Breakfast, boys."

From one and all come funny stories, fish stories, odd stories, ghost stories, good stories and bad, but we drew the line at off-color stories. The children, too, contribute their share - songs, stories or skits they had arranged, contributions from their stay at scout camps, cleverly performed. It was getting late – time for refreshments. Children gazed into the hot embers as they speared their wieners in anticipation. Dads and mothers slipped juicy hot dogs from the tines of my pitchfork into open buns.

We look back upon a certain campfire gathering with some embarrassment and amusement. Rain had necessitated postponing it until Friday night. While the other kids toasted and munched their savory hot dogs, a good Catholic mother with a sizable brood count- ed off the minutes on her wristwatch. Her children stood poised and ready to go. When at last the two hands of her watch stood together at twelve, she gave them the signal. In a hurry and scurry, with sparks flying this way and that, these children raced to the fire to roast their own hot dogs. I never anticipated such a predicament.

These informal gatherings have accounted for many lasting friendships among our patrons - in one case, at least, resulting in mat- rimony.

The plank seats about the campfire were empty now, although red flames still licked hungrily at blackened pitch stumps. The evening had been a good gathering, mixing city and country folks, fishermen, bird watchers, hikers, nature lovers all. We came to the Northwoods country, a family of five, in search of security and a livelihood a great city had denied us. As babes-in-the-woods, we pit- ted our wits and family know-how against a new and strange envi- ronment. With Nature as a partner, we gambled our all in the recre- ational business. Over the years, weekly campfire gatherings had become an established order and in this wilderness setting, captured the imagination of both youngsters and grownups

Yet time has a way of altering things. Of the family group who so long ago had hitched their wagon to a star, only three remained to carry on. Three of our children were forging their own lives now, with Bruce soon to depart as well. As Flora and I tarried before the lambent flames, we talked quietly of earlier days, of hardships we had encountered, the privations and disappointments that had been ours. Nor did we forget the good things, the happiness we found in our very closeness with nature, the fun and adventure we had in the new environment. But retrospection ceased when Flora turned abruptly to the present.

"Charlie," she said with new timbre in her voice, "I thought the campfire was much better than usual tonight, didn't you?" I did not reply. "The singing and all, I mean, and the way you held the children's attention with those exciting Indian stories." Still I held my tongue. "And the grownups," she went on, "why, you could have heard a pin drop when you told the story of our coming here and our long search for a place on which to settle." Her subtle intent did not escape me, and I knew with certainty what was to follow, for it had been the same the last campfire, and the one before that. When she finally finished building me up as a story teller, she laid a hand affectionately on mine.

"Charlie," she said with feeling, "surely you won't disappoint me again tonight. Promise me now you will write that book, get started on it at least, before you have forgotten the details." There it was, just as I had expected. "Do you know," she continued, "the more I think about it, the more convinced I am that you can do it. Why, with that imagination of yours, you could make a real Swiss Family Robinson out of it, only yours would be true." I felt the warm presence of her fingers on mine as she said pleadingly, "Come on now, Charlie, what do you say?"

Not until the following morning did I comprehended the full meaning of my reply – it struck me like a blow. What did I know about rhetoric, I who had never composed so much as a line for publication? Under these circumstances, this journal came about. My struggle with the pen and words, Flora's with the keyboard. But what was this compared to the struggles that had so shaped our lives?

LAKE LIPSIE PINES

Chapter 43

LESSONS

"Why, there's Harris," Mother called one day as she rushed out to greet him in his Model T. Of course this was not his first visit home by any means. Whenever his summer work with the State Geological Survey brought him into our northern territory, he managed a quick trip to Lake Lipsie Pines. As usual, his car was loaded with rock specimens of all kinds, some of which he dumped in a pile for me. How good it was to have him at the table that evening as he poured out his experiences for our eager ears.

"So you've got a B.A. attached to your name," his mother said as she passed the food. "We were so sorry we couldn't go down for your graduation, but you know what the spring months are in this business. We just couldn't spare the time, or the money, either, to be truthful."

"Oh, that's OK," he replied. "I was only a little frog in a very big puddle anyway."

"Not to us, you wouldn't have been. When you get through with this survey, what are your chances for something permanent?" she continued.

"That's just what I came home to talk about," he said. "I'm not quitting school. I'm going another year and get my masters. My time is still not worth very much these days, you know, so I'll always regret it if I don't go on now."

"That's fine if you can manage it, but how in the world can you make it work?" Flora had voiced my own sentiments, and I listened intently as he proceeded.

"Well, I can have my old job again, waiting tables and that will take care of my meals. Then I've had several jobs that the school has passed on, analyzing materials, you know, jobs commercial concerns hire the school to do. I can expect some more of that work. With this summer's survey, I'll make out, if the aunts will help me one more year, and I'm quite sure they will."

"How I wish we were in a position to give you a hand, but we're still borrowing ourselves, you know," I replied.

"Of course you can't," he said. "Say, Pa, I sure wish you could go along on one of these trips with me. You'd get a real kick out of it. I get into some of the wildest places – canyons full of rapids and water-falls. And woods! Pa, you don't know what wild country is until you've traversed the west end of the Pemkee Range on foot. I'm certainly getting acquainted with the northern part of the state."

"Do you ever run across much evidence of volcanic action? Come to think of it, I don't suppose so. Maybe an occasional boulder of lava brought down from Canada by the glaciers?"

"Now that's where you'd be surprised. The northern part of Wisconsin is mostly lava. In fact, there are hundreds of flows piled one on top of another, to a thickness of more than fifty-thousand feet."

"Fifty-thousand feet!" Bruce exclaimed. "Why, that's almost ten miles. I don't believe it. They surely haven't dug down that far," he said sarcastically, to which Mother added her own skepticism.

"Just how do they know?" she queried.

"Well, it's simple. The same lava flows that tilt down beneath Lake Superior on Keweenaw Point in Michigan, you know, where they mine copper, can be traced southward into Wisconsin and even into Minnesota, for that matter. This is the same stuff that they quarry over at Dresser Junction. Tap rock, they call it. Geologists have reason to believe that the volcanoes were active during the Keweenawan Period at least three-fourths of a billion years ago."

"You didn't answer the question," Bruce said.

"I know I didn't," Harris answered, "you didn't give me time. The thickness is the easy part to explain – it's like this. Every time a lava flow poured out and began to cool, the first minerals which crystal-lized were a type of lodestone – magnetite they call it. This stuff is heavy, so it sank to the bottom of each flow as they piled one on top of another over many thousands of years, maybe even millions! Then the bottom seemed to have dropped out of what we call the Lake Superior basin. Of course there was no lake then. All of the lava flows in northern Wisconsin and Michigan tilted steeply to the north and were beveled off by later erosion. So today we can take our magnetic instruments, compass and dip needle, that is, and detect the presence of the bottom of each lava flow even though most of the bed rock is covered by glacial drift. You can walk for mile after mile across upturned edges of the lava flows, never suspecting that they are there under a hundred feet or so of drift. Further east of here, in the Frog Creek country north of Hayward, the edges of the lava flows outcrop in long parallel hog-back ridges."

"If those are the same rocks that produce copper in Michigan, what are the chances of mining down our way?" I queried.

"Not too good, Pop. There seems to be just enough to tease the prospectors, and that's about it."

"How about iron? You mentioned something about iron formation on the Penokee Range."

"Yes, I did. That's even older. At least a billion years, back in Huronian time. There's not much chance for iron mining down here near Spooner. That is, unless someone discovers a new iron range. Come to think of it, that isn't impossible," he added somewhat reflectively. "No one really knows what lies south of the lava flows beneath the cambrium sandstone. You know they discovered the Cayuna Iron Range over in Minnesota completely buried beneath younger cover. Maybe someone will do the same thing here some day. Who knows? There's a long stretch on the geologic map between the Cyuna Range and the Penokee. Plenty of room for several Huronian iron ranges."

"Well, you'll never discover them, so quit worrying about it. What I'd like to know is how geologists account for all the lakes in the north country?" Bruce questioned. "But make it short and to the point and leave out that billion year stuff. My mind can't go back that far."

"It won't have to this time. Do you think you could stand looking back, say ten or fifteen thousand years?"

"Back? That's almost like looking into the future," Mother said, "after that billion year trip we just took. Do you mean these lakes are not more than fifteen thousand years old? Why, I thought they had been here since the day of Creation."

"Yep, Mom, they're not very old. They're what's left after the glacier melted. The Cary ice, that is, or was it the Mankato? Darned if I know. There is something special in the way these lakes in the northwestern part of the state were formed, come to think about it. They're located in a pitted outwash plain and that accounts for all the sand."

"You mean that's where all the sand comes from that I sweep up off the floor every day?" Mother interjected. "There ought to have been a law against outwash plains. Just what is an outwash plain, anyway?"

"I'll make this real brief," Harris said. "An outwash plain is made of the silt, sand and gravel that were washed out from the front of a melting glacier. I guess I don't have to tell you that this north country was covered with an ice sheet a mile or so in thickness; not just once but several times. Anyway, these lakes were formed when outwash material buried large icebergs left from a previous glacier. The buried chunks of ice slowly melted and the overlying outwash slumped in, forming lake basins scattered over the country as we find them today."

"That seems like an odd explanation," Flora said, "but I can't think of a better one. I know of some deep hollows that are dry without any lakes in them. How were they formed?"

"Probably the same way, but the chunk of ice was smaller, so that today the bottom of the hollow is still above the watertable."

"Well, that's one geological term even I know the meaning of," Bruce spoke up, the one on whom we depended most for driving the many wells needed for water supply at the house and cabins. And it was Bruce closing the bedroom door, indicating that he had enough geology for one evening.

"Well, Charlie," Flora said after we, too, had turned in for the night, "it's evident that college has done great things for our boy. He's becoming quite a man already."

"He certainly is," I agreed, "quite a man." Just before dropping off for sleep, I kept recalling when I was a lad of just fourteen, how I had to quit the eighth grade and help hustle a living for our family. Education is a wonderful thing, I concluded as I dozed off into a sound sleep.

Chapter 44

TRUE AUTUMN

What once had been a tangle of underbrush beneath the tall pines along our lakeshore was now an orderly stretch of frontage, its natural beauty further enhanced by low, spreading roofs that now dotted its length. Slowly but surely, our building sites were being converted into sources of revenue. To the south, beyond Air Pocket there remained room for two more cabins, and already this rise of ground had felt the impact of Bruce's tractor and earthmoving scoop, awaiting the day when further activity would begin. Then there was a site or two further back on the horseshoe rim. Though not on the lakefront proper, these sites had a splendid view of the water through the boles of our big Norways down in the park. The long stretch directly before the bathing beach was still virgin, as it was the day we had first pitched our tent on it, and so it would remain, tempting though it was as building frontage.

We had reached a point in our schedule where the end was nearly in sight. Another year, perhaps, or two at the most, would see our building program finished. With seven going cabins now completed, all contributing toward the financing of the few to follow, and still another well along, came hope that we were over the hump at last.

To dispel any unwarranted exuberance on our part, time, once our ally, had seemingly turned her back on us, and been subtly nibbling away at our economy from the first, in the form of depreciation. Up to now, upkeep and repair had been the least of our troubles. The cabins weren't any the worse for wear, for they seemed as sound as the day they were christened, but not so their furnishings, things such as upholstery, mattresses, floor coverings, chairs and the like were all showing the effects of time in one way or another. Had this deteriorating process confined itself to our inanimate possessions, we might have accepted it philosophically. When it reached out to the barnyard and touched LuluBelle, our black Jersey, this was quite another matter. LuluBelle had had her last calf – it seemed incredible. A cow might die, to be sure, but to wear out like some old piece of machinery! Why, she looked as sound as the day we had gotten her. If it had been Bruce's tractor that had gone haywire, a new part here and another there might well have put it in shape again. Yet where genes were concerned, well, all the king's horses and all the king's men couldn't put LuluBelle back together again.

"I feel like we are losing one of the family," Flora said sorrowfully as the Jersey set her dainty feet on the buyer's ramp. Butcher's block or sausage mill, it mattered little now. We would miss her for her own gentle self more than for the trickle of gold that had come daily from the cream separator. The twenty-six dollars we had gotten, though more than she had cost, would do little to assuage Lois' feelings when she got her mother's letter.

The shop, so vital to our carrying on, was hardly the busy place it once had been. Since Harris' going, I found little opportunity to  take advantage of its machinery. Bruce, however, spent many hours there each day. He disliked working in wood. "Wood either shrinks or swells – you can't depend on it," he said. He was concerned mostly with the fabrication of steel. Though some of the things he made were not immediately essential to our progress, the time usually came when they were needed. With his welding equipment, he frequently helped some farmer out of a jam. Of more importance was his mastery of concrete. This was something he liked and something that was to absorb his mind for years to come. With the

322

fashioning of foundations and floors in his competent hands, I spent most of my time on log work, and rounding up ridge poles and rafter material for the remaining cabins.

Log work, whether in the woods, at the mill, or on concrete foundations, is strenuous indeed. Logs that I once handled with facility were becoming harder for me to manage, heavier with each passing year. Obviously the time was not far distant when a stronger back than mine would be needed to help with construction.

As our business expanded, so, too, did our need for more boats, and rather than interrupt our cabin schedule, we broke down and purchased two metal boats to the tune of eighty dollars.

Nature's most gorgeous array of color is found not in the rainbow's illusion, nor even in an ethereal sunset, but rather in October's woods. We eagerly look toward this gala event each fall, as it is something real, with substance, and so close we breathe its very spirit. October is when frost fingers tint each leaf according to its kind, and set the woods ablaze in ripened color. We stand amazed at its bountiful expanse and shrink to nothingness in our attempt to comprehend its meaning.

To the oak it lends a purple hue and tucks a royal robe about the undulating hills. Autumn sets the horizons in seas of lavender and decks our acres in a pageantry of splendor. Feminine birches hug the water's edge and nod approval to mirrored reflections, as with slender white fingers they adjust their golden tresses.

These are dazzling days indeed, and we drink deeply of the crisp bright atmosphere that filters through the sunlit foliage. We shun our darkened interiors and forget our daily tasks, for we have ringside seats in this festival of the wilderness. Each day we set our feet toward some fresh and colorful spectacle, perhaps to the doghills across the lake, for they appear as an immense and gorgeous bouquet within a bowl of azure, or toward the purple tints of the cut-over pasture where the cows feed leisurely and unappreciatively.

We pass through groves of slender aspen, where amber light sifts through shimmering leaves, and thrill to the maple's gay banners that flash like flaming tongues of fire. Oh, to be able to drink it all in. Only within the shade of pines do we rub unreality from our eyes, for like somber hued chaperons, these tall trees lend not color, but dignity, to the occasion.

As quickly and silently as it came, this galaxy of color, this orgy of the wilderness fades away, and we return to the drab of our every-day living. This has been a time of thrill and inspiration, but one, too, of regret. This parade of exotic loveliness has passed unviewed by those who need it most – the city dwellers.

Just before Christmas in 1938, we got the sad news that Mother Walker had had a stroke. We had started for a social gathering at the Town Hall, and stopped into the store on the way. There the telephone rang our own three long ring party-line signal, and Flora answered it. I got the gist of the long-distance call as she talked, an urgent request for her presence; her mother had had a stroke. There was little else we could do but make hasty preparations for the long trip. However, there were complications. Our neighbors were anxiously awaiting our light plant on the truck. More than this, our Chevy was torn down and its parts lay scattered about the shop.

"Better take me back to the house, Charlie, then go on to the Town Hall with the generator. Maybe you can get Walt Sylvester to help Bruce with the car."

Jenny Walker

The boys worked through the night, assembling the motor and mounting it, and at sunrise we were driving over the old familiar route back to the city from whence we had come.

We reached the old homestead quite in time, but I was never again to hear that voice that had once sent us on our way with courage and forthrightness. On the living room wall of the big, square house and over the signature of our daughter was a nearly life-sized portrait of her grandmother. There was the familiar face, and the thin, blue veined hands lying idly in her lap. In retrospect, I could hear again those words of long ago: "Charlie, I know you and Flora will succeed, for you both have the cajene to do it."

"Flora, how in the world do you spell 'cajene'?" I asked. "I'd like to see just what it means."

"Why, it means initiative, ingenuity and ability, I'd say," she answered, taking over the big dictionary.

"Let's see – no, not cagene, or cajene, or cageen, or cajeen either. Had you tried the k's?" she asked.

"Yes, and the ch's, too," I replied.

"Let's try quajene. No, none of the qu's. Gracious, don't tell me there is no such word, when I've been brought up on it," she said as she followed ever more remote leads. "Well, I guess we'll have to accept it. There just is no such word."

"Well, there is now," I said, as I adopted my own spelling.

Chapter 45

RETURNING FRIENDS

Beside the winding two-track road that serves the northern part of our premises is an old white pine of extraordinary size, which stands as a patriarch among lesser pines that long ago had sprung from its abundance of cones. Although it had reached its maximum growth many years ago, somehow, by oversight perhaps, it escaped the woodsman's axe, but not the ravishing hand of the elements, for some long forgotten storm robbed it of its majestic crest. I often stopped on the sandy road to peer up and ponder at the new top which nature had so cleverly improvised.

One particular March day, late winter snows lay in blotches in the needled boughs. Though my approach had been slow and my footsteps muffled, I was not surprised when a feathered creature took flight, as I had startled it several times before while snowshoeing. The white blanket around the big trunk was littered with telltale balls of fur, remnants of undigested rodents. To me, this had but one meaning – an owl's nest. I stepped back to better scan the top, and there it was.

We had often heard the mating call of great horned owls during winter nights and not infrequently their far-away answers, but that these birds actually nested and hatched their young at this season of the year was quite unthinkable. Perhaps this was only an old nest with no relationship to the bird that had just taken flight, but that wouldn't account for the fur balls. To satisfy my curiosity, I had Billy

O'Mara, a neighbor who had come over to help with our ice harvest, place a ladder against the tree to investigate. I could only watch as he pulled himself from the ladder and made his way higher up through snow-laden branches.

"What does it look like?" I shouted when I saw him reach the nest.

"There's a young owl all right. Do you want me to take him?" he shouted back down.

"Well, what do you think, Billy? Is he old enough?"

"I don't think so. He's just a big ball of fuzz."

"Better come on down, Billy. We'll leave it there a couple of weeks longer," I answered.

Sometime in April we finally took the young bird from the nest. It's soft, fuzzy body had grown and now had a showing of feathers. A stone's throw from our house, we built an enclosure for this fledgling with chicken wire sides and top. How little I appreciated the responsibility I had taken unto myself, the care of so young a creature. I knew that most young subsist on their mother's milk, but having access to no such medium, I substituted milk from our cows.

"Flora, how does one go about feeding milk to an owl?" I asked.

"Why, by using a little cajene," she replied, walking over to the medicine cabinet and returning with a glass medicine dropper. From the start, I made it a practice to give a shrill whistle before entering the cage and soon to my satisfaction, I found the bird waiting, as it were, with open mouth. Owls cannot, however, live on milk alone, and this one in particular, craving something more solid, one day swallowed the milk, dropper and all. With spring came fish, frogs and slithering things from beneath boards and stones to augment his diet, though getting them was a time-consuming job. While cleaning the enclosure one day, among other fur balls, I found one containing my medicine dropper, rubber nipple, glass and all.

One memorable day the mother owl took over this chore from me, and started feeding her own. Flora called me to the window, and sure enough, there was the mother owl, trying to maneuver the carcass of a rabbit beneath the wire enclosure. Not to be thwarted of her own prerogative, from that day on, she courageously set about feeding her offspring. Finding bodies of such things as squirrels, gophers, chipmunks and even snakes was not uncommon. Even more remarkable were the remains of a wild duck, a skunk and even a turtle.

Needless to say, it was a happy solution for me. Usually whenever the old bird came, there would be a commotion in the park and bird life in general would make itself scarce. On one occasion the old owl swooped down, narrowly missing Flora's head, as it drove a prowling dog from the vicinity of the pen.

Though of considerable size, the wire enclosure offered no opportunity for flight, and as the young owl matured, I could only wonder if its flight instinct would carry through. Would it spread its wings in flight when the time came? The growing bird seemed contented enough on its perch, its great eyes immovable within their sockets and ever staring. Perhaps other owls are more or less blind during daylight hours, but not this one. One day I watched his big head turn slowly, eyes fixed, not unlike a cat stalking a mouse. What was the occasion? A large black ant reconnoitering about in the bright sunlight.

The day finally came when his trim, barred feathers proclaimed him a mature and fine specimen of his kind. Reluctant as I was to part with his company, I realized I owed him his freedom. A shrill whistle brought him to attention, and as I entered his enclosure with a tidbit, he hopped on my outstretched arm. Flora joined me, and we stood on the doorstep anxiously awaiting the outcome. With little ado, the great bird, no doubt responding to instinct, took off, and did not falter in his flight as he disappeared over the tree tops.

Though I whistled frequently the next day, hoping, but little expecting, my only answers came as echoes over the water. At sunrise the following morning, I repeated my whistling calls, and to my astonishment and joy, the owl came swooping from the forest and alighted on my outstretched arm. Thereafter I called the bird at will. When it failed to respond, which was seldom, I was sure it was out of hearing range.

We found it common practice for vacationers to visit other resorts through the lake area, sometimes as a matter of curiosity and other times to find better fishing or even better accommodations. On one such occasion, shortly after Labor Day, a family dropped in to investigate our housekeeping facilities for the following summer. Flora's hands were busy with bread dough, but not too busy to pull the bell cord to summon me. Their children had taken to our park immediately upon their arrival and as we followed, the parents told me they were looking for a place where there were lots of birds. Their interest was further evidenced by binoculars and a small volume on the subject.

"We're just beginners and we've got a lot to learn," the woman explained as we made our way down to the lake. After showing them through Wigwam, I led them up the open trail along the lake.

"What kind of birds do you have around here, Mr. Palmer?" the man asked as he shooed the children along.

"Well, of course birds are pretty quiet now. The Martins left a month or so ago and it's too late for the Orioles, but during spring and summer there are all kinds here in numbers. There goes a Pileated Woodpecker now. See, you can tell by his flight, but he's gone now there beyond that hill. It's not often, but we do see a Bald Eagle once in a while and there are owls..."

"Owls! Do you ever see those big ones with ears like a cats?"

"You mean the Great Horned Owl. And we have the smaller varieties, too. Would you like to see an owl? Maybe I can call one from the woods for you."

The woman stopped in her tracks, and for a moment I thought I had lost a prospective customer. Suspicion, hope and doubt swept over her face as she said, "You don't really mean it, do you, Mr. Palmer?" But mine was not a shot in the dark, for I had seen the owl not an hour before, in a darkened recess of the old white pine.

"Now if you folks will be very quiet, I'll see what I can do," I said, and walking slowly down the wooded trail, I whistled the old familiar call. From over the tree tops the big owl came, his great wings banking as he circled for a landing, and I winced as his talons sank into my arm. My prospects mouths hung open and speechless for several moments.

"Can you call that big woodpecker we just saw?" the astonished woman asked.

Chapter 46

DUET

"Charlie, what are we going to do about Bill's wages?" Flora asked one day in May. "Unless we get some deposits pronto, we're going to be flat broke in less than two weeks." Materials needed for building the last cabin had used up our funds faster than we had anticipated, but we had vowed we would borrow no more money and we must still stick to that resolve.

"It looks as though we'll have to sell something, but what will it be?"

"Charlie, how about your horn? No one here will ever use it again." I knew that was true, but hated to part with it none-the-less. For many a year I had played in the old Clyde Band. How proud I had been when I first acquired the old tuba, all silver-plated outside and gold-lined inside the bowl.

"It ought to be worth something," she continued. "You paid a hundred dollars for it, didn't you?

"Yes, but I'd get about ten dollars for it now," I said.

"Surely it would bring more than that."

"Who would buy it?" I asked.

"Well, the high school has a fine band. Maybe they would be interested. Let's get it down from the attic and polish it up."

As I rubbed away at the black tarnish of years, the genie of my young manhood rose to remind me of those days - those evenings of band practice with good friends, magic nights of band concerts on the prairie near the church. There, on balmy summer evenings, up on the lighted bandstand, we played to an audience scattered about in the moonlight. I most enjoyed Sousa's marches, Stars and Stripes Forever or Washington Post March. They were the most fun for a tuba player. Flora's favorite was the haunting Poet and Peasant Overture, pretty sophisticated music for such amateurs, but under Al Hancock's skillful leadership, we rendered the selection very credibly. During intermission, Art Whitney and I would seek out Toots and Flora on the edge of the crowd and go for a brief stroll. Ah, to be young once more. As I rubbed, the silver and gold luster re-emerged, and I hated more than ever to part with it.

When morning came, Flora telephoned the high school. Yes, they might be interested. I could spare no time, so she offered to take it to town. As she drove past the pasture where Bill and I were setting out three hundred pine trees we had gotten from the Conservation Department, she waved to us.

"I'm going to ask forty five for it," she called confidently.

"Good luck," I scoffed.

She was back before dinner, her errand accomplished, and I went to the house to get her story.

"Well, how did you make out?" I asked.

"Mr. Antholz evidently knows horns," she reported. "He looked it over very carefully, testing all the valves and keys or whatever you call them. He said we had done a good job of cleaning it, but it was an old style, one that would probably be used only for parades. Well, right then the price went down, mentally. When he got out a catalog to show me the difference in the present styles, I got a good look at some of the prices. Three or four hundred dollars or more! So when he asked me what I wanted for it, I screwed up my courage and said, 'Would forty-five be too much?'"

"He just smiled in a quiet sort of way and said, yes, he thought it would be. 'Well, how much will you give me?' I asked, and he answered, 'I'll pay you twenty-five dollars for it.' I gave a quick thought and said, 'Can you pay the money at once or will you have to wait for a board meeting?' 'No, you can have it at once.'"

"'Then I'll take it', I said, 'I'm just that hard up.' His secretary must have been a mind reader, for the check was in her hand when I turned around."

The day finally came, as we knew it would, when Flora and I were left alone to carry on as best we might, since Bruce, too, had taken his departure. Although we had conditioned ourselves for this very hour, it still left us overwhelmed and lonely. Our cherished family unity was broken now, those huddles from which our strategy had come, gone forever. If Bruce's going was a matter of concern for his parents, it was doubly so for himself. He was returning not to an atmosphere of hope and opportunity, but to the same environment of despair from which we had fled so long ago. Those six years which had changed and matured Bruce had done little for that stagnant city from which we had escaped.

It seemed only yesterday that Harris had gone, and now his brother had taken his few belongings and set out to find employment amidst the hordes of unemployed. He spent days in preparation, leaving nothing undone, no stumbling block that might hinder his parents in their endeavors. His last hours were spent in the shop that had meant so much to him, putting everything in order and caring for his tools and equipment.

"Pa," he said as we talked over his plans, "I'm going to get a job where I can learn more about mechanics and drafting, and later on I want to take a course in engineering if I can manage it."

"But Bruce," I replied, "there just aren't any jobs to be had now - you know that. Half of Chicago is walking the streets looking for work, something, anything to do."

"Yes, I know all that, Pa, but I've got to make a break sometime, you know, job or no job. Now that we've got seven cabins finished, I figure you and Mom can get along without my help."

"Yes, Son, you've got to go sometime and I suppose it might as well be now, only it would be a lot easier if only you had some prospect of a job. Say, I'll tell you, something just occurred to me. I'll give you a letter to Frank Schwinn: he can find something for you to do in the bicycle factory. I'm sure he'll do that much for me."

"No, thanks, Pa. I've thought it all out. I've got a plan of my own and I want to carry it out in my own way."

So Bruce left us. He had gone with the confidence of youth, sure that he could cope with any and all situations that might confront him. Never before had we felt more helpless and alone. We pushed our chairs from the breakfast table the next morning with the realization that only time and busy hands could dispel the aching void in our hearts.

Other things were developing, momentous things that would, for the time being, overshadow everything else. Lois was to be married in June! The news fell on our ears like a bombshell, though we had heard its whistling approach for some time. Was it possible that this child, consort of kittens and calves, had at last grown to womanhood? Where indeed had the time gone?

"Must be we're getting old, Pop," Flora said that evening as we laid plans for the coming event. Lois had had her first two years at the Art Institute by virtue of scholarships, and it had been good news, indeed, when later we learned that she had been awarded another, this time from the Chicago Conference of Club Presidents and Program Chairmen. This was a golden event for our daughter when, at the finish of the term, she was a guest at their May breakfast in the Stevens Hotel, and it thrilled her through and through.

"And that's not all," she wrote. "Do you know what, Mom? I sat at the speaker's table along with Lynn Fontaine, Alfred Lunt and Frederick Stock."

Kenny Huth finished high school along with Lois, and though he had kept steady company with her ever since, somehow we felt we hardly knew him.

"But, Charlie," Flora said, "that's the way it was with Ruth's Ed. We seldom saw him before they were married, and you know how quiet and reserved he is. Well, if Lois does as well as Ruth, she'll have a gem for a husband."

We heard from Bruce, and to our surprise he had gotten a job with the International Harvester Company. While waiting in their employment office, who should enter but a patron of ours who immediately recognized him.

"Why, Bruce, what on earth are you doing here?" he asked.

When he was duly informed, he set wheels in motion, with the result that Bruce was given an interview with the head of the tractor research division. Among other things, his examination called for a sample of his drafting. Having none in his possession, he worked the night through, and the following day he submitted a detailed drawing of an injection pump, sketches which he had worked on long ago and filed away. The upshot of it all was a chance to work at assembly drawings. More to his liking was when he was put in the Research Engineering Department somewhat later, working on plans for a mechanical cotton picker they were developing.

Chapter 47

RUNNING TO COMPLETION

When Winter relinquishes its icy hold and our little world responds to the first breath of spring, Nature's time for convalescence is at hand. During this interval of adjustment, all outdoors is unkempt and bedraggled. Our lake becomes a sea of slush ice, black and formidable, and all the highways are scarred with frost boils. Rivulets of water gather into dirty pools as belated snow drifts give way to the warmth of the sun. Chunks of ice, like great eggs, drop from fenders, and cars are never so spattered and muddy. Overnight our park becomes a reservoir of melted snow covering the playground and even the horseshoe stakes. Thanks to providence, this is an interlude of short duration, for suddenly one night, the frost leaves the ground. Beneath our big trees concentric rings of pine needles mark the water's gradual recession.

Our spring work then begins. The ice wall along our beach must be graded, and spring raking begun. Caulking and painting our wooden boats is a major undertaking, too. Though Flora undertook cleaning our cabins, it was my job to paint the floors, and there were many repairs to be made, and many times a stronger man was needed for heavy lifting. Clearly we couldn't carry on alone, what with a cabin waiting to be finished. As was so often our lot, we were fortunate that help was again provided, by Pete Hart. We were happy to secure his help once again.

On the southern boundary of our property, a pine clad hill over-

335

looks the rippling waters of the lake. Though windswept and bleak during winter months, it is a haven of cool breezes during the summer. I had long ago determined to crown this choice location with a cabin worthy of so fine a site. From its apex, one could scan the entire area of the lake, from the inlet on the north to the southernmost shore lines. Directly across, cradled within a dip in the horizon, was the outlet creek that wound its way through acres of dank, lush bottom land to merge finally in the waters of Rice Lake.

A freshly troweled floor was not only a reminder of Bruce's foresight and perseverance, it lay now as a challenge to the new order of things. As I scanned its length and breadth, I remembered the strong backs that had hitherto made things possible, and was overcome by my own inadequacy. Logs are heavy things and aging backs do not remain supple forever, but the fact that we were alone and shorthanded had in no way altered our aims, though it had pushed our goal back a little further. Thanks to Pete's help, much of the heavy work had already been accomplished. Sufficient logs for the cabin lay neatly stacked around its foundation. Only the heavy ridgepole and long rafters were still wanting, but now Pete was engaged with many spring clean-up jobs around the place. Another pair of hands was obviously needed and we turned to another neighbor.

Billy O'Mara was built close to the ground. He was strong and "Timber" was his middle name. To him, cabin logs were but toothpicks, and his rough, callused hands were the mark of a true woodsman. His keen wit made him a pleasant working companion, and I felt fortunate, indeed, to secure his services. He knew where the tall trees grew that might furnish the required ridgepoles and rafters.

Work had progressed on our new cabin to the point where we were ready to place the ridgepole. It was thirty feet long and about a foot in diameter at the big end. Cut green a few weeks earlier, it was indeed a heavy brute, and to get it in place would be  no mean feat, but I had worked out the procedure in detail and was anxious to go ahead. Monday morning came, but no Billy. This had happened too often to surprise me, but I hated to be the victim of his vagaries.

"Flora," I said, "Billy hasn't shown up again. I'd just like to show him I'm not totally dependent on him. If you'll give me a hand, I think between us we can get that ridgepole in place."

"You and me?," she exclaimed. "Are you crazy?"

"Well, you, me, the truck and some block and tackle."

"All right, I'm game," she answered after some consideration.

With the help of our gear, we pulled the butt end up the hill to the bedroom wing. I had left the top of the window frame off there, and we hoisted the big ridgepole up until it rested on the bottom of this open window frame. Still at the wheel of the truck and with Flora to signal me, I inched it forward and upward until the end rested on the opposite wall, on the lake side. Before it would be in proper alignment, it would still have to go ten feet forward. This accomplished, it was necessary to hoist the tail end up, level with the front. Our problem was to improvise a place to anchor a pulley above the open window frame, but once this was solved, we made short work of first hoisting the log, then shoving a board across the window opening. Once it was safely supported, we heaved a sigh of relief.

Both front and rear center gables had already been built to their correct heights, the ends of the logs ascending stair-like toward the center peak. Billy would have made short work of lifting the ridgepole up each step, front and rear, but it was all I could manage to lift an inch at a time and Flora to shove a short piece of board under. When the heavy pole was at last in place, we were two tired but triumphant people. I was already fitting rafters into place when Billy showed up the next morning with a sheepish look on his face.

An early customer who lived in Berwyn, just beyond our old hometown, showed up over Memorial Day, and Flora saw it as her chance to go back with them for Lois' wedding.

"I can come back on the train. Surely we can afford that much," she said. And so she had gone.

The plan all along had been that Lois and Ken honeymoon here at Lake Lipsie, but Flora's fortune in being able to attend the wedding made for an odd first night for the newlyweds – they sat up on the night train, Flora facing them, all the way to Spooner. Jenny Wren, our eighth cabin, was waiting for the newlyweds, and they were the first to occupy it.

The two stood arm in arm looking out over the water one day when Lois called, "Pop, look out there! There, those two things. Are they loons or geese or what in the world are they?" I saw at once that they were neither.

Jenny Wren

"Why, they're deer. Run quick and get the glasses," I said. Sure enough, the binoculars showed two deer swimming our way from the far shore. Lois and Ken set out at once in a canoe. That any creature so poorly equipped for swimming could possibly make its way across was quite beyond my thinking. The deer had evidently been chased, and had taken to the water as a means of escape, but now they encountered a new enemy, and milled about, unable to outdistance the canoe. Finally, after setting them on their course again, the couple withdrew a distance, feeling sorry for the creatures.

Slowly the deer came in our direction. Finally a yearling fawn dragged its tired body from the water, and it stood dripping wet, its legs spread apart, too exhausted to pay any attention to Flora and me. The doe, wiser and stronger, turned and walked unhurriedly through the shallow water to a distant brushy point where she disappeared into the woods.

Ever since the boys' departure, we had discussed the advisability of selling our livestock. To begin with, we were in need of working capital, and furthermore, try as we did, we could not keep abreast of major jobs, much less minor ones. Pete had solved at least one of these problems, so the matter of our cattle was forgotten until fall. Not wanting to see our garbage go to waste, we purchased another pair of porkers, hoping that two properly labeled garbage cans at each cabin would solve the problem of glass mixed with hog cuisine.

Unlike their predecessors with their roving nature, these little piggies stayed at home, where they quickly established themselves in the graces of our family as pets. As a matter of sentiment, we used the old names of Tom and Jerry. Tom, the more active of the two, found it convenient to attach himself to me, while Jerry, the lazy one, usually sunned himself beside the back door, awaiting Flora's appearance. They would have to be penned before the resort season started.

Though the work on Top Notch, our latest cabin, progressed only slowly and intermittently, a well defined trail tied it with our shop, and finally to the network of paths about the grounds. Unlike other

Top Notch

paths, however, much of this trail had been cut by the stubby hooves of Tom, who never missed a chance to be at my heels. A call from Mother or a trip for a needed tool would bring him to his feet to follow me with dog-like devotion.

One warm June day, as Tom lazily watched me apply stain to the logs, my sense of humor got the better of me. With my brush I set to work on his sleek anatomy. He only grunted with satisfaction when I turned him over to complete the job. His pink skin seemed to have a special affinity for the dye, and the warm sepia stripes about his white body might well have been nature's own work. Though I was proud of the result, Flora, with no eye for the esthetic, failed to appreciate it. As for Tom, he, I'm sure, doubled his affection for me. However, my gilding the lily nearly cost us our new hire, for when Billy O'Mara showed up and set eyes on Tom, he stopped in his tracks.

"My God, what's that thing?" he shouted.

When his surprise turned to indecision, I answered, "Oh, that? Why, it's only an ordinary pig with a little 'pig'ment on him."

There were times when Tom's devotion went a little too far. Though he never quite made it to the mail box behind my car, he lost a lot of good pie shortening trying to do so. I was working on the upper structure of Top Notch one day when I heard a swish of wings overhead. Some mallards circled the lake indecisively a few times, then dropped to the shallow water some distance from the cabin. Tom followed behind me at a double dog trot as I rushed home for my gun. While he lay puffing at the back door, I slipped quietly out the front. "If I can make it across the park without him seeing me, I'll be all right," I told myself. At Birch Hill I stole a look around the corner. No pig. Good! The rest'll be easy. Through underbrush and popple I picked my way along the shore, rising now and then to peer at my quarry. I crept on all fours through a dank swale, and again was under cover of the woods. Quietly now I rose, prepared to let go with both barrels, when "Oink, oink, oink" rousted my prey before I could get a shot off. My pal, squealing his delight, had found me.

When I think back to our first hard and trying years and recall the fun, wit and humor that somehow accompanied them, I am at a loss to understand the serendipitous mix, unless the answer lies within those timeworn pages where Grandfather Adams says of his parents, "They put into my composition about all the fun that normally should have been distributed throughout that large family." Could it be that fun, wit and humor are characteristics handed down, generation to generation, in the genes of my great grandfather, old Isaac Adams? Well, I like to think so and they will remain a goodly part of my legacy.

Forest fires are an ever-present danger in heavily wooded areas of the north, most often in the proverbial dry spell between the disappearance of winter's snow and arrival of spring rains. More than once, ashes from distant fires fell on our own roads, reminding us that we were not too far from Hinckly, Minnesota, where 413 were killed in a holocaust back in 1894, or the one in 1871 when over 1200 people were killed in a fire at Peshtigo, right here in Wisconsin.

There is never a year that there are not a number of fires in our area, and every spring there is anxious scanning of the sky for telltale smoke. Watchmen in fire towers, lanes for quick access through woods and good fire fighting equipment generally keep blazes localized. Trucks loaded with water tanks are equipped to jet down wells in a matter of minutes, where the water table is known to be favorable to the undertaking.

Billy and I were working at the new cabin when we spied a small cloud of smoke near Rice Lake. Just a brush fire, no doubt, but we kept it under an uneasy surveillance as we worked, and it was soon evident that it was getting out of control. When flames became visible in the tree tops, I rushed to call Flora. She needed no prompting and soon we three were watching in fascination. Finally Flora could stand it no longer.

"I'm going to drive over there where I can see better," she declared. I tried to dissuade her, but finding she was determined, I went along, not wanting to risk her getting into danger. From our new vantage point about a block from the road that skirted an open field and the woods beyond, we watched with mounting excitement as the fire blazed through tree tops toward the edge of the field. Tractor pulled breaker plows had piled up furrows of fresh soil there, and it was evident that it could be brought under control at that line. A warden, who was scouting near us, came over to our car and handed me a backpack sprinkler outfit, directing me to patrol the edge of the area. I knew he was quite within his rights, and not too reluctantly, I left Flora in charge of the car and followed him.

Now that the forefront of the fire was being contained, there was time to check on the flanks. I was put with a group of CCC boys who were reconnoitering the edge of the fire where it had run along a swampy stretch, occasionally running out into small stretches of higher ground. Suddenly I heard a cry of "help" from behind me and turned to see the last boy, flailing his arms and crying for help as he slowly sank in a muck hole. I had side-stepped that spot when I had passed, as the unusually green grass coverage made me suspicious. Shedding my pack, I ran to him, grabbing a pole as I went, and reached him none too soon. He frantically seized the pole I flung in front of him, and between us, we managed to remove his encumbering pack. I could barely pull him out and he could do little to help himself. He was one frightened lad laying on the ground, and a frightened man, too, for I was not sure I could save him. As I worked my way back to the car, I pondered the coincidence that had brought me into this picture at all.

Chapter 48

YOU CAN'T STOP PROGRESS

The Wisconsin Indian Head Country is not only a region, it is an organization as well. Representatives from fourteen northwestern counties incorporated to form it, its name suggested by that likeness to an Indian profile formed by the rivers on its western boundary. Its purpose is to promote its recreational industry. Though it started as a modest venture, it soon attracted not only members of the resort industry but commercial interests serving the area as well. Local Chambers of Commerce and County Boards joined as the vacation business became the largest industry in the area.

I was a member from the start and served as publicity chairman for a number of years. An early venture was renting a booth at the big Outdoor Show held each February in Chicago's Stockyards Amphitheater. From our booth, for a reasonable fee, members could hand out their brochures, often signing up business for the coming season. I had taken advantage of this opportunity on a number of occasions, and not being at all bashful about expounding the attractions of our place, had secured enough business to make it worth the time and expense involved.

One year, for the sake of color, the organization decided to send down an Indian from the Couderay tribe, and we arranged for Johnny Frog, their chief, to go. It was Johnny's first city experience, and as we rounded a bend on the crowded south side elevated train, he grabbed my arm, saying, "You take care of me in the city, Mr. Palmer. I take care of you in the woods."

343

I was staying with my daughter, Ruth, in suburban Riverside, and we invited Johnny out to dinner one night, to give Robin and Kathie the thrill of meeting a real live Indian. As we sat down to the table, Johnny asked, "May I say a prayer?"

"Of course, Johnny," I replied, and standing, he raised his hands and prayed in his Indian tongue.

From the start of the show it was evident that taking him had been a good idea, for Johnny was a born showman. He was quite used to meeting the public, since his tribe had staged Indian dances in Hayward for many years. So the next year we decided to take him again.

February came and when I went up to the Reservation to make final arrangement with him, he asked, "Sure I come, but can I bring a friend with me this time?"

"Is he a good Indian?" I asked. "He won't get drunk?"

"Oh, yes, he good Indian," Johnny answered, and so it was arranged.

Babe Begay was a fine specimen of a man, but like most Indians, very reticent, though on the long trip down to the city I learned that he was a Navaho who had come to Hayward to visit the Chippewas, and had married one of their women. When we reached the amphitheater, we unloaded our gear at the Indian Head booth, then set out to find lodgings for them. That accomplished, I bought them meal tickets at a nearby restaurant before going back to the amphitheater. As a precaution, we crossed and re-crossed Halsted Street a number of times, my attention directed to Babe as the newcomer, until I felt they could negotiate it safely by themselves.

The show had been going for three days when Babe came to me with a problem. "Mr. Palmer," he said, "my wife made some beadwork for me to sell, but I have no place here. What can I do about it?"

"Why didn't you tell me before, Babe?" I said as I cleared a spot on the counter for his wares. Disposing of them proved to be no problem at all.

On the last evening as we were dismantling the booth, I was

344

arranging for the return of some taxidermy we had borrowed from a man on the far northwest side of the city.

"Take a Halsted street car to Madison," I said to the lad who would undertake the errand, "transfer west and go to Western. Transfer again, going north to …" Just then a hand rested on my arm and I turned to hear Babe say, "Mr. Palmer, you're not telling him the best way. If he'll take the south side El to the loop, go over the bridge and catch the Logan Park El, then get off at …"

"Babe!" I said, stunned.

"Well, I'll tell you, Mr. Palmer," he said, "I drove a Yellow Taxi in Chicago for four years."

The day we made our first trip to town over the newly paved county road was truly a red-letter day in our calendar of events. With other resorts springing up in the lake region, the county had seen fit to blacktop Highway A out as far as Byrnes' Store, the western limits of their jurisdiction. Not only did this benefit us personally, but our patrons as well. This was to become an asset of consequence in our future advertising - "Blacktop pavement to within a mile of our property." Considering the newly constructed telephone line that paralleled the highway, things were looking up in the resort business.

"Flora," I called, "did you see this ad in the Advocate? 'Delco light plant with batteries for sale.' What do you say we look into it?"

"Of course, a Delco plant wouldn't take care of all the cabins, would it?"

"No, but it would be a start. Think of the luxury of having ample electricity here in the house, and I'm sure we would get some business we are missing now."

"OK, let's look into it," she said.

We got the outfit for eighty-five dollars and trusted to luck that we could secure the wire somewhere. However, we had a problem when it came to finding the heavy-gauge wire required for a low voltage system. Because of the war, new wire was rationed to essential industries, so junk yards were our best bet, and we traveled far afield in search of them. Returning from Eau Claire one day, we were indeed fortunate to discover a supply in a junk yard in Chippewa Falls; not only the heavy wire needed for outdoors, but some suitable for inside wiring as well.

We were able to supply current for five cabins and for several 32 volt motors we purchased. We housed the outfit in one end of the garage where it bothered no one as it operated through the evening hours. We shut it off at ten o'clock, there being enough residual power stored in the batteries for emergency night use. Though far short of unlimited 110 volt current, it was a great help.

Necessity never seemed to be satisfied, regardless of our achievements. We were constantly in need of more things. It was this very need that spurred us on our way. We had gotten our saw mill by dint of personal sacrifice and ingenuity. Now with no sacrifice, no cost to us and no effort on our part, things of importance to our project were coming our way. Along with the telephone line and the newly paved highway, another convenience was coming, one our patrons would especially appreciate. A new and sizable structure was rising at the site of the small tar-paper store.

Byrnes Store

Charlie Byrnes resembled his father in many respects, though he lacked the elder's intriguing homely philosophy. He and Mary, his wife, envisioned a place of business quite beyond my own expectations. From the day he hauled the big cement mixer from our place to the day he opened his new store, I was an interested observer. Imbued with foresight and courage, the two put themselves to the task, gambling their all on the future even as we had done.

Time has proven the wisdom of their foresightedness, for nowhere in the country about is there a more modern or finer country store. Here now you can fill up with gas, step inside, push your shopping cart about, fill it with cuts of choice meat, fresh vegetables and a variety of frozen foods. To be sure, it is not a Joe Larabee country store with horse collars and a heterogeneous display of accommodations common to a country store. Instead, it's a tidy and well ordered city store in a country setting where both courtesy and cleanliness are dispensed.

Chapter 49

BLOCKS AND ROCKS

Experience made me efficient and the work progressed routinely and now *Hide Away*, our last cabin, was finished. We now had

Lake Lipsie Pines, Spooner, Wisconsin   by Bence

Hide Away

ten cabins in all — a four bedroom, three three-bedrooms, five two-bedrooms, and a single. With each new one built, we not only added the work of servicing it but of raking away last season's leaves. Since we left every tree standing not actually in the path of building sites, the amount of leaves we carted away every spring was fantastic. Even before this task was finished, it was time to start mowing, which must be kept up regularly at intervals all through the summer. As we extended our groomed park farther and farther each year, the whole place took on the appearance of a rustic park dotted with log cabins, and it was getting a reputation as one of the beauty spots of the area. We meant to keep it so.

Saturdays are busy days on a resort. All hands begin as soon as the first cabin is vacated, if indeed we are up that early, since it is a long trip home to Chicago, Peoria or Indianapolis, and frequently patrons leave before dawn. Not infrequently, a new patron has driven all night and appeared before his particular cabin is vacated. Since those who had to return only to Eau Claire or Minneapolis are loath to pack up and leave early, it eventually became necessary to specify hours for departure and arrival.

Flora never enjoyed housework and it was a grim joke on her when confronted with spring cleaning. Washing windows alone was a huge task, for we had built our cabins to be light and airy. One day she counted the sashs and found there were 184 of them with six panes to a sash and two sides to a pane – the computation became an exercise in higher mathematics.

"There I stand," she said, concentrating on the dirty glass, "when right before my eyes is a whole world of beauty to be enjoyed."

We had been furnishing bedding and doing laundry for several years, and found a mangle was a necessity as soon as we had electricity to run the motor. As we added more cabins, it became necessary to have a cleaning woman on Saturday and Monday as well. Neighbor women were available for that service, and we gained not only their help but good friendships as well.

Vacationers as a rule are a congenial lot, happy and easy-going. No longer inhibited by formality or restraint, they lay aside camouflage and become their real selves, at least for the duration. Perhaps it is this very characteristic that makes our business so rewarding. Although our weekly campfires are communal affairs and well accepted, it was the closer, individual contacts within the cabins that I remember most.

"Here comes the ice man," someone would shout as they heard our pickup stop outside the door. A sink filled with unwashed dishes or an unswept floor were enough to bring forth apologies. "You know we're on our vacation, Mr. Palmer."

Icing was a time for good fellowship, and often my reward was a cold bottle or a tasty bit from within the crowded icebox.

Wanting to make a good impression on a new guest one day, I lost no time answering a special call for ice, even though it was a hot Sunday. I was greeted cheerfully enough by the lady of the house who said her husband had just gone out on the lake. After a moment's talk, I made ready for the lift, smiling the while. The box, a cylindrical type, was roomy but much too high for easy icing, as the opening was at the top. My thin, wet shirt clung to my back as I bent over the tongs, and with a jerk and shift of position, I hoisted the heavy cake and balanced it momentarily on the top. But in the heaving process, my expanding chest collapsed my stomach and I felt my trousers slipping, and so, too, the ice. To let the heavy cake go crashing through the box was unthinkable but my pants! God forbid! The big cake started sliding and instinct or reaction or call it what you will, made the decision. The ice did not slip, but...I was subjected to a feminine scream, then a burst of laughter to accentuate my dilemma as the ice settled neatly into its resting place.

"Something there is that does not love a wall," Robert Frost wrote. I had a picture in my mind of a wall I would like, one I would like to build.

A road skirted our house, and across from its uneven edge, rose a modest hill. By building a wall at the foot of this hill, we could fill in back of it, forming a bed for flowers, ferns or shrubs. Many trips with our truck were made to secure the rocks I wanted, quartzite lying along the roads north of Spooner, a task I could hardly have attempted without the help of Billy's strong back and arms.

Though started as an overtime project, I was soon completely absorbed in it, which was as well since there would be a good ninety feet to be laid. Considering my inexperience, the work went along well. At the front end, the wall terminated as the face of a rock garden. Here a large iron kettle hangs from a tripod where each summer thereafter a profusion of ivy and coleus has grown.

Some years ago, a topographical survey was run through our place, and when I learned our general elevation, I asked the surveyors to locate a spot exactly a thousand feet above sea level.

"Well, Mr. Palmer, right here on this wall seems to be just that," he said, indicating a stone by the rock garden. I marked it so, in gold-gilt paint.

Chapter 50

GOOD WITH THE BAD

While we carried on here, Hitler was gaining victory after victory in Europe. We no longer felt confident that we might not be drawn into the struggle. The Maginot Line fell, Germans were marching on Paris. Oh, the horror of those nightly broadcasts telling of the strafing of refugees along their line of advance.

America could no longer trust to isolation. She must be prepared – and so the draft. At the time of the first World War, I was a married man with four small children and I was not called. Now it would be different: we had grown sons. Sure enough, Bruce was in the second draft call. We waited with apprehension, for he was a conscientious objector. In answer to the examiner's questions, he said he would not take life nor destroy property. Would he serve in the Medical Corps? Yes, he would do that. So it was decided.

He was stationed at Camp Grant in Rockford, Illinois, serving in what they called the housekeeping detail. His work was to make cabinets and other equipment for the barracks, unready as they were for the influx of men. In fact, he made himself so useful that they kept him on for a second three-month stretch. At the end of that time, he was home for a short leave, and it was then that he had poured the concrete for what was to be the last cabin.

In the meantime, Harris had gotten his Masters Degree and was working at Camp McCoy in the southern part of the state where a new road was being built. His job was to locate road materials for the contractor. The following spring he was hired by the U.S. Engineering Corp to help with road construction.

All illusions that we would not be drawn into the struggle, that our boys might escape actual service, were lost that fateful Sunday of Pearl Harbor infamy. Flora said she had a hard ball, as big as an apple, in the pit of her stomach as she listened to that broadcast. Who will ever forget that hour?

Later Harris was inducted from Camp McCoy where he was working. His term of service was relatively short. As he was helping to unload a truck, an iron bar fell on his foot, breaking bones in the instep. Even when he had recovered, he was incapacitated for any immediate military service and was soon discharged.

The season of 1943 started out with misfortune. On a late June afternoon while I was up at Byrnes Store, the western sky darkened ominously with a big black cloud whose extremities drooped threateningly toward the earth. Gathering my mail, I rushed home.

"Get the chickens in, Flora," I shouted. "There's a bad storm coming. I'll tend to the boats." We had bought a hundred baby chicks that spring, to augment not only our own rationed meat supply but that of our patrons as well.

I just got back to the house when the wind struck with fury. On the lake side, the screens were so plastered with leaves that we could barely see, but at the back door we watched trees swaying wildly. We must have been in the center of the disturbance for in a few minutes the wind reversed its direction.

When at last we went out to survey the damage, we were horrified. The worst damage was along our lake shore where twenty-six good trees lay prone. Many were uprooted, the soil soft from a week of rain. Luckily there were still many trees left, and no significant damage had been done to cabins, which seemed like a miracle. Our hearts were sick at the havoc that had been wrought in those few short minutes. We later learned the other edge of the black cloud had wreaked its fury farther to the northwest where at Fish Lake a cabin had been overturned, one woman had been killed and two others injured. Then we felt ashamed to mention our own ill fortune.

By early spring it became evident, as we had anticipated, that this would not be a good business year for resorts. Reservations were coming in slowly, and no wonder, for who could plan at such a time, though it was really surprising how many there were who managed to save up gasoline rations for a trip. Often several would pool their resources to make such a trip possible. Fish they would if fish they possibly could.

To see cabins empty in the height of our season was a new experience for us, and adding up the results at the end of the summer was disheartening, for we had done hardly more than half of a normal business that summer. Yet we were in no worse shape than the other resorts. Gasoline rationing had struck us all a heavy blow.

Of late, acute inflammation along with severe suffering, sometimes in my toes, sometimes my ankles, was recurring frequently. Was it gout? Was it arthritis? Our doctor decided to send me to Wisconsin General Hospital in Madison for further diagnosis and treatment.

As luck would have it, I had both! Of course it was well to know, but no fun at all to be put on a gout diet. Meat substitutes only added to my overweight appearance. Prompt recognition of the symptoms and taking colchicine tablets forestalled most attacks. Only when I temporized, when I asked "is it gout or is it arthritis?" that it got the better of me. Flora insisted, "That's gout, Charlie, when you get so short tempered. It always affects you like that. I know, I'm on the receiving end."

She would be right. One thing I know, gout is no fun. Neither, of course, is arthritis, whose encroachment gradually stiffened my joints. I always enjoyed working with my hands, and it was a frustration to me when tools would slip from my grasp. Still, I knew that many victims were afflicted far worse, with suffering and worse crippling. I was still able to carry on.

If gasoline was rationed, the crop of new babies was not, for the previous fall Ruth and Ed had had a girl, Jill, their third child, and to Lois' and Ken's great joy, a baby boy, Mickie, came to their family circle in August. Both children were to spend many weeks here at Lake Lipsie Pines, as had Kathie and Robin. Lois had generally managed more than a two week vacation here with us, and now that babies had begun to arrive, we would have it no other way. Later, two brothers, Jonathan and Lindsay, came to join Mickie, and often the children stayed the summer through. City streets were no place for children whose grandparents had a summer resort with a playground and beach to be shared. Our home, too, was full of interest to them.

I have before me an essay written by Kathie which is a good example of her early impressions of Lake Lipsie Pines.

Grandmother's House.

There is not a place that bears so many sweet memories to me as my grandmother's house. It is a small white frame house with a country air, located about a mile off the county highway on a sand road in northern Wisconsin. Down a grassy slope to the front is the lake, with a sandy beach and many boats on the shore, for Grandmother's house is at a resort. Stately pines tower over the little house and shade it from the sun in summer and protect it from the storm in winter.

The wood stove in the kitchen is always going, and when a meal is ready, Grandmother rings the dinner bell which is perched on top of the roof. When it clangs, the family comes in from the garden and workshop to taste another delicious meal served in the cool back room of the house.

The living room is a collector's delight. There is a red rock fireplace which Grandfather built himself. On the shelf above it there is an old glass clock with four balls that turn round and round. A sword hangs under the shelf, and over the fireplace is the head of a deer with huge antlers.

To find more of these treasures, one must look in the attic which contains more Indian relics and many fishbowls of arrowheads.

Grandmother's house is like a treasure chest in which you keep digging deeper for more pleasures on rainy days.

"What would you think of our buying the old home, Pa?" Lois wrote. "We are pretty crowded here now with Mickie." Buying the old home was an idea to be sure. Its rent had been going to Flora's sisters who had loaned us money so often and so willingly. Flora's inheritance from her mother's estate had also canceled a goodly amount of the debt, and now if we could sell, we might at long last be free from debt and standing on our own two feet.

Built by a contractor for his own home, it was a substantial house when we had bought it the year before Lois was born. It was old-fashioned, of course. Removal of a partition had helped, along with the installation of hardwood floors and a half bath where the pantry had been.

"What is your father working on now?" a friend once asked Ruth.

"Oh, he's putting a bathroom in the pantry," she replied.

When I chanced upon an ad for a second hand heating plant from an old home being wrecked on Prairie Avenue, I hurried out to investigate. This proved a good buy, but over one of the fireplaces, a bronze relief panel of Apollo driving his four horse chariot of the sun interested me even more. Not daunted by my now-depleted bank account, I visited the owner of the building in his downtown office.

"So you admire that panel, too," he said. "I promised it to a woman who was very keen about it. I told her she could buy it if I ever sold the place. You know, that house used to belong to the judge who sentenced the Haymarket Rioters. I'll see if I can find her address. If I can't, I'll let you know."

I don't know how I had the nerve to make my petty offer of fifteen dollars when I got his word, but it was all I could afford. The owner was satisfied that the panel would be appreciated, and I came home exultant and happy. Now it was going to be the Huth children who would continue the old custom of hanging Christmas stockings from the ears of the horses, as ours had done before. Many more changes would be accomplished as the years went on, adding convenience and originality. In what had at first been a barn, later converted to a garage, now housed a ceramic studio where Lois spends many happy and creative hours.

So it was our home no more, but it was still in the family.

Handmade tapestry of Lake Lipsie Pines made by Lois Palmer Huth in 1940, now hanging in Top Notch.

Chapter 51

FAMILY TRADITION

The circle had swung full around, for now Harris was home again, this time with a wife, Frances. She was the sister of one of his college pals and it was a lucky day when he met her. They came home with a plan for their future. Harris wanted a summer resort of his own. This came as a complete surprise to us. Was it for this he had put in those three years at Madison? We remembered the wish he had made years ago on Bruce's birthday, that he and his brother would have the best resort in the state. Had he been subconsciously harboring that dream all this time?

I offered him a partnership with us, but he felt that was an opportunity that rightly belonged to Bruce, should he want it, as Bruce had stayed with us longer in the first place, and was not yet free to make his own plans. Yet I believe that being on their own also had much to do with their decision.

Behind our shop we had built a small frame building which we first called our dormitory, where the men had slept in the summer – Bruce, Harris, Dick, Harold or sometimes a visiting friend. With the installation of a sink, stove, cupboard and work counter, it now became Spare

Tire, living quarters for Harris and Frances. They would help us here while scouting the countryside for the place of their dreams.

Their ideals, like ours, were high and places which met them were not for sale. For one thing, they wanted to locate near enough to our place to be able to make use of our tools and equipment. Going further afield, they finally called on our naturalist friend, Karl Kahmann, near Hayward. Karl suggested a piece of lakeshore he had owned for years, on Diamond Lake near Cable. Though this was farther away than they thought to settle, they drove up to investigate. It was love at first sight.

"Pop, I think we've found the place at last," Harris said that night. "I want you and Mom to drive up with us tomorrow and look it over."

"Well, tell us about it," I said.

"You never saw such trees, at least not around this part of the country. The lake is about the same size as Lipsie and crystal clear. There's a good sandy beach, too. Karl has about eight acres there. I don't want to spoil it by trying to describe it. You'll have to see it for yourselves."

The trip up was through a type of country we were not unaccustomed to, and as we neared our destination, we saw nothing to warrant his enthusiasm. But as we left the highway onto the road that served the lake, suddenly there it was!

Our own enthusiasm mounted as we drove on and at the end of the road, we reached the site. This forest was quite different in character from our own – giant hemlocks were everywhere with their feathery needles and tiny cones, and beneath them grew smaller balsams, both trees we did not have. Determining whether the hardwoods were maple, oak or basswood was difficult, their foliage was so high above us. To lend even more variety were yellow birch, quite different from the white birch so plentiful at Lake Lipsie. Though not as graceful, they grow much larger and are valuable as a source of veneer.

As impressive as the standing timber were the prone trunks of old giants, moss covering their decaying surfaces. A path along one of these led down to the lake. Before us lay a nice sandy bathing beach with ample room along the shore for a play beach as well. A little creek entered the lake here, to be spanned at some later time by a rustic bridge. Beyond this was more of the same lakeshore, more forest. Important, too, was the lay of the land favorable for cabin sites. This was indeed a beautiful spot.

We were glad that just as Flora's folks had helped us out at our start, we could, even if in a more modest way, do the same for Harris.

The work at our resort was tapering off in the Fall, so Harris helped with the harvest at the cranberry marsh while Frances did substitute teaching in the Spooner schools. When a full-time teaching position opened up unexpectedly, Harris applied for it and they moved into town.

The next fall, their first baby came. They named him Cary, but Frosty they promptly dubbed him and through the years, that name has stuck.

Progress the next summer at Diamond Lake was slow work, with only one man to do the heavy lifting. Yet their cabin was steadily taking shape and it was a beauty, too. Harris was developing into a very capable man.

Wanting to get into his own field of geology, he secured a position teaching at Parsons College in Fairfield, Iowa.

Four years after Frosty was born, twin boys, Robert and Warren, arrived. The next year Harris was offered a better position; as an associate professor – he would teach geology at the Wisconsin State Technical College at Platteville. This pleased us all; not only was it a step up in his chosen field, they would be considerably nearer to us now. Long summer vacations afforded him time to proceed with his resort project and a second, rental cabin slowly took shape, this one

Star o' the North

with inside plumbing. They were proud of it, and we of them, for Frances, too, had done her share and more. 'Star o' the North' they named their place, and a star it was indeed.

Even with our ten cabins, we often had folks drive in, and upon seeing our park and beach, bemoaned the fact that we were fully booked. We, of course, hated to turn them away. When Harris and Francis moved up to their place, the simple two-room Spare Tire became available for such overflows, and from that time on, was filled nearly every week of our season.

Chapter 52

FIRE AND ICE

If December 7, 1940 was a day of tragedy, June 6, 1944, D-Day, was one of excitement and even rejoicing. Surely the war would be over soon now that the Allies were invading. Flora rang the big bell atop the house and I ran down to Air Pocket to tell the news to early vacationers there.

The reality was it would be many months yet before the war was really over, months before Bruce would finally be home. Yet at long last that day came. On a crisp autumn day, we awaited the arrival of his train. I became aware there were other families on the platform, there for the same reunion. There seemed a strange sense of anticipation – joy tempered with a vague concern.

A small dot of light and far-away scream of a steam whistle drew all eyes down the track. Gray-black plumes of smoke rose above the trees and the dull orange headlamp grew steadily brighter. As the great Northwestern steam engine pulled close, its gleaming bell cried out the arrival and our group backed away as the steam jets hissed past us. The dull green cars screeched to a stop, and we searched up and down the train as khaki uniforms began to step off. As my eyes swept past the closest car, I saw his toothy smile, so long absent from our midst, looking down at us from the car platform. I knew Flora had seen it too when I heard her soft gasp. A moment later he tossed his duffel bag down and wrapped his arms around his mother. Flora was not prone to tears, but that day was an exception. Perhaps I had underestimated her concern for him all these years.

Bruce insisted on driving home, remarking at every little change he noticed in town, and all the way out to the lake. He could not stop talking, relating not what he had been through, what he had seen, but what he had been planning for the resort. There seemed no end to it.

His return brought a new energy to the house. He immediately sought his civilian clothes as Flora prepared a hearty lunch. With food in his mouth, we were able to ask a few questions which had been hard to field during his marathon descriptions of plans for the future. Lunch was abruptly over when he excused himself to look over the premises. He bounded down through the park, and was gone over an hour. When he returned, he went through his bag until he found the list he had worked on for so long.

That evening, he detailed the many projects which had obviously been his diversion for so many years away from the place, and what a list it was. Some were quite plausible, and would be just what our patrons would enjoy, but he had many which sounded like wild dreams to me, of a scope beyond our means, and even a threat to the natural land as it lay around us. However, now was not the time to criticize his efforts. And what of his job in Chicago?

Bruce had never been comfortable unless a project and the tools for its accomplishment lay before him, and his return found nearly all his time back in the shop, to the dismay of his mother, I'm sure. If he was not at a task in the shop, he was off acquiring new tools or supplies with his own funds, diligently saved from his government checks. He was especially enthusiastic about the new welding equipment he had purchased, describing how vital it would be to the metal work in his many plans. The line shaft in the shop hadn't run so long since he had left, and I liked to think it meant progress, though I was not certain in what form it would emerge.

The autumn evenings closed out daylight far sooner than Bruce would have preferred, but he then turned to his sketches to fill the evening hours. One evening, as I sat reading, I glanced at the window before me, and thought it odd that the golden glow of the sunset was persisting. The next time I looked, the glow was brighter yet, an impossible feat which brought me from my chair toward the window. As I approached, I sensed things were quite wrong – the light was coming from a direction away from the lake, and was not steady. My worst fears were cemented when I reached the window – the shop was ablaze.

For a moment, my mouth was unable to cry out, so horrified was I by the sight. Finally I gulped a deep breath.

"Fire!" I shouted. "The shop is on fire!" Bruce came running, Flora not far behind. We all fought for the door, rushing out into the cool night air only to be basked by the intense heat of the blaze whose voracious tongues were consuming everything. Bruce fetched a large bucket of water, but could not even get close enough to throw it at the angry, roaring blaze. I felt Flora's hand at mine and took hold of it. She squeezed ever so hard. My chest went tight as I watched the very nerve center of our building program fall to the unstoppable fire. I had never felt so helpless, as all the tools that had helped us shape our new life perished. My eyes saw the flames, my mind recalled all the winter days within those walls fashioning the details that highlighted our cabins. It was all being swept away. As the flames broke through the roof, I thought of our old Orioles Nest, there up in the rafters, the soft early mornings with the glass slid open, the gifts of nature laid before us in bird songs and fresh dewy smells. My teeth clenched and I could no longer stave off the tears. Flora's arm slipped around me as I sobbed.

"I know," she whispered. "I know."

Autumn, while not a demanding time of year, still has certain tasks which one must fall to if winter is to be met prepared. With the sudden loss of both our tools and many supplies, there should have been within me an urgent drive to insure that we would meet these known demands. Yet, for days I felt whipped – no energy, and no will to move on. This was a helpless feeling, for in addition to losing the tools upon which you could place your hands, I seemed to have lost the tools within me that had always pushed me forward, ever forward. The practical tools could be replaced, if only I could find within me the key to actually get up and begin the rebuilding. The depression wouldn't even let me believe that such a turning point was not far away, as indeed it was not. Weeks passed before I slowly began to understand that while a major setback, it was not unlike other challenges we had assumed and conquered.

Much later, when I was fully engaged in our recovery effort, Bruce shared that he felt it was a spark from his welding that day which had started the fire. Angry at himself for such a loss, he had already planned the replacement building, located behind rather than beside the house, and to be constructed entirely from concrete. I felt this was a severe over-reaction, but the die had been cast, and over the next few years, the concrete structure emerged and grew. Fireproof it was, but it always felt cold to me, never inviting me in to ply my craft within its walls as had our lumber structure. Yet it was indeed home to Bruce's many efforts.

In addition to replacing the multitude of hand tools which were the staples of any craftsman, Bruce began to assemble larger pieces of equipment, one of the most impressive being a huge electric generator, driven by an even larger Diesel engine, an engine so large, it had a small gasoline engine mounted atop it used just to start the Diesel. This, he planned, was to be used to light the entire resort well into the evenings as well as energize new power tools he was buying. I was skeptical to say the least, but he labored for two months installing it in a corner of the shop, then readied it for a trial run.

Of course, we were invited to be present the afternoon he pronounced the Diesel ready to run. He had secured a used automobile battery which would power the starter motor of the smaller gasoline engine. When Bruce pushed its starter button, the engine spun with a whine, then caught hold and began to fire up. Since it was only to run during the startup of the larger engine, this smaller engine had no muffler, and the noise from it resounding off all the hard concrete walls was hardly music to our ears, but we had to show our support. Both Flora and I had already covered our ears as Bruce prepared to clutch in the large Diesel. As he engaged the main engine, the smaller one labored and slowed as the sleeping giant was roused. When the Diesel fired up, it was terrifying, at least to Flora whose devotion to Bruce was typically steadfast, but tested past her limits here. She fled as if fearing for her very being. While I stood my ground, hands pressed all the harder to side of my head, my body shook and I measured my resolve. Bruce turned with a grin of accomplishment, standing right beside the throbbing monster. I knew at once we were of different minds here.

Wiring up all the cabins for the level of power he had in mind would take Bruce a while, but he was immediately at this task, welding metal poles to carry the wires across our property. As he worked, I sought the words to tell him that I could not accept the roar of his new dynamo in exchange for electricity to provide light, light that currently came from far less invasive equipment. My problem was solved a few days later when I encountered a man walking through our property.

"Can I help you?" I called out as the man walked a directed path, sketching or writing and referring to a map. At first he did not acknowledge me, so intent was he on his task.

"Would you be Mr. Palmer?" he asked as I approached. I confirmed that I was. He introduced himself and told me he was from the Rural Electrification Association. The long promised extension of the electric power lines to our remote area was actually coming to reality. He was there to scout the exact route for the power lines, which would be coming right in between our house and the new shop. I thought this development would disturb Bruce, whose investment of funds and time in the generator was substantial, but as he joined us and asked about the lines, he seemed quite enthusiastic.

The REA lines came as promised, and Bruce had prepared for them. Our house was the first to glow steadily from this silent power source, and it was soon connected to each cabin in turn. While this was indeed a godsend, we were to find that it was also fragile. A tree branch falling miles away, a thunderstorm near or far, often left us in our original powerless state. Bruce responded with the reassignment of his generator as a backup source, and so it served for many years.

The introduction of a steady stream of electric power changed our world in ways we had expected, but also in ways we had not. We always thought of light as the primary asset it would bring, but Bruce's shop quickly became not only more productive with power tools, these tools often performed tasks previously simply not attainable with hand tools. Yet perhaps the greatest labor savings was to come as the result of a discussion one evening.

Flora had long known the benefits of mechanical refrigeration as many in her Homemakers group had this modern appliance in their kitchens as had our Cicero home. On one of our trips to town, she noticed an advertisement in the Co-op store as we were buying groceries. New, lower cost refrigerators were being offered at their appliance outlet near Trego. That night we talked about this opportunity, not simply for our own home, but the cabins as well. We figured how much our ice was costing us each year, and it seemed that over ten or twelve years, the cost of these appliances would nearly be recouped, to say nothing of the ice hauling labor to be eliminated. In the long run, it might pay, but we would have to come up with the money for twelve boxes none-the-less. Flora then informed us that some smaller print at the bottom of the ad indicated that payments could be arranged.

Within a week, we had arranged a payment plan and made the

required down payment. Now all that was required was the transporting of this sizable load to our property. Bruce and I set out in the truck and trailer, with the notion that we could get all twelve on one load. With a bit of maneuvering we did  indeed stand six cartons on the truck bed and six on the trailer, though the last two were hanging a bit off the edge. We felt confident that our rope had the load confined, and set out to get the load home before lunch. The shortest route was not the smoothest route, but was selected anyway. I encouraged Bruce to take it slow, which generally he did.

As we turned onto Little Bass Lake Road, we were about three miles from home and feeling good about the run. Our conversation had turned to repair work required on the boats, and I was hardly watching the road. Suddenly Bruce's end of the discussion stopped, and the smile left his face. I turned forward and noticed we were going too quickly toward a turn.

"Brakes," I shouted tersely, but it was evident that if he had them, he would have used them. The road dropped sharply, then turned quickly left to cross a small creek. As Bruce fought to make the turn, the entire truck tipped slightly, then thankfully regained its footing, but not until we heard a sizable splash behind us. The truck rolled to a stop on the uphill turn, then slipped backward, still without stopping power. When it came to rest on the culvert, we jumped out to assess our losses. There beside the road lay two of our precious cartons. Fortunately they both had landed in a bog-like area running beside the creek, which had cushioned the fall sufficiently to have prevented any damage.

We counted ourselves quite lucky, and proceeded to work the loads out of the mushy ground and back up onto the trailer. Significantly more attention was paid to the rope securing the loads before we set back out at a crawl in first gear, the remaining two miles taking longer than the preceding ten. To this day, our family refers to that little creek as "Refrigerator Creek".

Chapter 53

STARTING THE LAST CHAPTER

One thing that distinguished this winter from all others before it was our ongoing discussion in the house, a discussion I never foresaw, but certainly was inevitable. We were approaching our twenty-fourth season, and it was becoming more and more difficult for us to manage an operation of this size. Retirement should not have seemed such a drastic step as we did not plan to move. Bruce was willing to buy the resort and continue its operation, thus we could assume as much a role in it as we chose.

By the time the ice began to show signs of dissolving, we had made our decision and formal sale documents were prepared. In April of 1954, Bruce became the new owner of Lake Lipsie Pines. When our season opened in June, I found the operational portion had not changed very much at all. Flora still kept all the records, I managed some fix-up jobs and hob-knobbed with our patrons, and still hosted the campfires each week. Bruce hired cleaning help, for the Saturday cabin turnovers as well as for wash days. All in all, we wondered why it had taken all winter to make the decision.

One part of the operation that did change was that Bruce was now in charge, and some things which we had disagreed upon before, he was now able to implement freely. Although I still disagreed on some, I realized it was his resort to run now, and so he did.

We had been patching up the old steel and wood boats for many years, and watched as other resorts improved this key part of the

367

patrons' experience. Bruce studied various brands of boats, and declared AlumaCraft as the finest of its type. He would need ten boats just to replace the fleet of one per cabin, and needed at least two extras for folks with larger families. In addition, Bruce felt two canoes would be a popular rental item, by the hour or by the day. When he finished, his list called for thirteen boats and two canoes, and a total cost which was certainly hefty. Rather than consider a less expensive line, Bruce discovered that if he advertised as an AlumaCraft dealer, he could obtain this fleet at dealer prices.

This proved to be the solution he had been looking for, and one Monday he set off to Minneapolis for his first load of boats. The venture eventually took three trips, and Bruce would not put the new crafts in the water until he had carefully applied numbers to each boat and set of oars. Even the anchors and rope were new, as he retired the old fleet entirely, selling a few to locals glad to have a bargain boat, even if it required a bit of upkeep.

Still squaring himself in the driver's seat, Bruce then arranged for what was to become a signature item of the resort in the following years. He had heard that many of the vehicles used in the war were being disposed of by the armed services. He made some inquires, and was quite excited to find that Jeeps were being sold for $100 apiece in Chicago. He was aware that these were not operational, but felt by getting two of them, he could combine parts for one which would be usable. The purchase took some arranging, since these vehicles would arrive at the Chicago port by boat, and he would have to get them off the docks promptly. When the time came, he set off for Chicago in the truck.

Bruce was pleased with his purchase when he returned and unloaded them, and lost little time disassembling both of the Jeeps. All parts were scrubbed in kerosene to clean them up. He found that many smaller parts such as piston rings, gaskets and spark plugs would need to be purchased new. He was pleased to find they were common parts available in Spooner, but bristled at having to pay the new prices. As he completed each subassembly, he painted it to make everything look new. He worked diligently and finally a single complete Jeep emerged from the apparent chaos of parts.

The day he would crank the engine over finally arrived. Bruce connected a used battery which he had fully charged. Once the connections were tight, he moved to the ignition switch, flipped it on and pressed the starter button on the dash. The engine lurched a partial turn, but froze. He hit it again and again. Each time the engine made a small bit of a turn, but that was all. The ignition was switched off.

"I knew it was tight with those new rings and main bearings, but I didn't expect this," he mused. "I'll bet two batteries will give it the punch it needs." He produced a second battery, along with a short piece of heavy wire, and within ten minutes was ready to see what doubling the voltage to the starter would accomplish.

Again the ignition was switched on, and when the button was pressed this time, the starter fairly screamed as it drove the engine rapidly. There was but a brief delay, then the engine fired up and roared to life. I had come to know that such a success is always followed with Bruce's full mouth, toothy grin, and this certainly was no exception. He had resurrected one live Jeep from the ashes of two fallen ones – his very own Phoenix.

Nor was Bruce done with the vehicle once it was fully operational. He was immediately at work designing a dump bed to replace the seats in the rear of the body. By the end of the season, this modification was complete, and he was able to easily transport one-third of a yard of sand from his many excavation projects as well as easily pick up the garbage and take it to the dump in a vehicle far easier to drive than the truck.

The Jeep became such a signature item on the place due to its attraction to all the visiting youngsters, and Bruce regularly participated in the fun by giving rides. These rides were hardly confined to the roads of our place. He delight-ed in the screams he could induce by veering off roads into smaller saplings of the woods, diving down a steep sand embankment, or speeding down our shoreline in a spray of water. Nearly every patron from that time on took a photo or two of this, the most sought after tool of our operation.

Having Lois' children all summer long became a routine, year after year. They were assigned tasks according to their abilities, and were quite helpful, especially during the Saturday turnovers. They were paid a small stipend, which allowed them to buy small items on trips to town.

In addition to having the three Huth boys about, there were visits from other children, both relations and friends. The Swenson children, though not summer-long guests, were frequent visitors, and Harold's son Gary was a frequent resident at Blanche Walker's Many Pines cabin just across our north border. With Harris' efforts at his Star o' the North resort about sixty miles distant, their boys were often among this group of youngsters as well. Added to this mix was Charlie Byrnes' son, Gerry, of about the same age as Mickie.

For reasons best known to this younger age group, one afternoon Mickie, Jon, Frosty and Gary returned from a hike to Byrnes Store each sporting a corncob pipe. A cardboard display of these twenty five cent items had somehow tickled their fancy, and each parted with the required funds. It was reminiscent of the felt hats of the previous generation. For the ensuing week, everywhere they went, those pipes protruded from their faces.

One particular day, this normally effervescent group looked a bit under the weather, and it took a bit of cajoling to ferret out the truth of the matter. I found that after many days of empty pipes, they felt they were ready to try the true purpose of the devices. To their credit, they did not attempt to procure tobacco, but when the substituted sawdust from Bruce's shop was ignited with illicit matches, the result was hardly the effect they had envisioned as acrid smoke bit their tongues. Not only did the true smoking aspect of these pipes leave their imagination quickly, even the daily appearance of the empty pipes seemed to have lost its great appeal.

Bruce had few indulgences, but one he long savored was a bit of chocolate every so often. To this end, he had purchased an entire box of Hershey milk chocolate bars, and it was placed on a shelf in his bedroom, among hundreds of papers and other items of his interests.

Mickie was his uncle's shadow during his summer stays, and it was obvious that his interests were parallel to his uncle's. Despite the glory of a bright summer's day, he would often as not be inside the shop with Bruce, assisting or following his own devices with the plethora of tools at his disposal. This close kinship undoubtedly brought him into Bruce's bedroom often enough for him to spy the sacred box of chocolate. No one knew they also shared this passion as well.

"Somebody's going to get docked!" a booming voice echoed from Bruce's room one evening toward the end of that summer. A moment later, Bruce entered the living room, the box of Hershey bars in one hand, a partially unwrapped piece of mahogany paneling in the other. The story was quickly discovered.

Mickie's abilities with Bruce's power tools came to a unique advantage one afternoon much earlier that summer. Locating some one-eighth inch thick paneling material, Mickie cut about half a dozen small rectangles, each carefully sized. He then had sneaked into Bruce's room, slipped the white wrapper from several of the rich brown sleeves, carefully opening them and removing the chocolate, substituting the identically sized lumber, then re-wrapped and returned them to the sleeves. The bogus bars were not simply returned to the box, they were carefully positioned at the bottom layer of the box. To Mickie, it must have appeared such a box would certainly last well past the end of the summer and his safe departure.

While Bruce was obviously annoyed at the loss of his precious chocolate, I believe he was secretly pleased at the inventiveness and skill of his nephew, as no real docking took place.

Relieved of the routine demands of day to day operations, I was enjoying some of my pastimes, including time to organize my Indian artifact collection, mounting many groupings on boards for presentations. Large easel-type frames were constructed to hold many of these boards, and could set up a rather large display. I had always had a bit of a reputation as a collector and minor expert, and now enjoyed being asked to give talks with my display about the area and had even done it several times right in one of our cabins.

There was always such a strong interest in Indian lore in our area, I decided I could satisfy a demand of our patrons by making small plaques, with a color postcard of a chief in full regalia surrounded by about eight arrowheads. These were not prime arrowheads, but certainly the average observer wouldn't feel shorted. Displayed on our front porch along with postcards and other items, I was kept busy filling a brisk demand for these displays.

My other interest in semiprecious stones resulted in my amassing a huge collection of raw stones including agates which were underfoot on every walk. One evening as I mulled over the purchase of a tumbler drum to polish these stones, Bruce asked me to describe the device. As I spoke, he sketched, and in a short time, he had a plan, offering to build my required machine. His talents at welding made short work of the drum, and as the base took shape, two old washing machine rollers were installed as the rolling base for the drum, which would rotate with stones and abrasive materials inside it for over a day. Our collaboration was a great success, and I was most pleased when my first lot of highly polished stones emerged and were rinsed off. I held up one outstanding example - light shone off its polished surface and radiated through its translucent body, a feast for the eyes. Occasionally one may find a stone so polished by the natural action of stream waters and sand, but it is rare. I now had the ability to unveil many of nature's hidden gems at will, and was always eager to see the results when the drum was opened.

Four years had passed since we sold the resort to Bruce, and the pace of life was quite suitable. Letters this particular Spring began to talk about formulating some plans for a celebration during the coming August, for on the 11th of August, 1958, Flora and I would celebrate the true milestone of our 50th wedding anniversary. There was no place we would rather celebrate than right down in the bowl of our own park, and the guest list grew and grew. Space was hardly what we would be short on, but rather tables and chairs, though I was assured this was being seen to. Not only were our local friends planning to celebrate with us, a surprising list of far-flung friends and relatives from as far as California and Oregon were accepting invitations.

Family Gathered at 50th Anniversary

Nor were we allowed to help in the planning or preparation. In the days immediately preceding the gala, Bruce groomed the park area and readied other areas for the arrival of many cars. The menu included an entire chicken for each guest as well as several tables of shared dishes, the origin of which I couldn't imagine. Flora was summarily whisked from her own kitchen early on the actual day – I believe a first in our 50 years – and we spent the entire day reliving most memorable and pleasant recollections with nearly one hundred family and friends. Perfect weather was among our guests and though taken for granted, was kind to us all.

From well before the celebration, we had been encouraged to commemorate this occasion with a trip, perhaps the following winter. This possibility came up again and again that day, and among many possibilities discussed, a trip south, deep south, during our winter months had the most appeal. Eventually, as we pursued the possibilities into the autumn, we came to believe Cuba would make the sort of adventure we yearned for, and I secretly planned to ferret home some of the famous cigars at the conclusion of the trip. The plan took some months to arrange, but finally we were booked, a trip to begin just days after celebrating Christmas at home.

The trip down was a bit more arduous than I had expected, but never before in our lives had we dreamed of walking a beach and basking in the sun in December. We were in a small hotel in Havana, a city chosen for its liveliness, and every day, every night, it was living up to its reputation. We were basically quiet country folks, yet I am always ready to experience something new. Havana was all new – music, food, language. Every night seemed a celebration to these folks, and the noise was unlike any even Chicago had shown me.

One night near the end of our stay the tone had changed, though the fervor was still evident. The most obvious difference was gunfire. While it was not menacing, we were a full week past New Years, and I was unaware of another, perhaps Latin holiday. I inquired around until I got an explanation that General Batista had fled the country on New Years day, and this day a man named Fidel Castro was arriving in Havana. I was assured this was a great and peaceful step for Cuba, but we were happy to depart the unsettled country the next day.

Never had the peace of our quiet Lake Lipsie home been so cherished as in the days following our return from that island off Florida.

Chapter 54

HEAVEN

Well over a decade after starting this story at Flora's urging, I was still at it. Now, however, I had to dictate the words, my fingers unable to control a pencil any longer. Arthritis progression had turned them into knobby, thick appendages whose talents had steadily declined. Even small tasks I previously had found some comfort in were becoming impossible – I simply could not make my hands, so long the executor of my dreams, perform the required tasks.

Flora never backed from the task she had set me to, indeed she had helped from the very onset with proofing and typing that seemed would never end. Now she even had to transcribe the words, but it seemed a labor she enjoyed, setting down all the memories so as not to be lost. She had a sense that what was being preserved, the story of our venture, was something to be shared with many who by circumstance or opportunity had not experienced such events in their lives. Fortunately, her love of books showed her that our experiences could be shared in written words. As the pile of papers grew past two inches thick, and revision after revision churned more and more paper through her typewriter, I wondered at her resolve, but shouldn't have.

Each Thursday night around the campfire, I still enjoyed re-telling stories and events without the worry of getting it down on paper, looking into the eyes of each listener, seeing the response. That's where I could savor the telling, the sharing, but as I had to lean more and more on my pitchfork for support, I knew Flora had been

right those many years ago, pleading to preserve it all.

In March of 1962 I suffered a heart attack, my first close call with eternity, and it made earlier bouts with gout seem trivial in comparison. If I thought I felt frail after all those years of log lifting, I now knew what frail meant. Any exertion, even within the house, sapped what energy I thought I had banked up and left me feeble. Patience was not my nature, but I had no other choice. Gradually I could stand and walk about the house, and finally ventured beyond the confines of our walls, if only to savor the sweet smell of nature from our lawn. Never, however, would I feel it were too much to press onward, for I was endowed with sufficient cajene to handle even this setback.

Months passed before I could begin to make significant forays into the depths of our property, to break from constant watchful eyes of Flora and Bruce. My mind had been eased of its burden of handling so many other manual tasks as I focused upon such a simple task as walking. I was encouraged by the opening of our twenty-eighth resort season and the visits and many best wishes of those repeat patrons who were told of my infirmity.

I took relief in communing with nature. Although my arthritis was beginning to challenge my legs and hips, with my carved walking stick, I could and did routinely strike out to walk the property and revel in the unchanging world of wildlife and flora our property had always provided to us.

One late afternoon on a warm day that July, during one of those walks which Charlie savored as his private time, he stopped to rest, propping himself against a large White Pine along the road just down from the garden. He never returned from that walk. Bruce later found him sitting peacefully there, the birds still serenading him, as if attempting to allay his burdens.

An era ended that afternoon. The founder and soul of Lake Lipsie Pines had become one with the land that he so loved. Yet Flora and Bruce were not to be swayed from continuing the resort operations any more than previous hardships had. Bruce provided muscle and ingenuity while Flora continued business operations and mingling with the guests. Bruce had had the campfire pitchfork passed to him, though he struggled with filling the host position.

The ensuing four and a half years saw some technical innovations, but Flora could put less and less into the effort. Reminiscent of the feeling of solitude and loss of direction which settled upon Charlie and Flora when the boys had first left, something seemed to say that Lake Lipsie Pines was in fact far more than a place – it was an interaction of people, Palmers and patrons, but the Palmer strength had always been gleaned from the consolidation of the entire family. As it fell more and more upon Bruce alone, the magic began to fade.

Charlie and Flora Palmer

It was a cold and snowy day in January of 1967 that it all changed. Just before the previous Christmas, Flora took a bad fall in the kitchen. She lingered in the Shell Lake Hospital for a month, then on the 19th of January, she left all of her gathered family, departed the precious Lake Lipsie Pines she had loved so, and at last joined Charlie after his four and a half year wait for her.

We all have had memorable places in our lives, some more than others. The Palmer's lives were especially rich, and it's not clear even now why they were so fortunate. Charlie and Flora used to say it was heaven, there upon the shores of Lake Lipsie. With their new perspective high above the old Orioles Nest, perhaps they could see it was pretty close.

EPILOGUE

by the Editor

If you enjoyed the foregoing story, you will likely not enjoy this epilogue – it has neither a happy ending, nor even a pleasant interlude. Yet it is the story of Lake Lipsie Pines and its final frontier developer, Bruce Palmer, from the time of Flora's death until this writing, and there is a thread of a happy ending, with a Palmer descendant retaining and preserving a small piece of the land.

Bruce A. Palmer

The chronology is easy to lay down, the reasons for it not so. This is an outside view of the actions of a very private man, a man with goals he could never seem to reach, but never stopped reaching toward. A man whose creative mind went far beyond the mechanisms and inventions everyone saw, but never really broke out of the confines of the quiet land to which he ultimately retreated.

After Flora's death, Bruce was inspired to write to the many long-time patrons of the resort and among other things, declared the resort would continue as "a living memorial to my parents who founded the resort with so much intrepid courage and developed it with tireless ambition." This was what any patron and certainly all the family would be pleased to hear. And continue it he did, for but two years.

During those two last years as a continuing glorious vacation repose for its patrons, Bruce came face to face with feelings and values within himself. He found that he was far from the warm and conversation seeking nature of his parents, whose life goals centered around the personal interplay that had given Lake Lipsie Pines its gracious personality. Bruce found his goal-oriented drive was thwarted by the demands of his customers, demands that increasingly highlighted a split between their seeking of recreation while he sought a deeper life fulfillment through work and some sort of resolving of life's deeper issues.

The Judeo-Christian work ethic is widely used to describe the internal motivations of the American worker, and I suppose Bruce fits that mold as far as self-motivation goes. I know of few who worked as long and as hard in their life as my Uncle Bruce. I was aware of a developing conflict as far back as the last years of Charlie's life – fights between Charlie, retired but still the soul of LLP, and Bruce who now owned the resort, but already was struggling to find reward in simply applying his skills and inventiveness to the many needs of such a place.

In retrospect, the very forging of life from the earth that had been his beginnings never left Bruce. He learned well the lessons Charlie taught, by example or by necessity, of making do with little and wasting nothing. As the world became more extravagant and wasteful around him, and late twentieth century America has been a model of that in so many ways, he specifically objected, and with no one but himself to be concerned with, Bruce more and more left the mainstream to at least self demonstrate how to stem such a tide.

Thus in those pivotal two years, the recreational demands of vacationers, who in their other fifty weeks of the year toiled with their own work struggle, seemed to fly in the face of something inside Bruce which continued to demand frugality and never-ceasing work. How could he continue to be a part of such frivolity?

So, at the close of the 1968 season, Lake Lipsie Pines, the Mecca of those who loved the same rustic communion with nature that Charlie envisioned, sought, developed and shared for over thirty years, closed forever. Bruce never married, never shared the Lipsie land with anyone else after that time.

Bruce left the land even before closing the resort, taking a twelve year job as a lab director at the University of Wisconsin at Platteville, where his brother Harris was a professor. He returned to the Lipsie land each summer, bringing with him what would appear to most as the oddest assortment of materials. Deep within him a plan was burning, a plan far outside himself. Letters to family and others over the next twenty years or more gave clues, even specific details of a plan he called SOECO, an acronym for Socio-Economic, a plan to train economically disadvantaged young people to be self-sufficient and develop valuable hands-on skills. The LLP land was to be home to this "camp".

To this end, he began to collect "supplies" which would be the raw materials and equipment such an endeavor would require. In true Palmer fashion, he obtained these materials at pennies on the dollar, much of the equipment non-functioning but needing only the skilled hands and inventive mind he possessed to restore their full utility, though he never quite got to most of those repair tasks.

Those outside the Palmer family will wonder at the detail to follow, will question the mind that would actually carry the collection to the extreme described, but there is both insight and humor that would be lost in any editing of this portion of the true story.

Certainly the collecting and frugality were always there. I recall as a child spending summers there, the hundreds of coffee cans of bent nails, miscellaneous screws and fittings and other items defying description which filled the new shop. Yet first and foremost, Lake Lipsie Pines was a resort, so both the shop and its treasures were set back, mostly a behind-the-scenes part of the operation. However, once the land was no longer serving others, the entire eighty acres was open for repose of this new inventory. In addition, the ten beautifully hand-crafted cabins, so long the home away from home for so many, became instant inside storage opportunities.

Today, we have simple tags for defining people and their behavior. What developed with Bruce in this incendiary mix of storage opportunity and ambition would today likely be tagged OCB, obsessive-compulsive behavior. Understanding the basics of Bruce's plan, one could understand the general concept of gathering some items, but the degree to which he actually continued, well, I'm afraid avoiding such a diagnosis would be improbable. Stories abound of those with friends or relatives with such a problem, whose houses are crammed with anything from old newspapers, clothing or huge balls of string. I apologize if it seems the Palmers are simply claiming undue bragging rights, but those stories are but fleas on the dog.

To set the stage, a trip into the narrow roads of Lake Lipsie Pines in the late '90s would wend you past a road grader, bulldozer, crane, several buses, a log loader and cars, trucks and tractors too numerous to tally. Machinery, from common machine tools like lathes and milling machines were supplemented with scores of other devices whose original utility had been lost and could not be divined even by a trained engineer like me.

Only a Snapshot

Should any crabgrass still seek an opportunity to climb skyward, smaller parts and metal scraps filled in the gaps until the entire acreage likely began skewing compasses within the county. But you have not yet even opened your car door...

Any attempt to again savor the charm of even one of the formerly cozy log cabins would be futile. Those where entry was still possible displayed a semi-organized collection of materials whose description ran the gamut from aircraft radios to hydraulic cylinders, tar paper to electric motors. Into the confines of one tiny cabin were packed the entire inventory of fourteen aluminum boats and two canoes. How one person could even manage that is a puzzle amidst so many more.

A humorous but classic example of Bruce's waste-not life style came shortly after a promotional mailing of maxi-pads arrived in his mailbox. The simple irony of such a promotion arriving at a confirmed bachelor's mailbox should bring a chuckle, but our ever resourceful Bruce easily topped that. Involved in a roof repair, he lost no time in tying the pads to his knees to cushion the job a bit.

In the early '90's, when Bruce was in his late seventies, he was diagnosed with Diabetes and developed heart problems as well, which eventually required a pacemaker. More than one friend of our family, upon being told of his new pacemaker, quickly asked, "Did he make it himself?" This may have slowed him down, but it did not stop him. He did finally get deflected from his efforts by the same Old Man Winter that so early had challenged their entry upon this land. His efforts to redesign the heating system of the house, a task of such a scope I could not expound upon it here except to say one entire wall of the house was removed, the original heating plant was gone and the solar portion of the new plan was, well, a long way from operational. With winter breathing down his frail neck, a caring neighbor offered him a place in their home for the winter, and Bruce finally did something quite sensible – he accepted.

The Ken Christner family opened their hearts and home to him, and through the long winter months, Bruce found something long missing in his life – community. He delighted in their three young children and became an instant member of the family. If there was heart mending to be done, it was begun here. This also renewed his interest in his extended Palmer family. A surprise to no one, the heating plan stagnated almost entirely, and for the next two winters, Bruce ventured back to his origins in Cicero, Illinois to stay with his sister Lois. His health could not keep pace with his continuing ambition, however, and on November 2nd, 1997, Bruce died. He finally recognized his mortality in his last few days, and was completely at peace with his impending death. Only in those last days did he finally acknowledge that "I guess I've left one heck of a mess up there for someone."

Bruce was cremated per his wishes. We traveled back to LLP to spread his ashes at two places on the land he loved yet seemed to have desecrated.

The final stage of the Lake Lipsie Pines story obviously begins with the "heck of a mess" Bruce left. Actually, it began with several decisions within the family. Certainly a developer would have bought the land, "collection" and all, but to what end was unclear. I reasoned that if development was done by the family, the financial gain would be significantly better, and the goal would be within our control. Because Bruce never married, the estate fell to nine heirs, all nieces and nephews, who remarkably, all agreed with that concept. I was months from retirement, and already had a development plan in mind. A corporation was formed, Palmer Properties LLC, and I began...

Charlie's grandson and my brother, Jonathan, and his wife, Grace, had long sought a piece of the land which Jon also spent every childhood summer plying. Bruce, of course, had had other plans, and often said the last thing he wanted was to have the land divided and used for simple recreation, though recreation was the very reason for its formation. Nothing more than the massive collection of hardware had been done regarding SOECO, and the only practical outlook for this underlying pristine land was, in fact, private lots. Grace's position as a teacher and Jon's self-employment allowed them to spend the summer on the land. They had the foresight to know any money they could earn in the cleanup effort would be needed for their plan to restore and expand Top Notch cabin as their own. They did not, however, know what they were getting into. Hired by the LLC, they began what was to become the first of two "summers from hell".

Again, retrospect provides such clear and obvious parallels, views simply unattainable from any other perspective. Here again was another level of pioneers, forging their way over this same land, toiling, enduring hardship, yet gleaning fun and sharing all nature so close at hand. Pioneers with Bobcat loaders and chain saws, you may ask? Just ask them if it felt like pioneering. Most of the first summer was spent simply moving and organizing in preparation for a huge auction, an auction I simply could not believe was going to rid our venture of ninety-five percent of the "Bruce resources" that the auctioneer boasted he would do. While much of America watched cable television in air conditioned homes, Jon and Grace headed up the dig-out, retrieving items from piles of porcupine droppings, rotten wood and filth, all so it could be purchased by unknown bidders. That there were other SOECO-like visionaries out there waiting for access to low priced resources seemed hardly realistic.

I was wrong. Ninety-five percent of the stuff did sell. More importantly, the land was again beginning to look presentable, attractive even. Oh, there was a lot yet to do, but now the promise was actually beginning to be visible. In the days following the sale, winning bidders loaded their purchases. Not simply a multitude of cars with trunks opened, this was an industrial operation, with loaders, cranes and huge trucks churning up the once placid sand. The bidder loading steel with a magnet-crane told us he loaded over 200 tons, and said it was the largest accumulation by a single individual he had ever seen. Bragging rights! To further lend scope to this endeavor, the remaining five percent of the "stuff" required fourteen boxcar sized commercial dumpsters over three summers to remove. Fourteen! We even had to purchase a used Bobcat loader to haul and dump everything into these dumpsters.

In the rollover year 2000, after most of the cabins were cleared, three were too far deteriorated to save and demolition was arranged. In addition, the old homestead which Lou Arnold had designed and funded, which had housed the Palmer clan for every year after the Oriole's Nest, my boyhood home for all those joyous summers, Bruce had simply torn apart too far to save – it also became a casualty of the wrecker shovel. Between the demolitions and other clean up efforts, Jon and Grace again toiled in the heat and dust, Tom Sawyering help from many friends and relatives who ventured in to see it all.

Amidst the despair of the destruction of these historic structures, one preservation opportunity bouyed us. A chance meeting at the county courthouse put me in touch with Karen Benson, the then director of Burnett County's Forts Folle Avoine. This fort, a recreation of the 1802 fur trading outpost, is built on the original site which was discovered in 1969 by Harris and Frances Palmer as he pursued his lifelong archeology fascination.

Harris Palmer House - Burnett County Historical Library

Karen asked if we would consider donating one of our cabins to the Forts, to be used to house the historical research library. We were only too pleased with the opportunity to see one of the very cabins Harris helped create preserved in a park he helped found. Crows Nest, the first cabin of Lake Lipsie Pines, was dismantled log by log, moved to the Forts and re-erected (less interior walls) by volunteers, and stands today as the Harris Palmer House, the Burnett County Historical Library near Danbury, Wisconsin.

Interspersed with the cleanup effort, Jon and Grace began work on Top Notch. Never modernized beyond running cold water, the new plan called for two additions to be added, the primary one containing a bathroom and greatly expanding the kitchen, the other a large screened porch. The project began with a log restoration team who tore into rotten logs and rafters until

Top Notch - A Restored Gem

Jon could only hope they knew how to reassemble it. They framed out the new log walls using vintage logs from the cabins which had been torn down. The project proceeded over two years, and required a new driveway, well, septic system and modern plumbing, gas heating stove, roof insulation, all new electrical wiring and a compliment of new kitchen cabinets.

Meanwhile, our surveyor had mapped the lines and driven the stakes that were to define the new Lipsie Pines, a series of nine lakefront lots of about two-plus acres each, one hundred and fifty feet on the lake, deep woods, paradise awaiting now not patrons, but owners. Though somewhere in the 80's or 90's the lake had reverted to its turn-of-the-century "Lipsett" name, I chose Lipsie Pines as a reflection of the long and sweet history under the Lake Lipsie name. A new road cut across the land to access the new lots. I had envisioned a plan which, like Charlie's, retained the bowl-like park as undeveloped, commonly owned land for a gathering of this new community. To market we went, brochures and maps in hand. June had many lookers, but no buyers. By mid-July, I felt we needed the larger net which professional Realtors could provide, and signed a deal. Traffic increased, but no offers. The Realtor's caution about the common park land was resounding louder; there were questions about the liability should someone get hurt there, who would keep the peace, clean it up? Everyone worried, no one eyeing the possibility of gathering with friends and neighbors. Everyone wants to be by themselves, the Realtor kept saying.

First parting with the land, then the park. I knew I had to relent, but it was hard. Painful, in fact. The new stakes our surveyor drove were through my heart as the park disappeared and the lots behind the park pulled themselves up to the lake like a hungry woodsman at the dinner table. Business-wise it was obviously the correct decision since within two months, we had sold three lots, one being half the park.

I find it ironic that the birth of the old Lake Lipsie Pines resort was the direct result of a faltering economy, its glory years due to a growing post-war boom, and its 'demise' due to a robust era in which so many can afford their own private lakeshore property.

But would these new owners even care to know this story, the long and meaningful story of how that piece of land came to be there for them? Would anyone outside the family care? I re-read Grandpa's manuscript and knew it needed to be both finished and edited, enhanced with photos found in the old homestead before its demolition, then published. Ultimately it would be Grandpa, that grand old man of people and stories that would again spin his tale for those who would listen. This Epilogue – I guess it's more for me and readers thirsty to have all the facts. I rest easy in the fact that I'm of that pioneer Palmer blood. I had twelve tender years on that land that shaped me in ways I'm still discovering. I've just spent another three polishing that land, and myself, some more. That's reward enough.

Thanks, Charlie. I never really had a chance to say that!

Glossary

Back house - Outhouse or privy

Bailiwick - One's own area

Blaze - To mark; a term used in forestry / logging work

Boles - Trunks of trees

Blotto - A Palmer tradition, to be yelled upon the crossing of any State line.

Cajene - A Palmer word meaning initiative, ingenuity and ability

Catercorner - Diagonally across, as on opposite corners

Dooryard - The area outside a door: ie. present usage of front yard or back yard

Felts - Boot linings made of felt for cold weather

Grubbing - To root out, as in clearing land of pervasive roots

Hoyden - A tomboy

Indian - Native American, and a still-used term if used appropriately

Jag - A load of wood, as on a truck - slang for intoxicated

LLP - Shorthand for Lake Lipsie Pines, the Palmer resort

Mattocks - A pick-ax type garden tool for loosening soil

Nimrod - A hunter

Norways - A local name for Red Pine trees

Pitch stump - A tree stump (typically pine) rich with sap (pitch)

Rick - To stack firewood neatly

Sawyer - One who runs the saw rig at a mill

Shank's horse - Traveling on foot (on shank's horse)

Shinny - A simple hockey-like game on ice

Slabbed - To cut a flat on a log by running through a saw

Squaw - Today a politically incorrect term for the wife of an Indian, used here for historical accuracy

Stoker - One who feeds fuel (typically wood or coal) to a boiler

Swale - A wet depression in the earth or marsh

Tonneau - The body of a car

Tonsorial - Pertaining to barbering

Turnip - Slang for a pocket-watch

Verdure - Greenery, growing plants and trees

Victuals - Food-stuffs

Partial List of items found on the LLP property during the clean-up after Bruce Palmer's death.

1 drum	Choir Robes	2 Drums	Phone Books
1 drum	Tin Foil Scraps	30 Yrs	Newspapers & Flyers
1 box	Orange Juice can Tops	1 Box	Yogurt Lids
230	Plastic Milk Bottles	250	Plastic Oil Bottles
70	Plastic PB Jars	1 drum	Old Socks
4 drums	Torn Clothes	150 drums	Machine Parts
400	Egg Cartons	13	Cars (none operable)
2	Trucks	2	Buses
1	Road Grader	1	Caterpillar Tractor
1	Log Carrier	1	Crane (Truck Mounted)
4	Farm Tractors	1	Fork Truck
1	Jeep	3	Lathes
60	Electric Motors	2300	Coffee Cans
43	Business Machines	1 ton	Tar Paper
100	Light Fixtures	150	Florescent Bulbs
20 rolls	Fiberglass Insulation	1 load	Railroad Rails
83	Windows	25	Mattresses
200 tons	Scrap Metal	50	School Lockers
130	Tires (ALL sizes)	8	Bicycles
250	Broken Tools	1 drum	Inner Tubes
1 set	Church Pews	120	Hydraulic Cylinders
85 sets	Metal Shelving	2	Milling Machines
15 coils	Steel Cable	1	Gasoline Pump
2	Aircraft Wing Tanks	2	Saw Mill Spindles
asst	Radios incl. Military	13 rolls	Plastic Pipe
30	Meat Storage Lockers	4 drums	Milk Cartons
1 drum	Junk Mail	4	Lawn Mowers
3	Washing Machines	1000+	Old Magazines
100+	Coils of Wire	10,000	Brd Ft Lumber
4	Sinks (various)	3	Toilets
5	1000 Gal Oil Tanks		

NOTES:

• A 'drum' refers to a 55 gallon metal drum.

• The 200 tons of scrap metal was said to be the largest accumulation by a single person in the State.

• The 2300 coffee cans were filled with screws, nails and small items too varied to even describe.

• Misc. materials classified as hazardous waste and costing thousands to have removed by licensed hauler.

ABOUT THE EDITOR

Mike Huth is the author's grandson, and a beginning author in his own right. With one novel, many short stories and a stage play in his portfolio, Mike set about to bring the Charles Palmer manuscript to the audience Charlie had intended. The development and sale of the family property where the story took place spurred the renewed interest in the manuscript. Smoothing, restructuring and completing the inherently engaging tale became a labor of love culminating in this book.

Mike engaged others in the family, adding to the text, inserting photos and verifying timelines. He admits the effort was as consuming as authoring his own work, but stresses that the story is not his but all Charlie's.

Writing is a significant departure from Mike's 33 years as an engineer. Now retired from the tech world, he thoroughly enjoys wordcrafting, even the research that accompanies it. Unable to explain from where his ideas spring, it has become part of the mystery he enjoys - being struck with ideas at the oddest places and times. Not unlike most authors, a significant pleasure is positive feedback from his readers, and he regrets Charlie never had that, not in the written work. But since this text is little more than a transcription of his lifelong verbal story telling, in which Charlie always received deserved praise if only in facial expressions, Mike knows Charlie knew the same reward.

Most of this true story takes place along the shores of a small lake in Northwestern Wisconsin. It was a summer resort near Spooner called Lake Lipsie Pines. Although the story is far more about people, some readers may find this map helpful to cement the events and places together. It is a mixed era map–the location of both the old roads and cabins are shown with the new road and lot lines.

The resort is gone now, the land divided and sold, but it will never really die in the minds of many, and with this book, perhaps many more. To those who now own or even visit the land, perhaps the map will have even more of a special meaning. For the rest, it's enough to know it was a real place, a special place, a place easily conjured up in your mind, as you will find in the story within. But you may want to peek back here every so often and see just where the Palmers were in one chapter or another.

MAP DESIGN BY CAROLINE HUTH AND DAVID GRAY
COVER DESIGN AND BOOK LAYOUT BY CAROLINE HUTH

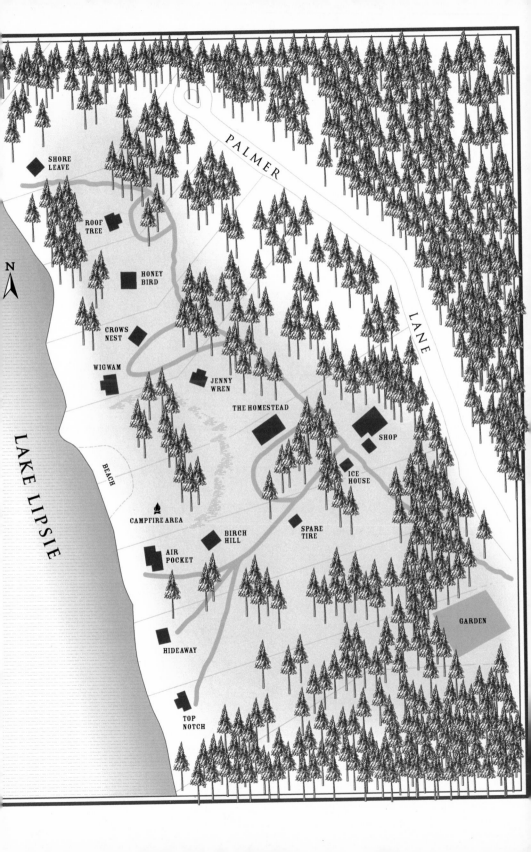